POLICIES AND OPINIONS
AT PARIS, 1919

POLICIES AND OPINIONS
AT PARIS, 1919

Wilsonian Diplomacy, the Versailles Peace,
and French Public Opinion

BY

GEORGE BERNARD NOBLE

HOWARD FERTIG

New York · 1968

FOREWORD

THE ills of present-day Europe, if not of the world, can in large measure be ascribed to the devastation and dislocation of the World War, and to the failure of the peacemakers of 1919 to reestablish a viable international order. Instability in international relations has persisted in spite of the epochal work of the Peace Conference in creating the first comprehensive institution designed to preserve peace and to organize the normal relationships between states. The failure of the peacemakers was due partly to faulty methods of procedure, partly to misunderstanding of the dynamics of national and international policies, and partly to the sheer impotence of the negotiators to shape the course of events in the midst of the surge of national passions, against which the best will in the world, and even greater intellects than those assembled at Paris, could scarcely have prevailed.

It is easy now to look back and point to these errors of method and of content, but it is difficult to appreciate the unprecedented handicaps which faced the statesmen. The Paris Conference has often been compared with the Congress of Vienna, and has already been linked with it as one of the world's outstanding diplomatic failures. In two important respects it was fundamentally different from its predecessor. The problems themselves with which it had to deal were far more difficult, arising, as they did, out of the infinite complexity of an interdependent world, and involving the re-ordering of the lives of whole peoples. "Politics" had broadened its scope enormously since 1815. Even more important were the imponderables of national psychology which plagued the diplomats of Paris in a way unknown to those of Vienna. Metternich, Alexander and even Castlereagh could very largely have shaped the settlement of 1815 to the conceptions of right and expediency entertained by themselves or their governments, without the intervention of popular democracies. Not so the negotiators of 1919, who had to take account of the turbulence of popular feelings, inflamed by falsifying war-time propaganda and distorted by a stupid censorship—for which, ironically enough, the governments themselves were largely responsible. After a war waged in the name of democratic principles, though with weapons of virulent nationalism, the peacemakers found themselves balked at times by the fact that their own democratic constituencies were demanding the application of extremely nationalistic principles in the peace settlement. It was as could have been anticipated.

All these factors have to be taken into account in studying the interplay of governmental policy with public opinion, and in exposing the errors of the past, errors which could scarcely have been avoided in January 1919, for the vicious circle was already complete. Their avoidance would have had to be sought in policies that went before. A peculiarly tragical aspect of the case is the fact that recent trends in European politics seem ostensibly to justify many extravagant fears and claims of the 1919 period. To what extent are these portentous developments the natural outcome of pre-existing trends? And to what extent have they been called up from the "vasty deep" by the very forces of 1919 which sought to take arms against them? To these questions, unhappily, no definitive answer can be given.

The Social Science Research Council, by means of a generous grant-in-aid, made it possible for me to return to Paris to pursue work indispensable to this study. It was in Paris, while attached to the American Commission to Negotiate Peace, in 1919, that my interest was first aroused in this subject. The officials of the Bibliothèque de la Guerre at Paris very kindly gave me special facilities without which my research could not have been satisfactorily completed. Likewise the officials of the Stanford University Library and the Hoover War Library have extended invaluable courtesies. For all these opportunities and privileges I am deeply grateful. It ought to be remarked that occasional statements in the text, made without citation of authority, are based on confidential papers in the Hoover War Library. These can be checked up by reference to Dr. Ralph H. Lutz of that institution. Above all, I must thank Professor Parker T. Moon, of Columbia University, for his patience in reading my manuscript and his helpfulness in offering criticisms and suggestions. My thanks are also due to Miss Gerda M. Andersen for her assistance at the Bibliothèque de la Guerre, to V. L. O. Chittick and Edward D. Sisson for reading manuscript and proof, and to Matilda Noble and Bryce Wood for their assistance in getting the manuscript into shape.

G. B. N.

CONTENTS

ix

POLICIES AND OPINIONS
AT PARIS, 1919

CHAPTER I

THE SETTING OF THE PEACE CONFERENCE

"Our democracy prides itself, among other things, on being a régime of opinion.

"Unfortunately with us there is really no opinion: there are only newspapers. They alone raise their voice in the silence of the public, and claim to express what those who are silent would think. The 'powers that be' pretend to accept this interpretation of the journalists. Thus, the democratic principle is safe, and the power of the press is consecrated."

(Robert de Jouvenel, in *Le Journalisme en Vingt Leçons*.)

" 'Quand il s'agit des Boches, je crois tout', . . . Ce fut le cas de l'opinion pendant la guerre."

(G. Demartial, *La Mobilisation des Consciences*.)

1. VERSAILLES AND PARIS

THE selection of Paris as the center of peace negotiations at the close of the World War had an important bearing on subsequent conference events. A number of cities had been under consideration by the Entente leaders for the honor of being host to the Peace Conference: London, Brussels, The Hague, Geneva and Lausanne, as well as Versailles, or Paris. President Wilson at first favored Lausanne or Geneva, and Lloyd George agreed with Colonel House that the Conference should not be held on French soil, but rather in a neutral environment, preferably Geneva; while Orlando of Italy, promised to favor the American choice.[1]

The French, however, were not to be casually brushed aside. Did not her sufferings entitle France to this honor? Was it not the Hall of Mirrors, in Versailles, in which the German Empire had been proclaimed in 1871? Where, unless in Berlin itself, could the collapse of the Bismarckian dream be more fittingly celebrated? When the matter was discussed between Clemenceau, Lloyd George and Colonel House, on October 29, the French Premier was determined that the peace should be consummated at Versailles. There was little public discussion of this subject, but the French point of view was shrewdly presented in the semi-official *Temps* (Nov. 3), in what was probably an inspired leader. "The city chosen as the seat of the Congress should be chosen because of its sacrifices, its heroism and martyrdom, or because of its history, and of past events which lend meaning and significance to those of today." Brussels might have been chosen for "noble and just reasons". Nevertheless, the choice should fall upon Versailles, said the *Temps,* not only because France had "borne the heaviest and bloodiest share of the war", but also for the reason that since Versailles had been "the cradle of the German Empire", it ought also to be "its grave". Mr. Wilson yielded, doubtless as a friendly gesture to France, and on November 8 cabled his acceptance of Versailles to Colonel House.[2]

In actual fact, Paris, with its superior accommodations, became the center of deliberations between the Allied and Associated Powers, though the treaty was finally signed in the Hall of Mirrors at Versailles.

The choice of Paris meant that the French people, who had so vital a stake in the peace settlement, were to furnish "the atmosphere wherein the Peace Conference decisions" were to be taken.[3] This was important because of the peculiar degree to which, in France, more than in any other great country, the driving force of opinion is concentrated in the nation's chief city, from which a multiplicity of newspapers and other instrumentalities dominate the national scene.[4] The Conference was thus peculiarly exposed to the winds of French opinion, the significance of which was heightened by the fact that President Wilson and Premier Clemenceau often found themselves in almost fatal disagreement over major peace policies.

The decision was subsequently the source of regrets in Anglo-American quarters. Colonel House later confessed that it would have been better to locate the Conference elsewhere, away from the "intrigues of Paris";[5] and Sey-

mour wrote: "We were hampered by the atmosphere of
Paris. . . . Everyone was afraid of being called a pro-German." [6] Mr. Wilson's threat in early February to have the
Conference moved from Paris was indicative of his subsequent feelings,[7] and Lloyd George, during the turbulent days
of late March, bitterly remarked to the Council of Ten that
the atmosphere of Paris was becoming intolerable.[8]

2. PUBLIC OPINION

In analyzing the drift of French opinion in relation to
the clash of Wilsonian and Clemencist policies, one recognizes the difficulty of starting from a hard and fast definition
of public opinion, and realizes the impossibility of precise
measurements. One can hope to attain only to approximate
accuracy.

Indeed, if public opinion be viewed in terms of a rational
process, as is frequently done, then perhaps it is the wrong
term to use in this connection. If public opinion is "the
social judgment reached upon a question of general or civic
import after conscious, rational public discussion", after
"experiences have been recounted, hopes and fear expressed,
and results weighed",[9] one would be rash to employ this
terminology in connection with the surging currents of
French feelings during the war and the Peace Conference
periods. How much more is this true if one accepts the
qualification of President Lowell, that for a real public
opinion to exist, "the bulk of the people must be in a position
to determine of their own knowledge, or by weighing the
evidence, a substantial part of the facts required for a
rational decision".[10] Such conditions were conspicuous by
their absence in France, as in most other countries, during
those crucial months. Free access to the facts was notoriously lacking, and it can scarcely be assumed, under the
circumstances, that reason prevailed over blind emotion, at
least for the public at large.

Perhaps it would be more realistic to define this concept
simply in terms of the "pictures inside the heads" of groups

of individuals, without regard to the process by which they got there.[11] The public opinion of a given group would be "the pictures which are acted upon" by that group, or by leaders of the group. When one approaches the highest combination of groups, the nation, it naturally becomes increasingly difficult to discover a common set of "pictures" throughout the heterogeneous groups comprising the national unit. Hence public opinion generally tends to be "public" to a given group or set of groups, rather than common to the nation as a whole. Lippmann has shown how extremely difficult it is to create a public opinion common to the entire nation.[12]

Viewing the flux of opinions during the Peace Conference, one can find a few instances in which this unanimity within the nation is clearly visible, if the actions and expressions of representative leaders and representative organs of opinion are reliable guides. Numerous other instances occur in which unanimity is far from realized among the various groups. In such cases the various factors must be weighed with a view to appraising the relative importance or preponderance of a given view.

In evaluating the currents of French opinion, one must take into account, primarily, the press, the party groups in Parliament, and non-party associations engaged in propaganda work. Of these the first two are more important, for the reason that their representative character is more obvious, and their general significance can be much more accurately estimated. They may therefore be regarded as better guides for the purpose of this inquiry.

3. The Press and Public Opinion

The precise relation of the press to public opinion is a perennially debated, and persistently recurring question. Does the press reflect public opinion, or does it make it? The probabilities are that neither alternative is a complete statement of the case, and that both reflect a large part of the truth, the degree to which the press either reflects or makes opinion, depending on the circumstances. There is much truth in the statement that there are two sorts of questions for the public, those as to which the public feels itself competent and those as to which it believes itself incompetent; those where a point of view exists already, and those in which it does not exist.[13] The press, it is said, tends to be all-powerful in the latter type of cases, and is relatively impotent in the former. Within limits this formula is sound, though the difficulty of fixing the limits is obvious enough. That there is always an undefinable "no-man's land" between the alternatives makes the problem a constantly baffling one. Francis Delaisi remarked on the ambiguousness of this relationship in saying that "the press does not represent public opinion, though it does make it—and it generally reacts to it. There is a give-and-take relationship."[14] The press, during the course of the Peace Conference, could scarcely have altered the conviction of the great majority of Frenchmen that the peace settlement should be severe on Germany, yet, in particular instances, the leading organs of opinion could have made a wide variety of solutions acceptable to the public, so long as these were interpreted as answering generally to the demand for harshness. On the other hand, it could have created, and did in fact create, a public opinion favorable to a more Draconian peace than had been demanded or expected prior to the Armistice. Speaking of the power of the "heavy press" of Paris (five or six leading dailies) de Chambure says "it covers more than ten millions of readers; it is able to create, to shape or to check, no matter what current of opinion; no power in France is more real than that which it exercises".[15] This is doubtless an overstatement, but F. L. Schuman is not far wrong in saying that "all commentators are agreed that the most important single factor in the formation of opinion, however it may be defined, is the daily press".[16]

In this connection the question arises as to the influence of the censorship on the formation of public opinion. A recognized policy in all countries during the war period, the censorship continued in France throughout the Peace Conference. No one had complained against its harshness during the war more than Clemenceau, who, before his premiership, changed the name of his paper from *Homme Libre* (free man) to *Homme Enchaîné* (chained man). When he took over the government in November 1917 the name of his paper was changed back to *Homme Libre,* but the only change in the censorship policy was a degree of added rigor; and when the war gave place to the Armistice, the policy continued with unabated severity, in spite of complaints coming equally from all sections of the press.[17] Although the American peace delegation had actually been in Paris since December 14, the French press, as late as January 10, was forbidden to announce, even unofficially, the names of the French delegates.[18] The *Intransigeant* was forbidden (Dec. 6) to reprint from the *Journal de Genève* (Swiss) an item relating to presumed French claims at the Conference. The *Débats*[19] remarked (Dec. 5) that for several years the censor had not permitted any news to come through regarding Montenegro. *Bonsoir* was seized three times during the week of April 25, 1919, once for attempting to reproduce an interview from the *Daily Mail* with Marshal Foch, a second time for mentioning the seizure, and a third time for printing an article from an American paper.[20] The *Information* was suspended for eight days, March 2 to 9, for attempting to publish alleged new Armistice conditions, an item which had already appeared in the English press.

The methods of the censorship were such that even the press itself frequently did not appreciate the full extent of the distortion of the news. Every day the news agencies, Havas and Radio, obtained "official information" from the government offices. This was put in one file to be given out to the press. In another file each agency placed information obtained from non-official sources. Inquiry was then made of the censor as to which of these items might be given out to the press. Those matters denied by the censor to the press were secreted in a third file. Since most of the information carried by the press came through the agencies, the result was that the newspapers themselves frequently did not know the nature or extent of the censorship. Furthermore, the government restricted the papers that were allowed to enter France, and many foreign newspapers were not seen even by the newspaper editors themselves. Many papers from abroad came only to the agencies. Thus, in a double sense, the editors were restricted and handicapped in their relations with the public.[21] The Socialist *Populaire* (Jan. 10, 1919), after confirming the existence of the above system, added that the letters of special correspondents were opened at the frontier and some of them taken. "Of those that remain, the censor sees to it that we do not use them."

Against this system the French papers did not cease to protest, the principal argument against it being, as the *Débats* put it (Nov. 23, 1918), that the French position was being weakened by "forbidding the press to explain and defend French interests". The total effect of the censorship régime was undoubtedly to limit the competence of the public to form intelligent opinions on matters often vitally connected with the peace. Since the people were denied many important facts, a really enlightened opinion could not be said to exist, and the quality of French opinion was to that extent lowered. This did not alter the fact, however, that, with regard to major aspects of the peace, a consensus of opinion existed, within particular groups, or indeed, in some cases, within the nation as a whole. It is doubtless equally true that the fact of the censorship did not reduce the power of the press over public opinion. It may, in a limited number of cases, have made individuals more skeptical of the information actually published, but the total result was to place the public more than ever at the mercy of the editorial interpretations of the events bearing upon the peace. When it is borne in mind that in the French press as a whole the editorial columns play a vastly more important rôle, relatively speaking, than in American newspapers, the significance of this situation becomes even more striking.

Because of the multiplicity of French newspapers, and because of the fact that they represent all shades of opinion, from reactionism and nationalism, on the extreme Right Wing, to Socialism and anti-nationalism on the extreme Left Wing, it will be well to classify the organs of the press, from Right to Left, so that the various papers may be more easily placed in their proper sectors of the journalistic political rainbow. It will also be useful to indicate, within this general grouping, the relative influence of the respective journals. A three-fold classification will be made on this score. The newspapers in the most influential group will be indicated by the use of large capitals; those in the middle category will be put in small capitals, and those in the third group will be given in italics. With this double classification, from the points of view of political color and of relative influence, it is hoped that the reader may be able to follow the activities of the press with more interest and understanding.

Naturally, any such classification is rather hazardous, and is certain to provoke some differences of opinion. Many such differences of opinion have already been encountered on the part of those whose personal experiences would incline them to place particular papers in one classification rather than another, whether from the point of view of political color, or of influence. The only recourse has therefore been to follow the indications of the greatest weight of evidence. A source of some difficulty in this connection is the fact that sometimes a paper may be relatively moderate, or even radical, in general internal policy, while pursuing a nationalistic foreign policy. The *Matin* was a striking case in point at the time of the Peace Conference. This was likewise true of practically all the papers of the moderate Left, and also, as will be seen, of the moderate Left parties in the Chamber of Deputies. The classification as Left, Center or Right, in other words, both in the case of the press and of the parliamentary groups, is more strictly relevant to internal politics than to foreign policy.[22]

Figures relating to circulation can be only approximate, for on this matter utmost secrecy prevails, with some exceptions, in the offices of the respective papers.[23] Other than the newspapers themselves, only the Ministry of Interior and the Havas Agency (which controls the advertising for practically all the French press) have exact circulation figures, and naturally their files are not open to the public. In making an estimate, therefore, one must again weigh the best available evidence from a variety of sources.[24] The classification which follows will, for purposes of convenience, group the Paris and provincial journals separately, and it will relate to the period of the 1919 Peace Conference.

THE PRESS OF PARIS, 1918-1919 [25]

THE RIGHT WING PRESS [26]

L'ACTION FRANÇAISE—Léon Daudet, Jacques Bainville, Charles Maurras; [27] Royalist; organ of *"Parti de l'Action Française";* importance extended beyond limits of Royalist group; 60,000 to 80,000.

La Libre Parole—Joseph Denais; anti-Semitic; independent Catholic; specially a partisan of annexation of Left Bank; less important than formerly; since disappeared; 10,000 to 20,000.

LE GAULOIS—Arthur Meyer, René d'Aral; Catholic and Royalist, but anti-*Action Française;* organ of Society and men of affairs; now merged with *Figaro;* 15,000 to 25,000.

LA LIBERTÉ—Georges Berthoulat, Marcellin; Catholic; militarist; one of most widely read (in Paris) afternoon papers; 25,000 to 35,000.

L'ÉCHO DE PARIS—"Pertinax", Marcel Hutin; nationalist; Catholic; representative of views of General Staff and of Foreign Office (though not always those of Clemenceau); widely read in army circles; one of the "Big Five"; about 300,000.

LA CROIX—Official and leading Catholic organ, published by the clergy; ultramontane; anti-Royalist; editions in provinces; about 100,000.

L'Avenir—Organ of "Union of Economic Interests"; close to "Committee of the Left Bank"; 5,000 to 10,000.

L'Éclair—Independent clerical; less important politically; now disappeared; 10,000 to 15,000.

LA VICTOIRE—Ultra-patriotic organ of Gustave Hervé, who, before the war was anti-patriotic; quite a vogue during war; anti-clerical, 30,000 to 40,000.

LE FIGARO—Alfred Capus; organ of Society and men of affairs; said to be close to Clemenceau; 20,000 to 30,000.

LE JOURNAL DES DÉBATS—Auguste Gauvain; independent; circulation among the "élite"; influence out of proportion to circulation; established 1789; 20,000 to 25,000. (Cited as *Débats*.)

THE CENTER PRESS

La Démocratie Nouvelle—Lysis; André Chéradame; organ of the "Sillon", Social Catholics; strongly nationalist; now disappeared; 10,000 to 15,000.

L'INTRANSIGEANT—Léon Bailby; conservative republican; militarist; widest afternoon circulation; 300,000 to 350,000.

LE MATIN—Stéphane Lauzanne; one of the "Big Five"; very patriotic; circulation estimated from 1,000,000 to 1,500,000.

LE JOURNAL—Saint-Brice; one of "Big Five"; close relations with munitions interests; about 1,000,000.

LE TEMPS—Jean Herbette, Ph. Millet; leading semi-official organ; opportunist; nationalist; greatest influence; about 70,000.

L'Excelsior—Largely pictorial; less important politically; about 100,000.

LE PETIT PARISIEN—One of "Big Five"; close to government; organ of middle class; widest circulation; 1,800,000 to 2,000,000.

LE PETIT JOURNAL—Organ of Pichon, Foreign Minister; one of "Big Five"; clientele, middle class; about 500,000.

PARIS-MIDI—Organ of Louis Loucheur, industrialist and member of government; Albert Milhaud; about 25,000.

L'INFORMATION—Léon Chavenon; leading economic and financial organ; about 25,000.

Le Petit Bleu—Reputation for extorting money from business concerns on threats of exposure; circulation very small, but copies sent to each senator and deputy.

THE LEFT WING PRESS

Le Rappel—Edmond du Mesnil; organ of the "Committee of the Left Bank" and advocate of annexation; very patriotic; since disappeared; about 10,000.

L'HOMME LIBRE—Eugène Lautier; formerly owned by Clemenceau; close to government; about 10,000.

LE RADICAL—Senator J. Perchot; organ of Radical Socialist Party; patriotic; about 10,000.

L'ŒUVRE—Organ of Gustave Téry; independent of party, but Radical Socialist tendency; widely read in provinces; 100,000 to 150,000.

Bonsoir—Closely affiliated with *Œuvre;* journal of the boulevards; now disappeared; small circulation.

LE PAYS—Gaston Vidal, Victor Basch, etc.; advanced radical tendencies; less important than formerly; now disappeared; about 10,000.

La France Libre—Compère-Morel, Arthur Rozier, Adrien Veber; established July 1918 by the "41" Socialists who differed from more radical policies of *Humanité* and the party majority; patriotic; since disappeared; 5,000 to 6,000.

L'Heure—Socialistic; Marcel Sembat one of chief contributors; since disappeared; small circulation.

LA BATAILLE—Léon Jouhaux; organ of General Confederation of Labor; now replaced by *Le Peuple;* 5,000 to 10,000.

L'HUMANITÉ—Marcel Cachin; official organ of Socialist Party; Communist since 1921; about 150,000.

LE POPULAIRE—Jean Longuet, Paul Faure; organ of Left Wing Socialism; now the official organ of Socialist Party; 25,000 to 30,000.

La Vérité—Paul Meunier; primarily pacifist organ; since disappeared; small circulation.

Le Journal du Peuple—Henri Fabre, Séverine; organ of extreme pacifism; since disappeared; small circulation.

Several observations should be made on the above classification. It is not to be assumed that opinion was uniform within any one of the three major sections of the press. There was a fair degree of uniformity within the Center group, but on the Right and Left Wings there were important cleavages. This was especially marked on the Left, where the Socialist and pacifist press differed more radically from that of the moderate Left than the press of the moderate Left differed from that of the Center or even the more moderate elements of the Right. Indeed, it ought to be borne in mind that Clemenceau himself was a member of the Radical Socialist group of the Left, and that the bitterest opponents of his war and peace policies were among the Socialists, also of the Left. On the whole, it may be said that the major foreign policies of the government were supported by all three sections of the press except that of the extreme Left and, occasionally, a small fraction on the extreme Right. These elements may be designated the "governmental" press, and, if the extreme Right be added, they might be classed as the "patriotic" press, in contradistinction to the Socialist organs which were frequently charged with being unpatriotic.

The Paris press may be divided into what are commonly called "journals of information", and "journals of opinion". The journals of information are those which in the emphasis on news features, as compared with editorial opinion, most nearly approach the American conception of a newspaper. In the journals of opinion the editorial policy more obviously dominates the news columns. The *Petit Parisien, Matin, Journal, Petit Journal* and *Écho de Paris* are commonly listed among the first group and are referred to as the "heavy press", because of the weight of their influence throughout the country.[28] They also comprise the so-called "Big Five". From the point of view of prestige and power in influential circles, however, it ought to be noted that none of them is equal to the *Temps,* which should probably be classed as the heaviest member of the so-called heavy press.

The above classification suggests that the real importance of a paper is not measured solely by its circulation, though circulation is, of course, important. In fact, so far as the journals of information are concerned, it is of dominant importance. With the remainder, however, the significance of a paper may be contingent on its relations with the government or the character of its clientele. This is best illustrated, perhaps, by such papers as the *Débats,* and the *Temps* at the time of the Peace Conference. The *Débats,* for example, had a dignified tradition, dating from 1789; also an able staff, headed by Auguste Gauvain, eminent and respected authority on foreign affairs. Though its circulation was limited, its influence was of the first order. Even more important was the *Temps,* dating from 1861 and universally regarded as the mouthpiece of the Foreign Office. Ably written, its editorial columns often surrounded with the atmosphere of an official pronouncement, its weight is brought to bear on the entire press of France. As one

Paris director of a leading provincial paper remarked: "At five P.M. each day every Paris editor of the various provincial journals has before him a copy of the *Temps,* which he reads carefully before sending out his despatches destined to appear in the respective provincial organs on the following morning."[29] Whether the policy of the provincial paper agrees with or differs from that of the *Temps,* it is bound to be influenced, in one way or another, by that organ's editorial and other columns.[30]

It is generally conceded that the Paris press exercises an important influence on that of the provinces. In important national crises the attitude taken by the leading organs of the Paris press will very probably become the government policy, and "no effort on the part of any provincial paper would have the slightest chance of altering it when Paris has made up its mind."[31] De Chambure says that the heavy press of Paris is the source of inspiration for most of the provincial organs, adding that in no case are these latter uninfluenced by the former. If the *Temps* be included in the heavy press, this appraisal is certainly accurate.[32]

The extent of the direct influence of the Paris press naturally diminishes with the lengthening distance from Paris, and beyond two hundred miles it decreases rapidly. The result is that in the provinces there exist a number of papers of high rank, which, though they maintain offices in, and direct connections with Paris, involving a certain dependent relationship, nevertheless enjoy an important prestige in their own right, over a comparatively wide radius. No study of French opinion should fail to take them into account. It is an interesting fact, indeed, that the leading organs of the Radical Socialist press are in the provinces, as, for example, the *Dépêche* of Toulouse, the *Progrès* of Lyons, and the *France de Bordeaux.* Other comparable organs of the conservative press are the *Petit Marseillais* of Marseilles, the *Petite Gironde* of Bordeaux, and the *Ouest-Éclair* of Rennes; though these are by no means equal in importance to comparable conservative organs of Paris.[33]

These six papers, along, perhaps, with the *Écho du Nord* of Lille, would constitute what might be called the heavy press of the provinces, though they are not commonly so called. A selected list of the provincial press is given below, in which the papers are grouped according to their political complexion, and also classified from the point of view of relative influence, as of 1918-1919. Here as in the case of the Paris press, evidence is not always decisive, and opinions differ; hence one can hope only for approximate accuracy, particularly in the classification as to relative importance. Accuracy in estimating circulation is even more difficult to attain, hence figures will be omitted, though it may generally be said that those organs of the first rank—certainly the first six named above—enjoyed a circulation of 300,000 or thereabouts, in a region covering several departments.

REPRESENTATIVE PROVINCIAL NEWSPAPERS, 1918-1919

NEWSPAPERS OF THE RIGHT WING

LE NOUVELLISTE DE LYON—Royalist; Catholic; regional.
JOURNAL DE ROUEN—Regional.
La Dépêche (Lille)—Departmental.
L'ÉCHO DU NORD (Lille)—Major regional.[34]
L'OUEST-ÉCLAIR (Rennes)—Major regional.
L'ÉCLAIR DE L'EST (Nancy)—Regional.
L'ÉCLAIREUR DE NICE ET DU SUD-EST—Regional.

NEWSPAPERS OF THE CENTER

LE PHARE DE LA LOIRE (Nantes)—Regional.
LA PETITE GIRONDE (Bordeaux)—Major regional.
LE LYON RÉPUBLICAIN (Lyons)—Regional.
LE PETIT MARSEILLAIS (Marseilles)—Major regional.
La Dépêche (Brest)—Departmental.
LE PROGRÈS DU NORD (Lille)—Regional.
L'EST RÉPUBLICAIN (Nancy)—Regional.

NEWSPAPERS OF THE LEFT WING

LE PROGRÈS DE LA SOMME (Amiens)—Regional.
LA DÉPÊCHE (Toulouse)—Major regional; official Radical Socialist organ.

LA FRANCE DE BORDEAUX ET DU SUD-OUEST—Major
    regional.
LE PETIT PROVENÇAL (Marseilles)—Regional.
LE PROGRÈS (Lyons)—Major regional.
LE POPULAIRE DE NANTES—Regional; advanced radical.
LE POPULAIRE DU CENTRE (Limoges)—Departmental; Socialist Left
    Wing.

While the Paris press consists chiefly of journals of opinion, the provincial papers stress news rather than editorial comment. Or at most, they follow the example of the *Écho de Paris,* in striking a balance between these two features. Even in the leading provincial papers, such as the *Dépêche* of Toulouse, the *France de Bordeaux,* or the *Petit Marseillais,* or the Left Wing Socialist *Populaire du Centre,* leading articles are often contributed by persons outside the regular staff, such as eminent members of a party or by authorities from various walks of life. Contributed in this way, these articles, however worthy—and they are generally of outstanding merit—tend to lose some of their timeliness, or edge, since they generally arrive a few days after the event. Moreover, they frequently come from Paris, and thus tend further to emphasize the intellectual leadership, if not dominance, of that city.

4. THE POLITICAL PARTIES

The grouping of the press of Paris and the provinces from Right to Left, in accordance with the political color of the respective papers, is reproduced in the party groups of the French Parliament, and especially in the Chamber of Deputies, to a degree which is unknown in the legislative bodies of the United States. Just as every color of the political spectrum is reflected in one or more organs of the press, so in the Chamber the semi-circle of deputies, composed of some twelve different groups, changes color gradually from extreme radicalism on the Left to extreme reactionism on the Right. The following table will give a picture of the groups as they existed June 25, 1919, on the eve of the Chamber debates on the Treaty with Germany:

GROUPS OF THE RIGHT

Des Droites (Conservatives)	10
Liberal Action	18
Non-inscrits (not inscribed in a group)	8
Democratic Republican Entente	57
Total	93

GROUPS OF THE CENTER

Independents	23
Democratic Left	5
Republican Left	49
Radical Left	56
Radical and Socialist Republican Union	16
Total	149

GROUPS OF THE LEFT

Republican Radical and Radical Socialist	156
Socialist Republicans	25
Unified Socialists	93
Total	274 [35]

To divide the Chamber into three presumably clear-cut sections is, in fact, quite impossible. It is difficult to tell precisely where the Left ends, and the Center begins. It is much more difficult, if not impossible, to state precisely where the Center ends and the Right begins. There is a degree of overlapping between most of the groups, for, if political parties in France, with the possible exception of those on the extreme Left, manifest a large degree of fluidity, the groups in the Chamber, which are the nondescript forms into which the parties are organized for parliamentary action, are even less stable in composition, though they generally manifest somewhat greater homogeneity in policy.

Within any one of the three major divisions of the Chamber (Left, Center, Right), one would not expect to find complete harmony of views on major problems. The most striking cleavage of opinion, however, was manifested within

the Left Wing, where, particularly in matters relating to
the peace, a rather sharp line could be drawn between the
Socialists and the more patriotic groups farther to the right.
Whereas, on matters of domestic policy the Radical Socialists and the Socialists were generally able to find much
common ground, their views on foreign policy, and particularly with regard to the peace settlement after the war,
tended to diverge widely. At their national congress of
September 1919, the Radical Socialists were able to repeat
their old slogan, "No enemies on the Left", but they felt
bound to add: "except enemies of the country"; and their
party program, while affirming their attachment to peace,
vigorously affirmed that "The Radical and Radical Socialist
Party is ardently patriotic." [36] In the Chamber, therefore,
as in the press, it was very largely a case of the Unified
Socialists against the patriotic parties, though this is not
to suggest that there was agreement among non-Socialist
groups, or even among the Socialists, as to all points of the
peace program.

The fact that the political cleavages within the Chamber
of Deputies on peace policies corresponded fairly closely to
those in the press outside, raises the presumption that the
press was not, in general, out of harmony with public
opinion. Perhaps one should not infer that a given preponderance of opinion in the press could be translated into
an equal preponderance of identical views among the public
at large, in spite of the fact that the press, even when it
does not reflect the views of its readers, does very largely
mold them. Yet, when this coincidence of views occurs
between sections of the press and corresponding groups of
parliament, it seems reasonable to conclude that this coincidence is not merely accidental, but that the views represent
the opinions of corresponding groups among the public.

It may be, however, that the party groups in parliament
are not truly representative of the public, and cannot therefore reflect its opinion. Naturally a party's representative
character can never be more than approximate on any spe-

cific question, owing to the complexity of issues that cloud every election. Nevertheless, when party divisions are based, as in France, on differing social and economic concepts (as contrasted, for example, with the major parties in the United States) one may assume that the policy of a given party represents the general political outlook of its constituents. The presumption in this case would be, for example, that the international ideology of the Socialist leaders, as translated into peace policies toward Germany, would prevail with the Socialist masses. The same would apply, generally, to non-Socialist parties.

The elections of November 1919 furnished a species of test, imperfect, to be sure, of the degree to which the various groups in Parliament had represented the popular mind during the peace negotiations. It is true that the election was not a mere popular vote on the question of ratifying party attitudes on the Treaty. There were other serious issues, internal in character, growing out of chaotic economic conditions, and sometimes involving alarming strikes among the workers. But these issues were such as to permit the so-called National Bloc to raise the cry of "Bolshevism" against the Socialists, and thus to give added force to the anti-patriotic stigma already attached to them as a result of their attitude regarding the peace settlement. In spite of these facts the Socialist vote, which was approximately 1,400,000 in 1914, rose to approximately 1,700,000 in 1919, thus amounting to twenty-five per cent of a total vote of about 6,800,000, whereas, in 1914 their vote was but sixteen per cent out of a total of 8,700,000 votes cast.[37] Making due allowance for extraneous issues in the election, it seems reasonable to infer that during the peace negotiations the Socialists were not misrepresenting the Socialist constituency. Indeed, the increase of some 300,000 popular votes might suggest that the views which they advocated during the peace negotiations were representative of a somewhat wider circle [38] than the actual Socialist membership in parliament at that time would indicate.

On the other hand, the elections of November recorded a distinct triumph for the ultra-patriotic parties, as contrasted with the moderately patriotic ones. The Radical Socialists of the Chamber, for example, relatively moderate, but never accused of lack of patriotism, were cut down from 172, after the 1914 elections, to 86 after those of 1919,[39] while the ultra-patriotic Democratic Republican Entente rose from a total of 57, before the elections, to 183 in the new parliament.[40] On the whole, it might be said that the election tended to swing slightly to extremes, though the greatest gains went to the more patriotic parties, thus giving them a species of vote of confidence for their attitudes toward the peace settlement.

There seems to be ample justification for the conclusion that the parliamentary groups and the press represented fairly accurately the dominant trends of opinion in France during the Peace Conference.

5. NON-POLITICAL ASSOCIATIONS

Another important factor in the expression or in the making of public opinion on war and peace policies was the numerous non-party associations which either sprang into existence during the war, or on the approach of peace, or which, if already in being, turned at least a share of their energy into these channels. An appraisal of the work of such organizations in terms of public opinion is naturally an extremely difficult task, since there are few definitive criteria. The amount of published material is clearly no guide, for a small, well-financed group can, in this respect, outdo a much larger less pecunious organization. The spread of such an organization's influence is not easily estimated. The fact that such groups are more obviously propagandistic than the press inevitably reduces the par value of their publications. Furthermore, the relatively irregular character of their propaganda activities makes hazardous any generalization as to their real significance.

Taking all these factors into account, however, one cannot help being impressed with the widespread and energetic propagandistic activities of a great variety of French groups during the war and the peace negotiations. Our task is not to make a complete analysis of them,[41] but rather to note their general character. The overwhelming majority of those organizations dating from the pre-Armistice period seem to have been designed to fortify the morale of the French masses, and to build up resistance against any possible propaganda efforts of the enemy.

Naturally, supreme patriotism for France, and bitter hostility toward Germany, were the universal leitmotifs in a time when any sign of weakness or conciliation was stamped as "defeatism". A large number of these groups (apparently a majority of the most important ones) were brought together in a central organization known as the "Union of the Great French Associations Against Enemy Propaganda", which carried on its activities throughout the period of the Peace Conference, and which was headed by the eminent historian Ernest Lavisse, and by the President of the Chamber of Deputies (later President of France), Paul Deschanel.[42] A mere enumeration of the most important of these confederated bodies is impressive:[43]

1. The Committee of University Entente.
2. The National League of Economy.
3. The French Renaissance in Alsace and Lorraine.
4. The National People's Aviation League.
5. Brothers and Sisters of the War.
6. The Catholic Propaganda Committee.
7. The Protestant Propaganda Committee.
8. The French League.
9. The Union of Departmental Committees.
10. The Book Committee.
11. The Rural Cinema.
12. The Friendly Union of Alsace-Lorraine.
13. The Union of Republican Youth.
14. The Effort of France and its Allies.
15. The Civic Friendship.
16. The Erckmann-Chatrian Society.
17. The League of Moral Education.

18. The Jewish Propaganda Committee.
19. The Society of Literary Folk.
20. The Friends of the University.
21. The League *Souvenez-vous*.
22. The Club of French and Colonial Officials.
23. The Society of Veterans of the Land and Sea Armies.
24. The Michelet Committee.
25. The Village Conference.
26. The Hearth.
27. Union of Fathers and Mothers Whose Sons Have Died for the Country.
28. The French University Alliance.
29. The Farmers of France.
30. The National Federation of Societies for Military Preparation.
31. The Moral Aid.
32. The Civic League.
33. The Federation of Agricultural Associations.
34. The Feminine Effort.
35. The National Women's Council.
36. The French Touring Club.
37. The French Union.
38. The Society for Popular Lectures.
39. The National Association for Economic Expansion.
40. The Circle for Lay Teaching.
41. The League of Patriots.
42. The National Union of Cantonal Delegates.
43. The Seine-et-Oise Committee of Propaganda.
44. The Association of French Doctors.
45. The *Ligue Patria*.
46. The Press Association of the East.

The general attitude and tone of the activities of the central organization were expressed editorially in its information leaflet of March 1, 1919. Referring to Germany as "The Permanent Peril", it said, "We must take guarantees. . . . They can never be too certain. The Germans will always be Germans." Another leaflet, of February 1, picturing a still powerful Germany before a glorious, but wounded, France, enjoined French children to remember that they could never be friends with Germans.

The various societies affiliated with the Union naturally

varied somewhat in tone, but were not far apart in their
general views as to the rigor of the terms which the peace
should embody. The Catholic and Protestant Propaganda
Committees both demanded a crushing peace. In the weekly
Protestant bulletin of February 18, 1919, it was argued that
the German people were in a less advanced stage of evolution, so that they were "incapable of elevating themselves to
an understanding of universal principles of morals and of
justice", and that therefore Germany could not pretend to
equal rights with other nations.[44] The "Village Conference",
under the direction of Victor Cambon, Gaston Deschamps,
Abbé Wetterle, etc., sought, by means of tracts and regional
conferences, to maintain the morale of rural communities.
While disclaiming political motives, its publications poured
fire and brimstone on Germany and exhorted the people to
maintain the national unity.[45] The "Michelet Committee",
under Edouard Driault and Gaston Roux, based its propaganda on "the history of our glorious past", hoping that the
French people "enlightened by the history of the last hundred years", would realize the necessity of establishing the
peace "on inviolable frontiers and on guarantees of absolute
security".[46] The "Civic League" was one of the most active
and most passionate of the affiliated societies. Under the
presidency of Ernest Denis, Professor at the Sorbonne, and
including some fifteen other professors on its committee,
it preached hatred against Germany and urged internal
solidarity upon all Frenchmen. The French University
Alliance, including such eminent names on its list as Ernest
Lavisse, Maurice Croiset, Émile Picard, Émile Boutreaux,
Georges Lecomte, Louis Marin, and a variety of faculty
members from the Universities of Paris, Lyons, Caen and
Rennes, expressed doubt as to whether the German people,
which had "not changed their spirit for two thousand years",
would succeed in changing it in the ensuing two thousand
years.[47]

There were other, and even more patriotic groups, not all
of which were affiliated with the "Union". There was the

Action Française group, the Military League, the French
Maritime League, the Federation of the National Leagues
for the Defense of the Rights and Interests of France, the
Committee of Action of the Young Patriots, the Anti-
German Club of France, and a number of others.[48] There
were also other specially interested groups, such as the Committee of the Left Bank, the Union of Economic Interests,
and the National Committee of Action for the Integral Reparation of Damages Caused by the War.[49] All of these made
their voices heard.

Amidst the babel of tongues of special-interest and
patriotic groups, the voices of moderation, of pacifism and
internationalism were scarcely audible, though at times they
rose in fairly clear tones. Pacifism did not, to be sure,
necessarily mean generosity toward Germany. The French
Association for the League of Nations,[50] most influential
proponent of the League idea, specifically proposed to keep
Germany out of the League until she had convinced the
world of her good faith. Even the more advanced pacifist
group, the Peace through Law Association,[51] in addressing a
note to Clemenceau, October 8, 1918, took the precaution to
remind him that though they were "pacifists", they were
"not defeatists. During four years, we have brought to the
war of justice the constant and resolute support of our
propaganda."[52] In January, 1919, furthermore, the French
pacifists refused to meet with those of Germany and neutral
countries for the purpose of discussing the organization of a
durable peace, because, said Ruyssen, the facts of the war
had become a part of history, and because it was "morally
impossible either to forget them or to refrain from
passing judgment upon them".[53] Likewise, the League for
the Rights of Man and of the Citizen,[54] truest guardian of
the doctrines of 1789, and closest perhaps, in spirit and
letter, to the ideas of Woodrow Wilson,[55] strongly supported
the "sacred union" against Germany during the war, hoping, in this way, to save both the country and liberty.[56] The
Confederation of Labor was the most powerful of the non-

political organizations which, in the period preceding and following the Armistice, raised its voice in favor of internationalism, and which whole-heartedly accepted the ideals of Woodrow Wilson.[57]

In early 1919, the Left Wing intellectuals were beginning to assert themselves in the hope of breaking down the prejudices of the war; and on April 6, 1919, Barbusse and a small circle of other writers began the publication of *Notre Voix,* a weekly organ which, it was hoped, would be "the voice of intelligence and kindness", and which was dedicated to the theory that Germany was not alone responsible for the war, and also to the reconstruction of society.[58]

Viewing the activities of the non-party associations as a whole, and admitting the difficulty of appraising them accurately in terms of public opinion, one remains impressed with the tremendous disparity between the great number and authority of the voices raised in behalf of nationalism and militarism and the few lifted up in behalf of moderation and conciliation. One current of propaganda was a mighty torrent; the other a tiny trickle. The voice of pacifist internationalism was practically hushed during the fury of the war, and the flood of propaganda flowed almost entirely from the mills of the super-patriots. This was natural enough, yet it remains true that the persistence and the volume of the nationalistic forces were bound to exercise a determining influence on the thinking of the nation as a whole.

Aside from the Confederation of Labor, which occasionally expressed itself in favor of moderation and a decent peace, the anti-nationalist forces remained comparatively unorganized and inarticulate. Official repression, unofficial pressures and inadequate resources combined to hamper their activities and to limit their influence on the course of events. In proportion to their numerical importance, the forces of pacifism and Socialism found far less adequate expression through unofficial *ad hoc* organizations than through parliamentary and journalistic channels, where they were better represented and in a stronger position in relation to the government. But here, as in the case of the press and of parliament, the Socialists, with the Left Wing of the labor movement, and a small number of ardent pacifists from Radical Socialist ranks, were aligned against the very much larger patriotic groups farther to the right.

NOTES

[1] Seymour, Charles, *The Intimate Papers of Colonel House*, 4 vols. (Cambridge, Mass., 1928), vol. iv, p. 217. Hereafter cited as *House Papers*.

[2] *Ibid.*, p. 218. Seymour says the President was afraid of enemy and Bolshevik influence in Switzerland. His estimate of the Swiss environment had apparently changed also, as he stated to the Colonel that Switzerland was "saturated with every poisonous element and open to every hostile influence".

[3] This fact, as R. C. Binkley says, gave a somewhat "higher importance" to the movement of French opinion during the Conference. Binkley, R. C., *Reactions of Public Opinion to Woodrow Wilson's Statesmanship from the Armistice to the Peace of Versailles, 1927*, p. 161. Typewritten manuscript in Hoover War Library.

[4] Julius M. Price, commenting on this situation has said that during the past 150 years "in every political crisis the national sentiment has been singularly affected by the trend of events and the ethical atmosphere of Paris. . . . Whatever the prevailing influence in the capital . . . it is usually intuitively expressed in the general tone of the whole nation. . . ." *Fortnightly Review*, June 1922, vol. 117, pp. 977-985.

[5] Thompson, C. T., *The Peace Conference Day by Day* (New York, 1920), p. 187.

[6] Quoted by Nicolson, Harold, in *Peacemaking, 1919* (London, 1933), p. 77. Nicolson says Paris was "too self-conscious, too insistent, to constitute a favourable site" for the Conference. *Ibid.*, p. 76.

[7] Thompson, *op. cit.*, p. 187. George D. Herron wrote that "The beginning of the tragedy was the meeting-place of the Conference. The choice was fatal both to Wilson and to the principles he had pronounced." *The Defeat in the Victory* (London, 1921), p. 28.

[8] Minutes of Supreme Council, in Miller, David H., *My Diary at the Conference of Paris* (Privately printed). Hereafter cited as *Miller Diary*.

[9] King, Clyde L., in Graves, W. Brooke, *Readings in Public Opinion* (New York, 1928), pp. xxiii, xxvii.

[10] Quoted in Graves, *op. cit.*, pp. 95 *et seq.*

[11] Lippmann, Walter, *Public Opinion* (New York, 1927), p. 29. John D. Dafoe takes this rather neutral attitude regarding the process by which public opinion is formed in defining it as "an expression of dominant conviction backed by an intention to give effect to it". Wright, Quincy (ed.), *Public Opinion and World-Politics* (Chicago, University of Chicago Press, 1933), p. 7.

[12] See *ibid., passim;* also Lippmann, Walter, *The Phantom Public* (New York, 1925), *passim.*

[13] Chassériaud, R., *La Formation de l'Opinion Publique* (Paris, 1914), p. 20.

[14] Personal interview, May 6, 1931.

[15] Chambure, A. de, *Quelques Guides de l'Opinion en France, 1914-1918* (Paris, 1918), p. 181.

[16] Schuman, F. L., *War and Diplomacy in the French Republic* (New York, 1931), p. 374. Cf., also Jouvenel, Robert de, *Le Journalisme en Vingt Leçons* (Paris, 1920), p. 7.

[17] The censorship was finally abolished October 12, 1919, the day following the ratification of the Treaty by the Senate.

[18] *Information,* Jan. 10, 1919.

[19] *Journal des Débats,* cited as *Débats. Europe Nouvelle,* November 30, cited a whole category of interdictions by the censor, among them being comments on the American elections of early November. On December 28 it wrote: "Thus we have only one right in France, that of keeping quiet."

[20] Great Britain, General Staff, *Allied Press Supplement to Review of the Foreign Press.* Published by the War Office. Vol. vi, p. 1. May 7, 1919. Hereafter cited as *Allied Press.*

[21] Statement to author by Francis Delaisi, April 23, 1931.

[22] The papers on each extreme, however, are much more consistently radical or conservative in foreign and domestic policies.

[23] As one newspaper editor remarked, to ask a paper for its circulation is much the same as stopping a man in the street and asking him how much money he has in the bank.

[24] The figures given are the result of a variety of estimates from individuals with special information or from other sources of authority, e.g., a report of the British General Headquarters, 1918, which is on file in the Bibliothèque de la Guerre, Paris; the German *Handbuch der Auslandpresse, 1918* (Berlin, 1918), which purports to estimate the circulation of some of the papers of that time; Hayes, C. J. H., *France, a Nation of Patriots* (New York, 1930), pp. 431-470.

[25] This list does not purport to include every Paris paper, but only those having real political significance.

[26] Within each group the political color changes relatively from "Right" to "Left" as one reads down.

[27] The names of individuals refer to leading personalities connected with the paper—directors, foreign editors, etc. The figures represent estimates of circulation.

[28] The *Intransigeant* should also be ranked among the journals "of information", though its influence is less widespread than that of the "Big Five" above referred to.

[29] Statement of M. Olive-Villard, of the *France de Bordeaux,* August 1931.

[30] The situation is naturally somewhat similar in relation to the Press of Paris. And this is true in spite of a common and well-grounded suspicion that the *Temps* at times stoops to receive money for matters carried in its news or editorial columns.

[31] Price, J. M., *Fortnightly Review,* June 1922, vol. 117, pp. 977-985.

[32] Chambure, *op. cit.,* p. 182. This situation lends added significance to the fact that the Peace Conference was held in Paris.

[33] No Socialist paper of the provinces, at that time, compared in importance with *Humanité,* of Paris.

[34] The *Écho du Nord* was not actually available for examination, but is noted merely because of its importance.

[35] For various reasons—the war, etc.—the Chamber was short of its full quota of 612 by some 94 members. *Annales de la Chambre des Députés; Débats Parlementaires,* June 25, 1919, p. 2624. Hereafter cited as *Annales de la Chambre.* A discrepancy of 2 between the total of the groups (516) and the total actually in the Chamber (518) is accounted for by the President of the Chamber (Deschanel) and one other member not being included in any of the groups.

[36] Parti Republicain Radical et Radical-Socialiste, Bulletin, No. 30, November 1, 1919.

[37] It is irrelevant, from our point of view, that, owing to the combination of the "patriotic" groups against them, the Socialist representation in the Chamber was actually cut down. La Chapelle, G., *Élections Législatives des 26 avril et 10 mai, 1914* (Paris, 1914), *passim;* also his *Élections Législatives du 16 novembre, 1919* (Paris, 1920), *passim;* Buell, R. L., *Contemporary French Politics* (New York, 1920), p. 194.

[38] Perhaps slightly over 20 per cent.

[39] La Chapelle, *Élections Législatives des 26 avril et 10 mai, 1914,* p. 264.

[40] Buell, *op. cit.,* p. 204.

[41] See Dahlin, Ebba, *Public Opinion on Declared War Aims in France and Germany, 1914-1918* (Stanford University, 1933), *passim.*

[42] The verbatim reports of the Union were widely distributed. They were sent, for example, to all prefects, sub-prefects and to all rectors and inspectors of academies. *Temps,* September 23, 1918.

[43] See Union des Grandes Associations Françaises Contre la Propagande Ennemi, weekly bulletin, 2nd year, no. 25, July 8, 1919. French titles for the Societies:

1. Comité d'Entente Universitaire; 2. Ligue nationale des Économies; 3. Renaissance française en Alsace et en Lorraine; 4. Ligue Nationale populaire de l'aviation; 5. Frères et Sœurs de Guerre; 6. Comité Catholique de Propagande; 7. Comité Protestant de propagande; 8. Ligue Française; 9. L'Union aux Comités départementaux; 10. Comité du Livre; 11. Cinema à la campagne; 12. Union Amicale d'Alsace-Lorraine; 13. Union des Jeunesses républicaines; 14. Effort de la France et de ses alliés; 15. Amitié Civique; 16. Société Erckmann-Chatrian; 17. Ligue d'Éducation morale; 18. Comité israélite de propagande; 19. Société des Gens de Lettres; 20. Les Amis de l'Université 21. Ligue Souvenez-vous; 22. Cercle des fonctionnaires de France et des colonies; 23. Société des Vétérans des Armées de terre et de mer; 24. Comité Michelet; 25. Conférence au Village; 26. Le Foyer; 27. Union des pères et mères dont les fils sont morts pour la patrie; 28. Alliance Universitaires; 29. Agriculteurs de France; 30. Fédération nationale des Sociétés de préparation militaire; 31. Aide Morale;

32. Ligue Civique; 33. Fédération des Associations agricoles; 34. L'Effort Féminin; 35. Conseil National des Femmes; 36. Touring Club de France; 37. Union Française; 38. Société des Conférences populaires; 39. Association Nationale d'Expansion Économique; 40. Cercle d'Enseignment laïque; 41. Ligue des patriotes; 42. Union Nationale des Délégués cantonaux; 43. Comité de Propagande de Seine-et-Oise; 44. Association des Médecins de France; 45. Ligue Patria; 46. Association de la Presse de l'Est.

[44] Bulletin in Hoover War Library. See also Emonet, B., *Nos Buts de Paix* (Paris, 1919), issued for the Catholic Committee of Propaganda. In Hoover War Library.

[45] Bulletins in Hoover War Library.

[46] Driault, Edouard, *La Victoire, Ses Leçons et Ses Promesses,* Pamphlet (Versailles, 1919), in Hoover War Library.

[47] Bulletin of the Alliance, October 1918. In Hoover War Library.

[48] See *Action Française*, May 26, 1919. French titles of above: le groupe d'action française, la Ligue militaire, la Ligue maritime française, la Fédération des Ligues nationales pour la défense des droits et intérêts de la France, le Comité d'Action des Jeunesses patriotiques, le Club antigermanique de France.

[49] French titles: Le Comité du rive gauche, L'Union des intérêts économiques, le Comité national d'Action pour la réparation intégrale des dommages causés par la guerre.

[50] L'Association Française pour la Société des Nations.

[51] L'Association de la paix par le droit.

[52] *La Paix par le Droit,* issue of November 1918, p. 332.

[53] *Ibid.,* January 1919, p. 48.

[54] La Ligue des droits de l'Homme et du citoyen.

[55] Binkley, *op. cit.,* pp. 196-198.

[56] Guernet, Henri, *La Ligue des Droits de l'Homme, La Guerre et la Paix* (Paris, undated), excerpts from minutes of 1917 Congress. Pamphlet in Hoover War Library.

[57] *La Paix par le Droit,* November 1918, p. 365; *L'Avenir,* vol. v, no. 35, March 1919, p. 115. In April 1918, the Republican Coalition was organized, based on strict Wilsonian principles. This group was composed of several hundred leaders from Socialist and pacifist Radical Socialist ranks, but its total effect was merely that of a manifestation of principles, for the Coalition engaged in no organized activity. See files of *Humanité,* April 6, 1918, and after.

[58] Copies in Hoover War Library.

CHAPTER II

THE COMING OF THE ARMISTICE

"We grudge her [Germany] no achievement or distinction of learning or of pacific enterprise such as have made her record very bright and very enviable."
(Woodrow Wilson, in address of Fourteen Points.)

"It is not with madrigals or imprecations that we shall induce Germany to occupy what President Wilson calls 'an enviable place.'"
(*Temps,* January 13, 1918.)

"Le plus terrible compte de peuple à peuple est ouvert. Il sera payé."
(Clemenceau to French Senate, September 17, 1918.)

1. President Wilson's Program Defined

THE Peace Conference was preceded by a considerable period during which the peace program was gradually taking shape. As early as December 1916 the German government had proposed forthwith "to enter peace negotiations", but the war map at that time was so favorable to the Central Powers that discussion of terms was felt by the Allies to be highly undesirable.[1] Prime Minister Briand characterized the German move as "an attempt to weaken the bonds of our alliance, and to undermine the courage of our people";[2] and the Allied comment on it, in reply to President Wilson's request for a statement of war aims, was that any offer based on the existing war map would not express the real strength of the adversaries, and that a peace based thereon would be solely to "the advantage of the aggressor".[3] Although the Allies, on January 10, 1917, followed up this statement with a somewhat fuller statement of objectives, they apparently did not desire that this should be followed by peace parleys, and the year 1917 passed without a definitive formulation of peace objectives by the various belligerents.

29

Meantime, the United States had entered the war, and President Wilson was becoming the leading expositor, among Allied statesmen, of liberal principles of settlement. Furthermore, he believed in broadcasting these principles to the world. In a series of trenchant addresses, beginning with that of the Fourteen Points, January 8, 1918, and climaxing with his Five Principles of September 27, he sought to crystallize the war aims of the Western Democracies.

His example was not, however, eagerly followed by his Allied colleagues in Europe. Although British political leaders talked relatively freely on peace objectives, those of Italy and France preferred a policy of silence.

The diplomatic year was inaugurated by the important addresses of Lloyd George and President Wilson, on January 5 and 8. The situation seemed to both of them to demand further clarification of war policies. Russia had collapsed, and the Bolsheviks were advocating a peace based on the principles of "no indemnities and no annexations".[4] Socialist and labor unrest in England lent special significance to the fact that Lloyd George addressed his statement of principles to representatives of the Trade Unions.[5]

Both speeches aroused widespread discussion in France, but Wilson's pronouncement, doubtless because of its greater precision and comprehensiveness, and its loftier moral tone, soon eclipsed that of Lloyd George in public interest. It was the Wilson program which shortly became the center of controversy in relation to peace objectives.

The French government did not manifest the same lively approval of Wilson's Fourteen Points as it had of Lloyd George's pronouncement. A telegram of congratulation was sent by Clemenceau to Lloyd George, but no comparable public notice was taken of Wilson's statement. This neglect was probably not due to the French Premier's failure to read the President's Fourteen Points, although he later remarked jestingly that he had not done so.[6] The same official coolness toward Wilson's program was manifest, January 11, in the Chamber debates on this subject. Cle-

menceau refused personally to answer the Socialist interpellation on "the diplomatic conduct of the war" and caused
Pichon to reply for the government. In somewhat evasive
terms, and without stating the French policy positively, the
Foreign Minister sought to counter the allegations of the
Left groups that there were divergencies between French
policy and that of Wilson. Referring to "publicity of diplomatic agreements", he turned to the Socialist group and
said: "Tell your Maximalist [Bolshevik] friends to keep us
a little better informed. (Disturbances on the Left.)" Scanning the other points hastily, Pichon read in full the declaration on Alsace-Lorraine, in which Mr. Wilson favored righting "the wrong done to France by Prussia in 1871". "This,"
said Pichon, "was the most applauded point of all the Presidential declarations." [7]

The public reception of Wilson's pronouncement was
somewhat more enthusiastic than that of the government.
Coming, as it did, during a dark period of the war, when
Russia was in collapse and when the American effort had
not really materialized, it brought hope and inspiration to
the French masses. The Left Wing press voiced warm approval, while most of the Center and much of the Right
Wing also found it satisfactory. The conservative *Débats*
(Jan. 11) remarked that the Fourteen Points were the
complement to Lloyd George's speech, and that Wilson had
got down to "solid and concrete proposals". The *Œuvre*
(Jan. 10), of the moderate Left, felt that he represented the
"living consciousness of his fellow citizens". To the *Dépêche*
of Toulouse (Jan. 20), the great provincial organ of
Radical Socialism, the peace of Wilson was the "peace of an
arbitrator", bringing with it the healing of wounds.[8] Even
the organs of the extreme Left approved,[9] and Mayéras, in
the Chamber, stated the dominant Socialist attitude in saying, "Here is what we think of the Wilson proposals. . . .
We accept all of them, even those which might be disquieting. For what reassured us, is that some are presented as
being open to discussion. In certain places Wilson writes

'*devra*'; elsewhere '*pourra*'; elsewhere '*serait*'. He has taken the honest precaution to give all the shadings to his thought." [10]   Thus Mayéras caught the fine distinctions which, according to Colonel House, had been carefully worked out by the President.[11]

There were, nevertheless, significant reticences, reservations, and qualifications in the press of the Center and the Right. Sometimes there were outcroppings of sarcasm.

The *Temps* (Jan. 10), in its first reference to the speech, limited its comments to Mr. Wilson's proposal to right "the wrong done to France" in the matter of Alsace-Lorraine. Observing that it was Mr. Wilson's first specific reference to Alsace-Lorraine, it added that his words in this connection would "make his name popular in the smallest French villages". This was the point, incidentally, which was greeted with the most universal approval throughout France. Even the extreme Socialists admitted that Germany had violated the principle of the "rights of peoples" in 1871.[12]

On the following day the *Temps* (Jan. 11) discussed the address more at length, conceding that it was "one of the greatest political events of the war". Though people would say that the President of the United States was "indulging in illusions", and though his policy was "adventurous in appearance", it might nevertheless be "clever and wise". Referring to the sacrifices which Wilson said the American people were ready to make for the cause, it concluded with a half challenge: "The European Allies wait with confidence to see them at their post of danger." Two days later (Jan. 13) the views of that semi-official organ stood out even more clearly, in its comments on Pichon's speech before the Chamber of Deputies. The great virtue of the Foreign Minister's address was not merely its complete understanding of the subject matter, but also its "clarity, which is not found in like degree in any other oratorical pronunciamento". The Allies were, of course, in agreement, but "a French voice has to speak to the French nation in precise language which embraces the contours of living reality, and does not lose itself in the clouds, even the most alluring ones".[13]

Nationalist feelings were well expressed by the *Écho de Paris* (Jan. 10) which divided Wilson's points into the "realistic" and the "idealistic". The "realistic", and fairly satisfactory ones, were those relating to territorial questions. The "idealistic", and highly unsatisfactory ones, were those referring to open diplomacy, freedom of the seas, removal of economic barriers, reduction of armaments, impartial adjustment of all colonial claims, and the League of Nations. Already the League of Nations was a "dream" to the "realists" of the Right.

2. DEMANDS FOR FURTHER CLARIFICATION OF ALLIED WAR AIMS

The pronouncements of Wilson and Lloyd George raised the question whether France, Great Britain and Italy should not unite with the American government in a joint diplomatic offensive against Germany. Could they not gain a great diplomatic advantage in placing before the world a collective statement of their war aims? Wilson and, apparently, Lloyd George favored such action.[14] Colonel House had endeavored to secure such a statement from the inter-Allied Conference, of December 1 to 3, 1917, but had been unable to win approval even for a resolution stating that the Allies and the United States "are not waging war for the purpose of aggression or indemnity".[15] The urgency of a vote in this direction seemed all the greater, in view of the Bolshevik program of a peace on the basis of no annexations and no indemnities, and in view of the German suggestions of willingness to enter into discussions on that basis. The only previous comprehensive Allied statement of policy— that of January 10, 1917—was made before the entry of the United States into the war, before the Russian collapse, and before the publication of the secret treaties. "President Wilson was acutely conscious of the conflict between the war aims of the United States and those of the Allies."[16]

The Socialists had, on December 31, 1917, read a group

statement in the Chamber of Deputies, to the effect that "the silence observed by all of the Allied governments on the general principles essential to the preparation of a durable peace, seems to us to create a state of moral inferiority prejudicial to our cause".[17] In the debate on war aims in the Chamber, January 11, 1918, this point was pressed by both wings of Socialist opinion,[18] which joined in a resolution insisting on the calling of an inter-Allied conference for the purpose of embodying the Wilson principles in a common declaration of policy. But the government was unwilling to comply with this demand. Pichon first argued that the declarations of the governments were identical in substance, even if not in form. Then he asserted that the Allies had indicated a preference for separate statements. Finally (and apparently this was decisive), France had contracts "which we cannot think of breaking", special reference being made to Italy, Serbia, Rumania and Belgium. By implication, Italy was the one most opposed to a joint statement. Consequently, the government refused to allow the Socialist resolution to be put to a vote, and another resolution, expressing confidence in the government for energetic prosecution of the war, was carried by a vote of 397 to 145.[19]

The proposal for a collective statement of war aims was supported not only by the Socialists. It had strong support in Radical Socialist circles, and even found advocates farther to the right. Gabriel Seailles, in the *Dépêche* of Toulouse (Jan. 6), argued persuasively that the silence of the Allies in this matter was playing the enemy's game, and that even though Allied statesmen had spoken separately, this was no substitute for a "solemn declaration" by which they would be drawn together and rendered immune to intrigues of the enemy.

The *Débats* was the only leading organ of the conservative press to support the plea for a joint Allied statement on war aims. Strongly sympathetic with the claims of the Yugoslavs, it pointed to the inconsistency of the Italian claims on the Adriatic with Wilson's Fourteen Points, and repeatedly urged the Allies to examine together "the general situation created by the events which have happened since the [Allied] reply to Wilson in January 1917". Dangers were prophesied if compromises failed. "It is clear that the United States is not making war for the 'war aims' of the *Idea Nazionale*." [20] It was a pregnant prophecy. Most of the Center and Right Wing press, however, not animated by special sympathies for the Yugoslavs, remained silent, apparently agreeing with the views expressed by such papers as the *Temps* (Jan. 13), *Homme Libre* (Jan. 12) and *Écho de Paris* (Jan. 24) that the dangers involved in an attempt to reach a common policy were greater than any possible advantage to be gained.

In spite of pressure, primarily from liberal sources, the Allied decision was cast against making a joint statement of war aims, as was evidenced by the pronouncement of the Supreme War Council on February 4. This, as paraphrased by the *Temps* (Feb. 5), amounted to saying that "since Germany did not want peace", the Supreme War Council had decided that its only immediate duty was to endow the military effort of the Allies with the greatest energy. [21] Though deplored by the radical press and the *Débats* (Feb. 5) as an avoidance of "the real question", [22] the moderate and conservative press, as a whole, received the pronouncement with tacit or express approval, and the *Écho de Paris* (Feb. 4) rejoiced in the apparent closing of the "oratorical dialogue" which had begun a month earlier.

The issue was not, however, entirely dead, for it raised its head repeatedly, especially in radical quarters, down to the eve of the Armistice. Furthermore, the failure to secure a joint Allied statement on war aims did not, in the view of radical opinion, and isolated groups farther to the right, relieve the French government of the duty of clarifying its own position more definitively.

The urgency of this course seemed all the greater, in view

of the increasing number of pronouncements in American, British, German and Austrian quarters. A veritable debate was, in fact, engaged in between Wilson and Balfour, on the one side, and Hertling and Czernin, on the other. From this debate the French government held strictly aloof. *Humanité* (Feb. 14), official Socialist organ, remarked that the French government seemed not to count any longer in these important matters.

The French government, during 1918, was, in fact, even less inclined than formerly to make clear its position with regard to peace terms. Though it had never consented to make a detailed statement of its case, several important pronouncements had been made earlier. The Chamber and the Senate, on June 5 and 6, 1917, after secret debates on the subject, and with the approval of the government, passed resolutions stating important general principles. The Chamber, by an overwhelming vote,[23] declared that it awaited "the liberation of the invaded territories, the return of Alsace-Lorraine to the mother country, and the just reparation of damages". "Far from all thought of conquest or enslavement of foreign populations", it looked forward to obtaining "durable guarantees of peace, and the independence of peoples, large and small, in the organization, now in preparation, of the League of Nations".[24] Premier Ribot, speaking in close accord with the sense of the resolution, said: "We do not desire annexation by force. We want simply that which belongs to us. . . . We must have an established justice, having as a guarantee this League of Nations which is taking shape today . . . and which, tomorrow, will be master in the world."

The Senate resolution, passed unanimously the following day, was markedly more drastic in tone. While confirming its faith in the "ideal of independence and of liberty for all peoples", it also confirmed France's obligations under her alliances, and demanded the restoration of Alsace-Lorraine, the punishment of crimes, the reparation of damages, and the "obtaining of guarantees against the return of an attack by German militarism". All reference to the League of Nations was omitted.[25]

When Clemenceau took over the government, and made his first official pronouncement before the Chamber of Deputies, November 20, 1917, the relative harshness of tone which characterized the Senate resolution became even more marked in his statements. "And when you ask me my war aims," said the new premier, "I reply to you: my aim is victory. . . . We must conquer in order to be just. Is that not a program?" As to the League of Nations: "You think that the formula of the League of Nations is able to solve everything. One must know what it means. . . . I do not think the League of Nations will be the necessary conclusion of this War."[26]

When, on December 27, 1917, debate on peace policies was again joined under pressure of an interpellation, Foreign Minister Pichon was again characteristically vague, though his tone was unmistakable. France's war aims were declared to be: "to conquer first"; "to assure the world a peace of justice and of fraternity." "Liberation of our territories . . . reestablishment of justice by the retaking of possessions taken from us by force, and in consequence, the reunion of Alsace-Lorraine with France. Just reparation of damages. . . . The guarantee of a durable peace by agreements for a general organization[27] with which you are familiar." On being asked to explain his last phrase, he replied: "It has to do with the League of Nations."[28]

Finally, in the debates of January 11, 1918, following the Lloyd George and Wilson speeches on war aims, Pichon again dealt primarily in generalities. Approval was expressed of the three principles enunciated by Lloyd George: the sanctity of treaties; a territorial settlement based on the right of self-determination, and the creation of some international organization to limit the burden of armaments and diminish the probability of war. Then, turning to Wilson's program, and scanning the Fourteen Points, he refrained from voicing specific approval, and satisfied himself, though not his Socialist interpellators, by saying that all of the Allied declarations were in accord, and that, "in their ensemble, they formulate one general opinion which leaves no obscurity, and no doubt as to their intentions".[29]

The French government could not be drawn farther than this in the elaboration of its diplomatic program. Indeed, after January 11, it seemed indisposed to go even that far again. Clemenceau, addressing the Chamber, March 8, on his diplomatic policy, said: "My domestic policy and my foreign policy are one. Domestic policy, I prosecute the war; foreign policy, I prosecute the war. Always I prosecute the war."[30] It is not difficult to agree with Professor Seymour's statement that the French government saw dangers in the Wilson program; that it feared lest the ardor of the Allied peoples might be cooled by indiscriminate peace talk. These fears were strikingly signalized by the refusal of the censor to permit the cabling of one of Carl W. Ackerman's articles, in which he advocated Wilsonian principles.[31]

In his determination to "prosecute the war" Clemenceau was resolved that the war should be strictly on the military front. No diplomatic offensives, involving commitments as to war aims, were to be tolerated. This decision was firmly adhered to in spite of a series of episodes which liberal and Socialist opinion, with occasional support farther to the right, regarded as providing excellent occasions for France, along with the other Allies, to speak out boldly on peace objectives. The Hertling-Czernin pronouncements of January 24 and February 25; the series of German "peace offensives" between March and July, and resumed again in September; the special pleas of Lord Lansdowne in behalf of a frank statement by the Allies of their war aims, all kept the question constantly before the Allied publics during the crucial days before the German collapse.

The Hertling speeches of January 24 and February 25 aroused no sympathy in France, even in Socialist quarters. While pretending to accept the Wilsonian principles, the German chancellor made reservations which practically rendered the acceptance a nullity.[32] Even the Socialist press in France found no good faith in the speeches. *Humanité* (Jan. 26) saw complete lack of harmony between the German position and that of Wilson and Lloyd George. "The masters of Germany have not yet come to the point," it said. Likewise it felt (Feb. 27) that von Hertling's pronouncement of February 25 was an attempt to dupe the Allies. Yet, in radical circles, this was regarded as all the more reason why France and her allies should clarify their own war aims.[33]

The German and Austrian "peace offensives" which preceded or followed the military offensives from March to July 1918, were aimed at engaging the Allies in semi-official peace negotiations while the German military position was still strong. Throughout these events the French government remained silent, except when Clemenceau rose to state that Count Czernin "had lied" in stating that the French government, early in February, had proposed peace negotiations to Austria.[34]

In this policy of silence the government had the support of practically all Center and Right Wing opinion, which appeared to be content that the government should talk as little as it saw fit, so long as it prosecuted the war with vigor.[35] Most of the Left Wing press, however, regarded the "peace offensives" as a splendid opportunity for a counter-offensive which would weaken the enemy governments with their own peoples. Even the *Débats* (June 16) exposed itself to criticism from the more nationalistic press for championing a counter-offensive on the diplomatic front. "Wilson understands how to use the diplomatic arm along with the military arm," it said, in arguing for a strong statement of principles. Leading liberal organs supported this position. Professor Aulard, writing in the *Dépêche* of Toulouse (June 16), thought it not enough to repeat the word "trap" whenever some statement came out of Germany, and the *Œuvre* asked why so many people should get excited "when the word 'peace' is spoken", since a reasonable statement of peace aims "would weaken the German forces rather than those of the Allies".[36]

The efforts of Lord Lansdowne, venerable British architect of the Franco-British entente of 1904, in his letters of March 5 and July 31, to bring on informal peace discussions were equally unavailing with the French government and with the bulk of French opinion.[37] While the press of the extreme Left naturally regarded the proposals as the embodiment of reason,[38] a majority of the moderate and conservative organs passed over the episodes in silence. Some of the more nationalistic papers were bitterly scornful. After the letter of March 5 the *Écho de Paris* (March 6) remarked that he "was an old man, broken by the war, who belongs . . . to a social and political order which is passing."[39] After his appeal of July 31 it stigmatized him (Aug. 2) as one of those who "have eyes to see and see not", and who "have nostrils but smell not".[40] Such, apparently, was also the opinion of the government, for it remained unshaken in its determination to pursue its offensive exclusively on the military front.

3. THE STRUGGLE OVER WILSONISM

During these months President Wilson had been dealing heavy blows also along the diplomatic front, hoping thereby to reinforce the military effort. Gradually a "Wilsonian" conception of the peace was emerging and taking precedence in popular thinking over all others. That this was a source of embarrassment to the French government has been suggested. That it should be a matter of controversy within French political circles was inevitable. In fact, the Wilson program soon became a thing to conjure with—and to interpret, according to the particular bias or preconception of the commentator. Gradually the lines of controversy became drawn primarily between the Socialist Left and the groups farther to the right.

It was unthinkable that direct and outspoken opposition should have developed immediately against a program which unpartisan opinion generally recognized as a reasonable statement of the case for a just and durable peace. Furthermore, the lofty tone of the entire pronouncement put forward as a sort of program of the Western democracies, could not fail to raise the prestige of the Allied cause at the expense of that of the Central Powers. Even conservative and nationalistic groups derived satisfaction from the dignity and sacredness which the idealistic pronouncement shed on their cause. In any case, violent dissent might have been disastrous, tending, as it would, to reveal discrepancies in Allied war aims, and thus to weaken their military effort.

For liberal and radical groups the Wilson program embodied a degree of precision and a general loftiness of purpose which that of their own government failed to manifest. In fact, it contained exactly the aims, which they hoped to realize. It promised also to open the road to the realization of an earlier peace than would otherwise be possible, by crystallizing the struggle into one of "democracy" against "autocratic imperialism".

But discrepancies were bound to develop, for Wilson's policies obviously could not be equally satisfactory to all parties. In this connection it is important to bear in mind that the Fourteen Points and Wilson's subsequent pronouncements could, at best, be only a scanty outline of the peace settlement, limited necessarily to a statement of general principles which would have to be elaborated and applied in detail. This was particularly true of the clauses not dealing with specific territorial aspects of the settlement. The attention which President Wilson gave to the use of such words as "will", and "must", and "should" in the Fourteen Points indicated his appreciation of the problems of application which would arise.[1] The inevitable lack of detailed precision resulting from this situation made it possible, to a considerable extent, for each commentator to see in Wilson's phrases what he wished to find there.

If it was inconvenient, for one reason or another, openly to reject the program, it might at least be interpreted. "Implications" of the various points might be pointed out; "inconsistencies" might be suggested, and even reservations might occasionally be made as to the time or manner of application of certain points.

Accordingly, the business of interpretation and application soon flourished, with the result that mutually antagonistic groups were shortly fighting among themselves for the right to claim Wilson's principles as their own. The tactics of the radical groups were to take possession of the Wilson doctrines and to challenge the government to accept them. This began on the appearance of the Fourteen Points. To *Humanité* they embodied sound Socialist doctrines. "In listening to Wilson," it said (Jan. 10), "one could hear the voice of Jaurès." Likewise, when the President announced his Four Principles of February 4,[42] he seemed to that same organ (Feb. 13) to proclaim the "ideal that Jaurès, before Wilson, had magnificently proclaimed". Again when Wilson, on April 6, after stating his willingness to discuss "a fair and just and honest peace at any time it is sincerely proposed", came out vigorously for "Force, Force to the utmost, Force without stint or limit", *Humanité* (April 9) said: "Wilson is the only one who speaks the language of reason and moderation." "Today," it said, "we are still at his side to uphold the noble policy of which he has become the honest, patient, tenacious champion." It was the same after the President's speech of July 4 in which he stated that there must be "no compromise", "no half-way decision", and in which he enunciated his Four Points.[43] "The Socialist principles are identical with those of Wilson," wrote *Humanité* (July 5). Finally, after Wilson's climactic pronouncement of September 27, in which he opposed "leagues or alliances" within the larger League, struck at special selfish economic combinations, and called upon the Allies to state whether they thought him mistaken in his interpretation of the issues, the Socialist press claimed his doctrines as their very own. *Populaire* (Oct. 4, 7), the organ of the more radical *Minoritaire* wing of the Socialist

Party, boldly proclaimed: "The Wilson theses are ours. . . . Wilson is not one of us, but it happens, by a curious intellectual phenomenon, that he has aligned himself with Socialist thought." [44]

Meantime, the Labor and Socialist Congresses were identifying themselves with the Wilson program, and calling for action based on it. The Inter-Allied Socialist Conference at London, February 1918, had unanimously acclaimed it.[45] The French National Labor Congress in July did likewise; and at the National Socialist Congress in July, at which the *Minoritaires* (formerly the more radical minority) prevailed over the old *Majoritaires,* the victorious Longuet motion, of the Socialist Left Wing, demanded peace on the joint bases of the Wilson program and that of the Russian Revolution.[46]

Nor were the Socialist groups content merely to declare their solidarity with the Wilson program. They proceeded to point out inconsistencies between Wilson's principles and those of the more patriotic French press, and to suggest the discomfiture of the semi-official and nationalist organs in the face of Wilson's pronouncements. "The pretended acclamations" given the Fourteen Points by the conservative press were pointed to, and it was suggested that Clemenceau and Pichon had the same enthusiasm for the speeches of Wilson and Lloyd George—"fifteen degrees below zero"— that they had previously manifested with regard to the appeals of Pope Benedict XV.[47] The "grimaces" of the Right Wing press at Wilson's address of July 4 were ridiculed.[48] "The men of little faith" were pilloried for their treatment of the Wilsonian ideals.[49] "There are two conceptions of the peace," said the *Populaire* (Sept. 27), "the Barrès-Hindenburg (Daudet, Maurras, etc.) conception, which envisages peace only through military victory, and that of Wilson, which opposes the prosecution of the war to the point of the extermination of peoples."

It is not surprising that the Socialist enthusiasm for Wilsonian principles was an irritating and exasperating spectacle for the patriotic press, since the embarrassing presumption was raised that Wilson and the French government were not in accord on the basic principles of the peace settlement. Accordingly, the more nationalistic organs strenuously endeavored to check the Socialist offensive, and to turn their weapons against it. On the one hand, while naturally abstaining from exuberant acclaim of the Wilson doctrines, they solemnly affirmed the solidarity of his principles with those of France. On the other hand, they stigmatized the Socialists for presuming to "monopolize" the President's program, and pointed out contradictions and inconsistencies which seemed to them to set the principles of Socialism in opposition to those of Wilson.

In spite of obvious misgivings with regard to the Fourteen Points, the *Temps* (Jan. 12) averred that the government would "interpret the considered opinion of France" if it adhered formally to Wilson's policies. When Mr. Wilson proclaimed his Four Principles of February 11, the *Temps* (Feb. 13) solemnly announced that "these laws conform to the French ideal". Likewise, following the promulgation of the Four Points of July 4, that organ (July 6) sardonically remarked: "They all conform to the most serene justice." Practically all the leading papers generalized in somewhat similar terms.[50]

Every opportunity was utilized by this press for the purpose of demonstrating the "inconsistency" or the "insincerity" of the extreme Left in its espousal of Wilsonism. The growth of the *Minoritaire* wing of the Socialist Party, and its apparent willingness to agree to a "peace of compromise", provided arrows for the quivers of these organs. The Socialists were accused of wanting peace "at any price", an allegation which Longuet hotly denied.[51] They were charged with wanting to substitute the League of Nations ("that marvellous plan") for victory.[52] The phrase, "bitter-enders" was hurled back and forth from one camp to the other. "All the Socialist and Anarchist agitators of the old world" were alleged to be "paying court to the capitalist dictator of the new".[53] The Radical Socialist *Dépêche* of

Toulouse (April 19) rebuked the extreme Left for confusing "a Wilson peace" with "an immediate peace"; and *Homme Libre* (May 28) confidently affirmed that Mr. Wilson was "closer to Clemenceau than to the Socialist party".

One of the leading patriotic organizations, the Civic League, issued a special pamphlet during July containing some of the most militant of Wilson's pronouncements. The publication was said to have been necessary by reason of the fact that "defeatists and false pacifists often seek to hide behind the high authority of President Wilson", and because they "pretend to set up a difference between the peace conditions of President Wilson and those of the other Allies".[54]

Repeatedly the *Temps* and other patriotic organs belabored the extreme Left for its "falsification" of Wilsonism. When the "Republican Coalition" was organized in April, an organization representative primarily of Socialists, but including also members of other advanced Left groups, and taking the Wilson program as the basis of its action, the *Temps* (April 10) denounced it for attempting to monopolize Wilson's ideas.[55] Later, in a long editorial (Aug. 31) that organ sought to contrast the "ideal of Wilson" with "the revolutionary ideal." "While the Socialists want a peace by compromise, Wilson wants a peace by victory."

Some justification for certain of the criticisms made by the patriotic press may be found in the developments that were taking place within the Socialist party during this period. The rise of the *Minoritaires,* and the drift of Socialist policy to the left had caused serious rifts within its ranks. The so-called "Forty" on the Socialist Right Wing, had broken away and, in July, established a paper of their own, the *France Libre.* A small group on the extreme Left, led by Loriot, was strictly Bolshevik in its policy. The dominant so-called *Minoritaires,* led by Longuet, were so outraged by Allied intervention in Russia, and so preoccupied with attempting to revive the Socialist International, that they easily justified the suspicion that they were dangerously sympathetic with the Bolsheviks.

This is illustrated by the resolutions which were voted at the Socialist National Congress, October 10, 1918. The moderate motion (*Majoritaire*) came out flatly for Wilson's Fourteen Points, and was replete with the name of "Wilson". This motion received 1212 votes. The radical motion (*Minoritaire*), avoided the mention of Wilson's name altogether, and said, "Only the International can assure the peace of peoples." While proclaiming the rights of peoples, "It does not expect from this war, directed on both sides by capitalist states dominated by territorial greed and annexationist desires, a just regulation of all these questions." Though it favored a League of Nations, it warned the workers that "so long as capitalistic struggles for markets continue, the peace of the world will be in peril".[56] This motion received 1528 votes, the Loriot group of slightly over 100 voting with them. The ex-*Minoritaires* seemed to have passed beyond Wilson.[57]

Perhaps further justification for the interpretations and criticisms on the part of the patriotic press may be found in what was apparently a distinct "evolution" in the views of President Wilson: a tendency, as it was expressed, for the President to become firmer as he came more closely into touch with "realities". After the address of February 11 it was said that his views were "being modified from message to message . . . tending toward the acceptance of the reality . . . of the war".[58] Mr. Wilson's address of April 6, in which he advocated the use of "Force . . . Force without stint or limit", was characterized as "probably the best adapted of all his pronouncements to hasten the peace". The President was congratulated on having oriented his policy in that direction,[59] and on having "the courage to give up his illusions, and to admit that the only way to convince Germany is to conquer her".[60] Wilson's Fourth of July speech was said to mark "the unbroken progress of an evolution";[61] and after the President's brusque reply to Austria's peace proposal of September 16, the *Débats* (Sept. 19) exulted in the "difference in tone and method". "It has taken

Mr. Wilson time, a long time," it said, "to penetrate German policy, and longer still to understand Austrian policy. But once he has penetrated the hypocritical protestations of Berlin and Vienna, he throws himself into the midst of the fight."

The fact, as previously suggested, that Mr. Wilson's ideas were frequently clothed in broad generalities, was itself a partial explanation of the conflict of interpretations. The idea of a League of Nations meant one thing to the radicals on the Left, and something entirely different to the groups of the Center and Right. The President's references to the use of force, to the treatment of Russia, and to a variety of other subjects were equally subject to wishful interpretations of widely differing character. The *Temps* (Nov. 8) might even find some excuse for its argument that the Fourteen Points meant that the Allies should not allow Russia "to stew in the infamous Bolshevik juice"; and the *Libre Parole* (Oct. 26) was not without justification in remarking on the "strange quality" of Wilson's notes, namely, that "persons of most widely differing opinions agree on them and see in them what they want to see, because they can interpret them at will".

4. THE SEPTEMBER PEACE PROPOSALS

The Wilson peace program began to take on added significance as the tide of battle turned definitely against the Central Powers late in July, and as their armies thenceforth continued to be rolled back. That the President would play an important personal rôle in the pourparlers leading to the Armistice was foreshadowed by the September peace feelers put out by the Central Powers. A growing consciousness of impending defeat was increasingly evident as the responsible ministers of Austria and Germany sought to retrieve their military disasters by diplomatic successes. Compromise and conciliation were manifest in the phrases of Foreign Minister Czernin, of Austria, as, on September 10, he advocated a "peace by understanding", and expressed the wish that "war as a political means" might be abolished.[62] In much the same vein the German Vice-Chancellor von Payer, on September 12, expressed the desire for a "lasting peace" on the basis of "no conquest". All territorial possessions existing before the war were to be "everywhere restored". Disarmament on land and sea was advocated, but Germany would not pay indemnities. It was a proposal which, a few months earlier, might have appeared magnanimous.[63] On September 16 Austria, in a note through the Swedish legation, proposed to President Wilson that the belligerents should enter informally into confidential "non-binding conversations" over the fundamental principles of peace, which conversations should not interrupt military operations.[64]

It was not to be supposed that proposals for informal, non-binding peace negotiations would be acceptable in influential French circles, in the midst of a triumphant military offensive, since the earlier "peace offensives" had been rejected at a time when the fortunes of war were far more doubtful.

Opinion of the Right, the Center and the moderate Left was solidly against taking these advances seriously. "Do the two Kaisers take us for idiots?"[65] "At the moment when the military action of Germany becomes defensive, its political action becomes offensive."[66] "The trap is too plain."[67] "The Allies unanimously reject this bad joke."[68] Such were the reactions of the patriotic press. *Écho de Paris* (Sept. 16) added that the fundamental danger of "conventicles of this sort" was that they were designed "to enervate the armies which, like our own, at the price of continual sacrifices, have to reconquer the war map which our enemies have constructed".

"Secret diplomacy" suddenly became anathema to the leading conservative organs. "The idea of a conference behind closed doors," wrote the *Temps* (Sept. 17), "is one of those projects which Germany and Austria periodically send out, like bait which fishermen take from one trap to another in the hope of enticing naïve fish."[69] Even liberal journals, and the *Débats* shifted from their former advocacy of an Allied definitive statement of war aims.[70]

Only on the extreme Left was opinion favorable to following up the lead which the Central Powers had given, though the Socialists were by no means convinced of the good faith of the enemy. The inter-Allied Labor and Socialist Conference, meeting at London, urged the governments to subscribe to the Fourteen Points, "thus opposing a policy of clarity and moderation to a policy dictated exclusively by changes of the war map".[71] Though the idea of secret negotiations was not pleasing to extreme Left circles, the procedure would have been accepted in the hope that the terms proposed might be made public in case the negotiations came to naught. "Then the people would be able to judge," said the *Populaire du Centre* (Sept. 17). President Wilson's crushing rejoinder to the Austrian démarche, brusquely refusing to entertain the proposal for a "confidential and unbinding discussion",[72] brought his first genuine disappointment to Socialist circles, where it was felt that a great opportunity had been lost to secure a collective statement of war aims, which might go far toward separating the peoples of the Central Powers from their governments.[73] On the other hand, to conservative and nationalist opinion, it was probably the most satisfactory of any of his pre-Armistice pronouncements.

On one point, however, a feeling of distinct uneasiness was developing in the patriotic press, namely, that Mr. Wilson was occupying a dangerously aloof position, diplomatically, from the Allies. He had stood apart from participation in the Supreme War Council, in order that he might preserve a free hand. It was now plain that he was being made the center of reference in matters relating to the peace. This situation had its dangers for the Allies, whose hands, it was feared, might conceivably be forced by him. Conservative and nationalist opinion, although it did not desire a joint Allied statement of war aims, did, nevertheless, strongly desire unity of "diplomatic command", so that Mr.

Wilson's freedom of action might be somewhat limited. *Écho de Paris* (Sept. 20, 21) forcefully expressed these fears, censuring President Wilson for acting independently of the Supreme War Council, and complaining that "he expressed himself as though he acted alone in relation to Germany". American representatives, it was urged, should join in periodical meetings of Allied ministers, a procedure "which President Wilson has always refused up to now".[74] Acquiescence in such a program by the American President, and surrender of his discretion, was less likely at that time, however, than earlier in the year, owing to the increasing harshness of influential French opinion on the subject of peace terms and to the Draconian character of Premier Clemenceau's own views, which were well expressed, September 17, in his references to this subject before the French Senate: "The most terrible of accounts between peoples has been opened. It shall be paid."[75]

5. THE OCTOBER EXCHANGES OF NOTES

President Wilson's relative independence of Allied diplomatic councils became a matter of acute concern when Germany, on October 4, made a formal request for an armistice.[76] The Fourteen Points were to be taken as general "bases" of discussion, though they were not unqualifiedly accepted. The German proposals were regarded in France as so inadequate that even the Socialists were unable to concede complete good faith. Opinion farther to the right naturally regarded them as a ruse of war, "an armistice trap".[77] "The beast, driven into a corner, draws in his claws and holds out to us a bloody paw," wrote the *Débats* (Oct. 7). As to the treatment which such a démarche merited, even the moderate Left organs joined in the cry that it should be forthwith rejected, as was evidenced in the affirmation by the Radical Socialist *Dépêche* of Toulouse (Oct. 7) that "only complete capitulation, total capitulation", would be acceptable.[78]

But what of the rôle assigned to President Wilson in the

drama? Was it not unusual to apply for an armistice to a political chief rather than to the military commander? And was it not especially bad form to apply to President Wilson as a sort of arbiter, rather than to the European Allies? One can understand how considerations of this sort stirred the commentators, in spite of the general exultation over the prospects of definitive peace. Even the liberal *Dépêche* of Toulouse (Oct. 9) questioned the propriety of the "detour by Washington", and saw in it a desire to attenuate the humiliation resulting from the defeat of Hindenburg and Ludendorff. Throughout Center and Right Wing circles there was not only profound suspicion, but also marked peevishness and injured pride over the whole affair. Grave concern was expressed, except in Socialist and certain other radical quarters,[79] that Wilson had been appealed to as an arbiter.[80] Others protested, perhaps too much, that France did not "feel any jealousy", or feel slighted over the situation, but added that the whole affair was a trick, designed to awaken strife among the Allies.[81] Some took a stronger line. It was suggested that it would be highly appropriate for Mr. Wilson to refer the matter to the Allies before going farther.[82] The *Intransigeant* (Oct. 7, 8) boldly suggested that the request for an armistice had "nothing officially to do with the Allies," adding that Mr. Wilson would not be able to answer in their name. The *Écho de Paris* (Oct. 6, 7) warned that the Germans were attempting to pay in ideology, "using the vocabulary of Mr. Wilson", and subtly assumed that the President would communicate with the Allies on "an affair which touches our national interests in such a sovereign matter".

President Wilson's brief reply of October 8 did much to calm fears and dissipate anxieties as to his course of action. Did Germany accept the Wilson program unreservedly? Would German armies evacuate Allied soil as a preliminary to the cessation of hostilities? Did the German Chancellor speak merely in the name of the "constituted authorities"?[83] Moderate opinion was satisfied with these pointed inquiries, while radical and Socialist circles were jubilant. The "Platonic attitude" of the reply was extolled. Its "superior humanity" was lauded.[84] Wilson was said by the Socialist press to have acted as though he were "penetrated with the same thought" as "French Socialism".[85] Leading organs of the heavy press manifested frank enthusiasm over Wilson's adroitness. He had "parried the German blow", and "achieved a coup comparable in its way with those of Marshal Foch," said the *Petit Parisien* (Oct. 10). His reply was "firm without brutality, haughty but without insolence", wrote Viviani in the *Petit Journal* (Oct. 10), though he significantly added that "certain persons would have preferred it to be more crushing". The *Matin* (Oct. 10), ordinarily more nationalistic than either of the above papers, seemed genuinely pleased, expressing the belief that the note would create the "maximum of disarray in Germany, and the maximum of discord among the enemy coalition".

Right Wing opinion and influential circles of the Center nevertheless remained fearful, feeling, as Viviani wrote, that the reply should have been "more crushing". Better still, the nationalist press, in general, would have brought the conversations to an abrupt end.[86] The *Journal* and *Écho de Paris*, both leading organs of the heavy press, were bitter. The *Journal* (Oct. 10) rejoiced that the Allies still preserved their freedom of action and the *Écho de Paris*, in a series of outbursts (Oct. 10, 11, 12), called on the Allies, and especially Wilson, to "put an end to this dangerous comedy", whose "inevitable end" will be to "divide and retard the conquerors, and to reanimate the vanquished". It stigmatized Wilson for acting alone, and insisted that the Allies must preserve their freedom of action, and "not sign any settlement except in consideration of their own interests, military, political and economic". The fear in nationalistic circles of a premature armistice was so great that President Poincaré felt impelled to send a note to Clemenceau insisting on the danger of signing an armistice while German armies were in occupation of any part of France or Belgium.[87]

The second interchange of notes between Germany and
President Wilson went much farther toward satisfying nationalistic fears, though only a complete breach of negotiations would have given complete satisfaction. No other note
of Wilson, in fact, ever won such universal acclaim from all
parties. Germany's second note continued to equivocate,
especially with regard to the evacuation of occupied territories and the internal democratization of Germany, though
it stated Germany's "unqualified acceptance" of Wilson's
Fourteen Points and subsequent pronouncements. On October 14 Wilson delivered a shattering blow in reply. Acknowl-
edging the "unqualified acceptance" by Germany of his
peace program, he denounced the "inhuman practices" and
"wanton destruction" wrought by the German armed forces.
The armistice conditions would be left to the military advisers of the United States and Allied governments. Furthermore the destruction of "the arbitrary power" which still
controlled German destinies was posed as an additional condition of peace.[88]

Here was satisfaction for everyone. The strongly militant
tone of his reference to armistice conditions was solace to
the nationalists. Even Poincaré felt that the note was "firm"
and "better than the preceding one", though he was convinced that Germany was "attempting blackmail".[89] The
demands for democratic reform gratified the extreme Left.
It was uncommonly strange to see both the *Populaire*
(Oct. 16) and the *Écho de Paris* (Oct. 16) greeting his
pronouncement with satisfaction. To the former he was "the
greatest individual that has risen out of the war. . . . It is
a Socialist of the extreme Left," said Phédon, "who renders
him this homage. And I do not know a French Socialist
. . . nor a French Syndicalist, who is not able to associate
himself with these words." Pertinax, of the *Écho de Paris,*
if not laudatory, was at least able to pronounce the note
fully satisfactory. "We find in it the language which, regretfully, we did not find in the first American response of October 8."[90] He could not fail to caution the President, however, that it should be his last word to Germany. This ob-

servation was in line with a number of insistent suggestions from the patriotic press to the effect that the matter had in effect been referred to Marshal Foch, though the *Populaire du Centre* (Oct. 17) issued a reminder that the armistice conditions had actually been referred to the military advisers of the United States and the Allies. The enthusiasm of liberal circles was well expressed by the *Dépêche* of Toulouse (Oct. 17), which found in the note "something of the eternal and permanent, something of human conscience and justice". It would be to the imperishable glory of Wilson that he had found it "necessary to speak to Germany, . . . as to a criminal seeking flight".[91]

The third exchange of notes threw the negotiations into a new perspective, and tended to confirm some of the fears of the nationalistic press. The German note of October 20 agreed that the conditions of evacuation of the Allied territories should be left to the military advisers. There remained but the question of fixing the details. Furthermore, it insisted that the German constitution had "undergone a fundamental change", and that it then rested on a democratic basis.[92] In his reply of October 23, Wilson continued to question the good faith of German constitutional reforms, insisted that the armistice conditions must make impossible the renewal of hostilities by Germany, and, finally, told the German government that he would turn to the Allies to see whether they, in turn, would accept peace on the basis of his program.[93]

Thus a new situation was posed, so far as the Allies were concerned. The German note itself had not altered the profound suspicion of German motives which prevailed throughout most French circles.[94] Nor was the "democratization" of Germany taken very seriously,[95] even by the Socialists, though Cachin insisted in *Humanité* (Oct. 22) that the time had passed when one could speak of "trap" and "maneuver".

Wilson's insistence on adequate military guarantees seemed satisfactory enough to patriotic opinion, so far as the armistice itself was concerned.[96] The important question now raised, however, was whether the Allies, in their turn, would accept the Wilson program as a preliminary basis of the armistice. This necessarily meant the acceptance of Wilson's policies as the basis of the subsequent peace, and was an alternative which leading organs of the Center and Right Wing press strenuously sought to avoid. They had hoped that the road to the armistice would lie exclusively along the "military" highway, and Wilson's second reply had given them some ground for hope. Now, however, it became apparent that an important detour was to be made along the "political" route. Colonel House was coming to Paris, and the Allied chiefs would be faced with the alternatives of accepting or rejecting the American President's program. It was awkward and unpleasant. The idea that the Allies, in the midst of their victorious march, should themselves be called upon to take pledges which they had not been willing to take in less prosperous times was indeed vexatious.

Furthermore, it looked as though Wilson, representing an "Associated", if not an "Allied" government, was coming into the peace parleys as an arbiter between the Allies and Germany. The German assumption, in its second note, that the Allies would also be pledged to Wilson's principles, had already been noted with some perturbation by such organs as the *Temps* (Oct. 14) and the *Débats* (Oct. 14). The distasteful implication, thought the *Temps*, was that the Allies themselves had been beaten, and it joined with a number of other papers in deploring the danger that Wilson was becoming more of a mediator than a belligerent.

Such implications, however, the leading organs of the patriotic press resolutely refused to accept. "There could not be any question of discussing peace conditions," said the *Temps* (Oct. 25), since the European Allies took no part in the preparation of President Wilson's programs. "The European Allies are confronted with a purely military problem." "At this moment it is a question only of the armistice, and not of conditions of peace," said the moderate

Petit Journal (Oct. 27). The statements of the Imperial
Chancellor to President Wilson were "non-existent for
France and her European Allies," argued *Homme Libre*
(Oct. 29). Pertinax wrote bitterly in *Écho de Paris*
(Oct. 26) that the Allies were "bound by nothing that
Mr. Wilson has said or typed". If the President made his
views prevail, he argued, it would be "at the expense of the
more realistic view of the Allies". If he should fail, his rela-
tions with the Allies would be strained. The armistice, in
such conditions, would not resemble "a capitulation".[97]

Socialist sentiment, with considerable support in Radical
Socialist circles, strongly favored taking the pledge, and vigorously denounced the gathering opposition to Wilson and
his program. "In proportion to the development of our success," wrote Longuet, "we see the growth of chauvinism
among us."[98] The liberal organ, *Œuvre* (Oct. 29), took
up the challenge that the Allies were not bound by anything
Wilson had said or typed, and replied that they were bound
by "something which in good French is called gratitude".
Humanité repeatedly denounced the methods of "the press
of provocation", and observed (Oct. 27) that the campaign was being visibly prepared "for the non-acceptance
of the Wilson peace".[99] The campaign in nationalistic quarters against Wilsonism became so persistent that the General Confederation of Labor, the League for the Rights of
Man, the Republican Coalition and the Socialist Party, all
organizations of the Left, joined in an effort to counteract
the propaganda, and on October 26 they warned the government against "lending its ear to the excitations of the
chauvinists of a press that is often more responsive to the
spirit of conquest than to the desire for justice". Indeed,
they argued plausibly that "the intentions of Wilson himself" had been distorted by a vicious propaganda.[100]

6. THE FOURTEEN POINTS AND THE ARMISTICE

Meantime, in a series of conferences from October 29 to
November 4, Colonel House was striving to induce the Allies

to accept Wilson's policies. The three European Allies, in the hour of victory, were definitely opposed to taking any pledges with regard to the basis of peace, although, once Great Britain had been reassured by a compromise on the "freedom of the seas" clause, the chief sources of resistance were France and Italy. Would acceptance by the Allies of an armistice automatically bind them to the Fourteen Points? House argued that under the circumstances it would; but Pichon was not willing to accept this point of view. He argued that the Entente Powers might inform Germany that they were "only stating terms of an armistice, not terms of peace".[101] The Colonel was able, finally, to make his view prevail only by suggesting that the President might be compelled to resort to further and rather embarrassing "open diplomacy".

During this series of conferences the French public knew almost nothing of what was going on. From October 29 to November 6, only three small communiqués were issued concerning the conference. On October 31 the *Temps* carried a small announcement to the effect that the Allied chiefs had come together, with their naval and military advisers. The precise purpose of the conference was not stated. Another small news note on November 3 announced that the Allied chiefs were continuing their deliberations. On November 6 the *Temps* finally announced that the "Supreme War Council of Versailles" had terminated its work (on Nov. 4) with "complete agreement among all participants".

No reference was made to the relation of Wilson's peace bases to the final agreement. Indeed, when, on November 5, Clemenceau appeared before the Chamber of Deputies to read the terms of the Austrian Armistice, he announced that the Supreme War Council had agreed on terms to be presented to Germany, stating that these had been sent to Wilson for approval. He made no reference to the Fourteen Points, and when Mayéras, of the Socialists, sought to bring up an interpellation for the purpose of discussing the question whether the French policy was in accord with the Four-

teen Points, the government refused to accept discussion, on
the ground that it "would tend to make it appear that there
possibly existed disagreements between President Wilson
and the Allies. . . ."[102]

Wilson's note to Germany of November 5, however, left
no doubt as to the Allied acceptance of the Fourteen Points.
Here again, most of the press seemed relatively indifferent,
in the midst of the gigantic events of the approaching armistice. Very few comments were made even by those Center
and Right Wing organs who had so bitterly opposed the
adoption of Wilson's policies. The *Écho de Paris* (Nov. 7)
could not, however, forbear a parting shot, stating that
the dialogue between Washington and Berlin had been
"unfortunate in the highest degree", and that "It probably
prolonged the war." The Socialist press was naturally
jubilant. The important point, said *Humanité* (Nov. 7),
was that the Allies had accepted the Fourteen Points.
Even the two reservations were "excellent" because "they
accentuate the acceptance of Wilsonian principles by the
Allies".

The final scene in this particular act occurred November
11, when Clemenceau read the conditions of the German
armistice to the Chamber, following which a resolution was
proposed to the effect that the French armies, Clemenceau
and Foch had deserved well of their country. The resolution
having been voted, the Socialists proposed to insert in it a
further statement to the effect that "The Citizen Woodrow
Wilson, President of the Great Republic of the United
States of America, has deserved well of humanity." Amid
cries from the Right of "Maneuver", "It is a maneuver",
and shouts from the Left of *"Vive* Wilson", the Chamber
finally supported the *rapporteur* of the Military Commission
of the Chamber, who argued that while he entirely favored
the proposed tribute, yet the two should be kept separate.
The vote against the proposed Socialist amendment was 365
to 136,—a few of the Radical Socialists and Republican
Socialists voting with the Socialists.[103]

On the eve of the Armistice intense distrust of Germany prevailed throughout all French circles, except on the extreme Left. This was accompanied by an increasing demand for an exacting peace. The German maneuvers leading up to the Armistice had not been a source of confidence, and since the October concessions to democracy were made only after great pressure by President Wilson, it is not surprising that the overwhelming majority of Frenchmen remained profoundly skeptical. The danger feared was that Germany might capitalize a so-called "democratization" of its political régime, and, by converting this into the coinage of Wilsonian ideology, purchase an easy peace, and thereby rob France of the "legitimate fruits" of its victory. "Enterprise of camouflage", "Democratic comedy",[104] were typical expressions of the feelings in patriotic circles. Even the *France Libre* (Nov. 7), of the Socialist Right Wing, warned that they were "playing a comedy behind a mask". In October a brochure was spread abroad by The Union of Great Associations, the central organization of all the chief patriotic organizations. It was specially distributed to the workers in all the large factories of the Department of the Seine. "People of France," it said in part, "you do not hate enough! Your hate is not sufficiently inflamed. . . . You still have illusions as to the German people. Strip off these illusions and look into the face of naked reality. You are dealing with a nation which has gone to the devil. . . . Arm yourselves, French people, with that mortal hate which does not recoil before anything. . . ."[105] A mere change from a monarchy to the forms of a republic was not enough. On October 2 the *Temps* wrote that "any political reform in Germany will be mere comedy as long as William II rules at General Headquarters". On November 10 it expressed prevailing feelings in saying: "We are now about to find ourselves faced with an unknown Germany. . . . It will be a force against which military guarantees will perhaps not be sufficient."

These feelings were reflected in a more unbending attitude

toward the peace settlement. With the victory, there was, as
Europe Nouvelle put it, a revival of "the old imperialistic
soul, the habitual companion through the ages of victorious
armies".[106] This was evidenced in the vigorous opposition
throughout influential quarters to the acceptance of Wilsonian principles as the basis of the armistice and the subsequent peace. It found expression also in liberal circles. In
October the *Dépêche* of Toulouse was calling upon the Allies
to demand "total capitulation" of Germany, and to "be
harsh",[107] whereas, earlier in the year, it had accepted Mr.
Wilson's program as "the peace of an arbitrator", and had
urged a liberal statement of Allied war aims. Even the
Right Wing Socialist organ, the *France Libre* had become
tinged with nationalism.[108]

A definitive peace program, however, had not, at that
time, become crystallized. Discussion of the subject during
the preceding months had, in fact, been discouraged. The
government itself had refused to participate in it, and had
added to the difficulty of free discussion by limiting the news
available, and by censoring the expression of opinion.
Humanité (May 26), referring to the Left Bank question,
said: "In France we are not permitted to speak of the affair,
whereas the English journals are discussing it freely." [109]
Certain it is that this great issue was scarcely mentioned in
the press during the ten months preceding the Armistice.[110]

There had been considerable general speculation on the
League of Nations, and much attention had been given to
Alsace-Lorraine, though it is notable that, in connection with
the return of Alsace-Lorraine to France, there was, in influential quarters, no suggestion that the Saar Basin should be
included with it.[111] During the two months preceding the
cessation of hostilities the phrase "Restitutions, reparations,
guarantees" was becoming increasingly current, but as to
what it meant, precisely, there was no agreement. All accepted it, even the Socialists, but their views as to reparations and guarantees, differed widely from those of groups
farther to the right. Like other general statements, the

phrase was susceptible of being interpreted according to the desires of the commentator, yet everywhere, except on the extreme Left, its implications were rapidly expanding at the time of the cessation of hostilities.

NOTES

[1] *Official Statement of War Aims and Peace Proposals, December 1916 to November 1918.* Prepared under supervision of J. B. Scott (Washington, 1921), p. 1. Hereafter cited as *Peace Proposals.*

[2] *Ibid.*, p. 7.

[3] *Ibid.*, p. 26.

[4] Dickinson, G. L., *Documents and Statements Relating to Peace Proposals and War Aims, December 1916-November 1918* (New York, 1919), p. 79; Fisher, L., *The Soviets in World Affairs,* 2 vols. (London, 1930), vol. i, p. 17.

[5] President Wilson's special objectives in formulating his Fourteen Points were, first, to answer the Bolshevik demand for a statement of war aims,—and to hold them in the war; second, to appeal to German Socialists, with a view to separating them from the Government; and third, to give notice to the Entente Powers of the need for a liberal revision of war aims. In this latter connection, Wilson had been especially disturbed by the Treaty of London, of 1915, with its proposals to transfer peoples of foreign nationalities to Italy. *House Papers,* vol. iii, p. 331.

[6] Aulard, A., *Histoire Politique de la Grande Guerre* (Paris, 1924), p. 294.

[7] *Annales de la Chambre,* January 11, 1918, p. 36. The fact that Clemenceau himself refused to participate in this important debate, following the Wilson and Lloyd George statements, is significant. *Humanité* (Jan. 13), adverting to this fact, said the reason for the French Premier's failure to do so was clearly the fact that he was not in agreement with Wilson and Lloyd George. "It is this disagreement which induces the Premier to impose certain formulas on his Foreign Minister, and to remain silent himself."

[8] *Europe Nouvelle*, a new and important liberal weekly, in its first issue (Jan. 12), hailed Wilson as the incarnation of "the highest moral authority", and said the message was the "most definite, the most wise, of any program that had been offered to the peoples bruised and bleeding from war." "The good sower has sown the grain in the furrow. The grain is going to ripen soon, and the soil of Europe is ready."

[9] The *Populaire du Centre* of Limoges (Jan. 31) remarked that it was a problem of a Wilson-Trotzky peace against the "Holy Alliance".

[10] *Annales de la Chambre,* January 11, 1918, p. 30.

[11] *House Papers,* vol. iii, p. 338.

[12] The only question on this point, as far as the Socialists were concerned, was as to the procedure for righting the wrong. Their proposal at that time was a plebiscite under the supervision of the League of Nations,

though they anticipated a return of Alsace-Lorraine to France. See *Humanité*, January 9, 1918.

[13] The *Action Française* (Jan. 13) thought Wilson's words would be warmly received in Berlin, even more so than those of Lloyd George; and the *Matin* (Jan. 13) subtly suggested that Mr. Wilson was not forcing anything on anybody.

[14] *House Papers*, vol. iii, p. 348.

[15] "What is still lacking," wrote House at the close of the Conference, "is intelligent diplomatic direction." *Ibid.*, pp. 287, 325.

[16] *Ibid.*, p. 151.

[17] *Humanité*, January 1, 1918.

[18] See speeches of Renaudel (*Majoritaire*) and Mayéras (*Minoritaire*). *Annales de la Chambre*, January 11, 1918, pp. 43, 27.

[19] *Ibid.*, pp. 39-43.

[20] January 11, 1918. See also January 18, 20; February 5, 9; June 8, 22.

[21] In stating that this decision manifested "the intimate collaboration of the Allies" the *Temps* conveyed a wrong impression if it meant to include the United States as one of the Allies; for the action of the Supreme War Council encountered serious objections from President Wilson, who protested against its conduct in making political pronouncements. *House Papers*, vol. iii, p. 370. Indeed, President Wilson specifically refused to have the United States represented on the political side of the Council, the President being thereby left freer to deal independently with the diplomatic problems that arose.

[22] *Europe Nouvelle* (Feb. 9), a leading liberal weekly, thought there would be a "tragic echo" to the "Vendean trumpet blast" from the halls of Versailles. It would come with the "blowing of the whistle" sending the men over the parapets of the trenches to the attack. The Allied leaders, it felt, had not heard the "clamor of the peoples", who were calling for "Peace! Liberty! Bread!" "Are these voices too distant . . .? Must they remain without an echo?"

[23] 467 to 52. Forty-seven of the opposition were Socialists.

[24] *Annales de la Chambre*, June 5, 1917, p. 1349.

[25] *Temps*, June 8, 1917.

[26] *Annales de la Chambre*, November 20, 1917, p. 3065.

[27] "*des accords d'organization generale.*"

[28] *Annales de la Chambre*, December 27, 1917, p. 3798.

[29] *Ibid.*, January 11, 1918, p. 38.

[30] *Ibid.*, March 8, 1918, p. 790.

[31] *House Papers*, vol. iii, p. 368.

[32] See *Peace Proposals*, pp. 246 *et seq.*, and 279 *et seq.*

[33] *Humanité* (Feb. 27) said there was only one way to answer Hertling's speech, and that was for the Entente Powers "to omit nothing in repeating with clarity that they pursue no ambition of conquest, that they do not desire to crush Germany". The *Populaire du Centre* (Feb. 28), a *Minoritaire* Socialist organ of Limoges, urged that the Allies could no longer postpone explanations "without exposing themselves to doubts as to the purity of their motives".

[34] See notes in *Peace Proposals*, pp. 298-322.

[35] The *Temps*, in repeated editorials, vigorously opposed the idea that talking of peace would hasten peace. See *Temps*, June 8, 10, 11, 1918. The *Écho de Paris* (June 5) said that the best response to all such maneuvers was that of the Allied War Council of June 4, with its "affirmation of our will to conquer". "Nothing but words," was *Homme Libre's* characterization of the episode (March 8). "All who suggest peace are living in a dream world. Down with dreams!"

[36] *Œuvre*, May 12, 14, 1918. The press farther left was naturally more emphatic. *Humanité* (May 5) remarked that the "present policy leads the world to think that we are fighting for strips of territory along the left bank of the Rhine".

[37] See Dickinson, *op. cit.,* pp. 169, 205. Lord Lansdowne had written an earlier letter in similar vein, November 28, 1917.

[38] *Humanité*, July 31; *Populaire du Centre,* August 7.

[39] *Europe Nouvelle* (March 9) referred to the coolness of the reception given the Lansdowne letter, saying it was as though the password had been given out to the press.

[40] In view of the biting comments made by several of the nationalist organs, it is interesting to note that Colonel House, who met Lansdowne in London, wrote of him, November 14, 1917: "Conservative that he is, we scarcely disagreed at all. . . . Lansdowne is a great gentleman . . . not merely in intellect and character. . . but in manner and in that intangible and indefinable air which comes as a gift from the Gods." *House Papers,* vol. iii, p. 237.

[41] *Ibid.,* p. 338.

[42] (1) Settlement to be based on essential justice of each particular case; (2) peoples and provinces not to be bartered about; (3) every territorial settlement to be in the interest and for the benefit of the populations concerned; (4) all well-defined national aspirations to be accorded the utmost satisfaction possible. *Peace Proposals,* p. 269.

[43] (1) The destruction of every arbitrary power capable of disturbing the peace of the world; (2) the settlement of every question of territory, sovereignty, or economic or political arrangement upon the basis of the free acceptance by the people immediately concerned; (3) the consent of all nations to be governed in their mutual relations by principles of honor and respect that govern individual citizens of modern states; (4) the establishment of an organized peace guaranteeing the free nations against every invasion of right. *Peace Proposals,* p. 351.

[44] Repeated articles in *Humanité* discussed "The Wilson Peace", and identified it with Socialist ideology. E.g., August 30, September 1.

[45] *Humanité*, February 26, 1918.

[46] *Ibid.,* July 30, 1918.

[47] *Populaire du Centre,* January 23.

[48] *Humanité*, July 7, 9.

[49] *Ibid.,* August 22.

[50] "The new map of the world," as outlined by Wilson, "contains nothing unacceptable to us," said the *Lyon Républicain* (Jan. 15), expressing a typically careful view limited to the strictly territorial aspects of the settlement.

[51] *Temps,* February 16.

[52] *Écho de Paris,* February 2.

[53] *Action Française,* February 4.

[54] Ligue Civique, *Bulletin* No. 5, July 1918.

[55] When, during the pre-Armistice October frenzy, the Coalition sought to counteract nationalistic propaganda and to explain "Wilsonian principles" to the masses, the *Temps* (Oct. 20, 22) bitterly charged it with endeavoring to persuade the "organized proletariat that President Wilson has only borrowed his magnificent ideas from international Socialism".

[56] *Humanité,* October 11.

[57] It is fair to say, however, that this motion did not accurately represent the real attitude of the *Minoritaires* toward Wilson. The motion was framed in extreme form partly to catch the Loriot group vote. Further, they had joined with the *Majoritaires* in a note to Wilson asking for peace on the basis of his principles.

[58] *Figaro,* February 13.

[59] *Temps,* April 8.

[60] *Gaulois,* April 7.

[61] *Homme Libre,* July 6.

[62] *Peace Proposals,* p. 380.

[63] *Ibid.,* p. 383.

[64] *Ibid.,* p. 386.

[65] *Victoire,* September 16.

[66] *Petit Journal,* September 14.

[67] *Homme Libre,* September 16.

[68] *Liberté,* September 16.

[69] See also *Débats,* September 17; *Figaro,* September 16.

[70] *Débats,* September 17; *Œuvre,* September 14, 16; *Dépêche* of Toulouse, September 17.

[71] *Humanité,* September 24.

[72] *Peace Proposals,* p. 396.

[73] *Humanité,* September 18; *Populaire du Centre,* September 19.

[74] See also, *Victoire,* September 20; *Journal,* September 18; *Débats,* September 19; *Intransigeant,* October 23.

[75] *Temps,* September 19.

[76] *Peace Proposals,* p. 415.

[77] *Matin,* October 7.

[78] *France Libre* (Oct. 7), of the Socialist Right Wing, felt that Wilson would be entirely justified in telling the Germans he would not talk with them.

[79] Socialists naturally rejoiced over the appeal to Wilson. The French National Socialist Congress, convening October 6, at once sent a note to Wilson felicitating him on being charged with the negotiations, and urging that, while taking "indispensable diplomatic and military guarantees", the Allied governments should not reject the German proposals without discussion. *Humanité,* October 7, 1918. *Bataille* (Oct. 7) and *Populaire* (Oct. 7) protested against the tendency of numerous journals to "dictate" to President Wilson as to the attitude he should take. Even *Œuvre* (Oct. 7), of the liberal press, applauded the reference to Wilson, and

THE COMING OF THE ARMISTICE 65

subscribed "in advance" to what he, with his "noble intelligence and moral probity" would do.

[80] *Petit Journal*, October 6, 7. This paper was perhaps the most moderate organ of the heavy press.

[81] *Libre Parole*, October 7; *Victoire*, October 6.

[82] *Liberté*, October 6.

[83] *Peace Proposals*, p. 418.

[84] *Europe Nouvelle*, October 12.

[85] Phédon, in *Populaire*, October 11.

[86] *Débats* (Oct. 10) admitted Wilson's skill, but thought many of his statements would have to be cleared up if the conversations were to continue.

[87] Poincaré says this letter was sent October 5. See his *Au Service de la France*, vol. x, *Victoire et Armistice* (Paris, 1933), p. 377. Aulard refers to this note as of October 12. *Histoire Politique de la Grande Guerre*, p. 376.

[88] *Peace Proposals*, p. 421.

[89] Poincaré, *op. cit.*, p. 388.

[90] See also *Débats*, October 16; *Temps*, October 17.

[91] *Europe Nouvelle* (Oct. 19) noted the "disarray" which Wilson's note had introduced into the ranks of those who had criticized Wilson's policy:
"These men, of which a certain Pertinax is the prototype, seem to have understood nothing of the great lesson which has emerged from the present conflict."

[92] *Peace Proposals*, p. 430.

[93] *Ibid.*, p. 434.

[94] *Matin* (Oct. 21) typically remarked: "The Boche humiliates himself in order further to deceive us." The note embodied "the sentiments of a barbarous people", lacked the "stoic force" of which France had given proof in times of distress.

[95] *Temps*, October 23.

[96] *Débats*, October 26; *Petit Marseillais*, October 25.

[97] See also *Temps*, and *Matin*, October 29; *Débats*, October 31. *Action Française* (Oct. 26) deplored the whole affair, "the debate in the public square"; fearing that Wilson was "promising Germany milder terms, and renouncing a capitulation if she becomes a democracy".

[98] *Humanité*, October 22.

[99] Cachin interpreted Wilson's position in relation to the Allies as follows: "Take whatever guarantees you like against Germany. But on one condition: that it is solemnly understood, in advance, that we have agreed in common on the principles of a just peace. . . ." *Humanité*, October 27.

[100] *Humanité*, October 27. This resolution was also put before the Radical Socialist Congress which was in session at that time, and was at first adopted overwhelmingly. After a speech by Herriot, however, who argued that the manifesto "denatured the thought of Wilson", the Congress refused to go quite as far as the manifesto proposed, and contented itself with unqualified endorsement of Wilson's program, while emphasizing France's rights to "restitution, reparations and guarantees". The original manifesto, apparently, was not sufficiently convincing in certain points,

stating only that "damages caused will be repaired", and that "peoples actually in submission to force will be liberated".

[101] *House Papers,* vol. iv, p. 162.

[102] *Annales de la Chambre,* November 5, 1918, p. 2559.

[103] *Ibid.,* November 11, 1918, pp. 2669, 2670. A somewhat attenuated
tribute to Wilson,—and the Chiefs of the Allied States,—was voted subsequently, on November 20. *Ibid.,* November 20, 1918, p. 2719.

[104] *Matin,* October 17.

[105] *Populaire du Centre,* October 20.

[106] December 14, 1918. The result, said *Europe Nouvelle,* was the
obscuring of the limits between what was just and what was unjust. "This
is a vestigial remains of past ages, and should be swept away by the irresistible breath of the new times."

[107] October 14, 1918.

[108] E.g., November 7.

[109] See also the *Temps,* November 21.

[110] The *Temps* referred to it vaguely only once (May 19), suggesting
that the Prussian territory on the left bank was a "danger for Britain as
well as for France".

[111] *Victoire* made an isolated reference to it, October 25.

CHAPTER III

PRESIDENT WILSON IN EUROPE

"It would have been very naïve to imagine that, after having proclaimed the tables of the new international law from the top of Mount Sinai, Mr. Wilson would lose interest in their application. . . ."
(*La Libre Parole,* December 3, 1918.)

"I have come to Europe to repair the damage caused by the war; I have no more pressing task. I must not lose a minute for other occupations. The contemplation of the ills of the war is not the way to repair them."
(President Wilson to Elizabeth Asquith.)

"We are moving toward a peace of conquest, of annexation and imperialism. . . .

"But Wilson is coming to Europe; and, furthermore, they will not be able much longer to gag all voices and silence the rising protests."
(Cachin, in *Humanité,* December 4, 1918.)

1. THE DECISION TO ATTEND THE PEACE CONFERENCE

THE proposal that President Wilson should himself participate in peace negotiations in Paris could not have been expected to receive an enthusiastic welcome in French official and conservative circles. His peace program had been the subject of violent controversy between various partisan groups. In the crucial pre-Armistice negotiations bitter opposition had been brought to bear, both in the patriotic press, and by French official representatives, to block the acceptance of his program as the basis of the Armistice and the peace. That President Wilson, who was not only the head of a government, but also the chief of a great state, should use his personal and official influence in the midst of the conference, was a source of serious misgivings.[1]

Clemenceau could scarcely enjoy the prospect of negotiating jointly with one whom he regarded as "the inspired prophet" and the "slave" of "a noble ideological venture".[2] There were, doubtless, other considerations, among which,

67

national prestige and personal pride were important. Clemenceau announced firmly to Poincaré that if Wilson came to France he would not be allowed to preside. "I represent France," said the Premier, "and will not yield the presidency to anyone." [3] Taking up the matter with Lloyd George, Clemenceau stated in a telegram that, since Wilson was a chief of state, he would not be "on the same line" as the others. [4] With these views Poincaré was in agreement, feeling that it was "shocking that a chief of a foreign state should sit in a conference in France". [5] Clemenceau's initial annoyance was all the stronger because of the general presumption that if Wilson came he would inevitably take the presidency. [6] These objections, which Lloyd George shared, were taken up with Colonel House, and transmitted to Wilson, in proper diplomatic form; but they were without effect, except to cause the President some annoyance, and to make him feel that the Allied leaders were trying to pocket him. [7]

Opinion in high places subsequently changed somewhat. At any rate, President Wilson's irrevocable decision was accepted more complacently, which was doubtless due, in large measure to Wilson's tactful gesture in yielding the presidency of the Conference to the French Premier. Clemenceau later told House that he "entirely approved the idea of Wilson's sitting in the Conference as a delegate", [8] a change of heart which Poincaré may have accurately explained in saying that Clemenceau "wanted to preside over Wilson". [9] Poincaré himself actually derived some consolation from the situation, observing rather shrewdly that "If he [Wilson] were not there, all the misfortunes which we may suffer would be attributed to his absence." [10]

The feelings in the governmental press were reflected in the treatment of the early news dealing with the subject. The first notice of the probability that Wilson would come to Europe was given in the *Temps*, November 7, without any comment from it or from any other paper. On November 15 the *Homme Libre, Ouest-Éclair* and *Progrès* of Lyons carried identical brief notes apparently coming from official sources, stating that "President Wilson has decided to come to Europe to participate in the Peace Conference". Each of these inspired notes then added, somewhat sardonically: "This piece of news will be received in France with deep joy." The following day the same item was copied in other papers.[11] Not only were these scanty references not elaborated in the papers in which they appeared, but the news of Wilson's coming was received with almost complete silence in the editorial columns of all the Center and Right Wing press, which was concerned primarily with developments in Germany, the advance of French armies into Alsace-Lorraine, and the immediate peace program.[12]

The prevailing silence was broken by occasional casual references which only heightened its effect. The *Écho de Paris* (Nov. 17), remarking that "Mr. Wilson seems to have resolved to come to Europe", listed this decision as one of the reasons for the delay in getting peace parleys under way. "Have you noticed," said an item in Hutin's column of that same paper (Dec. 4), "that President Wilson proposes to arrive in Paris Friday the 13th?" The *Débats* (Dec. 1) observed rather dryly: "It is said that before his departure the President will probably publish the letters he has received from European statesmen urging him to be present at the Conference." The *Journal* (Nov. 22) averred that "nothing could more usefully contribute to the disengaging of the Wilsonian principles from Utopian illusions and adapt them to practical ends" than for that "eminent theoretician" to come over and "get in touch with the realities of the war"; and the *Action Française* (Nov. 23) somewhat caustically expressed its preference for having him in Versailles rather than "in his ivory tower in Washington".[13]

President Wilson's popularity in these circles was not enhanced by his speech to Congress, November 11, on the occasion of the Armistice, nor by that of December 2, immediately preceding his departure for Europe. In his Armistice address he held out to the peoples of the Central Empires the promise of food supplies, and expressed his willingness "to await with patience and sympathy the awakening" of these peoples, till they should "choose the way of self-control and peaceful accommodation".[14] There was a general disposition in the press of the Center and Right to ignore this speech altogether. The comment which did appear was rather caustic. The President's view was alleged to be "very distant". "He speaks only in his own name. He no longer speaks for us," said the *Figaro* (Nov. 13). The influence of "several millions of American citizens of German descent" was stated to be evident in his moderate tones.[15] The *Action Française* (Nov. 14) saw a Europe dominated by Germany, with France still in danger, if the Wilsonian principles were applied. The *Progrès de la Somme* of Amiens (Nov. 15), near which the battle lines had swayed back and forth, unblushingly repudiated Wilson's "humanitarian invocation", and expressed its preference for Clemenceau's brief and cutting statement: "The most terrible of accounts between peoples has been opened. It shall be paid."

It was much the same with the speech of December 2, in which the President urged the necessity of his going to France to see to it that his ideals were not misinterpreted. The great majority remained silent. A few praised some references he had made to the special economic needs of France.[16] A few indulged in caustic comment.[17] A number of Right and Center papers in various parts of France printed the news note that after Wilson's speech to the Senate, only the Democratic Senators rose and applauded warmly, while the Republicans, and even some Democrats, remained silent.

But since Wilson had chosen to participate in the peace parleys, he must have the psychological preparation essential for that responsible task, and this would involve a survey of the pathway or ruin left by the German invasion. It was pretty generally felt that this was the one thing necessary to bring the President really into touch with the "realities" of the war. He would better understand the condition

of the invaded regions when he had "seen with his own eyes
the ruin left by the enemy".[18] "When Mr. Wilson has passed
through the devastated regions, when his eyes have seen and
his ears heard, he will enter the Peace Conference with the
stern desire to chastise the guilty and to prevent the innocent from suffering again." [19] Such were typical comments
from the patriotic press. Even the *France Libre* (Nov. 23),
of the Socialist Right Wing, was happy because it felt
that Wilson could not fail to judge Germany more severely
when he saw the damage the Germans had done. "With
Wilson in America we should be sure of having justice; with
Wilson in France we shall have enlightened justice." The
prevailing feeling on this subject in the North and East of
France was naturally even stronger.[20]

The importance attached to this Presidential pilgrimage
by all except extreme Left circles, which ignored it entirely,
is illustrated by the appearance in the Paris and provincial
press, December 8 and 9, of news items (apparently from
official French sources) stating that Wilson had requested to
be conducted to the cities and villages devastated by the
Germans.[21] That Wilson had made no such request seems
clear from the fact that it was not till December 9 that
Colonel House sent a radio message to the President telling
him of the insistence of the French and Belgian governments that he should visit the devastated regions, and
noting that the French were arranging for a three-day trip.[22]
The *Petit Marseillais* (Dec. 9) prominently displayed a
story of the alleged "conversion" of Colonel House by
Clemenceau. When House arrived and imparted to Clemenceau Wilson's peace principles, the Tiger is said to have listened deferentially, and to have remarked: "I agree with
you entirely, but have you seen the regions devastated by the
Germans?" "Not yet," replied the Colonel. "Will you do me
the honor of accompanying me on this visit?" said the Tiger.
The visit followed, during which House saw the desolation
of cities, towns and fields. "Those people are monsters,"
House said. "Very well," replied Clemenceau, "but were you

convinced of it to the same extent before having seen this cemetery of ruins?" "No," House is supposed to have said, "one must have seen it to believe it." [23]

The government's attitude was further signalized by the passage devoted to this subject by President Poincaré in his first speech after the President's arrival. It had been necessary, he said, for the American soldiers to see "for themselves the towns systematically burned, the mines inundated, the factories reduced to dust", etc., before they could realize the enormity of the enemy's crime. Then he concluded: "You will be able, in your turn, Mr. President, to survey with your eyes the extent of these disasters. . . . Your noble conscience will pronounce on the crimes." [24]

2. President Wilson's Arrival

While anxiety pervaded the most influential French circles as to the possible results of Wilson's participation in the Conference, the hopes of the working-class and Socialist masses had been profoundly stirred by the prospect of his personal intervention in behalf of his program. From the beginning, radical opinion had applauded Wilson's decision to join in the peace parleys, and had stigmatized the patriotic press for its alleged discomfort over the prospect. "Our reactionaries of the *Écho de Paris,* the *Action Française,* and the *Temps* are obviously secretly irritated," said *Humanité* (Nov. 30), and the *Populaire du Centre* (Nov. 28) denounced the "politicians" and "journalists" who "continue to use all their resources against this great citizen". Even the liberal organ, *Œuvre* (Dec. 13) denounced "the reactionary Frenchmen, militarists and imperialists" for having forgotten that the signing of the Armistice was directly connected with the acceptance of the Fourteen Points.

The enthusiasm in radical circles over Wilson's prospective visit had, by the time of his arrival, become almost a delirium. He was hailed as a deliverer, come to rid the world of the scourge of war and to free the peoples from the bonds of hate and fear. "Today he is the greatest moral personality in the universe," said one. "We salute in Wilson the man who will strike off the chains which bind one people to the yoke of another," said another.[25] Something of this spirit seemed, temporarily at least, to have been caught up by the masses as a whole, if the popular outpourings on the President's arrival at Brest and at Paris were any criterion. The unprecedented character of his visit, combined with the almost Messianic rôle associated with his name, could not fail to strike deep into popular emotions, and the contagion of the occasion swept through liberal circles and penetrated even conservative quarters. "It was a moment of unspeakable emotion in the crowd" when Wilson appeared at the station, commented the *Petit Parisien* (Dec. 15), which was not given to flattery or subtlety. "No matter what Wilson hears or sees later, he will never have it repeated. For never did such an ovation rise from any crowd in the world." "Never has a king, never has an emperor received such a welcome," said *Europe Nouvelle* (Dec. 14). When he passed the windows of the *Œuvre*, that paper's "League of Nations" banner was lowered before him. "Everywhere music, resounding national anthems, hard to distinguish because of the joyous cries which go up from the crowds. Tears fill the eyes. How can one describe the emotion?"[26] A "Passing Woman" wrote with religious fervor in that organ (Dec. 15): "Wilson, you have given back the father to his home, the ploughman to his field. . . . You have saved our fiancés; love blooms again. Wilson, you have saved our children. Through you evil is punished. Wilson! Wilson! Glory to you, who, like Jesus, have said: Peace on Earth and Good Will to Men!" The correspondent of the *Progrès* of Lyons (Dec. 16) wrote this appraisal: "When the King of the Belgians came there were a lot of people; on the arrival of the King of England, there was a crowd; yesterday there was a multitude of people who milled about, respectful and vibrant, along the course of the parade. In all our life we have not heard such acclamations." Even the *Temps* (Dec. 15) seemed, for the moment, to have been touched with the enthusiasm of the crowd. "Let us place ourselves in the spirit in which we live," it said. "The experiences of the past are not conclusive for the future. . . . We must have faith. It is this faith which the crowds today saw in the eyes of the American President."

The extent of the interest in, and, to a limited degree, the warmth of the popular reception for Wilson may be measured by the amount of space given him by the leading newspapers, as compared with that given to King George of England, and Victor Emmanuel of Italy on the occasion of their visits to Paris during those same weeks. The analogy is obviously not complete, for Mr. Wilson was not merely a chief of state; he occupied a dual rôle, and came as the herald of a new age. Yet the British and Italian kings had certain advantages. They embodied the majesty and attractions of royalty itself; they were personally very popular in France, and they represented the two leading European Allied states which for many months had borne the brunt of battle, with appalling sacrifices, before the United States had entered the fray. Furthermore, their peace policies, in general, were more closely in line with those of the French government, than were those of the United States. One would expect these monarchical heads to be acclaimed with immense enthusiasm. Such a welcome they, in fact, received. Yet the four leading newspapers (from the point of view of wide circulation—*Petit Parisien, Matin, Journal, Petit Journal*) gave practically fifty per cent. more space to President Wilson than to King George, and about eighty per cent. more than to King Victor Emmanuel. Lumping the four papers together, for the three principal days of the respective visits, the King of Italy was given thirty-seven columns of space, the King of England forty-four, and President Wilson sixty-five.[27]

There were, however, some rather interesting variations in the amount of space given by the various journals of opinion. Whereas, in the press of the Right, the margin in Wilson's favor diminished, in the press of the Left, and especially of the extreme Left, it increased markedly. The *Écho de Paris,* most representative of the nationalist organs, gave Wilson eight and a half columns, in three days, to an exactly similar number to King George, and to seven and a quarter to Victor Emmanuel. *Humanité,* of the extreme Left, gave Wilson a total of twenty-nine columns in three days, to only a trifle over one column each to King George and Victor Emmanuel.

Formal expressions of welcome to President Wilson came from all quarters. From the Ligue des Patriotes, on the extreme Right, to the Unified Socialists and Labor groups on the extreme Left, resolutions were voted and manifestoes framed. Of all these, however, the Labor and Socialist groups were by far the most active and demonstrative. Perhaps they felt the urgency of this action more keenly because of their belief that their point of view would not be represented on the French delegation to the Peace Conference. Colonel House records that on December 5 the representatives of the Socialists conferred with him concerning a plan to give the President a rousing reception.[28] A joint meeting of Labor and Socialist delegates framed a manifesto to the Workers and Peasants of France, proclaiming that President Wilson had "deserved well of humanity" for having placed "rights above interests" and for showing humanity "the road to a less painful and less bloody future". The workers and peasants were called upon to make President Wilson, on his arrival in France, feel that the hearts of millions of men and women were "close to him".[29]

The Labor and Socialist desire to make a special demonstration for Wilson, in the nature of a gigantic parade past his residence, was blocked by the government. Successive interpositions by representatives of these groups with Pams, the Minister of the Interior, and Premier Clemenceau, failed to shake their determination. Hence the proposal for a special manifestation was abandoned, and the workers were called upon simply to salute the President in the streets.[30] Nevertheless, a delegation from the Confederation of Labor presented Wilson with assurances of "the active sympathy of the workers", and of their passionate attachment to his "ideal of peace".[31] The Socialists likewise paid their respects. On the afternoon of the President's first day in Paris, twenty-five Socialist deputies presented themselves at his residence and pledged their fervent support to him whose Fourteen Points had "dazzled the peoples with their pure light", and had "contributed to the German revolution".[32]

In spite of the government's interdiction, various groups of the extreme Left sought to demonstrate before Wilson's residence that evening, but were unsuccessful, owing to the closing of the streets by the police. The correspondent of the *Progrès* (Dec. 16), a liberal paper of Lyons, wrote, "we have met sane people, by no means revolutionaries, who regretted that for three or four hundred metres around the residence of the President, all the streets were barred, and the traffic practically forbidden."

The Socialist and Labor activities were a matter of considerable concern to the government and to patriotic circles in general. Émile Hovelaque commented to David Hunter Miller on the government's anxiety over the "attempt of the Socialists to capture Wilson".[33] The activities of the censor were also an indication of this anxiety. The *Petit Provençal* (Dec. 17), a liberal journal of Marseilles, noted that "The censor of Marseilles has even gone as far as to forbid us to publish an account of a labor demonstration in favor of President Wilson. . . . We never supposed we should come to the time when we should have to defend them [the Allied chiefs] from their admirers."

The press of the Center and Right poured out its wrath on the radical groups for their tactics which tended to create the impression that Wilson and Clemenceau were not in harmony. If Wilson sympathized with the extreme Left peace policies, he certainly could not accept those of conservative and governmental circles. The patriotic press, therefore, turned upon the extreme Left groups, and not only stigmatized their conduct, but also vigorously affirmed the solidarity of Wilson's policy with that of Clemenceau. The Socialists were accused of attempting to take possession of Wilson for the purpose of furthering the class fight.[34] Confidence was expressed that Wilson was "the firmest and most loyal friend of France",[35] and that he would not be "taken in" by the radical tactics.[36] On the contrary, he would prove to be "the faithful guardian" and "highest guarantor" of the victory, said the *Figaro* (Dec. 7). He would act, not as an "arbiter" but "loyally as an ally", said the *Ouest-Éclair* (Dec. 7) with rather forced assurance. The Socialists were read completely out of court by the *Temps* (Dec. 12) which found it very strange that Wilson should be laid claim to by those groups which had not ceased "to shout for a peace of compromise" which the President had "formally denounced as dangerous".[37] "There are enemies behind the scenes," said the *Débats* (Dec. 17), "who everywhere insinuate that President Wilson pursues ends different from ours. . . . It is false, absolutely false. . . . There is not one of these [Fourteen] Points on which an accord cannot be established between Wilson and us."

A few powerful organs close to the government almost leaned over backwards in making gestures of good will. Pains were taken to acknowledge the strength of Mr. Wilson's position in the United States.[38] The *Petit Parisien* (Dec. 13) insisted that Wilson not only embodied the political thought, but also the entire soul of the American nation; while the *Matin* (Dec. 15) devoted two glowing articles to the American delegation, vigorously asserting that it "was really representative of America", containing, as it did, in addition to the chief of state, "the greatest sage" (Colonel House), "the greatest diplomat" (Henry White), and "the chief minister of State" (Lansing).

A glance beneath the surface of press comment, however, soon reveals that the cordiality of the welcome to the President was less unanimous in conservative-nationalist circles than a casual survey might have indicated.[39] The greetings of leading commentators, though outwardly cordial, were frequently accompanied by mental reservations or subtle qualifications. The *Journal's* headline (Dec. 16) read: "Wilson carried on the war as an idealist. Wilson will make peace as a realist." *Action Française* (Dec. 9, 14) having repeatedly stated its confidence in him, expressed its particular concern about "the way the enemy will be able to exploit him". Wilson must especially be "on his guard against certain pacifists". The *Croix* (Dec. 14), powerful organ of Catholicism, after lavishing its praise, concluded that he is too just not to realize that "certain of his plans ought to be revised". The *Écho de Paris* (Dec. 14) saluted him in terms of its particular view of the peace settlement. First, said Pertinax, we must have the "positive organization", consisting of "military, economic and political guarantees". After that, a generation later, can come the "idealistic organization" (Wilson's League). "In this spirit we salute the great chief of the American Republic." [40] *Homme Libre* (Dec. 14), having generally acclaimed Wilson's "many fine qualities", so seldom found "gathered in one man", expressed a sentiment which appeared in varying forms in many patriotic organs: "In the inspiration which he will find down there on our battlefields near our great dead he will, if possible, fortify still further his desire, which we share with him, of modelling at last a better humanity in a better world."

The press of the provinces naturally did not feel the thrill of Wilson's presence so strongly as did that of Paris. The liberal and radical provincial organs, which are relatively stronger than those of Paris, were genuinely enthusiastic. The conservative papers of the provinces, however, frequently ignored the visit editorially. The *Est Républicain* of Nancy (Dec. 16) was typical of a number. Making no comments on Wilson's arrival, it placed in the first column of its front page a long account of the "Twenty-one Conditions" laid by Senator Lodge before the Foreign Relations Committee of the Senate, which, it said, represented the Republican view of the peace. The *Progrès de la Somme* of

Amiens (Dec. 15), instead of commenting on Wilson's visit, carried a long article on Clemenceau, concluding: "Glory to Clemenceau through the ages." Practically all of the leading organs of the conservative press of the provinces carried with their welcome, admonitions to visit the devastated regions, or advice regarding the proper attitude toward Germany. Wilson "comes to judge the monstrous facts", said the *Petit Marseillais* (Dec. 14). "He comes to hear the eloquent prayer and lamentation sent up by the ruins, and this, without doubt, will go straight to his mind as well as to his heart." Even the correspondent of the *Petit Provençal* (Dec. 22), a liberal journal of Marseilles, after describing with touching enthusiasm the day "which saw the apotheosis of President Wilson", concluded by saying: "BUT THE LAST THOUGHT FOR EVERYBODY WAS THE SAME: HE MUST NOW GO SEE THE NORTH!"

3. CROSS-CURRENTS

In spite of grave questionings and forebodings in some of the most influential quarters, there is no denying that the popular welcome to Wilson was immensely enthusiastic. His very presence seemed at first to breed confidence and to inspire the hope, if not the faith, that he would speedily lead the way to a better and happier world. There was something ominous in the Messianic rôle cast for the President by his most zealous supporters. Its fulfillment would have required that he be both omniscient and omnipotent. Unfortunately, the events of the weeks which followed his arrival raised doubts as to his being either.

The first demand on the part of an impatient public was for a quick peace, so that life might resume its normal rhythm. President Wilson, however, seemed unable even to get the peace parleys started. He had sailed from the United States anticipating that the preliminary negotiations would begin December 17. A note in the press as late as December 6 fixed that date for the opening of the Conference. On December 8 it was stated that it was improbable that the preliminaries could start before Christmas. On December 14 a despatch announced that the preliminaries would be put off till about January 3. Another news note of December 17 conveyed the information that the opening date of the Conference could not then be fixed, but that it would doubtless take place during the first fortnight of January. The extent to which these delays were due to the internal political situation in England (the British elections, etc.) and to "Fabian tactics" of Clemenceau, aimed at strengthening his position with his public, is difficult to estimate. Colonel House seemed to feel that Wilson was being made the victim of a "waiting" game.¹ It is fairly certain that these postponements were not due chiefly to Wilson, since he had no time to lose, in view of the urgency of his return to America in February. Yet it was more than four weeks after his arrival in France that the first formal session of the inter-Allied leaders was held. It was, therefore, not evident to the public that progress was being made with the peace. An occasional news item noted that Wilson had conferred with Clemenceau. Then the President went to London, and later to Rome, for friendly visits and also informal consultations. So far as the public was able to know, however, there was no crystallization of the problems, or organization of the work of the Conference.

Perhaps a lack of political finesse on the part of the President was manifested in his failure to obey the injunctions to visit the devastated regions during this available interlude. France was anxious to show the wounds of her bleeding body to him who would play such a determining part in caring for them, and if he had managed to find time enough for this magnificent gesture, the psychological results on the patient would doubtless have been highly beneficial. Certainly, it would have offended very few, if any, and would have gratified a great many. The press continued to interest itself in the subject. The *Temps,* on the evening of December 16, noted that "Wilson will leave tomorrow for the old front". The next morning the *Intransigeant* stated that he was to have gone, but that "he stayed at home in his study". On December 18 the *Temps* announced the visit for another proximate period, and many other papers throughout France carried notes of successive proposed visits and postponements. These announcements were interrupted by Wilson's visits to the American troops, to England, and to Italy. On January 4 and 8 the *Temps* stated that the President would visit the devastated regions immediately after his return from Italy. On the 9th, however, it stated that the need for rest, and for conferences, kept the President at Paris. These repeated items, definitely announcing projected visits, were widely circulated, especially among the patriotic press of Paris and the provinces, and were not infrequently accompanied by editorial comments. The *Journal de Rouen* devoted three leading editorials to the subject during the first eight days of January. Noting, January 8, the announcement of the impending trip, it said, the visit was absolutely indispensable. "Only those who have seen nothing, and who have not wanted to believe in the sincerity of the populations that have suffered, are inclined toward indulgence for the Germans." The *Progrès du Nord* of Lille (Jan. 9), looking forward to the announced visit, said: "His arrival is awaited with impatience by all those—and they are numerous—who ask him to accompany words of comfort with acts of reparation." On January 10 the *Intransigeant* italicized prominently the statement: "The die is cast. Wilson will not have seen the front and its ruins before the conference opens." On January 15 it quoted an authority "sometimes well-informed", who stated that one of Wilson's reasons for postponing his trip was his desire, during the preliminary conference, to negotiate "as an idealist, and consequently, for the moment, there is no place in his heart for hate". Maurice Paléologue expressed the view that President Poincaré's "When You Have Seen. . . ." speech at the Élysée Palace on the day of Wilson's arrival, was a determining factor in the postponement of the President's visit. That the French President's words addressed to President Wilson carried an unwelcome challenge, with a suggested lack of confidence, is scarcely open to question. Yet, that these events played an important part in shaping French thinking on Wilsonian policies is also evident. On January 19 the *Heure* gave Wilson the friendly advice that his failure to make this visit was being used against him in important quarters. Finally, January 26, Mr. and Mrs. Wilson made a hurried one-day trip to Rheims—which came rather too late, and covered too small a sector of the front to capture the public imagination.

President Wilson's position before the French public was somewhat further weakened, during the four weeks following his arrival, and before the opening of the Conference, by the manner in which some of the leading organs of opinion played up news from the United States of a character hostile to the President. As far back as August the *Écho de Paris*, one of the "Big Five", had been receiving from its American correspondent, Welliver, news items, chosen exclusively from sources hostile to Wilson. A few other leading organs, such as the *Matin* (also of the "Big Five"), and *Action Française*, followed the lead of the *Écho de Paris*, in this manner of presenting American news, though with less consistency than the latter. Even following the Armistice, and before Wilson's arrival, when the editorial columns were silent on the political position of the President, four items from its American correspondent containing exclusively anti-Wilson news, were italicized in the *Écho de Paris'* most prominent columns.[42] On December 15, the day following Wilson's arrival in Paris, a similar article emphasized the opposition of the Republicans to Wilson; and from that date until January 9, no fewer than eleven articles, of increasing length and prominence, were devoted to exposing the hostility to Wilsonism in the United States.[43] The hostility of the American Senate to the League was repeatedly stated. The speeches of Senators Lodge, Knox and Thomas, opposing Wilson's program, or demanding the postponement of consideration of the League until after the peace settlement with Germany; hostile statements of Roosevelt, Senator Kellogg, and Nicholas Murray Butler; the confusion in America over the Wilson program, were all elaborated at considerable length, and presented in italics for French readers. The delays of the Conference were represented as being due, in American opinion, to President Wilson. Here again, the lead of the *Écho de Paris* was followed, somewhat less consistently, by a number of important organs." The so-called "Twenty-one Points" of Senator Lodge (actually drawn up by the National Committee of Patriotic Societies) were reproduced in practically all of the Center and Right Wing organs throughout France on December 16 or 17, and his later speech proposing the postponement of five of Wilson's Fourteen Points until after peace with Germany received almost equal publicity.

The direction of events was not unnoticed by the organs of the Left, which did not fail to protest against it. The liberal organ, *Œuvre* (Dec. 21), called attention to the "campaign on the sly" against Wilson. "Certain newspapers suddenly 'discover' that they have private correspondents, or special employees in New York, and let them cable pretended news to the effect that President Wilson has never represented America. In America everybody is against him", and "Wilson is . . . only a cloud-chaser, who brays at the moon". The *Pays* (Dec. 27) noted a "persistent campaign" carried on against Wilson by the "reactionary journals under cover of information coming from America, endeavoring to show that though he may be a prophet in this country, he is not a prophet in his own"." The *Populaire de Nantes* (Jan. 10), a vigorous Left Wing organ, referred to the "Bismarckian campaign" against Wilson. ". . . in our papers you read, side by side, flattering reports and hostile articles. Hostile? Oh, they do not directly attack the Wilsonian policy. The affair is arranged more cunningly. They simply give particular emphasis to all the manifestations against the President in the United States." That there was considerable justification for the allegations of these papers is beyond question, and this conclusion is not altered by the fact that

only the scantiest news favorable to Wilson appeared in the
Left Wing press, for the press of the Left did not have correspondents in the United States, and was, therefore, almost
entirely at the mercy of the semi-official news agencies
which carefully selected the news to be given out to the
papers.

Not long after Wilson's arrival, a vague uneasiness began
to creep into popular feelings. The exhilaration of the victory passed, but the sense of peace and security did not follow. "The war is finished, but we do not have peace", was
the expression of a prevalent feeling.[46] "The war is over.
Six weeks have passed since the signing of the armistice. We
are still in a state of siege," said the *Progrès* of Lyons (Dec.
29). "Victory does not bring serenity," said the *Dépêche*
of Toulouse (Jan. 4). "It has cost too dearly . . . life remains hard . . . peace seems to be but a dark and shadowy
idea." [47] The reasons ascribed for this situation were numerous. Each commentator had his special list. Purely
internal causes were admitted by many. The difficulty of re-
suming normal commercial and industrial life with the military régime still in control of national activities, the slowness of demobilization, even of those classes which could be
spared from the army without danger to the national security; the oppressive régime of the censor, restricting the
news and limiting discussion, were generally admitted to be
factors. But they all ultimately came back to the question
of the peace, which did not seem to be making progress.

In the midst of the prevailing uncertainty and confusion
with regard to causes, it is not surprising that much of the
blame fell on the shoulders of Wilson, in view of the rôle in
the peacemaking popularly ascribed to him. "America is
tending to resume her freedom of action," said the *Écho de
Paris* (Dec. 27), in complaining of the failure in the "evolution of a real peace program". It warned its readers
against the "new ideology".[48] The *Intransigeant* (Dec. 23)
averred that Wilson was trying to solve the problems of "the
past, the present and the future", and felt it would be better

to confine one's self to "a few concrete matters". Even the
Dépêche of Toulouse (Dec. 27) had serious misgivings.
Noting that Wilson had come to France with a large number
of documents, it remarked: "The documents are all right,
but ideas are better. Besides the documents, what principles
does our illustrious guest bring?" "During the past few
weeks there has been a prevailing uneasiness. Traditionally,
we are skeptical of idealism."

The hopes of the old *Minoritaire* Socialists were already
fading, and their profound suspicion of any bourgeois attack
on the international problem began to re-assert itself. The
Populaire du Centre (Dec. 22) strikingly characterized the
President from this point of view. Wilson, it said, "is a political leader of a new type. . . . Wilson is a great honest
statesman, and therefore a phenomenon without precedent
in the annals of secret diplomacy. . . . But his political
and social horizon has its limits. They are those of his democratic and bourgeois conception. Wilson . . . is the perfect
democrat, to whom there is lacking only one thing: a perfect
democracy—a society not based on the domination of class.
. . . Wilson is a force because he is an armed conscience.
But the régime is stronger than he is. And his policy . . .
can only triumph with the collapse of the régime itself. And
to bring about the collapse of the régime . . . the democratic
effort, which is not even conscious of the precise task to be
accomplished, is entirely powerless." [49]

4. RIVAL SYSTEMS IN CONFLICT

Toward the end of the year the divergence of views between President Wilson and Premier Clemenceau suddenly
stood out against the background of developing uneasiness.
Owing to the policy of silence regarding peace objectives on
the part of the French government during the preceding
year, the French public was not well informed as to the
degree of agreement or disagreement between Wilsonian
and Clemencist policies. Vague assurances from time to
time had created a general impression that harmony pre-

vailed. The acceptance of the Fourteen Points (with two qualifications) by the Allies as a basis of the Armistice, lent further weight to the public assumption of harmony. The struggle of the French representatives against the acceptance of the Fourteen Points in late October was a closed book to the man in the street.

On the very day of Wilson's arrival in Paris, however, the lack of harmony between fundamental policies could be seen between the lines of polite diplomatic phrases. The first important formal function was the luncheon given by President Poincaré to President Wilson at the Élysée Palace. The carefully chosen language of the toasts which followed could gloss, but could not conceal, the difference in points of view. Reference has been made to President Poincaré's challenge to President Wilson to visit the liberated regions. This was followed by an epitome of Poincaré's views of the peace settlement: "For the misery and sadness of yesterday, the peace must be a reparation; against the dangers of tomorrow, it must be a guarantee." And then the French President added: "Whatever precautions for the future we might take, alas! no one can affirm that we shall spare humanity the horrors of new wars." The future peace and organization of the world, in his view, was to be based on the intimate collaboration of the victorious Allied Powers.

President Wilson replied, also in glowing terms of friendship; but suddenly his thoughts veered to the subject of his major interest. "The thought of the people of the United States" had from the first, he said, "turned toward something more than the mere winning of the war. It turned to the establishment of the eternal principles of right and justice. It realized that merely to win the war was not enough; that it must be won in such a way, and the questions raised by it settled in such a way, as to insure the future peace of the world and lay the foundation for the freedom and happiness of its many peoples and nations." [50]

It is probably a good illustration of "wishful" interpretation (or of diplomatic finesse) that the *Temps*, the following day, was able to head its leader: "In Unison", and to say: "To each of the ideas expressed by Poincaré, Mr. Wilson replied with one that looked in the same direction." Continuing, however, it proceeded to interpret Poincaré correctly, and Wilson incorrectly, in saying that they both envisaged a League to be organized "in two stages", the first stage to be based on "the permanence of the fortunate relations of friendship and cooperation" of the Entente Powers —an undoubted species of alliance. The situation was naturally delicate, for it was not the time to emphasize differences which, with tact, might be harmonized. The entire governmental press pretended to see harmony in the two points of view, and was able to select persuasive statements from each speech lending color to that interpretation. But the press of the extreme Left did not mince words, finding the differences in "nuance" to be obvious, and important. *Humanité* (Dec. 15) pointed significantly to the fact that Poincaré failed to refer directly to the League of Nations— "one does not know for what secret reason". President Wilson had embarked upon a "glorious adventure", and the Socialists were with him.

A much clearer perspective of the clash of policies was afforded by the pronouncements of Wilson and Clemenceau toward the end of the year. Before making his pre-Conference pilgrimages to England and Italy, President Wilson had, on several occasions, discussed with Clemenceau some of the major peace problems; hence both men were apprised of the degree to which they saw eye to eye with each other. Their pronouncements, therefore, naturally took on unusual significance.

Speaking at the Guildhall in London, December 28, President Wilson said that the soldiers had "fought to do away with an old order and to establish a new one. . . . The center and characteristic of the old order was that unstable thing which we used to call the 'balance of power'—a thing in which the balance was determined by the sword which was thrown in the one side or the other; a balance which was determined by the unstable equilibrium of competitive interests." "From every quarter," he continued, "there comes the suggestion that there must now be, not "a balance of power, not one powerful group of nations set off against another, but a single overwhelming, powerful group of nations who shall be the trustee of the peace of the world." [51]

That Clemenceau would have broken his long silence on the subject of foreign policy, is doubtful, had not a large part of the Chamber manifested its determination that before taking final action on the financial votes it would obtain a statement of the government's guiding principles as to peace policy. M. Franklin-Bouillon, nationalistic chief of the important Commission on Foreign Affairs, joined with leaders farther to the left in demanding light from the government. It had been "more than a year" said Franklin-Bouillon, since there had been a "debate on foreign policy". "We are the only country, of the great democracies, which had not made known its so-called 'war aims'." [52]

Late on the night of December 29, the day following Wilson's Guildhall speech, Clemenceau broke his silence. France, he said, "finds herself at this time in a particularly difficult situation. . . . It is the country which is nearest to Germany. America is distant; it has taken her a long time to get here. And during that time we have been put to it, we have suffered . . . our cities and our towns have been devastated. Everyone says, rightly, that 'it must not happen again'. I think so too. But how? There was an old system, which seems to be condemned today, and to which I do not fear to say that I remain a faithful adherent at this time. . . . This system—solid frontiers . . . and balance of power—today seems to be condemned by certain very high authorities." Yet, said the Premier, it was "this system of alliances" which would be his guiding principle at the Peace Conference. [53]

The French Premier's concept of a League of Nations was then thrown into relief. "When I speak of international guarantees . . . I will say this, that if France is allowed to establish its own defense . . . I, for my part, accept with joy *every addition of supplementary guarantee* which may be offered to us." The League of Nations was thus assigned by Clemenceau to the secondary rôle of "supplementary guarantee", and, as such, it was, of course, highly acceptable.

The Premier said he had had several conferences with Wilson. "I should lie if I said that I was at once in agreement with him on all the points. America is far distant from the frontiers of Germany, as I remarked a little while ago. I have, perhaps, preoccupations which I would not say are foreign to him, but which do not touch him so closely as they touch the man who has seen his country devastated during four years by an enemy who was within several days of Paris. . . . Mr. Wilson . . . has a broad mind, open and elevated. He is a man who inspires respect by the simplicity of his words and the noble candor [*noble candeur*] of his spirit. (Applause. Interruptions on the extreme left.)

"*Renaudel:* This is abominable. This is a mere pleasantry.

"*Clemenceau:* I meant it for high praise.[54]

.   .   .   .   .   .

"*Albert Thomas:* Mr. President of the Council, if there are shades of divergencies between the policy of certain of our great allies and our own, perhaps it resides in a more ardent and more immediate faith in the realization of this common ideal.

"*Clemenceau:* I am not sure of that.

.   .   .   .   .   .

"*Albert Thomas:* Ah, Mr. President of the Council, how little the new spirit seems to inspire you at this time."[55]

The day following this declaration of policy, President Wilson was in Manchester. Colonel House had informed him of the contents of Clemenceau's pronouncement.[56] Speaking at the Free Trade Hall, he soon came to the subject that was nearest to his heart. After referring to the traditional aloofness of the United States from European politics, he said: "If the future had nothing for us but a new attempt to keep the world at a right poise by a balance of power, the United States would take no interest, because she will join no combination of power which is not the combination of all of us. She is not interested merely in the peace of Europe, but in the peace of the world." [57]

Was there a serious divergence of views between the two chiefs? If so, Wilson would seem to have against him a considerable portion, perhaps a large majority, of French opinion. The Clemenceau policy had been overwhelmingly supported in the Chamber, by a vote of 398 to 93. Only the Unified Socialists were counted against the government. Furthermore, the press of the Right, the Center, and a not inconsiderable portion of the Left were, in varying degrees, satisfied that Clemenceau should go to the Conference as the representative of the country. The *Petit Parisien* (Dec. 30), generally moderate in tone, emphatically stated that "It would have been an inexcusable mistake to bargain with Clemenceau about the confidence he needs. . . . The Chamber took care not to commit that blunder." [58] The *Écho de Paris* (Dec. 31) rejoiced that "the chief of our government intends to practice a policy of alliances".

Yet there was naturally great unwillingness to admit that the two positions were mutually antagonistic. The dangers involved were too obvious. It became the duty of French official and semi-official circles to demonstrate that the two views could be reconciled. The *Temps* (Jan. 1) came at once to the rescue. The utterances of the two men could be harmonized, it thought. "Though Clemenceau pins his faith on a system of alliances, and Wilson places his on a League of Nations, they are in reality the same." The apparent difference is explained by Clemenceau's words: "France is the country nearest to Germany; America is far away." Most of the patriotic press followed this line, though some did so with variations. It was argued that there was no difference in *principle* between America and France, and that it was expecting too much to hope that "a people on the other side of the Atlantic should accept immediately all the ideas that have ripened . . . in Paris under the shelling of the 'Big Bertha' ".[59] The *Journal de Rouen* (Jan. 1) thought Wilson would realize the significance of Clemenceau's views after he had seen the devastated regions. A number of organs quoted with approval the London *Times* leader, of January 2, arguing that at heart Wilson and Clemenceau were in harmony, the only difference being that Clemenceau wanted a more immediate solution.

President Poincaré sought to relieve the embarrassment in a New Year's interview given to the United Press and carried prominently in most of the governmental press. "The Agreement Between the Allies Is Complete," said the *Petit Journal's* headline (Jan. 2), carrying an excerpt from Poincaré's words in the interview. The French President did not anticipate any difficulty in arriving at complete agreement on all points, even on secondary questions. Further, "We are particularly happy over the visit of President Wilson," said the President. "He will certainly play a leading rôle in the Peace Conference."[60]

Yet even some conservative organs, which were less careful of appearances, admitted important divergencies. "The hour of negotiations approaches. The picture of conflicting interests and principles begins to stand out," said the *Intransigeant* (Dec. 30, 31). "Wilson says: League of Nations first. Clemenceau says: Guarantees first, which means alliances between the four great powers." The *Progrès de la Somme* of Amiens (Jan. 5) expressed a widely held view in saying: "The policies of reality and idealism are at grips."

The liberal and radical press frankly could not harmonize the points of view.[61] The *Progrès* of Lyons (Jan. 3), a leading liberal journal, placed the statements of the two leaders together, and remarked: "The semi-official organs try to show us, in Mr. Wilson and M. Clemenceau, two men who think alike on all points. It is asking too much of our credulity. . . . The disparity stares one in the face." *Europe*

Nouvelle (Jan. 4), an important liberal weekly, felt that the gulf between Wilson and Clemenceau was profound. "As between Wilson and Metternich, Clemenceau has chosen Metternich." "The dilemma is clear. It rests on principles." "If the policy of alliances is persisted in, America cannot be counted on."

The Socialist press used even stronger language. "M. Clemenceau sees in Mr. Wilson only the *'noble candeur'* of his spirit," said *Humanité* (Dec. 31). "*'Candeur'!* The President of the United States becomes a simpleton, an innocent, a kind of 'mutton-head'."

It was a critical period for the peace preliminaries. In some quarters of the conservative-nationalist press the campaign against Wilson became more intense. The attack lay generally, though not always, in the realm of subtleties and indirection. "American mysticism" was warned against by one.[62] "Idealism of Wilson: Realism of Clemenceau," wrote another.[63] "Vague aspirations" must not be given too much rein, said the *Éclaireur de Nice* (Jan. 5). The *Éclair de l'Est* (Jan. 3) followed the *Écho de Paris* in pointing to the "two conceptions of peace"—the "realistic", which would take positive and immediate guarantees against Germany, and the "idealistic, after the fashion of President Wilson, which would proceed according to juridical conceptions", and "which certain people call 'Utopian' in the presence of German bad faith". The death of ex-President Roosevelt at this time furnished an occasion for illuminating comment. "Roosevelt had seen . . .," was the concluding sentence of the *Journal de Rouen's* eulogy (Jan. 7).[64] "Wilson is the apostle of peace and disarmament," said the *Journal* (Jan. 6). "But he found a military guard even at the Vatican"; and the *Petit Journal* (Jan. 11) made the somewhat cynical observation: "It was in the Middle Ages, an epoch full of wars, that there was the most discussion of universal peace."

Liberal and radical opinion became alarmed lest the Wilsonian principles be shipwrecked. The great Radical Socialist journals of the provinces, such as the *Dépêche* of

Toulouse, the *Progrès* of Lyons, the *Petit Provençal* of Marseilles, the *Populaire de Nantes,* and the *France de Bordeaux,* joined with the *Œuvre, Heure,* and the more radical papers of Paris in support of the Wilsonian system. The *Progrès* of Lyons (Jan. 3, 7) felt it necessary to choose between Wilson, "the optimist" and Clemenceau, "the pessimist", and hoped that "the realism of Clemenceau" would allow itself to be convinced by the *"noble candeur"* of President Wilson. The *Œuvre* (Jan. 3, 7) expressed its determination to wait obstinately, and with *"candeur naïve",* for Wilson's alternative to the "international competition in cannons and munitions", for it thought "the old system acclaimed by Clemenceau" was "incapable of regulating the destiny of the world". *Humanité* (Jan. 10) expressed the feeling of the extreme Left in saying that "the brutal attitude of Pichon and Clemenceau and the imperialists of our country, renders more and more insoluble the problems placed before the statesmen of the Conference".[65]

Even moderate opinion of the Center was not unanimous in its assurance that Clemenceau had the better of the argument. The spirit of nationalism might go too far, and make it impossible for the United States and the Allies to reach a common agreement. *Opinion,* a weekly journal of moderate views, urged that it might even be desirable to re-examine the "basic premises" of the balance of power doctrine. "That concept," it said, was "essentially equivocal", in that it failed to weigh the imponderables. Wilson had been presented "in the guise of a dangerous ideologue who despises force". But the portrait was not exact. Ideology, if any, could rather be found "in other theses which, while supporting themselves on the realities of the past, neglect too much those of the present".[66]

The repercussions of these December clashes were so violent, and the anxieties aroused were so serious that official intervention was again necessary. On the evening of January 11, André Tardieu, right-hand man of Premier Clemenceau, addressing a distinguished Franco-Anglo-American audience, denied that there were two conflicting conceptions of the peace, and assured his hearers that complete harmony of views prevailed among the leaders of the Entente.[7] This official assurance probably aided somewhat in relaxing tense feelings. Much more important, however, in allaying the popular anxiety which had grown out of the events following Wilson's arrival was the actual opening of formal peace parleys on January 12. This served to turn public attention aside from fatuous contemplation of imaginary ills and to focus it on the specific problems of the Conference.

NOTES

[1] The *Journal du Centre* (Nov. 28) pointedly remarked that "it is not without a certain apprehension that all of these people ['certain politicians' and 'certain journalists'] learned that Mr. Wilson wished personally to be present at the deliberations on the conditions of peace. They tremble lest the President's ideas of justice triumph definitively, in spite of the ambushes and traps which the defenders of the outworn prejudices place in its route".

[2] Clemenceau, Georges, *Grandeur and Misery of Victory* (New York, 1930), p. 167.

[3] Poincaré, *op. cit.*, p. 410.

[4] *House Papers*, vol. iv, p. 209.

[5] Poincaré, *op. cit.*, p. 434. Poincaré says that King George remarked that if Wilson sat in the Conference, he (King George) and Poincaré should also sit in. *Ibid.*, p. 434.

[6] Deschanel and Dubost expressed the view to Poincaré that it would be impossible for a mere chief of government like Clemenceau, to preside over Wilson. *Ibid.*, p. 404.

[7] *House Papers*, vol. iv, pp. 209 *et seq.*

[8] *Ibid.*, pp. 209 *et seq.* House remarks: "It might be that he believes it will pull Wilson down from his high pedestal." *Ibid.*, p. 216.

[9] Poincaré, *op. cit.*, p. 434.

[10] *Ibid.*, p. 451.

[11] E.g., *Petite Gironde* of Bordeaux.

[12] There is little doubt that the treatment of this matter in the moderate and conservative press was influenced by official *directives*, as the suggestions and directions from official quarters were designated, and which were closely related to the policy of censorship. It is interesting to note a somewhat similar silence on the subject of the American elections of November 5. For four weeks, only belated news notes on the elections found their way into the papers, and none of these suggested the political significance involved. The *Correspondant* (Nov. 10), referring to this subject, said: "Our press has avoided speaking of it with a discretion that is almost

embarrassing." The writer ("Interim") added that several weeks earlier he had not been allowed to mention the subject.

[13] American opinion on the subject of Mr. Wilson's going in person to the peace parleys was divided. Opinion in Congress was apparently strongly opposed to the venture. See Houston, D. F., *Eight Years with Wilson's Cabinet, 1913-1920,* 2 vols. (New York, 1926), vol. i, p. 353; Seymour, Charles, *Woodrow Wilson and the World War* (New Haven, 1921), p. 250; Dodd, W. E., *Woodrow Wilson and His Work* (New York, 1920), p. 282. According to George Creel, Mr. Wilson felt that staying at home would be the more popular thing to do. *The War, the World and Wilson* (New York, 1920), p. 151. Secretary of State Lansing, who, perhaps, was not disinterested, felt that the President would be in a much more strategic position if he remained at home. *The Peace Negotiations, A Personal Narrative* (Boston, 1921), p. 15. Opinion in general throughout the country seemed somewhat more evenly divided, though the fact that tradition was against the President would weigh heavily with many. Liberal opinion was favorable, if the *New Republic* (Nov. 23, 1918) is a criterion. Such powerful papers as the *Baltimore Sun,* the *Brooklyn Eagle,* the *Christian Science Monitor,* the *San Francisco Chronicle,* the *Springfield Republican,* the *Newark News,* and the *Seattle Times* favored the President's plans, according to an analysis by the *Literary Digest,* November 30, 1918; while many other leading organs, apparently a majority, were hostile. The *New York Times* wondered whether the President had so little confidence in his men that he must go himself, and even the New York *World* thought the President would lose prestige by going. While the *Christian Science Monitor* said the President had the support of the "great majority of his fellow citizens", the New York *Evening Sun* alleged that ninety-five per cent of the people of the country viewed the expedition with misgiving and dislike. *Literary Digest,* December 14, 1918.

[14] Shaw, A. (ed.), *Messages and Papers of Woodrow Wilson,* 2 vols. (New York, 1924), vol. i, pp. 554-556. Hereafter cited as *Messsages and Papers.*

[15] *Journal de Rouen,* November 14.

[16] *Débats,* December 5; *Petit Journal,* December 4; *Action Française,* December 4.

[17] The *Gaulois* (Dec. 4) wondered whether Mr. Wilson was presuming to come to the Conference as an arbiter. The *Ouest-Éclair* of Rennes (Dec. 5), a vigorous conservative organ, warned against "revolutionary mysticism". "To pretend, as some do, that to perpetuate the 'peace of right' it is sufficient to draw up the statute of a League of Nations, is to lose one's self in a dream."

[18] *Temps,* December 5.

[19] *Ouest-Éclair,* December 5. "We have always thought it necessary for Mr. Wilson to see before his very eyes the spectacle of the devastation and ruin of which the Germans were the barbarous authors," said *Journal de Rouen,* December 4.

[20] See *Éclair de l'Est* of Nancy, December 9; *Dépêche* de Lille, December 13.

[21] See *Écho de Paris,* December 8; *France de Bordeaux,* December 9.

[22] *House Papers,* vol. iv, p. 243. That Mr. Wilson did not make the request seems fairly certain from a comment of Mr. A. H. Frazier, who said that when he first broached the subject the President remarked, "The French want me to see red. I could not despise the Germans more than I do already." *Ibid.,* p. 243. Possibly the Colonel had authorized the above news-note under pressure from the French government.

[23] The authenticity of this story cannot be vouched for.

[24] *Temps,* December 16.

[25] *Humanité,* December 14.

[26] *Œuvre,* December 15.

[27] The allocation of columns by these papers to Victor Emmanuel, King George and Wilson, respectively, was as follows: *Matin,* 6½, 8⅓, 16; *Petit Parisien,* 14, 11¼, 17¾; *Journal* 7⅔, 12¾, 18½; *Petit Journal,* 8½, 11½, 12¾.

[28] *House Papers,* vol. iv, p. 239.

[29] *Humanité,* December 11.

[30] *Humanité* (Dec. 15), in a heavy-typed appeal to the workers of Paris, said Clemenceau had forbidden the demonstration "unless President Wilson gave his personal approval". The labor and Socialist leaders, it said, feared that such a request might take on a discourteous character.

[31] *Humanité,* December 15.

[32] *Ibid.,* December 15. It is interesting to note that Wilson had known of the projected manifestation and had apparently not disapproved of it, for when the delegation was about to leave, a naval attaché asked Jean Longuet "whether the manifestation was going to take place soon, for the President would like to place himself at a window to see it pass and to salute it". Longuet expressed his amazement that the President did not know it had been called off, and gave his assurance that it was not the fault of the Socialists that it would not take place.

[33] Miller Diary, vol. i, p. 50.

[34] *Figaro,* December 16; *Temps,* December 12; *Victoire,* December 14; *Liberté,* December 14.

[35] *Temps,* December 12.

[36] *Figaro,* December 7.

[37] The *Action Française* (Dec. 15) damned them for displaying the red flag, and singing the "International" on the very night of the President's arrival.

[38] A number of papers had, somewhat earlier, copied notes from the London *Times* emphasizing the solidarity of the President with American opinion. The *Temps* (Dec. 5) pointedly remarked that in spite of the November elections "his prestige remains incomparable, and his power remains intact". Incidentally, this was the first time that editorial notice had been taken of the November elections.

[39] Some of the radical organs commented ironically on the "strange phenomenon" of unanimity. "On the words of command," said the *Vérité* (Dec. 17), "the reactionary press abandons itself to a very accommodating enthusiasm."

[40] The *Victoire* (Dec. 15) assured Wilson that the more he was "disposed to let France have all the restitutions, reparations and guarantees

to which she is entitled", the more France would "take to heart the cause of the League of Nations".

[41] See Thompson, *The Peace Conference Day by Day*, pp. 27-29.

[42] November 17; December 1, 4, 6.

[43] December 15, 18, 20, 23, 26, 31, 1918; January 1, 2, 5, 6, 8, 1919.

[44] Although the *Matin*, the *Temps* and *Homme Libre* had, on the eve of Wilson's arrival, generously printed a few items, editorial or otherwise, emphasizing Wilson's strength at home, after the triumphal welcome of December 14 they, along with a great many other conservative journals, found space, from time to time, for American news notes hostile to Wilson, but none for news in his favor.

[45] The *Vérité* (Jan. 7) asked why the nationalist press confined itself to one kind of American news, and why it refused to print such a speech as that of Senator Lewis, in which the Senator discussed the Wilson program favorably, and denounced the campaign against Wilson.

[46] *Éclair de l'Est*, December 27.

[47] "The exaltation of the first days [after the Armistice] has disappeared, and we are in a period of depression," said the *Journal de Rouen*, December 29.

[48] December 28.

[49] See also *Populaire* of Paris, January 2, 1919.

[50] *Temps*, December 15.

[51] *Messages and Papers*, vol. i, p. 584.

[52] *Annales de la Chambre*, December 29, 1918, p. 3328.

[53] *Ibid.*, pp. 3350-3351.

[54] *Ibid.*, p. 3352.

[55] *Ibid.*, p. 3354.

[56] Thompson, *op. cit.*, p. 59.

[57] *Messages and Papers*, vol. i, p. 591.

[58] It ought to be noted that the vote of the Chamber did not, and could not, accurately express its views on the subject of peace policies, as the final vote involved not only the matter of granting supplies to carry on the government, but also the question whether, on its policy, in the large, the government should be replaced.

[59] *Lyon Républicain*, January 7.

[60] Some attempts were made to explain away the implications of the *"noble candeur"* phrase of Clemenceau. A number of organs of the conservative press ridiculed the Socialists for suggesting that Clemenceau was dealing in subtleties. The *Petit Journal* (Jan. 2) carried an interview with someone in Wilson's entourage who was reported to have stated that he realized that the words had been used "in the sense of frankness and loyalty of spirit—in the English sense—rather than in the French sense which makes it a synonym of naïveté". Yet the phrase found currency in various quarters. The *Cri de Paris*, of January 5, enacted a dialogue between its puppets: *Guignol:* "My deputy is sure to be re-elected." *Guignolet: "Noble candeur!"*

[61] The *Dépêche* of Toulouse (Jan. 6) regretfully admitted that "the point of view of President Wilson does not agree entirely with that of Clemenceau".

[62] *Ouest-Éclair,* January 5.

[63] *Intransigeant,* December 30.

[64] The journals of information completely ignored the significant passages of Wilson's speeches in Italy—those in which he re-emphasized the necessity of supplanting the old system of "equilibrium" with the new one of "concert". The *Temps* (Jan. 6), however, chose this excerpt from Wilson's speech at Rome, and argued that though Wilson was right in his condemnation of the old system, and though it brings us to the League of Nations, yet this League must rest on "the intimate and permanent union of the victorious peoples".

[65] See *Populaire de Nantes,* January 8; *Populaire* of Paris, January 8.

[66] *Opinion,* January 11, 18, 1919.

[67] *Temps,* January 13.

CHAPTER IV

THE LEAGUE OF NATIONS

"A general association of nations must be formed under specific covenants for the purpose of affording mutual guarantees of political independence and territorial integrity to great and small states alike."
(Woodrow Wilson, in Fourteen Points.)

"Vous y croyez, vous, dans un monde bati sur la violence?"
(Clemenceau, *Humanité,* February 2, 1918.)

"Allons donc! la Société des Nations seule peut garantir la paix."
(Marcel Sembat, *Humanité,* November 7, 1918.)

"It is possible that a new era has dawned."
(*Petit Parisien,* April 29, 1919.)

1. THE FRENCH INTEREST IN THE LEAGUE OF NATIONS

ONE of the first major acts of the Peace Conference was the solemn affirmation by the Plenary Session of January 25 that the League of Nations should be an integral part of the peace settlement. This decision, which left to subsequent negotiations the elaboration of all details, raised a question which, in its implications, went to the roots of the entire French peace program, and related to a matter which few Frenchmen could view with philosophical detachment. The immediacy of the World War, the vivid memories of past wars, and the danger of future ones with an historic enemy whose frontiers lay so threateningly close, caused their thinking on the League to be dominated by considerations of the degree of security which it would provide for France.

French opinion on the subject of a League of Nations was not, however, well organized at the time of the Armistice. During the war a rigorous censorship and militant patriotism combined to restrict pacifist activities to a minimum. "Pacifist articles," defined as "those which tend to weaken the national defense", were forbidden by the censor to be published. The "Confidential Circular No. 1000" (the "Bible" of the censors) provided that publications in favor of peace could not be authorized "except when they specify that it is a question of a victorious peace, based on the triumph of right and justice".[1] The pacifist organ, *Universel,* was banned, even though its keynote was "more religious than pacifist",[2] and the *Bulletin des droits de l'homme* was whitened by the censor in the midst of an article reporting a conference on the League of Nations.[3]

Discussion of this subject was also discouraged by most patriotic Frenchmen. The idea that a League of Nations might be a practical contribution to the peace seemed too remote, as was accurately pointed out by Auguste Gauvain, who said that "in Europe, where there is too great reason to mistrust fine words, the thing was considered chimerical. Nobody was prepared to study the question with a view to a practical solution." [4]   Furthermore, conservatives and nationalists generally feared that any trafficking with the idea of a League would run the risk of endangering the more immediate and material guarantees which they deemed essential to the welfare of France.[5]

During the war period the organized peace movement was, accordingly, narrowly restricted. The Peace through Law Society, and the League of the Rights of Man did almost all that was done in this field. The former organization, moderate in tone, was assisted financially by the Carnegie Endowment for International Peace, but its resources during the war were so reduced that its publications were greatly reduced in bulk and frequency.[6] The latter was primarily a civil liberties organization, though its annual congresses of 1916, 1917, and 1918 devoted a considerable amount of time to the discussion of the problem of a League of Nations.[7] It was not until November 10, on the very eve of the Armistice, that an organization was established (The French Association for a League of Nations) comparable in representative character and importance to the League to

Enforce Peace, which had existed in the United States since 1915.[8]

The issue of the League could scarcely be ignored entirely in official quarters, especially after President Wilson had made it an issue of first importance in his "Essential Peace Terms" speech of January 22, 1917, and after our subsequent entry into the war in April of that year. Accordingly, a resolution of the Chamber of Deputies, June 5, 1917, renouncing all thought of conquest, included as one of its objectives, the achievement "of an organization, now in preparation, of a League of Nations"; and Premier Ribot paid his tribute to the idea.[9] It is significant, however, that on the following day, when the Senate voted a resolution patterned on that of the Chamber, reference to the League was conspicuously absent.[10] In July 1917 the Bourgeois commission was appointed to study the question with a view to elaborating a project, but when Clemenceau became premier in November, not only did the government show increased skepticism concerning the League idea, but it even prevented the publication of the Bourgeois report.[11]

Although, as has been noted, the reception given Wilson's Fourteen Points was at first overwhelmingly favorable, it was only in the Left Wing press that the fourteenth point, providing for "a general association of Nations", received a really hearty welcome. The Center press had very little to say on the subject, while the press on the Right manifested unabated skepticism. Under the title: "The Promised Land", *Action Française* (Jan. 18) glanced back through history, noting "similar attempts" from the time of the Greek Amphictyonic Council, and reached the satisfying conclusion that nothing had come of them. The *Écho de Paris* (Jan. 6, 1918) was willing to accept a League of Nations as long as it merely furnished "some carvings for the façade of our political edifice". The *Temps* remained silent on the subject of the League until May 27, 1918, at which time it conceded that the conception of the League proceeded from "generous idealism", but questioned very seriously whether such an organization was possible "so long as there are nations which still believe in force as the means of defending their interests". Shortly thereafter (June 11) it deplored the demands that were being made for the publication and discussion of the Bourgeois report on the League which was reported as being completed, and argued that talk of a League "does not hasten the end of the war", but rather, "it sows seeds of illusions and dissent". This idea, which was an expression of the Clemenceau policy, was fought vigorously by Left groups. Even Bourgeois, in commenting on the publication of his commission's report, remarked that the "discussion of the bases of the project . . . would not weaken the action of the armies".[12]

The profound distrust of the idea of a League remained unabated in Center and Right Wing circles with the approach of the Peace Conference, and continued to find encouragement in French official quarters. President Poincaré, speaking at Strasbourg, early in December, said: "The only guarantee of peace is that which the representatives of friendly and allied nations symbolized, in accompanying the French government to Strasbourg." [13] "The League of Nations is a fine dream for seducing the whole world," said the *Petit Marseillais* (Dec. 10), speaking out boldly, as many of the provincial papers were prone to do. The *Gaulois* (Dec. 26) wondered when we might hope to see "the League of Nations come down from the clouds of the theorizers". Elsewhere it was attacked on the grounds that it would loosen the ties of national sentiment.[14] The *Cri de Paris* (Jan. 19, 1919) staged a dialogue between its puppets: *Guignol:* "Then the nations will be just one big family?" *Guignolet:* "That is just what I fear."

The liberal and radical press vigorously attacked the anti-League attitudes of the conservative and nationalist papers. The *Dépêche* of Toulouse, which was typical, contested the claim that the League would "enervate the warlike virtues and strike a blow at national pride". It argued, on the contrary, that the idea of putting the collective force of nations at the service of justice, would be a stimulus to the young. "The dream of a League of Nations, if it is a dream, is a cordial rather than an opiate." [15] The Left Wing Socialists (*Minoritaires*) and Left Wing Syndicalists guarded against uncritical acceptance of the League ideal. The *Populaire du Centre* (Sept. 8, 1918) expressed this point of view in saying that while it recognized that the League of Nations represented "a serious effort toward a superior organization of humanity", and that while, therefore, they would not be numbered among its "detractors", nevertheless the *Minoritaires* must warn the workers against illusions, for they must remember that "there will never be real security in the world until capitalism is abolished". The *Avenir Internationale* stated the Left Wing Syndicalist case: "In our view the future safety of humanity lies in the international organization of peoples. There, only there!" [16]

For reasons stated above, public opinion had not, prior to the Conference, crystallized as to the details of a League of Nations. There were, however, two major schools of thought in France on the subject of the rôle which the League should play in the ultimate peace settlement. One, which was represented by the views of Clemenceau, as stated to the Chamber, December 29, regarded strong frontiers and a "system of alliances" as the indispensable foundation of peace. Anything additional in the nature of a League of Nations would be acceptable, as long as it in no way qualified the strength of the aforesaid guarantees deriving from the old order of diplomacy. [17] This view prevailed, in varying degrees, throughout the Right and the greater part of the Center. The other view ascribed to the League a much more important rôle, and regarded it as, in itself, a basic guarantee of the peace, assuming, of course, that it would be endowed with adequate powers and functions for effective action. This school of thought was supported by liberal and radical groups, with isolated support from the more moderate elements of the Center. Even the Socialists were by no means indifferent to French security. Only a negligible minority on the extreme Left thought in exclusively "internationalist" terms. Practically all those who supported the idea of a League did so because of their belief that it would contribute, directly or indirectly, to French security.

The question therefore was: which of the two basic peace systems—alliances, or League of Nations—would provide the greatest present and prospective security for France? In making this appraisal, every Frenchman was naturally affected by a variety of imponderables, such as his nationalistic "boiling point", and his belief in the natural goodness of man. Gabriel Seailles, writing on this subject in the Radical Socialist *Progrès* of Lyons (Feb. 5, 1919), presented the view which was typical of liberals and radicals, as contrasted with conservatives and nationalists. As to the value of alliances, he found himself led to conclusions diametrically opposite to those of Clemenceau. " . . . let us cherish no vain illusions," he said. "Variable as are interests and circumstances, alliances will give in the future just what they have given in the past; unstable, like the equilibrium which it is their object to maintain, they will bring back the war which they have always produced. To imagine that, by an impossible miracle of love, states will remain always grouped as they are today, is to neglect all the teaching of history. . . . The system of alliances leaves us in a Europe uncertain and disturbed, under the law and the menace of force. . . . Alliances or League of Nations: the alternatives bring us back to choosing between peace and war."

2. THE COVENANT AND THE "GENERAL TREATY OF PEACE"

In spite of divergencies of view with regard to the future rôle of the League in France's system of security, it seemed to be generally accepted that the League, in some form or other, would figure in the final peace settlement. Wilson obviously placed this at the head of his program, and the Allies were committed to it by their acceptance of the Fourteen Points. An important question which had to be decided, however, was whether the basic constitution of the League should be an integral part of the peace treaty itself, or whether the Entente Powers should first make the peace settlement with the Central Powers, and subsequently call together a congress of nations for the purpose of setting up a general framework for the preservation of international peace. Or, indeed, should they choose a middle ground, and include in the peace treaty certain general commitments with regard to the organization of peace, which should later be elaborated in a more representative congress?

The solution of this problem was important because of the fact that it would probably have a significant bearing on the character of the peace itself. If the organization of the general peace were to follow after the settlement with Germany, and be functionally unrelated to it, then the treaty with Germany would have to rest, so to speak, on its own bottom, and the guarantees of French security would inevitably tend to be those of the "old order". But if the peace with Germany were set in the matrix of a general international system, then the relative harshness of the pains and penalties of the treaty terms might be proportionally moderated. In the first case, the League would be strictly a "supplementary guarantee" as envisaged by the French premier. In the second, it might be elevated to the rôle of chief guarantor, not only of the general peace of the world, but also of French security.

President Wilson had taken a clear and unequivocal stand as to these alternatives. In his September 27, 1918 address he left no doubt as to the desired order of precedence, saying that the League of Nations was "in a sense the most essential part of the peace settlement itself". He thought it could not be formed *before* the end of hostilities, for that would make it "merely a new alliance confined to the nations associated against a common enemy". On the other hand, he thought it *unlikely* that it *could* be formed *after* the peace settlement. "It is necessary to guarantee the peace; and the peace cannot be guaranteed as an afterthought." [18]

The position of the French government was equally clear.

Faced with the determined stand of President Wilson, it chose the middle ground. Only the general principle of the League should be stated in the peace treaty, which should be primarily concerned with the details essential to the settlement with Germany. After the restoration of peace the statute of the League could then be elaborated.[19] Incidentally, it is interesting to note that this middle ground was also that of Wilson's two chief aides, House and Lansing,[20] and it was, likewise, the position of the British government. Hence, the subsequent decision to incorporate the Covenant in the Treaty must be regarded as a distinct personal triumph for President Wilson.

French opinion, before the Conference, was divided in its preferences as to the order of procedure. That of the Right would have preferred to postpone all consideration of the League until after the final treaty with Germany had been signed, while the radical groups favored the close union of the League and the Treaty. The actual trend of events seemed, however, to point in the direction of the middle course, which was probably most acceptable to the great majority of Frenchmen. The *Temps* (Dec. 29) accurately expressed the prevailing view in saying, that it was generally supposed that the work would proceed in stages,—"first, the framing of the peace, including a general statement on the League; then the setting up of the League". The precise number of steps in the process was a matter of indifference, as long as nothing more than the general principle of the League was inserted in the peace treaty itself.

The general impression was that the process would consist of three successive stages, and this was advocated by the widely representative organization, the French Association for a League of Nations, which, under the leadership of Léon Bourgeois, asked Premier Clemenceau, early in December, to pledge himself to accept the following procedure: first, a preliminary declaration by the Allies as to the general principles; second, the insertion of the general principles in the treaty; third, a universal congress to establish these principles between "all states called to membership in the League of Nations".[21] Even the League of the Rights of Man, an organization more strictly of the Left than the French Association, accepted this as the desirable procedure in December, 1918.[22] Only mild protests against this middle course were heard from the Left. Camille Ferdy thought the "free peoples who aspire to a new organization of the world . . . would not be content with a mere platonic manifestation", (a simple statement of principle) for this would have the effect, he thought, of adjourning "to the Greek Kalends the solution of the agonizing problem".[23] Renaudel, of the Socialists, who expressed considerable gratification over the pledge given by Clemenceau that the "principle of the League" would be included in the peace, nevertheless hoped that the Peace Conference would go beyond this.[24] Cachin, however, editor of *Humanité,* seemed to accept the middle course as a desirable alternative.[25] This generally complaisant attitude of the Left groups was doubtless due to their belief that such procedure would mean a quicker peace, bringing with it demobilization (the object of their insistent demands), and a quicker return to normal economic life.

Casual remarks in the patriotic press show how strong was the antagonism in those circles to the idea of the contemporaneous elaboration of the League Covenant and the peace treaty. The *Matin* (Dec. 24) observed that "many people" would prefer to commence by making the peace treaty, leaving all consideration of the League till later, which, it thought, could at that time be "only a theory or a chimera". But it expressed its willingness to accept the compromise proposal. "Mr. Wilson will ask only for a clause in the peace treaty affirming the general principle of the Great Project," said the *Petit Parisien* (Dec. 27). "This procedure is irreproachable." This same interpretation was generally, and perhaps justifiably, placed upon Wilson's Christmas Day speech to the American soldiers, in which he said he found "no differences of view as to the fundamental principles and aims" in the "minds of the great chiefs" with whom he had conferred. "All is then for the best," said the *Liberté* (Dec. 26). "Let us first sign peace, and then organize it afterwards."

Before the lapse of another month, however, events had taken a somewhat different turn, and it became apparent that the intentions of President Wilson had been misinterpreted. Rather than consenting to a mere statement of the principle of the League in the treaty, he had held fast to his plan outlined September 27, and had won the Allied leaders over to his point of view. For, at the plenary session of January 25, the Conference put itself formally on record, to the effect, first, that a League of Nations was "essential to the maintenance of the world settlement, which the Associated Nations are now met to establish", and second, that "this League should be created as an integral part of the general Treaty of Peace. . . ."[26] It was also resolved to appoint a committee to work out the details of the constitution and functions of the League. President Wilson, addressing the plenary session gave his appraisal of the importance of the step taken: "We regard it [the League] as the keystone of the whole program which expressed our purposes and ideals in this war and which the Associated Nations accepted as the basis of the settlement. If we return to the United States without having made every effort in our power to realize this program, we should return to meet the merited scorn of our fellow-citizens."

This triumph of the President was hailed with delight in radical and some liberal circles,[27] but there were evidences of considerable annoyance in the Center and on the Right, though comment, for the time being, was rather guarded. Reference was made to Wilson's pique over the protests of the small states who asked for more representation on the League of Nations commission.[28] Notice was taken of Wilson's "strange smile, which suddenly disappears and leaves the face rigid and lifeless".[29] The merits of the Smuts League plan were extolled, the argument being used that this plan would at least give France something in the nature of an alliance.[30] Some of the conservative journals of the provinces were more outspoken. The *Nouvelliste de Lyon* (Jan. 26, 27) quoted Pascal to the effect that "by becoming too much of an angel, one ends by becoming a beast", and expressed the hope that "these gentlemen of the Conference would come down from their Olympus to settle questions quite otherwise urgent; and, first of all, settle the peace". The *Ouest-Éclair* of Rennes (Jan. 26) warned its countrymen against eloquence and "ideology", which, it urged, should not be allowed "to distract us from the immediate realities which menace our lives and our interests".

Before many days had passed public opinion everywhere, except on the extreme Left, had become crystallized in the belief that it was unwise to attempt the extremely difficult task of elaborating the international constitution before the main lines of the peace with Germany had been laid. That "we should first have settled the peace conditions with Germany", was a characteristic expression of opinion even in the liberal press.[31] "Wilson's method is to subordinate the conditions of peace to a League of Nations. . . . In the meantime the Germans profit", was a sentiment frequently expressed in the Center and Right Wing organs.[32] "The plow has been put in front of the oxen", was an expression which echoed repeatedly in many editorial columns.[33] "Wilson's generous ideas bear bad fruit," said the *Nouvelliste de Lyon* (Feb. 13); "and it is the nation most ravaged by the war" which becomes the "first new victim of the American dream". "Let us have peace, and have it quickly," said another. "After that we shall be able to think of the new world." [34] Professor Scelle later remarked that the haste on the part of Wilson in the matter of the Covenant of the League, "could not but surprise even favorable opinion, and be a source of criticisms. It seemed that the Conference was abandoning the traditional and logical method of arranging the questions in the order of their urgency." [35]

Viewed in the light of the interests and desires of the great majority of the statesmen of the Conference, as well as of

French opinion, the resolution of January 25, declaring the union of the League and the Treaty, was remarkable. The situation was well characterized by Professor Aulard in saying: "Here is this Conference, which, although composed of ministers more or less caught in the spirit of the past (with the exception of the great Wilson) and whose ironical remarks, reservations and silences prove that they have no belief in a League of Nations, here is this Conference forced to play the rôle of a League, or rather, to call this League into being. . . ."[36] The subsequent attempt radically to modify the application of the January 25 resolution will be referred to later. Mr. Wilson's immediate problem was to give definite form to the League of Nations idea.

3. THE DRAFT COVENANT OF FEBRUARY 14

After the acceptance of the resolution of January 25, one of President Wilson's major preoccupations became the problem of working out the details of the League Covenant, in the hope that he might be able to carry a first draft back with him to the United States on his return in February. The process by which this task was accomplished has been the subject of some controversy. It has been said that the President wanted the Council itself to perform the function of working out the principles of the League; that the proposal by the Allied leaders to form a special commission for this purpose was a means of "getting it, at least temporarily, out of the way, so they could proceed to the business that really interested them", and that the formation of the relatively large committee (first fifteen, then nineteen) was a means of making the process "as unwieldy as possible", thus hampering the work of drafting the Covenant.[37] These assertions have, in turn, been vigorously denied.[38] On none of these points are the records of the Council of Ten definitive as to the precise intentions of the parties,[39] hence generalization on that basis is difficult. Whatever Wilson's initial intention may have been, there is little doubt as to the ultimate wisdom of the method devised; and if Lloyd George

and Clemenceau had any *arrières pensées* in urging this procedure, the results did not justify their anticipations.

As to the size of the proposed commission on the League,
there were undoubtedly differences of opinion between Wilson, on the one hand, and Clemenceau and Lloyd George,
on the other. Wilson favored a small committee of the representatives of the Large Powers, on the grounds that this
would be a "more elastic arrangement". They would be able,
as they saw fit, he felt, to call into conference the "thoughtful men representing the small powers". In this he was supported by Sonnino; but Clemenceau and Lloyd George argued that this was an opportunity to give the small powers a
hearing. Clemenceau thought it desirable "for the great and
small powers" to "get together", and "to let the public feel
that their work was connected". Lloyd George warned that
"the small powers were becoming restive, and felt that they
had been locked out, so to speak".[40] The Clemenceau-Lloyd
George thesis prevailed, agreement being reached on a committee of fifteen, five being representatives of small powers.
As a result of protests from the small powers the League
Commission, at its second meeting, despite Wilson's objections, gave representation to four additional small powers.[41]

One of the major articles of the Covenant was settled in
principle, and practically in final form, before the Commission of the League of Nations had its first meeting. This was
the provision relating to Mandates. Because of the fact that
the fundamental problem involved was one of high policy—
what to do with the German colonies and parts of the old
Turkish Empire, rather than the more general problem of
building the structure of international peace—it was the
Council of Ten which took jurisdiction in the matter. The
decision that the colonies should not revert to Germany was
quickly reached on January 24.[42] The determination of the
precise international status of these territories was another
matter, and several heated sessions of the Supreme Council,
between January 24 and 30, were necessary before agreement could be reached. The British Dominions asserted

perhaps the most vigorous claims for outright annexation. Japan and France followed suit, demanding the annexation of the German islands north of the Equator, the Cameroons and Togoland. Imposing arguments were assembled as bases for the claims—sacrifices made, economic and geographic factors, security, etc. M. Simon, the French Colonial Minister, was opposed to what he called "internationalism, pure and simple", "for humanitarian reasons. Similar experiments had been tried in the past and had failed ignominiously." [43] President Wilson espoused the idea of "trusteeship", arguing that if the Conference yielded to the demands for annexation, "The world would say that the Great Powers first portioned out the helpless parts of the world, and then formed a League of Nations." [44] Wilson's persistence was finally rewarded by the acceptance of a formula, on January 30, which eventually went, without much change, into the Covenant of the League. [45]

The bitterness of the discussion in the Conference over the German colonial spoils was reflected in the press. In spite of the fact that fairly innocuous communiqués were given out by the Council of Ten, certain members of the Supreme Council talked so freely, especially to the English press of Paris, that President Wilson felt compelled to threaten, January 30, that if it continued, he would "publish his own views". [46] French public opinion, except on the extreme Left, strongly resented the idea of "internationalizing" the German colonies. For several days, during the latter part of January, this was the chief subject of editorial comment, which, for the most part, supported the policy of outright annexation. History was appealed to to prove the fallacy of the Mandates idea. Some fears were expressed lest the mandate idea carry over to Alsace-Lorraine. Several hints were thrown out to the effect that Wilson's zeal was to be explained by his opposition to seeing the German colonies north of the Equator annexed to Japan. [47] The *Temps* (Jan. 29) argued that nothing in the Fourteen Points obligated the possessors of the German colonies to act as Commissioners

under an international control, and felt that these territories
"ought to be divided between such nations as the Conference thinks have the best claims to them". Several journals
stressed the danger of interference by the League in domestic
affairs.[48] The French Colonial League demanded that the
Mandates idea be definitively rejected.[49] Mr. Wilson was
criticized sarcastically in the conservative press. The President was pointed at as "the man of the Fourteen Points . . .
the arbiter who proclaimed peace without annexation".[50]
The Conference was warned not to follow "the noble apostle of the League of Nations".[51] "France does not like the
[Mandates] idea at all," said the *Phare* of Nantes (Jan.
29).[52] The radical press, while highly approving the Wilsonian idea of Mandates, feared that the ultimate solution
was not so good as the promise.[53] "This rush for the spoils
of the German colonies, after all the talk of fighting for
'the right' for four years, is one of the greatest shames of
history," said *Humanité* (Jan. 31).

When the League of Nations Commission began its work,
February 3, the French members felt that the procedure
adopted placed them at a serious disadvantage. The British
and Americans succeeded, at the first meeting of the Commission, in having a joint Anglo-American project (the so-
called Hurst-Miller draft) accepted as the basis of the Commission's discussions. The decision in Anglo-American
quarters to urge the acceptance of this draft was arrived at
so hastily that not even a French translation of it was prepared for the first meeting. Bourgeois acquiesced in the procedure only after having sought, without success, to obtain
a period in which to study the draft presented. It was a
rather bad diplomatic beginning, and Bourgeois experienced
no little embarrassment and pique over the episode.[54] Even
after the eighth meeting, when the text of the various articles
was referred to the Drafting Committee, there was not, in
"any proper sense of the word", a French translation, says
Miller.[55] The fact that this single draft was accepted as the
basis of discussion, however greatly it may have facilitated

the ultimate progress of the work, made the French program somewhat more difficult of achievement, for the text which had been provisionally adopted had a natural advantage, since changes could be made only by process of amendment.[56]

There were a number of points on which Franco-American views clashed in the Commission discussions. One of these was the question of League membership. That German membership in the League must be postponed indefinitely was the settled policy of the French government, and this was in accord with French opinion generally, except on the extreme Left.[57] While Wilson did not urge immediate membership for Germany, the French commission members wanted to put the bars excessively high, not only desiring to require a unanimous vote for admittance, but also proposing to make membership depend on the country's having no reparations to pay, and on its possession of "representative institutions which permit it to be considered as itself responsible for the acts of its own government".[58] The President not only successfully resisted this attempt to impose unduly exacting conditions of membership, but he also refused to yield to French insistence that the Covenant should include a complimentary reference to the work of the Hague Conferences—work in which Léon Bourgeois, one of the French members of the Commission, had played so honorable a part.[59] The French members, in their turn, balked the President in his desire to abolish the institution of compulsory military service. Nor would they tolerate even a proposal that the Council should "enquire into the feasibility" of abolishing it.[60]

By far the most important conflicts between the French and American policies in the Commission came over the problems of the control of armaments and the setting up of an international force with an international general staff. Even before the opening of the Conference, French opinion was practically a unit in insisting that if a League were created it should be endowed with powerful organs of supervision and control. The *Dépêche* of Toulouse (Dec. 27, 1918) expressed the views of the Right, Center and almost all of the Left in insisting that the League would amount to nothing unless it had "repressive and preventive instrumentalities; economic sanctions and military sanctions". The various organized groups which had expressed themselves on the subject of the future organization of the peace unanimously shared this view. Ferdinand Buisson, of the Socialist group, in addressing the 1917 Congress of the League of the Rights of Man, expressed perhaps a rather more advanced view in calling for the setting up of "a collective power, international and supra-national, provided with the three attributes which characterize sovereignty: legislative, executive and judicial powers. This last is the condition *'sine qua non'* of the existence of the League of Nations." [61] It should be noted that one of the major reasons why the nationalists were extremely distrustful of the League idea was their conviction that it would be impossible to endow that institution with sufficient force to make it a source of real security to France.

The original French project for a League, submitted to the Commission but not taken as a basis of discussion, called for "a military force supplied by the various member states", of sufficient strength to secure the execution of League decisions, and to overcome any forces which might be arrayed against the League. Furthermore, a permanent international staff was to be created, "to investigate all military questions affecting the League", and to inspect "international forces and armaments" in various countries.[62] At the eighth meeting of the League Commission the French delegation brought in its amendments on these subjects. It was proposed that the Executive Council should "institute an international control of military forces and armaments", and that, further, it should "determine the conditions which are necessary for assuring the permanent existence and the organization of an international force".[63]

On these two subjects—an international army and armaments control—the debate was prolonged, and the opposing parties were tenacious in their views. President Wilson urged the necessity of making a "distinction between what is possible and what is not. No nation will consent to control. As for us Americans, we cannot consent to control because of our Constitution". ". . . if we organize . . . an international army, it would appear that we were substituting international militarism for national militarism. . . . The argument which has been most employed against the League of Nations in America is that the army of the United States would be at the disposal of an international council. . . ." [64] Bourgeois insisted that there was a misunderstanding on the subject of "control". "The most important thing of all," he said, "was to have some means of verifying the quantities of armaments produced by each nation. . . . So far as the international army was concerned, it was not a question of a permanent army, but simply of making some provision for a military organization to be given to national contingents so that they could be rapidly coordinated against an aggressive State. If one could not do that the League became nothing but a dangerous façade."

Wilson argued that security would come primarily through the disarmament of Germany, but in reply to Larnaude's insistence on the inadequacy of the League for a long period of time—"perhaps . . . a hundred years"—the President added: "we cannot offer more than the condition of the world enables us to give." When Bourgeois asserted that France was asking for no special favors, that she was willing to have her armies and her military preparations, equally with all others, controlled by the League, Wilson was compelled to resort to a plea for "confidence in the good faith of the nations who belong to the League". Any control, by whatever name it might be called, would, he thought, be "too offensive to be adopted". [65]

In subsequent discussions, the French delegates dropped their demand for an international army, and an international general staff, but fought strenuously for "a permanent body" to "plan and prepare the military and naval program". In spite of this modification of their program, it was impossible to reach a common ground of agreement with President Wilson, who was supported by Lord Robert Cecil and a majority of the Commission.[66] So strongly did the French delegation feel on the matter, that they felt impelled to carry their plea to the plenary session of February 14, when the Draft Covenant was presented to the world. There the French demands for "control of munition factories and industries utilizable for war purposes" and for a "permanent organism" to "foresee and prepare the military means for insuring the fulfillment of the obligations", were formally placed before the Conference and world public opinion. The action was merely a gesture of protest, however, for the French government acquiesced in the document as presented to the Plenary Session.[67]

During the ten days of the League Commission's labors, the press had little to say on the subject of the League in general, or of the Commission in particular. As far as the actual proceedings of the Commission were concerned, the public had very little information, for a policy of almost complete silence was adopted by the Commission at the suggestion of President Wilson.[68] The President would have preferred to carry on the work of the Commission in such an informal manner as to exclude even minutes of the discussion. "He stated that he wished to keep his mind wide open, so that he could say the opposite of what he had said before if he saw fit." [69] The French members, however, insisted on a *procès verbal,* which was, in an imperfect fashion, established.

The communiqués issued to the public conformed strictly with the policy of withholding the proceedings "from the public until its whole work was accomplished". Only brief and barren notes were issued to the press. That of February 4, for example, stated that "the preface and the two first articles had been discussed", but as neither the preface nor any of the articles of the draft had been made public, no one was greatly enlightened. The communiqué of the 7th noted that appreciable progress had been made, and that a number of points had been handed to a sub-committee for elaboration. No mention, in these communiqués, was ever made of the issues that arose in the meetings, though of course the leading organs of the press, through their close contacts with official circles, could find out and indicate in a general way what were the major items under discussion. The public seemed not greatly disturbed over the situation, occupied, as it chiefly was, with the German armistice renewal. Such criticisms as there were (and these were fairly numerous) expressed concern over the fact that, to all appearances, France's immediate and primary interests were being sidetracked. Reports that rapid progress was being made in the League Commission tended, however, to allay uneasiness.

The presentation of the Draft Covenant to the Plenary Session of the Peace Conference, February 14, provided the first opportunity for public appraisal of a definite official project for a League of Nations. The amazing rapidity with which the Covenant had been whipped into shape had already, on the eve of the Plenary Session, been the subject of favorable comment in various quarters. For several days after February 14 the Covenant held the stage as the chief subject of comment. Except on the two extremes of opinion, the welcome accorded the Draft Covenant was surprisingly cordial. Even the more nationalistic organs were disposed, for a brief period, to accept it complaisantly. Comments, at times, rose almost to lyrical heights. Idealism had descended to reality, according to the *Homme Libre* (Feb. 15), which felt that though the instrument was "not a Bible", it was "capable of being more than that, since neither the Bible nor any evangelist ever prevented men from killing each other". The *Petit Parisien* (Feb. 15) warmly praised the "beautiful dream" and the "magnificent soul" of President Wilson. More nationalistic organs voiced varying degrees of approval. The *Liberté* (Feb. 15) regarded it as "the basis for a real League of Nations", while the *Victoire* (Feb. 15) hailed it as a "Charter of Humanity", and was inclined, temporarily at least, to "cease to smile at the prophet of Washington". A number of leading organs of the Center and Right were, at first blush, disposed to find in it a species of alliance among the Powers leagued against Germany, and it was precisely this appraisal of it that was a source of grave objection on the extreme Left. The *Temps* (Feb. 16) confidently affirmed that the victorious Powers remained "united to maintain peace, as they were united to win the war"; and the *Figaro* (Feb. 15) rather hastily concluded: "The mystic League of Nations has therefore become a League of the five Great Powers which conquered Germany." "However," said the *Démocratie Nouvelle* (Feb. 16), "let them christen it the 'League of Nations' to please Mr. Wilson."

The liberal organs, though not rapturous, were well satisfied,[70] while on the extreme Left there was considerable bitterness. A few Socialist organs found in it more of good than of evil,[71] but the dominant note in the Socialist press was that of frank disillusionment. "We do not find in this document . . . the general spirit of the messages of Mr. Wilson," said *Humanité* (Feb. 15). "This project cannot in any manner receive the adherence of democratic and popular parties throughout the world. . . ." The *Populaire* (Feb. 16) was finally convinced that "the proletariat can hope for salvation only through itself", and (Feb. 19) confessed its "error" in ever expecting that "the capitalists would be capable of restoring order to the chaos" into which Europe had been plunged. That the Draft Covenant was viewed as setting up a species of alliance, and was thus made more attractive to the conservative-nationalist press, was precisely the thing which made it obnoxious to the extreme Left.[72]

In no quarter was the new instrument accepted uncritically, and, naturally, further reflection upon it tended to make defects stand out. As the *Progrès de la Somme*

(Feb. 21) put it: "First, everybody cried: 'bravo, bravo, fine!' and then immediately afterwards everybody raised objections. Perhaps the project was too beautiful." There were two almost universal objections to the document, namely, the absence of provision for armaments control, and the failure to set up an international force. With regard to these matters, the French members of the League Commission had accurately interpreted French opinion. The liberal *Dépêche* of Toulouse and the Socialistic *Heure* of the Left were in agreement with the *Action Française* on the extreme Right, and the *Petite Gironde* of the Center, in deploring the absence of these provisions, deemed so vital to France.[73]

In addition to these widespread objections to the Draft of February 14, there were various others which were typical of particular sections of the press. From the Right Wing, and frequently from the Center, came the following criticisms:

1. The guarantees are inadequate for France: they lie only in "moral force".
2. It is only a slight improvement over the Hague Conferences.
3. Its language is vague.
4. It contains two conflicting theories—that of reduction of armaments, and that of national defense.
5. It is a dangerous compromise between the idea of a superstate and that of national sovereignty.

Typical criticisms from the Socialist and Socialistic press are the following:

1. It is an alliance of conquerors.
2. It is an association of governments rather than of peoples.
3. It lacks universality.
4. Armaments are not suppressed.
5. Secret diplomacy is not abolished.
6. War is preserved in articles 11, 12 and 13.
7. Obligatory arbitration is not provided for.
8. Rights of peoples are not sufficiently recognized.
9. The "delay" provided for in the declaration of war is illusory.
10. It will not control economic antagonisms.[74]

It was so easy to find imperfections in the document on second and third readings, that the spirit of criticism tended to increase, especially since the vision of peace seemed so out of harmony with the chaos of the passing hour. Wilson's return to America for a month naturally did not alleviate the developing uneasiness. In some important quarters the League became almost "an object of mockery".[75] "Mr. Wilson leaves with us a pledge, in the shape of a draft of a League of Nations, to console us for his absence," said the *Ouest-Éclair* (Feb. 16). "Strange coincidence," it averred. The document was "the definitive guarantee of peace". Yet, as each turn of the ship's propeller carried Wilson farther away, the German provinces of old Austria were electing "a national assembly on the issue of union with Germany".[76]

4. The Covenant and "Peace Preliminaries" Mr. Wilson's Absence

During the four weeks of President Wilson's absence from the Conference, after his departure for the United States, February 14, the happy union of the Covenant and the Treaty decreed by the resolution of January 25 was seriously threatened. Although it is impossible to explain the precise chain of events, or to interpret exactly what was in the minds of the various parties concerned, there seems no reason to question the statement of David Hunter Miller, that, "Undoubtedly, while Wilson was away from Paris, the idea of separating the Covenant from the Treaty revived, despite the resolution of the Peace Conference of January 25."[77] As to whether there was "an intrigue" against Wilson, which Baker asserts and which Miller, Churchill and Seymour deny, perhaps more may yet be revealed.

There were, doubtless, several reasons for the determination to reconsider, if not to break the resolution of January 25. One of these undoubtedly arose from the general discontent over what was considered the "cart-before-the-horse" procedure in taking up the League first. Another seems certainly to have had its origin in the proposal to impose on Germany very quickly a species of military "peace preliminaries". The discussion of this proposal grew out of the situation created by the third renewal of the Armistice with Germany, in February. The military chiefs wished to put new terms into the Armistice, but this was opposed by Balfour and President Wilson, supported by General Bliss, as being a very undesirable policy of "pin-pricks".[78] The upshot of the discussion in the Supreme Council was the decision, February 12, that, "Detailed and final naval, military and air conditions of the preliminaries of peace shall be drawn up at once . . .; these, when approved will be presented for signature to the Germans."[79] Thus the idea of a preliminary peace, under a very narrowly restricted form, was accepted by the Council. From these preliminaries, of course, the League of Nations would very naturally be excluded. This program was entirely acceptable to Wilson, though it had been opposed in the Council by Clemenceau, who argued strongly that the military terms should not be separated from the political.[80] He was afraid lest the imposition of the military terms on Germany might be followed by too great demobilization of the Allied forces, so that the later imposition of the political terms might be rendered extremely difficult.

Thus was created the idea of "peace preliminaries" divorced from the League of Nations. In the days which followed, while President Wilson was in America, it was sought to relax the narrow limits which had been fixed, February 12, for the preliminaries, though there was no apparent disposition on the part of the Supreme Council to expand them sufficiently to include the League Covenant. Clemenceau had remained hostile to the idea of preliminaries restricted to military, naval and air terms, and while he was confined to his room with an assassin's bullet in his body, he convinced Balfour (if convincing was necessary) of the desirability of adding territorial, financial and economic terms to the preliminaries.

On February 22 Balfour introduced a resolution proposing these additions, and as an important argument in support of his proposal, he cited the fact that "A general feeling of impatience was now becoming manifest in all countries on account of the apparent (sic) slow progress the Conference was making in the direction of Final Peace." [81] Both Colonel House and Secretary Lansing rallied to the proposals of Balfour, House saying he was very glad to see "that the Conference intended to bring about as soon as possible a preliminary peace". Lansing observed that it would be "a mistake to treat the military terms of peace as distinct from the other terms of peace". "He thoroughly agreed with Mr. Clemenceau's viewpoint." [82]

It has been argued that there was no inconsistency between the resolution of February 24, and the expressions of Wilson, of February 12, in which he is quoted as saying: "But he [Wilson] did not wish that during his unavoidable absence such questions as the territorial question and questions of compensation should be held up." [83] In view of the whole context in which the statement was set, however, it would be difficult to infer that Wilson meant to imply that territorial and financial questions should also be included in the preliminaries. This conclusion would seem to be emphasized by Wilson's message to House, February 20. The Colonel had notified the President that Marshal Foch was bringing pressure to bear to settle at once "the three principal conditions of the peace" to be imposed on Germany (the military, territorial and the financial) thereby insisting on expanding the preliminaries beyond the February 12 agreement. The President, in reply, pointedly stated: "I am not willing to have anything beyond the military and naval terms [settled] and believe that the Conference of Ten would be going very much beyond its powers to attempt anything of this sort." [84] It is quite probable that a real misunderstanding as to intentions developed between the Colonel and the President at this time, and it was doubtless facilitated by House's admitted desire to broaden the scope of the preliminaries. Though his loyalty to the President can scarcely be questioned, his interpretation of the "honorable compromises" that were "necessary" was undoubtedly different from that of his chief.[85]

The development of this new orientation of policy, in favor of broadened peace preliminaries, with the League left outside, was no doubt the product of misunderstanding, and of what was deemed to be the exigencies of the peace. In the absence of Wilson the attention of the Conference was riveted on the Treaty, and "European diplomacy gradually seemed to assume that the Treaty was the only question at issue, apparently overlooking the resolution . . . declaring the Covenant was to be an integral part of the Peace Treaty".[86] At all events, President Wilson returned to Paris to find a powerful move under way to present to Germany preliminaries including the major items of the peace settlement, but excluding the League Covenant.

French opinion was well prepared for this separation of the Covenant from the "Preliminaries". As a matter of fact, it had (except on the extreme Left) originally disapproved the idea of linking them together. The trend of events during Wilson's absence seemed to make a reversal of the January decision very natural and desirable. Whereas, the prevailing opinion in France was that the Draft Covenant was already much too weak, events in the United States revealed a powerful opposition to Wilson, determined to weaken the Covenant provisions drastically, so far as they applied to the United States.[87]

Patriotic opinion in France was undoubtedly alarmed over the American developments which seemed to portend a drift back toward the policy of "splendid isolation". Nor could it fail to admire the fight Wilson was putting up to prevent that alternative. Indeed, there was a disposition, for a time, to stress the merits, rather than the defects of the Covenant. Perhaps the League was not so bad after all. It was inadequate, to be sure, but it was something to build on, and needed only to be strengthened. Even the nationalist press was inclined to view the scene in a new light. The *Écho de*

Paris (Feb. 26), leading organ of this group, feared that American opinion was being misled, and observed that it was not the League itself that was open to criticism, "but rather the fact that it might suffer from too much idealism"; and it regretted that the opponents of Wilson's plan "place themselves in opposition to the idea itself rather than to the methods of constituting it". In a long and careful leader the *Temps* (Feb. 27) pointed to the grave dangers inherent in the trend of events. "If American opinion accepts the League," it said, "peace is assured for a long time. If it hesitates, the obstacles and risks on every side will grow. . . . Those who are campaigning against Mr. Wilson's scheme in the United States are not the partisans of a more realistic or of a closer League of Nations. They are the adversaries of any sort of League. . . . We should be simple indeed if, under the pretext that the ideas of Mr. Wilson do not satisfy us completely, we were to furnish arguments to those Americans who do not want to grant us anything at all." Other influential organs of the patriotic press expressed the hope that the American adversaries of Wilson would exert themselves by way of improving the League rather than by endeavoring to demolish it.[88]

It was not long, however, before the impression was created in French opinion that Wilson was playing a losing game in the United States. At least it seemed certain that if the United States Senate were to be induced to accept the League, the Covenant would have to be radically modified in a direction entirely unsatisfactory to most Frenchmen. The French press, during this period, watched the course of events with great interest, and carried news articles which tended, rather naturally, to emphasize the opposition encountered by the League project. Articles from the *Écho de Paris'* American correspondent repeatedly stated that Wilson seemed not to have won over any of his former Senate opponents,[89] though he also noted (March 8) that the capture of a Pennsylvania district by a Democrat (the first in fifty years) might indicate some popular support for Wilson.

A number of other Center and Right Wing organs carried frequent articles from American correspondents,[90] and the news agencies furnished further columns either direct from the United States, or from British sources. News favorable to Wilson and the League was not ignored, but the inevitable impression created was that the League would have a terrific fight ahead if it were to win out in the United States, and that even if it ultimately succeeded, it would be at the cost of drastic modifications contrary to French interests.

Before the President's return, March 14, these impressions had become definitely crystallized. Even the *Dépêche* of Toulouse (March 6), under the fat headline: "Wilson does not bring back to France the adhesion of the American Senators", carried an article to the effect that the resolution of Senator Lodge, proposing that the Senate reject the League, and that it call upon the American Commission to proceed at once to conclude peace with Germany, is "considered the death sentence of the League in its present form". The following despatch from the London *Times'* American correspondent was reproduced in various French papers: "My considered opinion is that the pact of the League of Nations will not be accepted in America without amendment."[91] On the day of Wilson's return to France the *Temps* (March 14) stressed the burdens that lay ahead of the Conference in giving a "definitive character" to the League, one of these being the time-consuming problem of convoking the neutral states for the purpose of securing their suggestions regarding the Covenant. On the same day (March 14), the *Petit Parisien's* American news despatch, while stating that American opinion was favorable to the League, went on to say that it demanded that peace be concluded at the earliest possible date. The New York *Sun* was quoted as saying that peace could not be rapidly concluded if the Conference went on "for hours, days and weeks discussing the League of Nations".[92]

What better reasons could there be for postponing the entire problem of the League until after a preliminary settlement had been reached with Germany? The desirability of this course seemed all the more obvious in view of the developing uneasiness over Conference activities.

From week to week the "general feeling of impatience", to which Balfour had referred, was increasing. Early in March public anticipations were aroused by promises that important commissions were soon to report, and that France's immediate interests were finally to be served. The press of March 3 announced that it was to be "a most important week" for the Conference.[93] Hopes were stimulated that the broadened "Preliminaries", including military, territorial and financial terms, were soon to be imposed on Germany. "When public opinion learned that the Conference was finally putting these items on its agenda," said the *Ouest-Éclair* (March 5), "it heaved a sigh of relief."

But these anticipations were not so soon to be realized. The achievements of the week did not live up to expectations, and at its end the feeling prevailed that the public was still "in the *entr'acte,* waiting for the curtain to rise on the presentation of the masterpiece of the Conference".[94] Again was heard the familiar refrain that preliminary peace terms should have been imposed on Germany before taking up the question of the League of Nations.[95] There was hope, however, that the failures of the preceding week might be redeemed, as was evidenced by the optimistic forecast of the nationalistic *Nouvelliste de Lyon* (March 9): "This week ought to be the Great Week—that which will see the definitive conclusion of the Peace Preliminaries." It assumed that the divorce of the Covenant from the Preliminaries was complete, and that the Conference would not, at that juncture, waste time talking about the League.

Expectations were further nourished by an official statement given out by Lloyd George to the English press of March 12. According to that Conference leader the definitive text of the conditions of peace would be drawn up within a week. This was reprinted in the French press of March 13, the very day of Mr. Wilson's landing in France. The assurance that the period of waiting was over, and that the Conference was about to pass from words to deeds, was emphasized by the *Temps* on the very afternoon of the President's arrival in Paris (March 14). The Supreme Council, it said, "is going to settle without delay the disarmament of Germany and the line of her new frontiers. It is clear that the entire peace hangs on these two problems."

5. President Wilson Upsets the Apple Cart

While Wilson was absent from Paris the Conference leaders, faced with the growing impatience of the public, had allowed themselves to raise hopes which were incapable of immediate realization, regardless of the relation of the Covenant to the Preliminaries. But they had also failed to appreciate fully or to interpret correctly the President's wishes and desires as to the peace program, as was revealed shortly after his return to Paris. Mr. Baker states that "the first well-informed man" with whom he talked after landing in France, remarked: "Well, your League is dead." [96] Wilson apparently feared that the life of the League was at least in danger, for, the day after his return to Paris, he instructed Mr. Baker "to deny the report, now everywhere current in Europe—and to some extent in America—that there would be a separate preliminary peace treaty with the Germans, excluding the League of Nations". [97]

This important news item, broadcast by the French press of the 16th, created a temporary crisis in Conference circles, which justified Wilson's suspicion that a policy in conflict with the January 25 resolution was in process of formation during his absence. The very afternoon of the day on which the Wilson pronouncement appeared, Pichon, the French Foreign Minister, and member of the French delegation, received the Allied press representatives. In the course of the interview he expressed his opinion that "one cannot think of inserting the project of the League in the Preliminaries of Peace". The *principle* of the League, he said, might be stated in the Preliminaries, but even this, he thought, "was

not necessary", since "all of the delegates to the Peace Conference are in full accord on the principle".⁹⁸ This statement
was obviously in direct conflict with that of President
Wilson, and could not be allowed to go unchallenged by the
American delegation which soon got wind of Pichon's remarks. André Tardieu, having been summoned to the
American headquarters, and interrogated on the subject, explained that surely the Foreign Secretary must have been
misunderstood. Upon the suggestion that perhaps it would
be unwise for the French newspapers to make use of the
Pichon statement, since it conflicted with that of the President, he obligingly "made a round of the French press",
says C. T. Thompson, and "kept the Pichon statement from
being printed".⁹⁹ Tardieu did in fact succeed in keeping the
objectionable remarks out of practically all of the Paris
press. Only the *Œuvre*, of the Left, and the relatively unimportant *Libre Parole*, of the Right, carried that feature of
the interview.¹⁰⁰ All of the governmental press obeyed the
word of command. While most of them omitted all references, the *Petit Journal* (Pichon's own paper) and the *Information* carried the general interview, conspicuously omitting the banned features. Even the *Daily Mail* yielded to
pressure, though the *New York Herald* displayed the clash
of policies. The press of the provinces, with very few exceptions, carried the entire interview. The *Phare* of Nantes
(March 18), one of the few exceptions, carried a careful
explanatory note from Paris, which threw light on the background of hopes and desires: "During the absence of the
President, there was a tendency, increasingly strong, to
attach very great importance to what is called the preliminary peace, which, it is hoped, will be signed next month."
"Nevertheless," it added, with an obvious note of regret,
"it is believed that the President remains firmly convinced
that the pact of the League of Nations ought to be incorporated in it, and not wait for the definitive peace. . . ."

The diplomatic skirmish continued, though the scene
shifted temporarily to the Council of Ten and the secret

meetings of the four heads of delegations. Meantime, the public was in a confused state of mind. On three successive days (March 18, 19, and 20) various organs of the press asked the question: "Definitive Armistice or Peace Preliminaries?" "On the one hand, will the Allies, in the form of a definitive Armistice, present Germany with the military, naval and air conditions . . . with a view to its disarmament? Will they, perhaps, add to these military conditions, territorial and financial clauses, still being studied, and make it a single diplomatic instrument, which would constitute the Preliminaries of Peace? Or, on the other hand, will the pact of the League of Nations be incorporated in the Preliminaries of Peace, in its totality, or simply in principle?" Such were the alternatives posed before public opinion—and debated in Conference circles.[101]

With regard to the relation of the League to the Preliminaries, whatever form they might be given, the Supreme Council took no definitive action, and for some time the matter remained a subject of public controversy. Not only the position of the French delegation, but also that of the British remained equivocal. On March 18, Lord Robert Cecil, apparently to offset a British press campaign against Wilson, announced that the Covenant would go into the Peace Preliminaries.[102] Two days later Lloyd George, whose relations with Wilson at the time were rather strained, announced to the British press representatives that "The question of including the League of Nations in the Peace Treaty has never been brought to my attention in any way whatever", thereby appearing to disavow Lord Robert Cecil of his own delegation, and to challenge the President's position.[103] The next day this interview was carried in the *Écho de Paris* (though not in the other papers), and the British Premier was made to say, somewhat ambiguously, that the Covenant would not be included in the Preliminaries as then prepared.

These diplomatic maneuvers aroused deep public anxiety. From the 16th to the 21st of March leading papers, from

Right to Left, voided their spleen on the idea of tying up the League with the broadened Preliminaries. The major arguments against it were, first, the immediate question of expediency—the alleged additional delay involved; and second, the time-honored argument of the "illogical character of the 'cart-before-the-horse' procedure". Only the Unified Socialist press supported the President's idea, and even it did so with much less ardor than that with which it had previously rallied to Wilsonian proposals.[104] On all hands the threat of added delay in the negotiations was made much of. "Indeed, it will take two months to put the project in question [the League] on its feet," said the *Petit Provençal*, of Marseilles (March 18), expressing the moderate Left sentiment that "it would be better at once to sign the preliminaries of peace", including territorial, financial and military clauses. "President Wilson has just had it decided by the Conference that the League will be an integral part of the Peace Treaty," said *Ouest-Éclair* (March 18) of the nationalist press. "In this way the hour of signing the Treaty is postponed two or three months!" "Already Germany is menacing us with a refusal to sign," said the *Liberté* (March 19). "What will she do in three months after she has been supplied with food?" "And here we are," said the *Nouvelliste de Lyon* (March 23) "waiting, holding up everything for the League of Nations." "Why should the roof be put on before the foundations are solidly laid?" was a typical query which struck at the logic of the whole procedure.[105]

These arguments were fortified by appeals to the state of opinion in the United States. The *Écho de Paris* (March 17) argued that "what American opinion really wants is for the preliminary peace terms to be concluded with Germany before we finish the League of Nations project". That paper's despatches from the United States followed the same line. It is interesting to note that, though clipped by the censor, these cables were allowed to discuss the "efforts made to defer the organization of the League of Nations and to hasten the conclusion of peace".[106] Elsewhere it was averred that Wilson's opponents in America were the Republicans, who were "partisans of a rapid peace, giving entire satisfaction to the legitimate claims of France, and leaving it open to discuss subsequently the future statutes of the League".[107]

In the midst of the confusion Colonel House sought to calm fears and revive hope. On the 20th of March he gave to the Paris *Daily Mail* an interview gilded with optimism. The entire treaty, he said, would be ready by Saturday the 29th, and he would be disappointed "if the Germans are not at Versailles within three weeks". Furthermore—coming to the vital part, and the *raison d'être* of the interview: "The League of Nations Covenant has not held up the work of framing the Peace Treaty in any way. . . . It has never taken up time needed by other commissions. We sat at night, or when the Council of Ten was not meeting." Unfortunately, however, this interview did not generate much hope or evoke public optimism. Very little editorial comment was spared it. A few organs of the conservative-nationalist press took occasion to characterize it appropriately. The *Débats* (March 22) said that all the world would like to hope that Colonel House was an accurate prophet. "But one cannot help feeling some doubt as to the probability of realizing these unanimous wishes." Noting that the Conference was faced with the "most formidable work ever imposed on statesmen", it expounded the familiar thesis that the logical thing would have been, to settle first the three or four most urgent questions, drawn up in a separate text, "thus avoiding the risk of holding up everything because of the desire to do too much at once". The *Figaro* (March 22) put it somewhat more baldly: "The entire peace in three weeks? What a beautiful dream!"

The problems of the Preliminaries and of the relation of the Covenant to them remained in an equivocal status for a considerable period. In fact, no official statement on the subject ever came from the Supreme Council. After the diplomatic flurry immediately following Wilson's return, these matters were apparently allowed to drift. On March 24

Colonel House wrote in his diary that he urged the President "to settle once and for all the question as to whether the League of Nations was to go into the Peace Treaty".[108] As late as April 25 the Council of Four was engaged in discussing what was referred to as preliminaries of peace.[109] The Wilson point of view was gradually, if tacitly, acquiesced in. This was due, in part at least, to the fact that the difficulty in working out the military, territorial and financial aspects of the peace was so great that the Covenant itself was ready for final action even before the so-called Preliminaries were completed.

6. REVISION OF THE COVENANT

Having reaffirmed the resolution of January 25, and beaten back official opposition, President Wilson pressed forward with the work of revising the Draft Covenant so that the peace settlement might not be delayed. This difficult task, complicated with even more thorny problems than those of the February discussions, was completed after two meetings with a group of neutral states (March 20, 21), and five sessions of the League Commission (March 22, 24, 26; April 10, 11), accompanied by delicate diplomatic negotiations on the outside.

During these discussions, as in the February sessions, French and American theses found themselves at odds with each other, and at this time, as earlier, the Wilsonian views generally triumphed over those advocated by Bourgeois and Larnaude, the French members of the Commission. The principal matters advocated by the French delegation in the revision period were: (a) The Belgian claim for Brussels as the seat of the League; (b) the Japanese demand for racial equality; (c) the adoption of the French language as the official language of the League; (d) the creation of a so-called "Financial League of Nations" as part of the League of Nations; (e) the re-introduced French amendment proposing "verification" of armaments, etc., and (f) the sister amendment providing for an international military organism to foresee and plan for the use of the military arm in the execution of League decisions. On all these points the French view failed of acceptance.

In support of the Belgian plea in favor of Brussels as the seat of the League, the French delegates argued that it would be "a profound lesson for humanity" to request "one of those Allied peoples which had suffered the most to give its hospitality to the institution which was to represent right in the world". As for President Wilson, he "yielded to none in his admiration for Belgium, but the present question was one not of awarding honours but of finding the best surroundings for international deliberation. The antipathies of the war should be set aside. . . ."[110] In consequence, the Belgian claim should also be set aside, as, by the overwhelming preference of the Commission, it was.

The Japanese claim for the recognition of "racial equality" seemed to Bourgeois to be equally deserving of support. This had been first urged by Baron Makino at the tenth session of the Commission, in the hope of effecting a trade with President Wilson, who was urging the acceptance of an article recognizing "religious equality". Rather than accept the Japanese proposal that the Members of the League should be pledged "to accord . . . to all alien nationals of States members of the League, equal and just treatment in every respect . . . making no distinction on account of their race or nationality", President Wilson preferred to withdraw his proposed "religious equality" article.[111] When Baron Makino, at the final session of the Commission, proposed that the principle be inserted, not as a regular article, but merely as a general principle in the preamble of the Covenant, the Italian, as well as the French delegations supported the proposal, Bourgeois saying that it was impossible to vote against "an amendment which embodied an indisputable principle of justice". President Wilson, however, supported by Cecil, was opposed, saying that he was afraid of the controversies "which would be bound to take place outside the Commission" over the proposal. Eleven votes out of seventeen were recorded in favor of the amendment, but President Wilson, as chairman, declared it lost, under the unanimity principle.[112]

The question of the "official language" of the Treaty had been fought out in the Supreme Council, and, much to the disappointment of French opinion, especially of the Center and Right Wings, English was put on a parity with French. In spite of this initial defeat, the French delegation still sought to make French the official language of the League of Nations, and Bourgeois introduced an amendment to this effect at the fourteenth meeting of the Commission. But he was unsuccessful in having it discussed or voted upon. President Wilson, as chairman of the Commission, ruled the amendment out of order, on the ground that the matter was within the competence of the Supreme Council, rather than that of the Commission on the League.[113]

Another matter which had aroused even greater interest in public opinion generally, was the project for a species of "Financial League of Nations", as it was popularly known, or a Financial Section of the League of Nations, as it was officially proposed. As early as the Plenary Session of January 25 M. Klotz, of the French delegation to the Peace Conference, proposed the creation of a Financial Section of the League, which has been described as "a kind of financial high command to mobilize the financial forces of the Allies and to enforce the execution of the Treaty".[114] Though the proposal did not itself incorporate a definite scheme for mobilizing the financial resources of the Allies, it was part of a general plan which looked to the sharing of France's financial burdens by her Allies who were stronger and who had suffered less. This idea was extremely popular throughout France, where the conviction grew that some such scheme of financial relief would surely be accepted. It was calmly assumed in many quarters, early in March, that a project was taking shape to relieve the financial burden. The *Progrès* of Lyons (March 9) expressed the current feeling in saying that the project aimed "to hand over to the League of Nations all of the financial charges of the belligerent countries arising from the war. A sort of international control would assure the service of interest and amortization charges." It said the idea was that each member of the League of Nations would subscribe to a great loan, in direct proportion to its financial capacity, and in inverse ratio to the damages suffered. "Is it not perfectly just," it asked, "that the sacrifices consented to by the Allied Nations in common should be equalized?" The whole matter was vigorously debated in the Chamber of Deputies on March 11 and on March 13, when Klotz remarked that he did not think that the League could live and develop unless it included a financial section, and stated somewhat vaguely that the Financial League of Nations was making progress toward realization.[115] When, on Wilson's return to France in March, the proposal for the Financial Section (somewhat watered down from Klotz' original proposal, though still with powers to control the execution of the Financial Terms of the Treaty of Peace) was brought to his attention, he immediately dismissed it from consideration.[116] Apparently the French members of the League Commission did not press the matter, though Klotz brought up the subject at the Plenary Session of April 28 (at which the Covenant was finally adopted), and the project was referred to the League for further consideration.[117]

The degree of importance which the French members of the League Commission attached to their amendments for armaments "verification" and for an international military organism, is illustrated by their persistence in urging these proposals. At the Commission meetings of March 22 and 24 the modified proposals introduced at the tenth meeting were again brought forward and argued at great length, but with no more success than on previous occasions.[118] It only remained for Bourgeois to take advantage of the opportunity provided by the Plenary Session of April 28, in order to state the French case finally and fully to the world. "Effective limitation of armaments is the supreme condition of peace. . . . Yet, if this limitation is to be real and effective, the possibility of verification must exist. . . . A system of mutual verification which does not call in question the good faith of any member, in particular, would be a common rule accepted by all in the interest of all. . . ." "By our second amendment . . . we request that the commission (the international military organism) should be entrusted with the task of foreseeing and planning the measures which the Council may prescribe." France has been wrongly accused, he said, of defending exclusively her own interests. But "even if she were protected by the strongest ring of mountains, protected by the whole ocean, protected by the most solid alliances, [she] would nevertheless . . . use the same language and formulate the same principles. . . ." [119]

While the amendments advocated or supported by the French members of the Commission were being rejected, those proposed by President Wilson were registering successes. The drift of events in the United States had finally convinced Mr. Wilson that without certain modifications the Covenant would run grave risks of rejection by the Senate.[120] He, accordingly, brought in amendments to the Draft Covenant proposing: (a) to exclude the League's jurisdiction from so-called "domestic questions"; (b) to provide for the possibility of withdrawal from the League; (c) to safeguard the Monroe Doctrine.[121]

The first point caused no difficulty. It was sent to the Drafting Committee almost without discussion.[122] The withdrawal amendment caused considerable debate, and was opposed by the French delegation in particular, especially in the form first proposed, namely, that after a ten-year period, withdrawal should be permissible with one year's notice. The French members objected on the grounds that the ten-year clause gave rise to the implication that the League was conceived of as limited in duration. "The essence of the idea of the League was that it was to be a permanent thing. The placing of a ten years' time limit would encourage the idea that the success of the League was not hoped for." Larnaude added that "for some time past national sovereignty had been a fiction", and expressed the fear that giving notice of withdrawal by any Great Power would throw the League into confusion. President Wilson argued that "sovereign states could not permanently be bound", but he did not entertain the smallest fear that any State would take advantage of the proposed clause. "Any State which did so would become an outlaw." Furthermore, "The sovereignty of their own country was the fetish of many public men. . . . Americans would have to be assured that they were not giving up the Sovereignty of their State. . . . The time would come when men would be just as eager partisans of the sovereignty of mankind as they were now of their own national sovereignty." [123] A compromise was eventually reached, entirely satisfactory to Wilson, providing for withdrawal on two years' notice, but omitting reference to the ten-year limitation.

The most important change proposed by President Wilson was that relating to the Monroe Doctrine, and for the achievement of this he had to win over practically the entire Commission, including the British, who tried to make a trade involving an agreement on the part of the United States not to build its navy up to the level of that of Great Britain. This British difficulty was solved in private negotiations outside the deliberations of the League Commission, [124] and thereafter, Cecil lent his support to Wilson's amendment. It was the French delegation which led the fight against it at the fourteenth and fifteenth meetings of the Commission.

Commenting on fears as to the nature of the Monroe Doctrine, the President assured his colleagues that there was no conflict between it and the League Covenant. The Covenant was, in fact, "an international extension of that principle by which the United States said that it would protect the political independence and territorial integrity of other American States". Fears as to the operation of the Monroe Doctrine were baseless, for any understanding which infringed upon "the territorial integrity or political independence of any State would be inconsistent with the Covenant", and any State which signed the Covenant would obligate itself "immediately to abrogate such inconsistent understandings". Indeed, the inclusion of this reference to the Monroe Doctrine was in effect "nothing but a recognition of the fact" that it was not inconsistent with the terms of the Covenant. If the United States signed the Covenant it would be "solemnly obliged to render aid in European troubles when the territorial integrity of European States" was threatened by external aggression. His American colleagues had expressed fears that the Covenant would destroy the principles of the Monroe Doctrine, and when he had assured them that this was not true, they then asked "whether there would be any objection to making a specific statement to that effect in the text".[125]

M. Larnaude nevertheless contended that if the Monroe Doctrine was not inconsistent with the Covenant, it was unnecessary to make specific mention of it, and Bourgeois argued that if the amendment were adopted there would be "two separate groups of States under the Covenant, the United States, on the one hand, and the European States on the other".[126]

After listening to repeated objections from various sources, President Wilson, about midnight of April 10, rose and delivered an extemporaneous and impassioned address which, as Mr. Miller says, "literally seemed to cast a spell over those present". The United States, in promulgating the Monroe Doctrine, had, he said, acted originally to stop the spread of absolutism. "The question now arises whether you are going to penalize the United States for her adoption of this policy, when you are engaged upon the drafting of a document which is the logical historical extension of the Monroe Doctrine to the whole world. . . . Are you now going to debate this issue, are we going to scruple on words when the United States is ready to sign a Covenant which makes her forever a part of the movement for liberty? . . .

Gentlemen, you cannot afford to deprive America of the privilege of joining with you in this movement." Though the French, supported by other delegations, urged either the definition of the Monroe Doctrine, or at least a specific statement designed to assure its subordination to the obligations of the League, this resistance ultimately gave way before the insistence of the President. "If there were anything in the Doctrine inconsistent with the Covenant," said Mr. Wilson, "the Covenant would take precedence over the Monroe Doctrine."

Thus President Wilson was able, very largely, to have his way with the League Commission at Paris, and to gain most of his major objectives; while the French representatives, outmaneuvered from the beginning, failed in their attempts to strengthen the instrument which they regarded as very inadequate.

7. THE FINAL COVENANT OF APRIL 28

Prior to the Plenary Session of April 28, when the final Covenant was published to the world, French opinion had taken account of the trend of events within the Commission on the League and had become increasingly uneasy. Though the official communiqués issued by the Commission were as barren as during the February sittings, the American and English press of Paris gave rather full accounts of the meetings, and these items were freely copied by French papers. Leading French papers also secured fairly detailed and direct news of the last two meetings of April 10 and 11. Special mention was made of Wilson's personal intervention in the debate in favor of Geneva as against Brussels; and the French plea for the adoption of French as the League official language was carried in full.[127]

During this period criticism against President Wilson was based partly on the allegation that he had abandoned guarantees that would make the League of Nations worth while.[128] "The League of Nations lies in bits on the floor of the Crillon," said the *Écho de Paris* (April 5). Even *Œuvre*

(April 5), of the liberal press was losing faith in the League. "A League which one can enter or leave at will, and which has no army, is no League at all." The *Matin* carried two full columns of Lauzanne's caustic criticism against the methods of the League Commission's work. The two French amendments, it said, "were discarded on the lively opposition of the American delegation", which thinks that though it is not contrary to French dignity to have "French administration of Togoland examined every two years", it is contrary to American dignity "that an examination should be made of the state of American armaments". The Japanese amendment, said Lauzanne, had received a curt "NO" from the American delegation. "Only the American amendment shared a different fate." Wilson was excoriated for his political tactics in the Commission. He had ruled that a mere majority vote was sufficient for Geneva to prevail over Brussels as the seat of the League, while a similar majority was not sufficient to secure the adoption of Japan's race equality amendment. "Thus at the Commission on the League of Nations," he said, "there are majorities which count, and majorities which do not count. They count when they are for you. They do not count when they are against you. . . . With such a system it is impossible to be beaten." [129]

The uneasiness of March and early April turned to bitterness and disillusionment on the presentation of the final Covenant to the world, at the Plenary Session of April 28. If the February Draft Covenant had a preponderantly "good press" on its first appearance, the April Covenant, at its début, met with extreme hostility or skeptical reserves throughout the entire press. Only isolated and relatively feeble voices were raised in its favor [130] The prevailing discontent was accentuated somewhat by the delays of the Conference, and by the feeling in patriotic circles that the League, as presented, was a poor recompense for the concessions which the French government was thought to have made on certain vital aspects of the peace.

The Plenary Session was satirized in various quarters. Under the title: "Simplicity and Duplicity", the *Phare* of Nantes (May 1) editorialized: "The League of Nations was born the afternoon of April 28 while President Wilson smiled to the Angels." Lauzanne again waxed sarcastic in the *Matin* (April 29). After weeks of waiting before the wall of censorship, he said, the public and the press had finally discovered, when they got behind the poster labeled: "The League of Nations", that "it was a grey, lack-lustre film, all arranged and fixed in advance". Considerable surprise was expressed in the leading papers that there was not a passionate debate over the failure of the French and Japanese amendments, and over the success of the Monroe Doctrine amendment. "At the beginning Mr. Wilson rose to read it [the Covenant]," said the *Écho de Paris* (April 29). "There was no comment. It was a simple catalog. This set the tone for all the discussion that followed. No controversy. No noise. No change. No voting. We are in a death-chamber, for the League of Nations is still-born." Another commentator said: "At the moment when everybody thought the debate was going to open, Clemenceau got up and said in an undertone, and very hurriedly: 'No opposition? Voted unanimously!'"[131]

A statement by Bourgeois at the close of the Plenary Session, to the effect that the League was a "somewhat shaky edifice, open to all the winds", was taken up and echoed throughout the press of the Right, Center and Left.[132] The "deception" was equally great in the nationalist and in the Socialist press.[133] In the liberal press, though the criticism was not, in general, so violent, it was no less pointed, and was sometimes bitter. The *Œuvre's* comments of April 29 expressed much greater disappointment than did those of February. "It was not the charter of international law which had been hoped for." Gaston Doumergue (later President of France), writing in the *France de Bordeaux,* thought that the League had lost so much of its original promise that it now remained but an empty "façade".[134]

The action of the Commission on the League in throwing out the French and Japanese amendments, while adopting that on the Monroe Doctrine, was the subject of universal criticism; and Belgium's failure to win the League capital for Brussels aroused sympathetic comment on the Right. "The Massacre of the Innocents" was the *Écho de Paris'* headline (April 29), referring to the failure of the various amendments. The "Three perfect capitulations" were commented upon by another—those of France, Belgium and Japan. The "fourth question" (that of the Monroe Doctrine) was the subject of a "success without a battle" for the Americans.[135] The position of special privilege in the League which the United States seemed to be assuming was the subject of widespread adverse comment; and it was alleged that the Monroe Doctrine clause had been inserted *ex officio*, on the initiative of the American Delegation, and without formal adoption by the League Commission.[136] The Covenant represented "the apotheosis of the influence of the United States", said another,[137] and the *Paix par le Droit* characterized the American insistence on its amendment as "an offensive and profoundly disquieting return to Monroeism, that is, of national, or continental egoism".[138]

Other objections came from various sectors of opinion. The failure to provide for a Financial Section of the League of Nations was assailed in all quarters. Criticisms coming from the extreme Left, in addition to those above-mentioned, were largely a repetition of those made against the February draft, special emphasis being placed on the exclusion of the ex-enemy Powers, the failure to reduce armaments or control private manufacture of munitions, and the "undemocratic" character of the League (governments rather than peoples being represented). The objections from the Right as well as from the moderate press could well be epitomized in the phrase "inadequacy of guarantees for France".

One comment which was freely made in February, was totally absent in late April, namely, that the League was a species of alliance. Not even the extreme Left press urged this point, which, in February, had been a major source of objection. Conservative opinion felt that this made it all the more urgent that the Allies should form a grouping of their own.[139] Indeed, the fact that there were rumors, in late April, of a special alliance in France's favor, contributed, in some quarters, to make the League less objectionable. The *Écho de Paris* referred to this rumor, concluding that "They [the alliances] will have to be beautiful, complete and eloquent" to justify the government's policy. The liberal organ, *Petit Provençal* (April 30) held a not greatly dissimilar view: "If it is true, as we are told, that this ideal pact is supported on defensive alliances, we can cherish the hope that it will be the end of wars. But I am convinced that this is the only condition."

However disappointing the League was, it is clear that most commentators felt that it was better than no League at all. Even the nationalist *Journal de Rouen* (April 30), with all its violent objections to the final Covenant, confessed that "it is of course better to have some sort of a League". The *Temps* (April 30) led the way toward this new orientation of opinion. After careful reflection— noting the disappointment of "the three delegations whom the League, as adopted, did not please", and leaving "facile mockeries and sterile recriminations to others"—it decided that after all, "the important thing is to have created the League". "The good-will and trust of nations are now necessary to make it live." The various disappointed nations (and France was one) could reserve their amendments for the future.[140] *Opinion* (May 3) epitomized the sober second thought of moderate (and doubtless the preponderant) opinion in saying: "It [the League] is a little monster, half vertebrate, and half zoophyte. It is a form molded by trembling hands. But perhaps the future of the world lies in this 'nothing'. We must not rail at it. We must not despise it."

NOTES

[1] See articles by Paul Allard in *Excelsior*, May 1 to 8, 1931.

[2] Beales, A. C. F., *The History of Peace* (London, 1931), p. 297.

[3] *Bulletin*, nos. 11-12, June 1918.

[4] *Débats*, April 30, 1919.

[5] Statement to author by M. Louis Aubert, May 1931.

[6] See *La Paix par le Droit* bulletins.

[7] See monthly bulletins of La Ligue des droits de l'homme. These did not reach a wide constituency, as they were not noticed by the press. There were, of course, occasional statements of a very general character by Labor and Socialist conferences favoring the idea of a League of Nations.

[8] In January 1917 the Ligue pour une Société des Nations was organized, but it was not representative in character, and was relatively inactive. Between January 1917 and May 1919 only two rather unimportant brochures were published. (See copies in Hoover War Library.) The new association, formed at the time of the Armistice, the Association Française pour la Société des Nations, with Léon Bourgeois as president, was very representative, including practically all shades of public opinion, from the Archbishop of Paris and Millerand on the Right, to Renaudel and Cachin on the Left.

[9] *Annales de la Chambre*, June 5, 1917, p. 1349.

[10] Tardieu, A., *The Truth About the Treaty* (Indianapolis, 1921), p. 82. It was the influence of Clemenceau which blocked reference to the League in the Senate resolution, according to Renaudel. *Humanité*, January 13, 1918.

[11] *Humanité*, July 7, 1918, quotes Bourgeois as saying that the government had forbidden any communication on the subject without its consent; and this, apparently, was never given.

[12] It should be noted, however, that the policy of the French government in the matter of publishing the League project was in line with the policy of President Wilson, who refused to permit the publication of any official or semi-official drafts in the United States, previously to the Conference, on the ground that it might provoke undesirable controversy. See *House Papers*, vol. iv, p. 49.

[13] *Temps*, December 11, 1918.

[14] *Écho de Paris*, November 28, 1918, and repeatedly thereafter.

[15] January 2, July 7, 1918.

[16] January 1919.

[17] G. J. Adam says Clemenceau "was quite willing to play about with Wilson's League of Nations and his self-determination", so long as they did not affect reparations and guarantees "by misleading France into believing in the efficiency of either notion as a safeguard on the Rhine". Adam, G. J., *The Tiger: G. Clemenceau* (London, 1930), p. 212.

[18] *Messages and Papers*, vol. i, p. 523.

[19] This was, in essence, the official French proposal with regard to "Principles and Methods" submitted to the Peace Conference. Tardieu, *op. cit.*, p. 88.

[20] See Lansing, *op. cit.*, p. 110; and *House Papers*, vol. iv, p. 203.

[21] *Progrès* of Lyons, January 13, 1919.

[22] See *La Paix par le Droit,* January 1919, p. 52.

[23] *Petit Provençal,* January 15, 1919.

[24] *Annales de la Chambre,* December 29, 1918, p. 3348.

[25] *Humanité,* December 21, 1918.

[26] Miller, D. H., *The Drafting of the Covenant,* 2 vols. (New York, 1928), vol. i, p. 76.

[27] "God be praised," said *Humanité* (Jan. 26), "our idea has been accepted as the basis of the final settlement." The *Populaire de Nantes* (Jan. 26) exulted that an end had finally been put "to the raillery against the pacifists who were treated as dreamers and mild lunatics".

[28] *Matin,* January 26, 1919.

[29] *Petit Parisien,* January 26, 1919.

[30] *Temps, Écho de Paris, Action Française,* January 26.

[31] *France de Bordeaux,* January 31.

[32] *Figaro,* February 10.

[33] *Ouest-Éclair,* February 7.

[34] *Liberté,* February 11.

[35] Scelle, G., *Le Pacte des Nations* (Paris, 1919), pp. 23.-30. These fears were natural enough, though they were to a large degree illusory, which Professor Scelle admits, in saying that the American delegation "manifested, from the beginning, a very pressing desire" to see the study of the political problems of the peace pushed ahead at the same time as the constitution of the League.

[36] *Dépêche* of Toulouse, February 5.

[37] Baker, R. S., *Woodrow Wilson and World Settlement,* 3 vols. (New York, 1922), vol. i, pp. 236-240.

[38] Miller, *The Drafting of the Covenant,* vol. i, pp. 82-85.

[39] Minutes of Supreme Council, Sessions January 21 and 22, as quoted by Baker, *op. cit..* vol. i, pp. 237-242; and Minutes of Supreme Council. B. C. 7-A, January 22, 1919, in Hoover War Library.

[40] Baker. *op. cit..* vol. i, pp. 241-242; Minutes of Supreme Council, B. C. 7-A, January 22, 1919.

[41] Miller, *Drafting of the Covenant,* vol. i. pp. 142-143.

[42] *Ibid.,* p. 105.

[43] Miller Diary, vol. xiv, pp. 36 *et seq.*

[44] *Ibid.,* pp. 36 *et seq.*

[45] This was not until after a bitter encounter with Clemenceau over the interpretation of the right of recruiting among the natives of the mandated territories "for defence of territory". Wilson, under pressure from Clemenceau, conceded that the phraseology would permit "France to raise troops in the African territories . . . in case of a general war"—meaning for the defense of France, rather than merely for the defense of the local territory. *Ibid..* pp. 72 *et seq.*

[46] *Ibid.,* p. 73.

[47] Noble, G. B.. *Current Intelligence Summaries,* Manuscript copies in Hoover War Library, January 27 to February 1, 1919. Hereafter cited as *Current Summaries.*

[48] E.g., *Écho de Paris,* January 31; *Nouvelliste de Lyon,* February 2.

[49] *Esprit Public en France,* Bulletin No. 13, February 1-8, 1919.

[50] *Progrès de la Somme,* February 2.

[51] *Victoire,* January 30.

[52] When it was semi-officially announced in Conference circles that the mandate would be, in effect, permanent, and that interference by the League would not be serious, the conservative press moderated its tone somewhat. *Temps* (Feb. 1), and *Débats* (Jan. 31).

[53] "Internationalized or not, the German colonies will certainly be shared between the victorious Powers," said the *Pays* (Jan. 30).

[54] Statement to author by M. Louis Aubert, April 1931. See also Miller, *Drafting of the Covenant,* vol. i, p. 131.

[55] *Ibid.,* p. 212.

[56] "Please note," said Bourgeois, in one of the heated discussions on the control of armaments, "that we are in a somewhat delicate situation, for we are always in the position of discussing a text that was never our own. We can act only by amending the text proposed by the Chair, and that gives our interruptions an aspect that I truly regret. If we had only had the French proposals on the one hand, and on the other the English and American, both side by side, we should have been able to compare the two texts; but since we have before our eyes but the one text, which represents one of the two sides . . . we can intervene only by means of amendments." *Ibid.,* p. 246.

[57] Only in extreme Left quarters could any sympathy be found for the idea of admitting Germany to the League. The Socialists were favorable in principle, but Cachin, editor of *Humanité,* was embarrassed when, in the Chamber of Deputies, December 27, 1918, the question was put to him as to German membership. "I know very well, at the present moment," he said, "there is a problem of immense difficulty." *Annales de la Chambre,* December 27, 1918, p. 3252. The liberal *Progrès* of Lyons (Jan. 7, 1919) and the Socialistic *Heure* (Nov. 29, 1918) agreed with the view that Germany should not at first be a member.

[58] Miller, *Drafting of the Covenant,* vol. i, pp. 164-167, 206, 234.

[59] Wilson shared with Cecil the view that any such reference might subject the League to criticisms from which the Hague Conference had suffered. *Ibid.,* pp. 229, 256.

[60] *Ibid.,* p. 171.

[61] *Bulletin des droits de l'homme,* Nos. 7-8, 1-15, April 1918. See also programs of the Association Française pour la Société des Nations, in *La Paix par le Droit,* December 1918; La Ligue pour une Société des Nations, pamphlet no. 6, July 1917; Délégation Permanente des Sociétés Françaises de la Paix, in *La Paix par le Droit,* January 1919; program of La Société Proudhon, in *Éclair de l'Est,* December 24, 1918; Syndicalist program in *La Voix du Peuple,* 1919, which latter stresses the "free cooperation of peoples", while naturally accepting the above-mentioned limitations on sovereignty.

[62] Miller, *Drafting of the Covenant,* vol. ii, p. 242.

[63] *Ibid.,* vol. i, p. 207.

[64] *Ibid.,* vol. ii, pp. 290 *et seq.*

[65] *Ibid.,* pp. 290 *et seq.*

[66] *Ibid.,* vol. i, pp. 244-260.

[67] *Ibid.,* vol. ii, p. 571.

[68] At the first meeting of the Commission Mr. Wilson urged the policy of secrecy, comparing the work of the League Commission to that of the American Constitutional Convention of 1787, "whose proceedings were withheld from the public until its whole work was accomplished", he said. *Ibid.,* vol. i, p. 233.

[69] *Ibid.,* p. 143.

[70] The *Dépêche* of Toulouse (Feb. 15) noted the "enthusiastic current in all nations", and remarked that world opinion would be happy over the League's creation. The *France de Bordeaux* (Feb. 16) thought it a compromise. "It is far from being perfect," it said. "But where is perfection?" "The project is not a Utopia," said the *Petit Provençal* (Feb. 15). "Some might even appraise it as a timid sketch of that which had been dreamed about." The *Œuvre* (Feb. 15) was more enthusiastic than any of the provincial liberal organs. It found its principles and aims "much loftier and more humanitarian than we had dared to hope".

[71] E.g., *France Libre* (Feb. 15), *Journal du Peuple* (Feb. 15), *Populaire de Nantes* (Feb. 15).

[72] "The League of Nations presents itself under the guise of a league of victorious governments," said the *Bataille* (Feb. 15), organ of organized Labor. "What bitter irony."

[73] There could be no serious League without a firm undertaking for mutual aid, said *Action Française* (Feb. 15). Without these guarantees, it would be "one more scrap of paper", said the *Petite Gironde* (Feb. 16). The *Dépêche* of Toulouse (March 14) thought the League would be only "a Platonic second edition of the Hague", if it had no gendarmerie; and *Heure* (Feb. 16) felt that "the central organ of the League is missing".

[74] *Current Summaries,* February 17, 1919.

[75] Noted by conservative *Petite Gironde* (Feb. 23, 1919).

[76] The pacifist, though not radical, organ, *La Paix par le Droit,* undoubtedly reflected the mature judgment of public opinion in saying that the "outline" which the Commission drew up "has aroused more disappointment than enthusiasm in public opinion. . . . While the details [of the project] abound in happy and bold innovations, the general inspiration is of an incontestable debility." It added a judgment which also represented the preponderant opinion in France: "The Commission . . . seems deliberately to have avoided the problem of limiting . . . the sovereignty of nations, and this omission naturally postpones to the Greek Kalends, the problem of disarmament." Issue of February-March 1919.

[77] Miller, *Drafting of the Covenant,* vol. i, p. 92. See also *ibid.,* pp. 76-100; Baker, *op. cit.,* vol. i, pp. 295-313; *House Papers,* vol. iv, pp. 321 *et seq.;* Churchill, W., *The World Crisis: The Aftermath* (New York, 1929), pp. 184 *et seq.;* Steed, W., *Through Thirty Years,* 2 vols. (Garden City, N. Y., 1924), vol. ii, pp. 289 *et seq.*

[78] Miller Diary, vol. xiv, pp. 283, 335-336; *House Papers,* vol. iv, p. 321

[79] Miller, *Drafting of the Covenant,* vol. i, p. 86.

[80] *Ibid.,* vol. ii, pp. 165 *et seq.*

[81] Miller Diary, vol. xv, p. 4.

[82] *Ibid.,* pp. 6-8. The resolution as finally adopted, February 24, stated

the precise items which were to be included in the preliminaries. In addition to the military terms, the territorial, financial, economic and "responsibility" clauses were noted, reference to the League of Nations being omitted. At House's suggestion, Lansing secured the insertion in the introductory clause of the words *"inter alia"*, in order, as the House Diary explains, to leave room for later inserting the League Covenant. This would, however, seem to leave the status of the League somewhat ambiguous. See *House Papers*, vol. iv, pp. 340, 341.

[83] See Churchill, *op. cit.*, p. 184; Miller, *Drafting of the Covenant*, vol. i, p. 94.

[84] *House Papers*, vol. iv, p. 336.

[85] Thus it was that, early in March, the Colonel had under serious consideration the idea of separating the League from the Treaty, so that the Senate might have the opportunity of voting separately on the two aspects of the settlement. Miller, *Drafting of the Covenant*, vol. i, p. 99.

[86] Thompson, *The Peace Conference Day by Day*, p. 245.

[87] In his idealistic challenge to his fellow countrymen, on his arrival in Boston, President Wilson manifested his awareness of the danger. "If America were, at this juncture, to fail the world, what would become of it?" he asked. "Think of the picture, think of the utter blackness that would fall on the world. . . . America made a little essay at generosity and then withdrew. America said, 'We are your friends', but it was only for today, not for tomorrow. America said, 'Here is our power to vindicate right', and then next day said, 'Let right take care of itself and we will take care of ourselves'. America said, 'We set up a light to lead men along the paths of liberty, but we have lowered it—it is intended only to light our own path'. . . . Arrangements of the present peace cannot stand a generation unless they are guaranteed by the united forces of the civilized world. And if we do not guarantee them can you not see the picture?" *Messages and Papers*, vol. ii, pp. 643-645.

[88] E.g., *Débats* (Feb. 27), *Liberté* (Feb. 27), *Gaulois* (Feb. 27). The Socialistic organ, *Heure* (Feb. 27), pointed to the embarrassment of the conservative press arising out of the new orientation of events. ". . . now the very people who were his opponents here are afraid of the opposition in America. . . . Suppose the United States returned to their pre-war policy of non-intervention in Europe? To separate the United States from us means to consign us to ruin. . . . Now the result alarms us." Other extreme Left organs, while praising the Boston speech, deplored the "halfway measures" of Wilson in regard to the League. E.g., *Populaire* and *Journal du Peuple*, February 27.

[89] March 1, 2, 5, 7.

[90] E.g., *Petit Parisien, Matin, Ouest-Éclair*.

[91] E.g., *Ouest-Éclair*, March 11; *Écho de Paris*, March 13; *Temps*, March 14.

[92] On the President's return it is interesting to note that, while he was welcomed back to France politely, and in some of the moderate press, warmly, the éclat and enthusiasm of the previous December were completely lacking. The changed tone of the Left is partly indicated by the fact that *Humanité*, which, on his first arrival, in December, had devoted

three pages in a special number to the President, on the occasion of his second arrival, it gave him only one-third of a column, without any editorial comment. It ought to be noted that a number of leading provincial nationalist papers, for instance, *Ouest-Éclair, Nouvelliste de Lyon, Phare* of Nantes, *Journal de Rouen, Petit Marseillais*, remained consistently hostile to Wilson throughout this period. A note from the *Phare*, March 14, is typical: "Here is Wilson back again. Would that he could now only understand that when one obstinately puts the plough in front of the oxen even the best soil can produce only tares!"

[93] *Current Summaries*, March 3, 1919.

[94] *Ibid.*, March 10.

[95] *Ibid.*, March 10.

[96] Baker, *op. cit.*, vol. i, p. 308.

[97] *Ibid.*, p. 311.

[98] See *New York Herald*, Paris ed., March 17, 1919.

[99] *The Peace Conference Day by Day*, pp. 247, 248.

[100] Perhaps these papers were not reached by Tardieu; perhaps they resisted pressure. In the case of the Socialist papers, they probably did not have the news of the interview. Twenty-eight Paris papers (all those having any importance) were examined in this connection.

[101] See e.g., *Temps*, and *Progrès* of Lyons, March 19.

[102] *Temps*, March 20.

[103] Thompson, *op. cit.*, p. 255. Steed, *op. cit.*, vol. ii, p. 296.

[104] For one day *Homme Libre* (March 17) strangely spoke a good word for the idea, hoping that it might mean that the whole peace would be that much nearer, but it soon fell away when this glimmer of hope faded.

[105] *Information*, March 18. "Why not disembarrass ourselves of Germany before trying to settle the affairs of the Universe?" asked the *Gaulois*, March 19. *Victoire* (March 19) expressed the hope that "perhaps Mr. Wilson would consent—which would conciliate his apostolic zeal, and our legitimate impatience—to incorporate only the main lines of his organization . . . in the Preliminaries." The *Temps* (March 21) reprinted, at considerable length, a leader from the London *Times* which argued strongly for concluding the Preliminaries with only the basic principles of the League included.

[106] *Écho de Paris*, March 17, 20.

[107] *Liberté*, March 20.

[108] "Tell them that the Covenant for the League of Nations would either be written into the Treaty of Peace or we would have none of it. . . ." *House Papers*, vol. iv, p. 390.

[109] *Ibid.*, p. 373.

[110] Miller, *Drafting of the Covenant*, vol. ii, p. 367.

[111] *Ibid.*, vol. i, p. 269; vol. ii, pp. 273, 323; *House Papers*, vol. iv, p. 314.

[112] Miller, *Drafting of the Covenant*, vol. ii, pp. 387 *et seq.* The Japanese, however, made a "reservation" on the subject, and at the Plenary Session of April 28, Baron Makino made an eloquent statement of the Japanese case. Miller Diary, vol. xx, pp. 111 *et seq.*

[113] Miller, *Drafting of the Covenant,* vol. ii, p. 363; *Temps,* April 12, 1919.

[114] Baker, *op. cit.,* vol. ii, p. 301; Klotz, L., *De la Guerre à la Paix* (Paris, 1924), Annexe II.

[115] *Annales de la Chambre,* March 11, pp. 971 *et seq.;* March 13, 1919, p. 1025.

[116] Miller, *Drafting of the Covenant,* vol. i, pp. 282, 292.

[117] Miller Diary, vol. xx, p. 126.

[118] Miller, *Drafting of the Covenant,* vol. ii, pp. 343-345.

[119] Miller Diary, vol. xx, pp. 116 *et seq.*

[120] Colonel House records that on Mr. Wilson's return to France in March he was at first quite unwilling to consent to any modifications in the Covenant. *House Papers,* vol. iv, p. 385.

[121] These provisions took care of three of the most common objections to the Covenant in the United States, and might very well have caused the President to suppose that he was making the really necessary concessions. Strong objections had been made to the territorial guarantee of Article 10 (e.g., even by Hughes), but the above three were the objections most generally raised. Miller, *Drafting of the Covenant,* vol. i, pp. 322 *et seq.*

[122] *Ibid.,* p. 331; vol. ii, p. 350.

[123] *Ibid.,* vol. ii, p. 357.

[124] *House Papers,* vol. iv, pp. 416-421.

[125] Miller Diary, vol. viii, pp. 282 *et seq.*

[126] Miller, *Drafting of the Covenant,* vol. i, pp. 442-450.

[127] *Temps,* April 12.

[128] See *Current Summaries,* April 4, 1919.

[129] April 14, 1919. This criticism is interesting as showing a state of mind, though of course there is a vital difference in the two cases, as Wilson pointed out in the Commission. The only way the League capital could be chosen was on the majority principle. It was a matter of "procedure", whereas the other proposal was a question of "substance", to which unanimity has generally, rightly or wrongly, been demanded in international conferences.

[130] E.g., *Victoire,* on the Right, somewhat oratorically referred to the "immortal glory of Wilson" that would derive from the pact, but then proceeded to criticize. April 29. *Vérité,* on the extreme Left, seemed pleased with Wilson's triumph over "prejudices, lies, rancours, hate". April 29. It likewise had severe criticisms to make.

[131] *Homme Libre,* April 29. Also *Journal, Petit Parisien, Matin,* same date.

[132] E.g., *Gaulois, Matin,* April 29; *Petit Provençal, Humanité,* April 30.

[133] "It is a League of good words," said the *Écho de Paris* (April 29). "The text voted on Monday at the Conference is laughable," said the *Populaire* (April 30). Even the *France Libre,* on the Socialist Right Wing, was unusually pessimistic, saying that now it would be for the "world of labor, politically and economically organized, to lead the workers". "The League of Nations was a beautiful dream; now it is a great deception." April 30, May 6.

[134] May 4. This term was very commonly applied to the League.

[135] *Matin,* April 29.

[136] *Journal,* and *Œuvre,* April 28.

[137] *Liberté,* April 30. The Covenant was frequently labeled an Anglo-American document. See *Current Summaries,* April 30.

[138] April 1919.

[139] E.g., *Débats,* April 30.

[140] *Débats* (April 30) chided France for not having taken the League seriously enough at first. Having first treated it lightly, and made it the "butt of any number of jokes", France suddenly turned about and demanded that it be invested with the most extended powers, only to find, at that time, that Wilson was moving in "precisely the opposite direction".

CHAPTER V

THE PROBLEM OF GERMANY

Senator Flaissières: We have no right to hate a people forever. We have no right to consider them as eternally unchangeable, for . . . just as individuals improve under a better environment, so the German people of today will evolve. (Protests on many benches.)
Senator Guilloteaux: Science will not transform a wolf into a lamb.
Senator Jénouvrier: And particularly, do not count on the evolution of the German people. (Smiles.)
(From debates in French Senate, April 18, 1919.)

1. German Recovery

THE problem of peace, as viewed by most Frenchmen, resolved itself primarily into the question of France's future relations with Germany; and the League of Nations, as well as every other aspect of the settlement, won approval only in so far as it contributed to reducing to a minimum the "danger from across the Rhine". The state of affairs in Germany, therefore, as affording an index to probable future German attitudes and policies, became a matter of intense concern to French opinion.

It has been previously suggested that the November Revolution was not greeted with enthusiasm in any quarter, except on the extreme Left. Even in those circles the comments were not without reservations. Almost everywhere the new Republic was the object of the greatest suspicion. Born, as it was, in the midst of defeat, and as the epilogue of diplomatic negotiations in which President Wilson had demanded fundamental changes in the German constitutional system as a condition precedent to the granting of an armistice, it could scarcely fail to carry questionable birthmarks. Accompanied, also, by the mounting wave of nationalistic feeling in France amid the enthusiasm of victory, it could not hope to avoid sharing the odium of the old régime. Whatever genuineness the Revolution may have possessed, one could not have expected the French people to believe in the possibility of an apparently over-night change of heart.

Some of the leading Center and Right Wing organs had, preceding the Armistice, consistently opposed the Wilsonian policy of admitting a distinction between the German government and the German people, and had warned against acting on the presumption that the people, as contrasted with the government, were honest. "The past attitude of the German, Magyar and Bulgar peoples does not permit this illusion," said the *Temps*.[1] So far as the Reichstag was concerned, it was repeatedly and plausibly said to be tarred with the same brush as the old régime, since it (even including the Social Democrats) had supported the war policy of the Imperial government. Having voted for the Treaty of Brest-Litovsk, for example, after the declaration of Wilson's Fourteen Points, was it not "placed in the same rank as 'those who have conducted the war up to this time' "?[2]

Unabated skepticism and distrust of the young Republic prevailed almost equally strongly in all quarters, from the Right almost to the extreme Left. "The more she changes, the more she remains herself," said one paper.[3] " 'Republic' is only a label. The difference between the leaders is one of caste," said another.[4] "You will better understand the German Republic when it has proclaimed Hindenburg its President," said the *Action Française* (Nov. 25). The Radical Socialist papers were equally vehement. They felt that there was no reason to change France's attitude, and pointed out that Ebert and Scheidemann had helped the Kaiser's government.[5] *Œuvre* (Nov. 10) very pointedly wrote that "in humiliating their Emperor" the Germans "are not responding to righteous indignation; they are only obeying their fears. They do not punish their sovereign for his crimes, but rather for the failure of his crimes. . . . Germany hopes to escape bankruptcy by a timely liquidation. They

are changing the name of the firm." The *Dépêche* of Toulouse argued repeatedly that the Revolution was, in large
part, a maneuver, and that Germany was already planning
revenge. The only way to convince a German that he was
beaten, it urged in one leader, was not only to throw him
down, but also to "beat his head on the pavement".[6] In the
Chamber of Deputies, when Cachin, asking for a definition
of government policy with regard to Germany, made reference to the German Republic, Raoul Mequillet, of the Left
Republican group (in the Center), shouted: "The Germans
are savages. . . . We do not want to have relations with
savages, vandals and assassins." Numerous other voices
joined in, shouting that the Germans had "conducted themselves like savages".[7]

Meantime, a certain degree of order in Germany was
evolving out of the relative chaos of December and early
January. On January 19 the elections for the Constituent
Assembly gave the Social Democrats forty per cent of the
seats—a much larger percentage than they had ever won
before. With the 163 Social Democrats, furthermore, were
associated 75 Democrats and 92 Centrists; and against this
block of moderates the two extremes gained only 91 seats.
To all outward appearances, moderation had triumphed
over the extremes of Bolshevism and nationalism. Though
it was generally admitted to be a victory for political democracy, this was far from satisfying French opinion. Indeed,
it seemed to cause increasing uneasiness, for, except on the
extreme Left, the results were interpreted as being, not a
swing of Germany toward anti-Imperialistic Social-Democracy, but rather as a swing of Social-Democracy toward
Pangermanism. "It returns to the plan of 1848," said *Paris-
Midi* (Jan. 22), "following the law of its profound and permanent thought." Even *Humanité* and *Populaire*, while expressing sympathy and hope, manifested uneasiness over the
prospect that Ebert and Scheidemann would tie up with
more reactionary elements.[8]

A few of the liberal papers of the provinces felt that the

elections were a "hopeful sign" for the future,[9] but for the most part, even this press joined with the Center and Right Wing papers in profound skepticism over the results. The *Dépêche* of Toulouse seemed as convinced as the most nationalistic that there had been no change of heart. "Germany remains, as a Republic, what she was as an Empire," it said, echoing the prevalent sentiment from Right to Left.[10] The radical *Pays* (Jan. 22) warned that, like the victory of the moderates in 1848, this Socialist victory was "the inevitable precursor of reaction"; while the *France Libre* (Jan. 23), of the Socialist Right Wing, averred that Germany had just sanctioned "the collusion of the Social-Democracy with the military and feudal empire. It is not merely a verdict of absolution and amnesty; it is a bill of approval and encouragement." The Center and Right Wing journals unanimously shared the point of view (held by many of the Left) that it was "an Empire without an Emperor".[11] "Whilst the victors are making speeches," said the *Temps* (Jan. 25), "Germany has just given herself a Constituent Assembly which will act as the pivot of her resistance and as a lever for her recovery."

It was just this aspect of the situation suggested by the *Temps*, that was the source of the greatest disturbance. Germany seemed to be showing an unmistakable disposition to return to "its former disciplined activity" and to put its house in order, while the Allies were still in the first stages of the peacemaking, and while they were, indeed, manifesting signs of confusion and lack of unity of purpose. Would this situation not be exploited to the limit by this new democracy, which seemed bent on erecting a stronger and more centralized system of government than Germany had previously possessed? In late January and early February a very definite opinion was fostered throughout the press (except that of the extreme Left), that a reorganized and consolidated Germany was getting on its feet with amazing rapidity, and that it was strenuously preparing to resist the demands of the Allies, and to promote divided counsels among them.[12]

The meeting of the Constituent Assembly at Weimar, February 6, tended further to heighten the tone of French feelings. The "pompous display" surrounding it, the "military music", the "flowers decorating the Chamber", the "numerous attendants", the "cinematograph operators", the "numerous police agents", and the "Imperial Eagle adorning the Presidential Chair" were described in detail.[13] Ebert's speech was the object of specially hostile comment, especially his remark that though Germany had lost the war, both Germany and her adversaries were worn out by it, and his statement that, "The idea of spoliation had come in consequence of the victories." Ebert's speech marked "a revival of insolence which approaches menace . . .," said one.[14] "Adorned with a new vocabulary, it is the old imperialism which rises in the footsteps of its disaster," said another.[15] The *Débats* (Feb. 7) caustically commented that the Weimar Assembly was meeting as a triumphant Empire rather than as a vanquished Assembly; and the *Matin's* large headline (Feb. 10) shouted: "The Germans talk as though they were not beaten." "The news which arrives from Weimar," said the *France Libre*, "shows us a Germany in full imperialistic reorganization." [16]

A violent outburst of feeling (from all except the Socialist press) was directed at the "German menace", and the consequent dangers against which the Conference should arm itself. There were several immediate reasons for this: the developments in Germany, the developments within the Supreme Council, and, behind it all, the feeling that President Wilson's absorbing interest in the League of Nations as the basis of the future peace inclined him to a certain softness and "idealism" with regard to Germany. The news coming out of Germany was alarming. Germany was reported to be on the point of hostilities with the Poles in the region of Posen. The election of David as temporary President of

the Constituent Assembly was interpreted as a swing toward
Pangermanism, and the election of Ebert as President of the
Republic was interpreted as confirming the imperialism of
the Social Democrats. A series of interviews with leading
German statesmen and industrialists, reported by the *Matin,*
and other papers, was alleged to confirm the dangerous
trend. Brockdorff-Rantzau, foreign minister, warned France
not to treat Germany like a pariah, or to push her to
thoughts of revenge.[17] Hugo Stinnes and Dr. Rathenau spoke
of the danger of Germany's going Bolshevik. Friedrich
Naumann was quoted as saying that in twenty years Germany would be at the head of the commerce and industry of
the world.[18] The speeches of German statesmen in the
Weimar Assembly stimulated further fears, and publicity
was given to a report of Foch to the Supreme Council, in
which he made alarming statements as to German military
capacity.

Within the Council of Ten the Wilson and Clemenceau
theses were at grips with each other over the question of
adding new terms to the Armistice on the occasion of its
third renewal in February. Clemenceau supported the report of the military commission which proposed to demand
of Germany the surrender of a vast amount of additional
war material, and to set up a control over factories and
workshops engaged in the manufacture of these articles.
Occupation of the Ruhr was threatened as a penalty.
Wilson, supported by General Bliss, thought "it was not
sportsmanlike to attempt to correct at that time the errors"
that had been made at the time of the original Armistice.[19]
He proposed, as an alternative, the renewal of the Armistice
on an indefinite basis, with a provision for denunciation by
the Allies on three days' notice, with the added proviso that
final military terms should be handed to the Germans at the
earliest possible moment. Clemenceau was strongly opposed
to this program, especially to the proposed separation of the
military terms from territorial and financial terms of the
peace. These leaders were also at odds over the question

of supplying the enemies with food and raw materials, and as to the general method of dealing with Germany. They also differed as to the seriousness of the danger arising from German threats. Wilson averred that "The Germans were beaten, and they knew it. Their spirit was broken, and they would not renew the struggle." [20] Clemenceau thought the right to impose new terms could not be contested on juridical or any other grounds. He feared the danger of "losing the fruits of victory". "In the last few weeks the Germans had become insolent, and recently an incident had occurred. Marshal Foch had been forced to use constraint to bring the German delegates to a meeting." "He knew the German people well. They became ferocious" when anyone yielded to them. [21]

The dissension within the Council was soon reflected in the press, in spite of the fact that the official communiqués were rather noncommittal as to what actually took place within the Council. There is reason to believe that a press campaign was officially encouraged. Mr. Baker says that "one day in February" at the time when the fight for the League was at a crucial stage, President Wilson showed him a memorandum of instructions from the French government to the French press (coming, as Wilson assured him, from an unimpeachable source), urging the press, among other things, to play up the point that Germany was willing and able to renew the struggle. [22] In view of the activities of the press at this time, and of Clemenceau's own conduct, there is no reason to doubt the authenticity of this memorandum, or that it issued during this period, for it was at this time that a concerted campaign, of unprecedented violence, began in the governmental press, supported even by papers which ordinarily did not follow the lead of the government.

All of the heavy press led the way with repeated articles of alarmist character, and most of the other organs of opinion, including the liberal press, followed suit. Conditions in Germany were represented as being most threatening. "The Weimar Assembly has been called to help the German government to establish order, to make closer the national unity, to annex Vienna and to resist the claims of the Allies," said the *Temps* (Feb. 8), thus summing up the various dangers envisaged. "It is the cry of the Hohenzollerns that Minister Preuss lets out at Weimar," said another.[23] The *Matin's* articles and interviews with leading Germans seemed to prove the dangerous rapidity of German recovery and the probability of increasing German resistance. The *Débats* (Feb. 9) thought the new constitution more to be feared than the old, remarking that, whatever its form of government, Germany "must be marching at the head of civilization". Even *France Libre* (Feb. 9) expressed fears of the "German menace".

Oil was thrown on the flames, and corroboration was given to the report that the press campaign was directly encouraged from above, by the personal intervention of Premier Clemenceau by means of an alarmist interview given to the Associated Press, which appeared in the French papers of February 10. The victory he said, was only "a lull in the storm". It was a Pyrrhic victory, for France was destroyed industrially, and had contracted large debts toward America and England. Germany, he feared, would start the war again, with the aid of Russia. After these statements he took the precaution to add some complimentary remarks about President Wilson, and referred to the "perfect harmony" which existed on the subject of his "splendid platform", on the basis of which we were tending toward "a higher and more healthy idealism in the conduct of the world's affairs".

This pronouncement of the Premier could not fail to excite public opinion further, since the interview was obviously designed, not for the purpose of complimenting President Wilson, but rather to paint the German menace in more threatening colors. The press of the Right, Center and moderate Left emphasized the importance and expressed strong approval of Clemenceau's action. "Clemenceau points out to the American people the rebirth of the German danger," was *Matin's* headline (Feb. 10), and the following day it wrote that the "cry of alarm uttered by Clemenceau . . . has stirred public opinion profoundly". His "vigorous and hardy pessimism" was characterized by another as "an act of ardent patriotism".[24] Others wrote in similar vein. The *Victoire* of the Right, and *Bonsoir* of the Left rejoiced equally that Clemenceau had thus, by speaking out, clarified the situation.[25] *Action Française* (Feb. 11) commented that Clemenceau "brings us down from the clouds of Wilsonian idealism to solid earth". *Écho de Paris'* American correspondent cabled that the interview had made a strong impression in the United States, where, he said, it was feared that Allied demobilization was proceeding too rapidly.[26]

Quite naturally, the sense of alarm was increased in moderate as well as conservative circles. Germany was said to be awake and "shaking her fists again".[27] The Armistice of November 11 was only a supplement to the famous collection of "scraps of paper".[28] The whole affair was a "frame-up of German militarism".[29] The sudden renewal of war was suggested as a possibility.[30] "We are at the most critical period since the ending of hostilities," said the *Matin* (Feb. 11). "How shall disaster be avoided?" asked the *Progrès de la Somme* (Feb. 12). "We confess we see no solution." [31]

President Wilson was attacked openly and bitterly. The *Figaro* (Feb. 10), carrying the Clemenceau interview prominently in its second column, devoted its first column to a scathing indictment of what Capus called "Wilsonian Equivocation", which, he said, was threatening to "plunge the world into a chaos of which Russian Bolshevism offers us only a feeble likeness". The equivocation, he said, "consists in this, that our conquered enemies rely on his ideas to contest the very reality of our victory, and tomorrow will invoke his name to refuse us its fruits". The Wilsonian method, he complained, consisted in subordinating the conditions of peace to the League of Nations. And France was the country "which runs the greatest risk from this maneuver". The "Internationale" and the Germans repeat

incessantly their desire for "the peace of President Wilson".
"Very good! But the kind of peace designated by this name
—universally respected—will, in the interpretation given it
by the Germans and the internationalists, mean the ruin of
our country. So long as the equivocation which contains
such disasters is not dissipated, the psychological disarray
will continue, and peace will continue to hang by a
thread." [32] Such an indictment should be read in the light
of the existence of an active censorship, which, had it so
desired, could easily have prevented the appearance of this
article. The *Écho de Paris* (Feb. 11) lashed out at the
"naïve persons" who, "with the guest from the White House
have thought that to rid the enemy of its dynasty was to
consecrate it to peace and to right. . . . Either the Wilsonian
credo means nothing, or it signifies a peace without victory." [33] The *Action Française* (Feb. 12) stated that though
Wilson possessed "a lofty spirit and ingenious views—which
might or might not be practical—" nevertheless he did not
know the "infinitude of the German knavery as did Foch
and Clemenceau". Even the Socialistic *France Libre*
(Feb. 11), thought Wilson would one day say "ungrateful"
to Germany when the "serpent" (Germany) had "eaten
away all the edge from the file of the watchmaker".

These violent outbursts of fears and recriminations were
accompanied by vehement demands for the application of
rigorous conditions to Germany in the renewed Armistice, as
well as for more speed in the work of the Conference.
Europe, it was alleged, would never be peaceful again till
the teeth of the "German beast" had been pulled. [34] The
heavy headlines of the *Petit Parisien* (Feb. 11) expressed
the prevailing desire: "GERMANY, BY THE NEW ARMISTICE,
OUGHT TO BE RENDERED INCAPABLE OF DOING HARM." Demands were made for the occupation of the Ruhr; for the
drastic reduction of German divisions; for the surrender of
practically all of Germany's heavy arms; for the withdrawal
of German troops in the disputed Polish territories; for the
debarkation of Allied troops at Danzig; for tightening the

blockade,—demands in line with those made by Foch before the Supreme Council. Others, chiefly on the Left, insisted on the complete demobilization of Germany, except for limited police purposes. The *Œuvre* (Feb. 10) joined the chorus of those farther to the right in demanding that the Conference, "before re-shuffling the world's map", should get down to the business of delimiting Franco-German frontiers. Let them "settle the hash of Germany at once, clearly and publicly". Then the diplomats might be allowed to "wrangle at their ease".

Throughout this upheaval of opinion the official Socialist press, while joining in the demand for a rapid settlement of the major terms of peace with Germany, refused to get excited, except to deplore the campaign, which, it stated, was promoted to alarm public opinion, and to display a "distorted picture of the German situation", so that Wilson would consent to new and more coercive measures.[35] *Humanité* (Feb. 11) expressed stupefaction that Clemenceau, the President of the Council, should lend himself thus to stirring up public opinion. "It is he [Clemenceau]," it said, "who, in organizing the resistance against the Wilsonian propositions, and in compromising France in imperialistic intrigues, has created the unrest from which we suffer at the time when the work of the peace ought to be about finished." The *Bataille* (Feb. 11), of organized labor, pointed out that Germany had practically no metallurgical supplies, and that the fighting, if any, would take place on German soil. "No, comrades," it said, "the war will not recommence." Indeed, when the first fever of excitement was over, a number of papers farther to the right admitted that after all, Germany was not really in a position to renew the conflict.[36] Even the *Temps* (Feb. 17) admitted that the conflict between the Poles and Germans had been exaggerated.

Meantime the Supreme Council had come to an agreement as to terms to be demanded of Germany in the renewed Armistice. On February 12 it was finally agreed by all, (a) that the Germans should be ordered to desist from attacks on the Poles and that a line of demarcation should be fixed behind which they would have to withdraw; (b) that the Armistice was to be renewed for an indefinite period, but terminable by the Allies on three days' notice, and (c) that the previous Armistice terms, which Germany had not completely fulfilled, were to be rigorously executed under conditions to be fixed by the Permanent Armistice Commission.[37] These decisions were not reached without heated debate. Clemenceau resisted vigorously the thesis supported by Wilson and Balfour in favor of the indefinite renewal, for, as a counter-part to this point, Wilson and Balfour urged that the military, naval and air terms should be drawn up within the immediate future and presented to Germany as a species of preliminary treaty. Clemenceau was bitterly opposed to separating the military terms from other peace conditions (e.g., territorial and financial terms), for he feared that their application might mean premature Allied demobilization. Though he strongly supported the Foch proposals for the addition of new and drastic terms to the preceding Armistice, with threats of heavy sanctions, he finally compromised in the direction of the Wilson-Balfour program.

These terms were presented by Marshal Foch to the Germans. Though the latter protested vigorously, arguing that they were given no reciprocal protection against aggression by the Poles, and that they were threatened with the exhaustion of their economic resources, they finally yielded on the 16th, after recording their protest in the name of Wilsonian principles.

The spectacle of the Supreme Council, finally united on a reasonably firm set of principles, was very gratifying to patriotic French circles, even though the French thesis had not entirely prevailed in the Council. It was reported in the press that negotiations would immediately be undertaken for the elaboration of the military and economic clauses, for demobilization, and for control of German factories, after which consideration would be given to the question of food supplies to Germany—prior Allied claims being respected.[38] The 12th was regarded as "an excellent day" by most of the press except that of the extreme Left.[39] Special satisfaction was felt that Germany had failed to divide the Allies.[40] Confidence was expressed that the Allies would be ready, if necessary, to give the "extra turn of the vise" on Germany.[41] Wilson actually received a modicum of praise, even from those who had attacked him most bitterly. He was quoted (correctly), with gratification, as having said in the Supreme Council that if the Germans refused to conform to the clauses of a "just peace" that he "would not hesitate one second to order the American army to make another attack".[42] The *Figaro* (Feb. 13), which had been so bitter a few days previously, congratulated the President, not without a touch of irony, stating that "The high and noble Wilsonian idea finally comes into contact with reality." A similar view was expressed in the *Temps;* and the *Écho de Paris* accepted the compromise without too bad grace. The *Victoire* (Feb. 13) expressed the prevailing view of the moderate and conservative press in remarking that the President had now shown the "spirit of conciliation" which had long been awaited from his "high wisdom".

The Allied unity of February 12, and the renewal of the Armistice February 16, while relieving the tension somewhat, did not dispel recurrent fears. The news from Germany still seemed threatening. Interviews with leading Germans continued to arouse misgivings. Erzberger was quoted as saying: "We shall not allow ourselves to be reduced to political slavery"; and as demanding the return of the German colonies.[43] Various others warned against driving Germany to Bolshevism.[44] Speeches of German leaders in the Weimar Assembly appeared no less portentous. Scheidemann, elected chancellor, set forth an alarmist government program: adhesion to the Wilsonian program; repudiation of any peace of violence; reestablishment of German colonial territories; German entrance into the League on a basis of equality; general and reciprocal disarmament; reinforcement of German unity by a strong central government. Brockdorff-Rantzau, appealing to Wilsonian principles, demanded the return of the German commercial fleet and German colonies; a plebiscite in Alsace-Lorraine; the union of Austria with Germany, and a rapprochement with Russia.[45]

Nor did the acceptance by Germany of the renewed Armistice restore confidence, for the terms were found, on second thought, not to be highly satisfactory. Even the *Heure* (Feb. 18), close to the extreme Left, commented on the weakness of the terms: no demobilization; no control of munitions factories, inadequate delimitation of Polish frontiers. Everywhere the demand was made for hastening the drafting of definitive preliminaries; and widespread suspicion of Germany remained unabated.[46] The major source of satisfaction was that the Entente Powers had remained united; but patriotic opinion was still convinced that "The Eternal Danger" of Germany remained.

2. THE PROVISIONING OF GERMANY

The question of supplying Germany with food and raw materials was closely connected with the problem of German recovery which, during early February, had so disturbed influential French circles. No sooner had the November Armistice been signed than Germany began to appeal to President Wilson for assistance in relieving its food crisis. These appeals elicited slight sympathy in France, except on the extreme Left, and stirred considerable indignation in most of the press, which saw in them a double example of German duplicity: an attempt to continue its separate negotiations with Wilson, thus separating him from the Allies, and an attempt to arouse sympathy for themselves by painting conditions in Germany in unduly alarming colors. It was natural that a suspicious French public should be disposed to believe that the enemy's needs were greatly exaggerated, and that France's own needs were greater. Even granting the seriousness of Germany's condition, there remained the formidable dilemma: the choice between the danger of driving Germany to despair and to Bolshevism, if the food blockade were rigorously maintained, and the danger of German rapid recovery and resistance to Allied demands if she were helped to her feet. For the most part this dilemma was not really faced, the easier alternative being followed of refusing to admit the seriousness of the case. The Germans were charged with trying to force the Allies "to choose between humanitarian sentimentalism and political prudence"; [47] and the public was advised to avoid "Useless Pity", on the grounds that talk of food relief for Germany was out of place as long as the devastated regions of Northern France needed help. [48]

President Wilson did not allow himself to be drawn into separate negotiations on this matter, though American policy was favorable to the extension of food relief work to the ex-enemy countries. Colonel House recorded on December 26, 1918, that the Entente countries were taking "a perfectly impossible stand. They are making it more difficult for Germany under peace conditions than it was under war": by the restriction of the German fishing fleet, by the prohibition of the use of German gold for paying for food, and by the establishment of zones which were not allowed to send or receive articles of commerce. [49]

The problem came before the Supreme War Council January 13, when the question arose as to the surrender of the German merchant fleet to supplement the shipping resources of the Allies during the Armistice period. It was recognized that some concession would have to be made toward the revictualling of Germany, though the French representatives sought to hedge it about with rigorous limitations. Two major difficulties remained to be surmounted. The first concerned the manner in which to approach Germany on the subject. Should the demand for the delivery of the merchant fleet be bluntly and unconditionally made of Germany by the Allies, thus leaving the subsequent revictualling of Germany as a species of act of grace on the part of the Allies and entirely within their discretion? Or, should the promise of food supplies accompany the request for the ships, and the whole transaction be put on the basis of a frank bargain between the parties? On this point, Marshal Foch preferred that the renewed Armistice should bluntly demand the German ships, thus leaving the Allies completely free to decide questions of policy. The British and American delegates preferred to put it more in the form of a bargain. "If you want food, then turn over your ships", was the form suggested by Balfour, and President Wilson urged the drafting of an agreement on this basis.[50] The final terms of the January Armistice renewal were a compromise between these two points of view. Article 8 provided that "In order to secure the provisioning of Germany and of the rest of Europe, the German government shall take all necessary steps to place the German fleet, for the duration of the Armistice, under the control . . . of the Allied Powers and the United States. . . ." It was also provided that "All questions of details . . . shall be settled by a special agreement to be concluded immediately." [51]

The second difficulty had to do with payment for the food supplied, and was even more thorny, for it involved a clash between conflicting interests of the Entente Powers themselves. Klotz, for France, recommended that the debt incurred by Germany for the food should be carried as part of the "general indemnity". The British and American position was that it should be paid immediately, or, at least, that it should have priority over claims for reparations. Clementel and Klotz pointed out that the sum would come to about $60,000,000 a month, and argued that it was "not right that the Germans should be permitted to pay for their food with money which they already owed for the reparation of the damages to France and Belgium". Wilson observed that "So long as hunger gnaws, foundations of governments crumble", and urged that it was imperative to act at once. Bolshevism threatened. The Allies did not expect to pay for the food which they now proposed to send to Germany. Germany must pay, not only for the food, but also for the damages inflicted on the Allies. He added, further, if the Allies did not feed Germany she would be unable to pay any indemnity at all. The difference in points of view was understandable, since Great Britain and the United States would be supplying the food, while France would be witnessing available securities flowing out of her enemy's coffers. A compromise was reached, giving priority to the new debt, but limiting it to a period of two months.[52]

The solution of the revictualling problem had made no progress when the time came for the discussions over the February renewal of the Armistice. Plans for implementing the January arrangements had not been worked out, and only a small part of the German merchant fleet had been turned over. The major difficulty seemed to be among the Entente Powers. On February 4, Hoover wrote to Wilson stating that "The French, by obstruction of every financial measure that we can propose . . . in the attempt to compel us to loan money to Germany for this purpose, have defeated every step so far for getting them the food which we have been promising them for three months."[53] In the February discussions Wilson urged giving Germany "the means of renewing her economic life", as a matter of interest to all the Allies. Lloyd George and Clemenceau thought that the Allies were not honor-bound to supply Germany with food, and Wilson agreed "that the Allies were under no moral obligation", but "he was proud as a moral man that on humane grounds it was not intended to let the people of Germany starve".[54] The matter was further argued in the meetings of February 10 and 12, but definitive conclusions were not reached, except that the Permanent Armistice Commission was empowered, generally, to supervise the carrying out of the terms of the preceding Armistices.

Meantime, discredit was being cast on the revictualling program by powerful organs of the Center and Right Wing press. The seriousness of German need was questioned. French correspondents in Germany sent back statements discounting reports of bad food conditions in certain parts of Germany.[55] News reports were carried purporting to prove that prices in Germany were lower than those in France. French children were said to be suffering as badly as those in Germany.[56] Public opinion was enjoined not to be influenced by the cries of famine and misery in Germany. After all, the Germans had started the war, and they should pay the penalty.[57] Fears were expressed that feeding Germany would enable her to get on her feet too rapidly.[58]

Anxiety was aroused as to the method by which Germany would pay for the food supplies, and as to the results which might be anticipated. Though the Supreme Council proceedings on this subject had not been made public, the journals close to the Foreign Office were apparently fully apprised of the tenor of the debates. The *Écho de Paris* and the *Temps* adopted the arguments used by the French delegates in the Supreme Council. "Will Germany's gold and other assets be dispersed to neutrals and to the United States while her war creditors are left in the lurch?" It was argued that the total assets of Germany should be sequestered and distributed according to the situation of each creditor.[59] Germany was said to be trying to tie up commercial relations with the United States, and this was naturally viewed with considerable alarm. The food and raw materials policy, it was felt, should be directed toward securing the necessary guarantees.[60]

French opinion had apparently become even more unyielding in this matter than the government itself, as was revealed when, on March 4, Clemenceau asked Colonel House to allow him "a little time to bring the French public to a realization of the importance of sending food into Germany".[61] This state of feeling was illustrated by the events accompanying the rupture of negotiations at Spa concerning the handing over of the German merchant fleet and the delivery of foodstuffs to Germany by the Allies. The Allied delegates were instructed to demand the unconditional surrender of the German ships. The Germans were instructed to promise to surrender them only in return for a definitive

arrangement concerning foodstuffs. Not a ton of food, they
pointed out, had been supplied them since the Armistice,
and they demanded a definite promise of regular supplies as
part of the bargain.[62] As agreement could not be reached
within the limits of the instructions, the negotiations were
interrupted.

The episode produced a wave of indignation throughout
the patriotic press. Although most of the papers carried the
official German reports of the incident, which naturally presented it from the German point of view, though in moderate
terms, almost none of the papers questioned the legal and
moral right of the Allies in making a categoric and unconditional demand for the ships. "Blackmail", "bluff",
"manœuvre" were the most characteristic terms applied to
the German conduct, except on the extreme Left.[63] Even
the *Dépêche* of Toulouse (March 10) said Germany wanted
"to blackmail the Entente". But she would yield quickly
enough, it said, "if the Entente shows its teeth".[64] Even the
Socialist press did not dispute the desirability of taking over
of the ships; and merely discounted the seriousness of the
incident. *Humanité* (March 8) pointed out that the delivery
of the German merchant fleet could be regarded, in the last
resort, as a measure of reparation toward the Allies. It did,
however, stress the importance of sending in food. "Only
fools can imagine," it said, "that it can be useful to starve
Germany, and drive her to despair"; and it supported its
position with a message from the Socialist Labor Party of
Holland which, having made an inquest in Germany, reported that the condition of the working class there was
"unbearable, desperate, and the cause of regrettable ex-
cesses. The lack of the most necessary foods brings about
a most frightful mortality, especially among children, old
men and pregnant women." [65]

Most of the press accepted the affair as proof, on the one
hand, that the conditions across the Rhine were not so serious as painted, and, on the other, that the danger of German
resistance to the Allies was as threatening as ever. Almost

no notice was taken of the report made public by an English Commission, which stated that Germany must be fed at once.[66] The *Temps* (March 9) actually argued that "in breaking the pourparlers . . . this official [Braun] has proved that the food crisis is not so tragic beyond the Rhine. . . . The German papers ought to admit that the Spa gesture gives the lie to all of their sinister predictions." This statement, however, ignored the fact that the initiative in making the break came from the Allies, not from the enemy delegates.[67]

Statements coming from the Quai d'Orsay to the effect that of course the Allies did not want to starve Germany, but that they would not be dictated to by her, were carried with great approval throughout most of the press. "The Allies cannot allow Germany to dictate conditions" were prominent headlines in Left Wing organs.[68] It was re-assuringly stated that France had too much outstanding in Germany to let her starve, even apart from humanitarian considerations.[69] "We are too humane to let her perish of hunger," said the *Matin* (March 9). But a strong policy was, in almost all quarters, considered essential. "The Germans are defeated and must know it," said the *Débats* (March 10), expressing the prevailing sentiment of the patriotic press. Under a title "Pity for the Hangmen", the *Phare* of Nantes (March 10) denounced the "soft creatures who cry out for mercy toward the Germans, their women and children". Painting a gruesome picture of German atrocities, it concluded: "ask us anything, but not that we should pity them." [70]

Official and semi-official statements from the Supreme Council seemed anxious to give the public the impression of an adamantine attitude toward the enemy. "The Allies would not put up with the demands of Germany." "The Supreme Council has decided to maintain its instructions, and to hold to the terms of the January 16 armistice." "The Allies repulse the German pretensions." Such were the semi-official notes appearing in the press.[71] Actually, the

Supreme Council was engaged in making important compromises, and in conceding, to a degree, the validity of the German contentions. On March 8 the Supreme Economic Council reported to the Supreme War Council on the subject, recommending that Germany, in return for handing over her ships, be guaranteed a specified quantity of foodstuffs.

Lloyd George was of the opinion (contrary to his opinion expressed February 7) that the "honour of the Allies" was involved in the revictualling of Germany. "Under the terms of the Armistice," he said, "the Allies did imply that they meant to let food into Germany. . . . But so far not a single ton of food had been sent. . . . The fishing fleet had even been prevented from going out to catch a few herrings. . . . The Allies were sowing hatred for the future. . . . The British troops were indignant about our refusal to revictual Germany." General Plumer had said that he could not be responsible for his troops if children were allowed to wander about the streets half-starving. Bolshevism threatened. "Six weeks ago the same arguments about gold and foreign securities had been raised, and it had then been decided that Germany should be given food."

Clemenceau denied that the honor of the Allies was involved, though agreeing that food should be sent "as soon as possible". "In the Armistice," he said, "no promise had ever been made to feed Germany." Balfour, however, thought "that almost a promise had been made". When Klotz intervened, asking that Germany be not allowed to pay for the foodstuffs in gold or by the sale or use, as collateral, of foreign securities, Lloyd George accused the French Finance Minister of spreading Bolshevism.

Clemenceau exclaimed "that his country had been ruined and ravaged, . . . over two million men had lost their lives . . . and yet what guarantees had France that anything would be received in payment for all this destruction? She merely possessed a few pieces of gold, a few securities, which it was now proposed to take away in order to pay those who

would supply food to Germany, and that food would certainly not come from France. In a word, he was being asked
to betray his country. . . ." [72] French consent was finally
given to a resolution stating, in effect, that in return for
Germany's acknowledgment of her obligations under the
January Armistice, the Allied representatives would proceed
with plans for revictualling.

It was on this basis that a bargain was struck, March 14,
at Brussels. Germany was to receive 370,000 tons of foodstuffs per month, up to September, in return for which her
merchant ships were to be handed over to the Allies, and
Germany was, along with certain other arrangements, to
guarantee payment by a deposit of £7,000,000 gold in the
National Bank of Brussels. [73]

Meantime, Secretary Lansing had sought to reduce the
intransigence of French opposition by a speech, March 11,
at a dinner given to the American delegation by the French
Foreign Press Club. He shrewdly argued for a quick peace
and for the shipment of food to the enemy. "We have
reached a crisis in the affairs of the world," he said. "We
must meet it without passion and without permitting our
judgment to be warped by a natural and unavoidable desire
for vengeance on a nation which has committed such atrocities as those the Germans committed. . . . Two words
explain the situation: food and peace. In order that Germany shall be able to resist anarchy and the hideous despot-
ism of the red terror, she must be able to procure food."
Raw materials, he thought, would also have to be furnished.
"It is not out of pity for the Germans that this ought to be
done, and done without delay; but because we, the conquerors in the war, would be the chief sufferers if that were
not done", for otherwise, he added, Germany would not be
able to pay her obligations.

Such a carefully weighed pronouncement by Lansing, who
was personally highly respected in all French circles, could
not fail to win over a few adherents to his point of view. [74]
The extreme Left needed no converting, and naturally found

it highly gratifying. *Humanité* (March 13) offered it to the
meditations of those "who each day cover us with insults".
Scattered comment from the moderate Left gave it mild
approval, though most of them, including *Œuvre,* failed to
comment. "Mr. Lansing poses the question of German revictualling as it ought to be posed," said the *Populaire de
Nantes.*[75] Several important organs of the conservative
press seemed to be converted, though a great many, especially of the Center, refrained from comment.[76] The Right
Wing journals, for the most part, were untouched by Lansing's words. It was said that though "bread and peace"
were necessities, if the Germans were fed first, there would
be no peace.[77] Lansing was twitted for "believing the Germans" when they said they had no food.[78] It was predicted
that there would be trouble, and that the French people
would be saying: "It is because America is sending its prod-
ucts into Germany that we are paying so dearly for food."[79]

The *Écho de Paris* made no comment on the speech, de-
voting its leader to the subject: "The Tunnel Under the
Channel." The *Temps* (March 13) showed that it, too, was
unconvinced. After a personal tribute to Lansing, and without disputing his statements as to the threat of chaos, or of
the necessity of sending food, it raised serious questions
as to the fundamental cause of the chaos. It was not lack of
foodstuffs. That played "only an incidental rôle in Germany". It was not lack of raw materials. That was "only
a local cause of unemployment". There was something else.
"As Hamlet said: 'There is something rotten'. Germany is
afflicted with a moral crisis which one cannot cure with
portions of victuals, or with bales of cotton."

The Brussels agreement of March 14 having once been
signed, moderate opinion was disposed to make the most of
an unsatisfactory situation, and the heavy press treated the
result as a "capitulation" by Germany[80] in the face of an
Allied ultimatum. The moderate press as a whole followed
this lead, and, though there was but slight comment, the
news articles assumed that Germany bowed to Allied de-

mands. The fact that the Allies had actually abandoned their intransigent position of early March, was not, however, ignored by journals of the Right, for whom it was gall and wormwood, especially when coupled with the concessions which France had so unwillingly made to Great Britain and the United States in the matter of payment. "Something has been accomplished," it was said, "an important achievement—but in favor of Germany." [81] "We are going to feed the Boche. But what about Northern France?" [82] The reports of German distress were still heavily discounted; [83] and the Entente Powers were harshly criticized for negotiating with Germany rather than dictating to her. [84] The financial arrangement was criticized as being very disadvantageous for France, and more profitable for Great Britain and the United States. [85] Occasional protests came from the Left; [86] and the *Temps* (March 20) harped on the familiar refrain that Germany was suffering, not from a lack of food, but from a "lack of morality".

3. DISARMAMENT OF GERMANY

If the "Eternal Danger" from across the Rhine were to be mitigated, the problem of Germany's military establishment could not be ignored. Hence, one of the most insistent demands arising out of the February crisis was that her military strength should be so reduced that Germany would be rendered "incapable of doing harm". This was viewed as an indispensable preliminary to French security. It had been anticipated that the renewed Armistice would go a long way toward the achievement of this goal, but when the terms of the new Armistice were made public, it was realized that this objective had not been attained. Indeed, the terms made no mention of disarmament. The Allies simply set up a procedure which would permit them to demand disarmament, by means of a three-day ultimatum. The reason for this was that the Wilson-Balfour plan, adopted February 12, proposed to draw up, as quickly as possible, the final military, naval and air terms to be presented to Germany as a sort of "definitive armistice", or preliminary treaty. The promise that this objective would soon be consummated served to offset somewhat the disappointment arising from that particular gap in the new Armistice.

Marshal Foch, having been asked on his return from the armistice negotiations at Spa, to proceed at once to elaborate the definitive military terms, drafted the Committee report toward the end of February and laid it before the Supreme Council March 3. The debate on its terms was joined March 6. The clash of policies at this time had to do chiefly with the question of the basis of recruiting for the German military forces, and, closely connected with this, the question of the size of these forces. The difference of opinion lay primarily between the French and British. Foch favored an army of 200,000, recruited annually. Lloyd George criticized this as permitting the passing through the army of 200,000 men every year, creating a trained force of 2,000,000 in ten years. Foch thought this not so important, relatively, since "staffs" would be limited.[87] However, Lloyd George insisted on voluntary enlistment for all branches of the service, with a minimum period of service of twelve years for all ranks. He was willing to leave the numbers at 200,000. In spite of French insistence that "the long-term voluntary army would make Germany far stronger than a short-term conscript army", Lloyd George was adamant. "He would never agree," he said, "to an army raised in Germany by short conscript service."[88]

On March 10 the revised proposals came before the Council, with the recommendation of the Drafting Committee that since the basis of enlistment had been changed, the numbers should be reduced to 140,000—that being the presumed equivalent, on a long-term service basis, of a 200,000 army on a short-term conscript basis. Marshal Foch then intervened, however, insisting that "if Germany were really to be limited to a mere police force, then 100,000 would be enough". General Bliss and Secretary Lansing both upheld the Committee report, arguing that "safety could not well

be ensured with less than 140,000", and pointing to "the
spirit of disintegration at work in Germany". Lloyd George
soon came around to the revised French point of view, and
agreement was finally reached on the basis of an army of
100,000.[89]

As between the Lloyd George plan for a long-term service
army and the Foch plan for a short-term conscript system,
French public opinion showed a slight preference for the
British Premier's program, especially after the figures had
been reduced to 100,000. But with the progress of events,
it became increasingly clear that neither system was really
satisfactory to the majority of French people. Diverse and
conflicting factors, each apparently valid in itself, played
upon their thinking and cut across the normal groupings of
opinion, so that classification along normal lines becomes
difficult. The precedent of 1806 and its aftermath argued
strongly against the short-term conscript system. Prussia,
having been limited by Napoleon as to the size of its army,
passed successive contingents of recruits rapidly through a
short period of service, thus building up a much larger
trained personnel than was anticipated by the limitation
provisions. The memory of these events apparently weighed
more heavily with the general public than with the French
General Staff, for it was Foch who had proposed to adopt
again the short-term system for Germany, and it was the
British Premier who had intervened against it. Journals
from Right to Left, without particular regard to political
grouping, approved the modified program, and provincial
opinion seemed especially pleased with the change. Lloyd
George was praised, and the British were complimented on
their clearness of vision.[90]

On the other hand, there were undoubtedly strong arguments against the long-term system. There was the question
of staffs—*cadres*. Would not a standing army, even though
small, make it possible to build a well-organized, highly
trained framework into which a much larger army could be

fitted if the occasion offered itself? This was universally viewed as a serious danger, and tended, to a considerable extent, to counterbalance the fears raised by the precedent of 1806. The leading organs, especially of Paris, feared a "trap" in the system of *cadres,* and in this matter they felt that Foch had shown considerable wisdom. The *Temps* (March 8) expressed a widespread misgiving in saying that "The Prussian General Staff would make of every soldier a future officer or non-commissioned officer"; and this opinion came equally from the Left.[91]

There was also the possibility, unwelcome to many, that the new basis envisaged for the German army might upset the French conscript system. Would it not strike at its very roots? This eventuality would have been pleasing to Royalist opinion on the extreme Right, which had constantly advocated a return to the professional army system.[92] But a change of this character was disturbing to faithful Republicans, for, was not a professional standing army historically a pliant tool for a *coup d'état?* [93] Opinion in advanced liberal circles acclaimed the military set-up prescribed for Germany on the ground that it was the first step toward ridding the world of the conscript system; [94] but conservative commentators, for the most part, viewed this feature with forebodings as to possible results.[95]

There was a powerful current of distrust of both systems, and a growing feeling that Germany would find a way to evade the consequences of either régime. As pointed out by the *Temps* (March 8), a small army, on long-term basis would permit the building of a framework for a much larger army, but it was no less true that the short-term conscript army would enable Prussia to put millions of men through the barracks. Either alternative was objectionable, and various other safeguards were suggested. One widely supported proposal was to deny armed contingents to the Reich as a whole, and to permit them only to the various states.[96]

Another, which seemed indispensable to most Frenchmen,

was that rigid control of indefinite duration should be established over German factories capable of making munitions. All hope of setting up any such control over German arms manufacture was blasted at a session of the Supreme War Council, March 17, when President Wilson refused to accept the report of the Military Commission which failed to fix limits to the Allied control over Germany, and required, among other things, "the notification [by Germany] of all orders to the Allies". The President objected, saying that "if the Allied armies were to be maintained forever in order to control the carrying out of the Peace Terms, not peace, but Allied domination would have to be established".[97] This intervention was decisive. Lloyd George concurred in the President's view, and the military control was restricted to the period covering the enactment of the necessary legislation in Germany.[98]

This action of the Supreme Council received a hostile welcome from patriotic opinion, which agreed that the proposed limitation provisions would be promptly evaded. "One can imagine the smile which this clause will cause among the enemies," said one.[99] Germany would consider the treaty another "scrap of paper", said another; [100] and the *Temps* hammered on the idea, expressed by many, that "We shall have only a temporary guarantee if we do not exercise permanent control." [101]

The episode further stimulated demands for the total disarmament of Germany. For some time this idea had been gaining headway. The extreme Left groups had from the beginning supported the total disarmament program in the hope that it would be the first step toward universalizing this principle. The fixing of a definite quota for Germany, as proposed by the Supreme Council, was condemned as "an artificial limitation" which would postpone indefinitely the realization of general disarmament. "Where then," it was asked, "are the snows of yesteryear, and the Fourteen Points that were accepted unreservedly by all the belligerents?" [102]

But there were others who, without other motives than the immediate safety of France, urged the total disarmament of Germany. This included practically all of the Radical Socialists in the Chamber of Deputies, and scattered support from the Right. The results of the deliberations of the Supreme Council had been so unsatisfactory, even to moderate opinion, that the matter was finally brought before the Chamber and a debate was precipitated by Raynaud, of the Radical Socialists, who presented a resolution, signed by 223 of his colleagues, and adopted unanimously by the Commissions on the Army and on Foreign Affairs. The purport of the resolution was that Germany should have "purely and simply police forces necessary for the maintenance of order, but no army"; [103] and the police forces were to be allowed only to the respective states. The Chamber was enthusiastic for the resolution, but the matter was not permitted by the government to come to a vote. The Foreign Minister assured the Chamber that the government was inspired by "the same thought as the authors of the proposal", and that it would endeavor to achieve the "principle of the ideas" involved, but that a full-dress debate on the matter could not be permitted, since the question was still before the Peace Conference.[104] In that body, however, the military proposals already adopted remained practically unchanged.

The "problem of Germany" could not be solved by halting, halfway measures, whether applied to armistice terms, food and raw materials policy or military provisions. Yet an overwrought, highly suspicious and ill-informed French public would scarcely permit its government to pursue a far-sighted policy with regard to any of these. Nor could a policy acceptable to patriotic French opinion be fitted into the context of policies acceptable to France's war-time allies and associates. The "problem" was therefore destined to drag on throughout the Conference and into the post-war world.

NOTES

[1] September 30, 1918.

[2] *Temps,* October 10.

[3] *Intransigeant,* November 22.

[4] *Gaulois,* November 15.

[5] *Radical,* November 15, 19.

[6] December 4, 23, 25.

[7] *Annales de la Chambre,* December 27, 1918, p. 3249. Occasional voices on the extreme Left were raised in behalf of the struggling Republican régime. Sembat, in the Socialistic *Heure* (Nov. 16), wrote that it was simple stupidity to regard the German revolution as mere "camouflage", and remarked further that, "The strength and violence of the popular movement which is shaking Germany to its base are such that the very people who speak of camouflage frighten us the next day by holding out the threat of Bolshevism. . . ." This remark was appropriate, for the stories of threatening famine and Bolshevism coming out of Germany were, by some of the conservative press, discounted as being further proof of German strategy in the interest of a softer peace, while others used them to emphasize the danger of Bolshevism, and therefore as an argument for stronger guarantees against Germany. E.g., *Temps,* repeatedly during December. On January 10 it argued that Russian Bolshevism was financing the German Revolution. The official Socialist press was very sympathetic, though it lacked complete assurance as to the *bona fides* of the Revolution. E.g., *Humanité,* November 13, 1918.

[8] *Current Summaries,* January 27, 1919.

[9] *France de Bordeaux,* January 24; *Populaire de Nantes,* February 2; *Progrès* of Lyons, February 4.

[10] January 23. See also *Petit Provençal,* January 24 and *Œuvre,* January 30.

[11] E.g., *Figaro, Rappel,* and *Journal,* January 22; *Avenir* and *Petite République,* January 23.

[12] *Écho de Paris,* January 28. The fight against the Spartacists in the streets of Berlin was said to be "only a curtain behind which to prepare revenge". *Progrès de la Somme,* January 29. Germany was becoming "more centralized than ever". *Écho de Paris,* January 29. The choice of Weimar as a meeting place for the Constituent Assembly was a "symbol of the dream of Germany's union against France". *Petit Marseillais,* January 30. "The watchword throughout Germany is 'To divide the Allies'." *Homme Libre,* January 27. "Germany remains menacing." "War-like Germany is raising her head." *Action Française,* January 25, February 1. "Take care! We must expect to be faced before long with a Germany reconstituted politically, if not indeed militarily. . . . Hun democracy is becoming daily more aggressive. . . ." *Homme Libre,* January 30. "Germany will not accept defeat." "The Free German people" continue the work of the old dynasty. *Figaro,* February 7, 8. Such were typical phrases broadcast by practically all except the Socialist papers in the two weeks following the German elections.

[13] *Matin,* February 7.

[14] *Petit Journal,* February 8.

[15] *Écho de Paris,* February 8.

[16] February 10.

[17] February 10.

[18] February 8.

[19] Miller Diary, vol. xiv, p. 236.

[20] *Ibid.,* pp. 279 *et seq.*

[21] *Ibid.,* pp. 236 *et seq.*

[22] Baker, *op. cit.,* vol. i, p. 153.

[23] *Homme Libre,* February 10.

[24] *Figaro,* February 10.

[25] February 12.

[26] February 12.

[27] *Petit Marseillais,* February 12.

[28] *Petite Gironde,* February 12.

[29] *Phare* of Nantes, February 12.

[30] *Liberté,* February 12.

[31] The fact that fears of almost identical character were expressed by such papers as the *Œuvre* (Feb. 13) and *France Libre* (Feb. 11) showed how general, as well as genuine, this state of public feeling had become.

[32] It was this editorial blast which caused Wilson to threaten to move the seat of the Peace Conference.

[33] The *Gaulois* (Feb. 12) dubbed the President a "philosopher and apostle", averring that his schemes were based on those conceived in 1915 when he considered that there should be neither victors nor vanquished in the war.

[34] *Homme Libre,* February 11.

[35] *Humanité* and *Vérité,* February 9.

[36] After all, we still "hold the enemy by the belly," said the *Pays. Allied Press,* vol. v, no. 15, February 19. "Without the purchase of raw materials . . . the Germans could do absolutely nothing," said another. *France de Bordeaux,* February 12.

[37] Miller Diary, vol. xiv, p. 379.

[38] *Temps,* February 14.

[39] *Humanité,* February 13.

[40] *Current Summaries,* February 13; *Temps,* February 14.

[41] *Victoire,* February 13.

[42] *Matin,* February 13.

[43] *Matin,* February 14.

[44] Rathenau, in *Matin,* February 12; Heinrich, *ibid.,* February 13; Scheidemann, in *Journal,* February 14.

[45] See *Current Summaries,* February 13 to 17, 1919.

[46] "The revolution . . . has an authorized air," said the *Dépêche* of Toulouse (Feb. 25). The *Temps* (Feb. 19) expressed the overwhelming feeling of the press in saying: "Formerly it was a question of forcing Germany to keep her promises. Now it is necessary to obligate her to keep the promise that she would keep her promises." "The renewal of the Armistice is not a deliverance to celebrate: it is simply a lesson to meditate, a work to continue."

[47] *Écho de Paris,* November 24, 1918.

[48] *Dépêche* de Lille, November 14.

[49] *House Papers,* vol. iv, p. 254.

[50] Minutes of Supreme Council, January 13, 1919, B. C. 1-A.

[51] Temperley, H. W. V. (ed.), *A History of the Peace Conference,* 6 vols. (London, 1920), vol. i, p. 479.

[52] Minutes of Supreme Council, January 13, 1919. B. C. 1-A.

[53] Baker, *op. cit.,* vol. ii, p. 40. Mr. Hoover was here referring to Article 26 of the November Armistice which stated: "The Allies and the United States contemplate the provisioning of Germany during the Armistice as shall be found necessary." Temperley, *op. cit.,* p. 468.

[54] Minutes of Supreme Council, February 7, 1919, Miller Diary, vol. xiv, pp. 236 *et seq.*

[55] *Action Française,* January 25, 26.

[56] *Petite Gironde,* January 26.

[57] *Temps,* February 18.

[58] *Gaulois* and *Figaro,* March 5.

[59] *Écho de Paris,* January 21.

[60] *Temps,* February 12.

[61] *House Papers,* vol. iv, p. 355.

[62] *Temps,* March 9.

[63] *Current Summaries,* March 8, 9; *Ouest-Éclair, Petite Gironde, Phare,* March 9.

[64] The *Populaire de Nantes* (March 10), even more advanced in its views, wrote that Germany would have to change her tune.

[65] March 9. The *France Libre* (March 8), somewhat farther to the right, joined in blaming the Allies for their attitude.

[66] See *France Libre,* March 8, which did call attention to it.

[67] The official French statement, while denying that the blame lay on French shoulders, admitted that the Allies were solidary with Admiral Hope in making the rupture. *Temps,* March 9, 1919.

[68] E.g., *Petit Provençal, Populaire de Nantes, France de Bordeaux,* March 9.

[69] *Figaro,* March 9; *Populaire de Nantes,* March 9, 10.

[70] Hope was expressed by the *Petite Gironde* (March 9) that the Spa episode would serve as a lesson to the Allies.

[71] *Temps,* March 9, 10.

[72] Miller Diary, vol. xv, pp. 258-281.

[73] Paris *Daily Mail,* March 16.

[74] See *Allied Press,* vol. v, no. 20, March 26, 1919.

[75] March 12. *Petit Provençal,* March 14, said, "strictly necessary food— no more".

[76] The *Débats* (March 13) said that of course it was desirable that Germany should escape from anarchy, and that the Allies should help her to do so. *Victoire* (March 13) favored feeding Germany, lest worse befall. *Homme Libre* gave qualified approval.

[77] *Phare,* March 14.

[78] *Journal de Rouen,* March 13.

[79] *Gaulois,* March 13. "Misplaced Tenderness," shouted another head-

line, in warning against the "humanitarian compassions of Mr. Lansing". *Nouvelliste de Lyon*, March 13.

[80] *Matin, Journal, Petit Parisien, Petit Journal,* March 16.

[81] *Nouvelliste de Lyon,* March 17.

[82] *Ouest-Éclair,* March 16.

[83] *Figaro,* March 16; *Journal de Rouen,* March 19.

[84] *Phare* of Nantes, March 19; *Écho de Paris,* March 18.

[85] *Écho de Paris,* March 18.

[86] *France de Bordeaux,* March 19, said, "They are without gratitude."

[87] Miller Diary, vol. xv, pp. 179 *et seq.*

[88] *Ibid.,* pp. 244 *et seq.*

[89] *Ibid.,* p. 288. An interesting sidelight on the general armaments situation, and on French policy, was thrown at this time by Balfour, who pointed out that there was no general plan for disarmament, and "that if Germany was held to 100,000, while France, Poland and Bohemia could have as many as they wished", Germany would say that "the Allied Powers were leaving them at the mercy even of their small neighbors". He suggested the need of some guarantee to Germany, if she were left thus defenceless. Clemenceau, however, thought this a matter which might be left to the League of Nations—"one of whose functions was to prevent sudden aggression by any of its members". *Ibid.,* p. 292.

[90] *Journal de Rouen,* and *Phare,* March 8; *Petit Marseillais,* March 12; *Figaro,* March 11; *Homme Libre,* March 12; *Pays,* March 13, 1919.

[91] "The sergeants of Scheidemann will constitute excellent staffs, instantly adaptable to a levy *en masse*," said *Europe Nouvelle* (March 15). See also *Intransigeant,* March 8; *Matin, Journal, Œuvre, Petit Provençal,* March 9; *Écho de Paris,* March 7; *Débats,* March 19.

[92] *Action Française,* March 13, 1919.

[93] *Populaire* (March 13), which favored the abolition of all armies, thought that as between the two systems, the "national army", based on conscription, was better than the long-term army, because it was "less servile".

[94] E.g., the *Pays* (March 13) enthusiastically remarked that "the disarmament of Germany has for its . . . corollary the disarmament of the whole world, and *the armament of the League of Nations*". This latter aspiration was doomed to disappointment.

[95] *Allied Press,* vol. v, no. 19; March 19; vol. v, no. 20, March 26.

[96] *Temps,* March 8; *Europe Nouvelle,* March 15; *Œuvre,* March 9.

[97] Miller Diary, vol. xv, p. 369.

[98] Later, the jurisdiction of the League was added. See Art. 213 of Treaty with Germany.

[99] *Intransigeant,* March 19.

[100] *Gaulois,* March 18; *Écho de Paris,* March 18.

[101] March 19. *Écho de Paris,* March 18, thought the merit of the control was that the collective surveillance would "perpetuate our alliance".

[102] March 12, 16. Also *Heure,* March 12; *Vérité,* March 9.

[103] *Annales de la Chambre,* April 3, 1919, p. 1525.

[104] *Ibid.,* p. 1525; *Journal,* April 4; *Temps,* April 5.

CHAPTER VI

REPARATIONS AND THE SAAR BASIN

"There shall be no annexations, no contributions, no punitive damages."
(Woodrow Wilson, in Address of February 11, 1918.)

"To make certain her safety was the first duty of France. To secure reparation was her second."
(Tardieu, *The Truth About the Treaty*, p. 280.)

"We must establish clearly and energetically our right to an indemnity, to a heavy indemnity (applause), and one that will have a privileged position."
A Senator on the Left: "These are the words for which we were waiting!"
(Ribot, to French Senate, December 17, 1918.)

1. REPARATIONS: ANTICIPATIONS

ALTHOUGH the reparations problem took second rank in ultimate importance to France, as compared with that of general security, it was capable, at times, of stirring even deeper feelings; and it occupied probably more of the time of the Conference than any other single question. Like the problems of the Saar Basin and the Left Bank, it came to a head during the latter days of March, and contributed its share to producing the major crisis of the Conference.

Before the Conference had come to grips with this matter, however, public sentiment in France, except for a minority on the extreme Left, had become crystallized into a concerted and inflexible demand that crushing and even fabulous sums be extracted from Germany. The sentiment of the post-Armistice period contrasted sharply with that which had preceded. At any rate, public expressions of opinion after the Armistice became markedly more exacting in character. The demand for heavy reparations from Germany was by no means new. It was a familiar member of the trilogy: "Restitutions, Reparations, Guarantees." During the months preceding the Armistice, however, the assumption was that this demand was governed by the principles asserted in President Wilson's Fourteen Points, Article Eight of which provided that "All French territory should be freed and the invaded portions restored. . . ." Reparations, in other words, meant that payment should be made by Germany for the direct damage and destruction arising from her belligerent acts. The principle had not been questioned. Hence there remained, presumably, but to fix the method of ascertaining the amount to be paid. On this point the Socialists alone had taken a definite stand, advocating an "impartial inquiry" for appraising the merits of claims, and fixing totals.[1]

The pre-Armistice negotiations between the Allies and the United States over the question of accepting President Wilson's program as the basis of the peace, did not, apparently, change the meaning of the reparations article of the Fourteen Points. In his note to Germany of November 5, the President called attention to the understanding of the Allies "that compensation will be made by Germany for all damage done to the civilian population of the Allies and their property by the aggression of Germany by land, by sea and from the air".[2] This was an even more explicit statement of Germany's liability for direct damage due to her belligerent activities, and as Gabriel Terrail says, it did not enlarge the interpretation, "it simply prevented the meaning of the word 'restoration', as spoken and written by Wilson, from being restricted".[3] The *Œuvre* (Nov. 7) drew the implication that no war indemnity would be claimed.

The terms of the Armistice itself, however, seemed to point in a somewhat different direction. Not only did that instrument, at Clemenceau's behest, make specific reference to reparations, but, on Klotz's insistence, Article Nineteen carried a significant reservation to the effect that "any future claims and demands of the Allies and the United States of America remain unaffected" by the other financial terms.[4] The meaning and effect of this formula were warmly debated later in the Conference, and interpretations by the public differed even at the time of the Armistice. The *Temps* (Nov. 13), which doubtless correctly interpreted the intentions of Klotz, asserted that the way was left open for "payments which would have rather the character of an indemnity than that of reparation", while the *Progrès* of Lyons claimed (Nov. 15) that it meant merely to assert the principle of reparation for damages, with the reservation that later the totals due and the methods of payment would be made known.[5]

In any case, public opinion was soon prepared to give the broadest possible interpretation to the "reparations" principle. The activities of press and parliament alike combined to bring about this result. On November 16 the *Matin* launched a campaign which it pursued with relentless vigor throughout the crucial stages of the peace parleys. Five days after the Armistice it felt competent to draw up the bill of German indebtedness and to assert: "GERMANY OWES FRANCE AT LEAST 340 BILLIONS." All the items making up this staggering total of nearly seventy billions of dollars due to France alone were but applications of "the admirable principles accepted by the nations at war, and formulated by President Wilson". The itemized statement of account was given:[6]

1.	Debt of 1870, with interest of 5%	60 billions (fr.)	
2.	Expenses of the war	140	"
3.	Pensions	40	"
4.	Reparations for damages	100	"
	Total	340 billions	

When Sir Eric Geddes, in late November, assessed the total Allied bill against Germany at 1,250 billions of francs (250 billions of dollars), and suggested that Germany could not pay all of it without causing injury to labor conditions in Allied countries, the *Matin* (Dec. 1) took the British minister severely to task. Sir Eric's fears were "incomprehensible". "How could Germany injure any class of the popula-

tion in paying for what she had destroyed?" The idea of
hesitating over the question whether Germany could pay
or whether the Allies could wisely receive payment was
anathema. "Who up to now has paid the 1,250 billions that
Germany owes to the Allies? Is it the enemy, or is it ourselves?" It might be admitted, in passing, that Germany
could not pay off the debt. But this was irrelevant. The
important thing was to force the enemy to recognize the
debt, for "the insolvent debtor remains a debtor by reason
of the single fact that he recognizes his debt". After the
debt had been recognized, the interest of which would be
62½ billions of francs each year, the Allies could take coun-
sel and decide each year how much of this sum they would
demand. Sir Eric should recall "the noble words of the
great world citizen, Wilson", who had declared: " 'Germany
will make restitution, Germany will make reparation'. . . .
Today, Sir Eric Geddes, you tell us that Germany owes us
1,250 billions. Why did the Germans declare war? Why
have the Germans forced us to spend these fabulous sums?
Sir Eric Geddes, who should pay the 1,250 billions?" If the
bill was a heavy one, then, "So much the worse for Germany."

Other important organs joined with the *Matin* in pressing
this campaign. The *Intransigeant,* of the Center, and the
Liberté and *Action Française,* of the Right were equally
vigorous. The *Liberté,* strongly supporting *Matin's* initia-
tives, differed only in feeling that the indemnities suggested
were inadequate. They should also have included a *penal*
indemnity, it thought, because of the violation by Germany
of her treaty obligations.[7] *Action Française* blithely asserted that Germany could pay an annuity of twenty-five
billion francs (about five billion dollars) every year for
forty years, and to the suggestion that Germany could not
pay the bill, it replied "Germany MUST pay." [8] On November 28 it reported that public opinion was "making
progress in craving wider and wider reparations", and on
December 4, it reported further progress.

The *Matin's* colleagues of the heavy press (the *Petit Parisien, Journal, Petit Journal,* and *Écho de Paris*) did not join actively in the campaign, though they gave it their sanction, and reported with approval the various developments. The *Temps* and *Débats* associated themselves with it even more closely. Having earlier suggested (as above noted) that the way was open to indemnities, the *Temps* (Nov. 29) frankly adopted a list clearly incompatible with the Wilson principles. Referring with approval to an article in the *Revue Politique et Parlementaire* on this subject, it listed the items which it agreed should be included as bases, among which were: (a) Material damages of every kind, direct and indirect, positive and negative, whether or not capable of being precisely defined; (b) the charges of the national debt; pensions and indemnities for victims of the war. "The capital value of all the lives sacrificed and all the human energies ruined." "These," said the *Temps,* "are the bases for the indispensable calculations." Furthermore, it agreed, "strict justice" would add a penal responsibility, which should be translated into "a supplementary indemnity".

Most of these journals concerned themselves with the method by which Germany would acquit herself of the gigantic obligations envisaged. The *Liberté,* in repeated articles, suggested ways and means, which were generally approved in other Center and Right Wing organs. Germany's public and private fortune, which, it said, was estimated at between five and six hundred billion francs, would be placed under a servitude. Long annuities and control of all public revenues would be necessary. Taxes would be levied on all German manufactures, on exports, and on railways, and her mineral resources would be mortgaged. Germany would pay in cash, in labor and in raw materials.[9] The *Débats* (Dec. 5) demanded the exaction of reparations, "up to the last centime", and carried with approval a long article analyzing the various German resources available. "It is not to our advantage to prevent them from breathing:

but the surplus above this minimum ought to come to us," was the conclusion.[10]

The adoption of the "war costs" plank at this time by the British government in its election campaign, played upon the situation in France, and encouraged pre-existing trends. Lloyd George's statements that Germany would pay the cost of the war up to the limit of her capacity, was widely quoted with approval, except that objection was sometimes expressed to raising the question of capacity. Everywhere it was recognized that the terrible totals would require a considerable period of time for payment. But, said Péret, in the *Petit Journal* (Dec. 3), "let the Boche work and carry the burden for many years to come. He wanted the war. Let him pay for it." This element of time was stressed by the *Écho de Paris* as an argument for the necessity of tightening the bonds of alliance between the victorious powers.[11]

In liberal and radical circles questions were raised as to the wisdom and justice of the exorbitant claims that were being built up. It was a bad piece of work, thought the *Œuvre* (Dec. 2), which charged that the *Matin* and its colleagues, with the best of intentions, were preparing the French people for serious disillusionment; since naïve readers would be led to expect fortunes to drop in their laps from Germany. The *Heure* (Nov. 19) rebuked those responsible for the campaign. Now that the enemy was beaten, it said, France was forgetting its promises and tearing up its engagements. Reparations had, during the war, been interpreted as meaning damages resulting from invasion. "When these engagements were taken nobody, or hardly anybody, considered them insufficient. Why should they be denied today?" There was, however, no disposition either in liberal or Socialist circles, to deny Germany's obligation to make reparation for damages caused. Reparation for damage done in the invaded regions was a matter of "simple justice", said *Humanité* (Nov. 20), and Cachin, in the Chamber of Deputies, said "certainly, reparations will be necessary. We are in agreement. President Wilson also." [12] Much Radical Socialist sentiment, however, was favorable to the thesis of those who were preaching "billions and trillions" up to the limit of German capacity. The *Dépêche* of Toulouse, noting with approval the Lloyd George campaign in England, wrote that "without indemnities . . . France would be ruined for centuries". Germany must pay "to the limit of its capacity", or otherwise, "Germany wins the war in losing it, and the word 'justice' has no meaning." [13]

The developments in Parliament contributed further to the growing expectation of fabulous payments by Germany. Finance Minister Klotz, in announcing to the Chamber, on December 3, the success of another loan, openly encouraged this anticipation. He referred with approval to Lloyd George's statement that Germany would have to pay the cost of the war to the limit of its capacity, and to Clemenceau's earlier statement that, "The most terrible of accounts between peoples" had been opened, and assured the Chamber that the French people were not to be called upon for further taxation at that time. The Finance Minister felt it his "sacred duty" first to draw up the list of reparations and restitutions to be demanded from the enemy. The Chamber could then say "whether it intends to make our country pay the costs of the war or to make the responsible party pay them". [14] The *Journal* (Dec. 4), commenting on the session, noted that the Chamber showed by its renewed applause that it had "no hesitation in that respect". From the Socialist benches, however, the charge was appropriately hurled at Klotz, that his policy consisted in saying, "We shall await the peace, and make the enemy pay." [15] At any rate, "Make Germany pay First" became the slogan which was publicly accepted as characterizing the policy of the Clemenceau ministry.

The parliamentary debates later in the month lent further encouragement to this growing demand. Dubois of the Right argued in the Chamber that the reservation inserted in Article Nineteen of the Armistice implied that reparations demands were absolutely unrestricted,[16] while Ribot, member of the moderate Left Wing of the Senate, pointed to the totals of France's indebtedness and argued that heavy indemnities were the only solution. Not only must France obtain from Germany the heaviest possible indemnity, but France's claims must have a preferred place among the various categories of payments which Germany would have to make. Furthermore, "If the resources which we find on the other side of the Rhine are insufficient . . . it is the duty of the Allies to . . . examine the state of their resources and see whether it is not strict justice . . . to pool at least a part of the charges of the debt and the resources which must serve to pay for it." [17]

The activities of the Commission of the Budget, and the debates in Parliament during February and March revealed an alarming condition of French finances; with the result that public feeling was even more deeply stirred. On February 18, Klotz appeared before the Commission of the Budget and was asked for a statement as to how the budget of eighteen billions, or more, was to be met. In reply, the Finance Minister said he preferred not to deal in definite figures, but would state only general principles. The totality of the debt was to be demanded of the enemy; a privileged position was to be demanded for certain French claims (reparations for damages, for instance); a financial section of the League of Nations was to be formed, it was hoped; a policy of close inter-Allied financial cooperation was to be pursued; the French tax-payer was not, at that time, to be called upon for more than was necessary to balance the immediate budget, but later a tax on capital was to be imposed, with payments spread over a number of years.[18]

The suggestion of the probability of a levy on capital was sufficient to underscore the seriousness of the situation, and the vagueness of the Finance Minister's statements gave further occasion for alarm. A feeling of disillusionment was beginning to take possession of the Budget Commission. Its report of February 27 expressed profound dissatisfaction with the government's planlessness, and entered an emphatic reservation on the project for a capital levy. This feeling was further emphasized by its insistence that "justice as well as interest demands . . . the pooling, by the Allied and Associated Powers, of all their war expenses".[19]

In the Chamber debates on March 7, 11, 12, and 13, discontent was rife. On all hands the government was bitterly attacked for its failure to provide a definite program of financial amelioration, and all groups, except the Socialists, demanded that heavy indemnities be included in the reparations bill. Even the Socialists advocated a rigorous policy toward Germany. "Germany first," shouted Barthe, of that party, when Péret was protesting that the capital levy should not be applied in France before Germany had been made to pay reparations.[20] "We are all agreed," said Vincent Auriol, speaking for his Socialist colleagues, "that these devastations must be integrally restored by the enemy." "It is only justice that the enemy junkers and capitalists, who systematically ruined our industries in the North, should repair the damages which they have caused. On this point there cannot be any disagreement. (*Trés bien! trés bien!*)"[21] Indeed, the idea of an indemnity was not repellent to all Socialists. When André Lefèvre, of the Center, stated his belief in a German indemnity, Marcel Sembat, of the Socialist group, spoke up, saying: "We all believe in it";[22] and Auriol himself seemed not hostile to the idea *per se*. He simply regarded it as impracticable, and regarded as of first importance the safeguarding of France's prior rights to reparations for damages incurred.[23]

The demand for a privileged position for France's reparations claims was a point on which all parties fervently agreed. It had been warmly acclaimed in the Senate, when advanced by Ribot, December 17.[24] It was further elaborated by Senator Touron, February 14, who stressed the demand for indemnities as well as reparations, but insisted that they should be distinguished for purposes of priority of satisfaction.[25] It was equally strongly emphasized by the succession of speakers in the Chamber debates of March 7, 11, and 13. There was very little rational consideration, except by the Socialists, of the subject of Germany's capacity to pay; [26] but that suspicion and doubt were gathering in other quarters was indicated by Lefèvre's remark: "I believe that the famous formula from which we suffer: 'Germany can pay', has a political origin"; [27] and also in Bouilloux-Lafont's comment that "as to the thesis that Germany can pay everything, I ardently wish that it were true".[28] This state of mind was also manifested in the widespread demands for a privileged position for France's reparations claims, and for immediate financial assistance from the Allies. A large loan would probably be necessary, explained Louis Dubois, of the Right, in order to make possible immediate recovery on the "formidable claim" which France had against Germany.[29] In seconding this idea, Vincent Auriol, of the extreme Left, interjected: "It is not our difficult situation; it is justice which gives us the right to make the appeal to our allies. (*Très bien! très bien!* from the extreme Left.)" [30] Throughout these debates stress was laid on the absolute necessity of a Financial League of Nations to support France's impaired financial structure. Auriol, of the Left, and Dubois, of the Right, were in complete agreement in judging this to be indispensable.[31]

Meantime, the clamor outside was more than equal to that inside Parliament. Resolutions were passed by patriotic societies, and billboards were covered with posters demanding a privileged position for France's reparations claims, and insisting that Germany be made to pay before France was called on for taxes.[32] The heavy press resumed a lively campaign to make Germany pay the entire expense of the war, in order not to crush the French tax-payer.[33] The *Matin* carried on its campaign with increased vigor. "WHO OUGHT TO BE RUINED? FRANCE OR GERMANY?" it began asking after Klotz' appearance before the Budget Commission. Germany, it thought, could pay the Allies some twenty billions a year, for twenty years, which would serve as interest payments. At the end of that time Germany could begin paying off the principal of the 1,200 billions owed. "It matters little whether it takes one, two or three generations for justice to be accomplished. Justice . . . is eternal, and is not concerned with limits of time." [34] During the ensuing month no fewer than sixteen special articles were devoted by the *Matin* to various aspects of this theme.

The patriotic press, for the most part, refused to consider the question of Germany's capacity to pay. [35] There should be no question of asking whether "poor ruined Germany" could pay, it was argued, but only of demanding the desired reparations. Ways and means could subsequently be considered. [36] It was freely asserted that Germany would actually be able to pay, [37] and the popular feeling resulting from the repeated statements that she would be made to pay was illustrated by a cartoon in the *Journal*, March 29, showing a lodger faced with a battery of creditors, against whom, in nonchalant manner, he defended himself by saying: "No, no, no. M. Klotz himself has said it. Germany should pay first."

Thus, the assumption that "Reparations" should properly include war costs became general, as, also, the demand for a privileged position for France. [38] On this point the *France Libre,* of the Socialist Right Wing, was as insistent as the most nationalistic; [39] and the liberal *Progrès* of Lyons (March 17) took it as a matter of course. The state of public feeling resulting from over-zealous propagandist activities was well described by *Europe Nouvelle* (Feb. 22). With the coming of overwhelming victory, public opinion, intoxicated with success, abandoned itself easily to the idea that Germany would have to pay the costs of the war. "This was the epoch of wild calculations, of senseless illusions. Journals and statesmen drew up the detailed bill to be presented to our enemies. 500 billions! 1,000 billions! 1,200 billions! Germany would pay everything, right to the last centime." "Now we are beginning to realize that the account is not so simple. . . . Financially our situation is desperate if we are left to face it alone."

2. REPARATIONS: DECISIONS

How greatly French policy was affected by the drift of public opinion it is difficult to say. The views of the Finance Minister seem to have been in harmony with the more extreme demands which came to be widely accepted. The blanket reservation inserted in Article Nineteen of the Armistice, on his insistence, suggests how far he was from accepting the strict "reparations for direct damage" principle; and his subsequent public pronouncements concerning reparations must have encouraged the developing intransigence on the part of the public. At all events, the French government eventually found itself faced with a political situation which made a rational solution of the problem appear impossible.

The French government's own policy seems to have undergone a change during the post-Armistice period. The original memorandum, drawn up by Tardieu, and submitted to the various governments in late November as a basis for the Conference program, apparently rested on the Wilsonian principle of reparation "only to the extent of the direct damage resulting from German attack".[40] However, the French thesis, as submitted to the Reparations Commission, February 1, proposed that indemnities for the "integral cost of the war" be imposed on Germany.[41] At the same time a privileged position was demanded for "certain categories of claims". Thus the French government associated itself with the claim for "war costs" which had been first officially advanced by the Lloyd George government in the preceding November-December election campaign. It would seem to have been an unwise move from the point of view of French material interests, since the addition of the total war costs would reduce the percentage of German payments to which France would be entitled.[42] An explanation of the French position may be found in one or more of the following factors: (a) the anticipation of being granted a preferred position in the matter of receiving payments; (b) an exaggerated belief in Germany's capacity to pay; (c) the desire to impose a crushing burden on Germany for an indefinite period; (d) the excited state of domestic public opinion resulting from a vigorous press campaign.

For over two months first the Commission on Reparations and then the Supreme Council struggled with this vexing problem. During February the issue of "war costs" consumed most of the time of the Commission, the American position being that the item was excluded by the pre-Armistice agreement between the Allies and the United States as to the bases of peace.[43] The Allies claimed, first, that there was "no controlled agreement", and second, that if there were, it included "war costs".[44] Article Nineteen of the Armistice agreement, with the sweeping reservation inserted by Klotz, was presumed to override any other consideration. The American members, during this period, stood firmly on the position that only "direct physical damage" resulting from military operations was covered by existing agreements, and when Wilson was appealed to during his temporary absence in America, he was equally adamant in opposing a policy which he regarded as "clearly inconsistent with what we deliberately led the enemy to expect".[45] War costs had therefore to be struck off the German account; and this Clemenceau and Lloyd George accepted, in the hope of finding some other way in which to saddle crushing payments on Germany. This alternative was considered to be a political necessity. In a conference with Colonel House on March 10, Clemenceau and Lloyd George both expressed the hope that "a large sum would be settled upon because of the political situation in the Chamber of Deputies and Parliament". They said they were perfectly willing to have the sum called reparations.[46]

The desires of the British and French leaders were satisfied by the addition of pensions and separation allowances to the reparations account, and this was satisfactory to the

French delegation, since the French percentage of the German payments would not thereby be reduced so greatly as under the application of war costs,[47] and it would, nevertheless, constitute a crushing addition to the German bill. The American delegation was divided as to the merits of the pensions case, but, toward the end of March, President Wilson was won over to a "liberal" interpretation of the "damages" principle of the pre-Armistice agreement.[48]

The major categories of "damages" were thereby fixed; but the problems remaining were the most difficult of all, and these were fought out within the Council of Four during the critical days of late March and early April. Should the Conference agree at that time upon a lump sum to be imposed on Germany? Should a definite term of years be fixed during which Germany would be required to pay the totals? How much, if any, attention should be paid to the question of German capacity to pay? These were the thorniest of all the reparations problems. The position of the American delegation was clear on all of these points. A definite global sum, it contended, should be fixed, of an amount which was within Germany's capacity to pay within a period of about thirty years. But on each of these points the French were unyielding in their opposition.

No definite sum could be fixed, because either it ran the risk of being too high, in which case Germany would refuse it, or it risked being too low, in which event France would not be indemnified for her damages.[49] Clemenceau preferred to postpone this problem altogether, leaving it to a commission to fix the totals and the annuities to be paid. The Premier's real difficulty is revealed by his statement that whatever sum the experts might compromise upon, it would still fall far short of the expectations of the French populace, and that no government accepting such a sum could endure.[50] On March 28 President Wilson finally yielded to Clemenceau's insistence that the matter be given over to a commission for later determination.

Clemenceau likewise vigorously contested the American

position that "all we should demand is Germany's utmost capacity for thirty years", and that, as Mr. Davis put it, "The enslavement of one generation was enough." [51] The "utmost capacity" formula was unacceptable, if limited to a term of years. Furthermore, asked Loucheur, "Since when is it enslavement to compel the payment of debt?" [52] The third, fourth, fifth, sixth and seventh of April witnessed the continuation of the debate on reparations, the French maintaining their position that capacity to pay should not be taken into account. The gigantic total should be made to stand forth, and then the Associated Powers could fix a term as well as the annuities. "I would say this," said Clemenceau, April 5, " 'Germany owes x for damages caused to life and property. This sum x the governments can reduce in the future if they see fit, but I am not prepared at present to consent to any reduction.' " The Conference might even agree upon a term, if it were understood that it could be extended in case payment within that period were impossible. If the Commission should decide "that Germany's total debt is sixty billion pounds [300 billion dollars] it will decide whether this can be paid in thirty or forty years". The Premier thought fifty years could be accorded, if necessary. [53]

It therefore became impossible frankly to face the problem of German capacity, though there was a feeling that ultimately the Reparation Commission would be governed to a certain extent by this consideration. An attempt was accordingly made to anticipate the popular disillusionment that would probably follow. Lloyd George proposed that a statement be included recognizing that the enemy resources were "not unlimited". When Klotz objected, the British Premier explained that only thus could he and Clemenceau justify to the British and French peoples "their acceptance of less than the whole cost of the war". [54] Thus on April 7, the Reparations issue was settled in all except matters of detail, though President Wilson, who was then ill, did not give his final approval until April 12. [55] On most points the

French theses had prevailed. A list of categories was drawn up; a commission was to determine the grand total within two years; an initial sum was fixed, to be paid within the same period, and a tentative period of thirty years, from May 1, 1921, was named during which the entire amount should be discharged.[56]

The period during which these decisions were made was the most critical of the entire Conference, for decisions on the Saar and the Left Bank were also hanging in the balance after several months of the Conference had elapsed. Furthermore, the procedures of the Conference became more secretive than ever, and public opinion was allowed to wander rather confusedly in a no-man's land of uncertainty. During this time no communiqués were issued, and the press gathered its information as best it could from those who maintained fairly close contact with official circles. Important gleanings, some accurate, some inaccurate, were made by leading organs on the subject of the decisions concerning Reparations. An agreement by the Conference on principles was correctly reported as of April 5, and the *Temps* (April 7) suggested the prospect of France's receiving "complete reparation for all the losses experienced". A report without foundation, on the 8th, stated that France's share of German payments was to be fifty-five per cent.[57] The *Temps,* of April 10, quoting the *Daily Mail* (Paris), stated correctly that twenty-five billions of francs would be demanded of Germany within the ensuing two years. On the 11th a report was widely circulated giving the erroneous impression that the war costs principle had been adopted by the Conference.[58] The *Temps* of the 14th reported that "appreciable progress" had been made on the 12th, but its account of the details was an inaccurate and incomplete statement of the situation.

In the midst of these reports, some true, some false, but all confusing and misleading because they revealed only parts of the picture, agitation in press and parliament continued. The *Matin* again led the patriotic press in a vigorous offensive,[59] demanding that, before everything else, Germany should be made to recognize her debt in full, including war expenses and pensions, though the total alleged debt due France was now reduced from 340 billions to 316 billions. No inquiries should be made as to German capacity. Unsuspected sub-soil riches might be revealed, or chemical discoveries might be made by Germany that would transform the economic world! The duty of the Four was to make Germany recognize her debt! [60] Furthermore, Germany would have to continue paying till the total debt was extinguished. It should always be borne in mind that "Germany must pay all".[61] Priority for the "reparation of damages" was of course insisted upon.[62] The report that a provisional sum of only 125 billions was to be asked of Germany was seized upon by the *Matin* and other organs to emphasize the gaping financial abyss that loomed for France if only this sum were demanded.[63] "VICTORY—OR RUIN?" shouted the glaring title over a prominent and heavy-typed box on *Matin's* front page (April 17). *"The war cost France 316 billions. Of the 125 billions which the Four are demanding of Germany, the French share is about sixty-six billions. It will remain for the French people to raise 250 billions out of their own resources."* France's population had, it said, been reduced to 35,000,000, whereas Germany's was 68,000,000. "Germany has not been invaded; its industries can be put into operation at once." France's war burden would be 7,443 francs per head, while that of Germany, even including the 125 billions, would be but 4,338 francs per person. Furthermore, Germany was contemplating the annexation of Austria. "If these figures mean nothing to the Four, they mean something to the French people!"

As the *Esprit Public en France* put it, a "wave of pessimism" was spreading.[64] It permeated parliamentary circles. Raoul Péret, president of the Budget Commission, wrote a strong leader in the *Matin* (April 13), asking when the "Famous account between peoples" was to be settled. France, he feared, was threatened with defeat by the very immensity of her victory. On April 10 the Budget Commission of the Chamber memorialized the government, asking that war costs be included in the reparations bill. On the same day a large majority of the members of the Senate issued a similar manifesto, demanding also that a penal indemnity be inscribed.[65] The following day over three hundred members of the Chamber signed a manifesto endorsing the demands of the Senators.[66] On the 15th the Budget Commission again passed a resolution on the same subject, saying in part: "It is the most elementary justice to demand of the enemy integral reimbursement for all the damages and the costs of the war, WITH PRIORITY FOR THE REPARATION OF DAMAGES. . . ."[67]

These feelings flamed out both in the Senate and the Chamber during their meetings of the 18th. In the Chamber Vincent Auriol, of the Socialists, led the attack. Was it true, he asked, that France was to get only a share of fifty-five per cent of a bill of 125 billions to be demanded of Germany? Was it true, that while the minimum estimate of France's reparations bill was 120 billions, France was to receive but this fifty-five per cent (sixty-six billions) in thirty years? "All of that is inexact," interposed Klotz, though without giving any positive enlightenment. Persisting in his inquiries, Auriol demanded to know whether the 125 billions would be a privileged claim for France and Belgium. Had the Allies accepted the equitable sharing of the war charges demanded by the Budget Commission? And, furthermore, what had been done about the financial League of Nations? Though the Chamber was overwhelmingly sympathetic with the Socialist speaker, the government, because of the Peace Conference, was able to avoid the responsibility of a debate, and the Chamber was compelled to be satisfied with the above-mentioned terse statement of the Finance Minister.[68]

Almost identical questions were being raised in the Senate the same day, where Senator Perchot, of the Left Wing, led the debate.[69] Particular stress was placed on "the principle of priority" for France's reparation for damages claims, and the Senator was still uncertain whether the bill against Germany included war costs, or only reparation for damages, and pensions. The press reports of the Conference, he rightly charged, were misleading and contradictory.

The parliamentary debates coincided with a general tendency to recognize, however reluctantly, that France was not to obtain full satisfaction of her claims against Germany. Apparently the full cost of the war was not being included, though this was not officially known until the Conditions of Peace were presented to Germany on May 7. The alternative was for France and her Allies to interpret as broadly as possible the "damages" clauses that were included in the treaty. This course was already being advised by the *Temps*. The term "damages", it said (April 17), could be interpreted to mean "any punishment" suffered by the population. "Everything possible must be included in 'damages'."

When the Conditions of Peace were presented to Germany on May 7, the broad lines of Reparations policy became clear, although only a summary of the Conditions was made public. Germany and her allies accepted responsibility "for all losses and damages suffered by the Allied and Associated Powers, wherever occurring", and Germany undertook "to make reparation for all the damages caused to the civilian population and their goods". Ten broad categories of damages were specified, including pensions and separation allowances. A Reparation Commission would, by May 1, 1921, make known the total bill to be ultimately assessed against Germany. Meantime, and irrespective of the ultimate bill, Germany would undertake obligations, on account, to the extent of 100 billion marks (125 billion francs), one of these being the payment, before May 1, 1921, of five billion marks in gold.[70]

There was a sufficient amount of certainty, and at the same time, of uncertainty, in the terms announced May 7, to win the conditional approval of most moderate as well as reactionary circles. The assumption of definite responsibility by Germany, the inclusive list of categories of "damages", and the payments on account seemed to offer a very substantial minimum. These could be used, as suggested by the *Temps,* as the basis for a very substantial structure, if the categories were broadly interpreted by the Commission, if France were given a preferred place in the receipt of reparations, and if the Allies hung together throughout the critical years to follow. Within these limits, Center and Right Wing opinion was satisfied.

The *Matin* (May 8) remarked caustically, in outlining the reparations terms that, *"it is understood definitely that Germany is exempted from the payment of war costs, which for France . . . amount to* 160 BILLIONS", yet there was a general disposition even in the Right Wing press to admit that the war costs idea was not a practicable one. Even the *Liberté* (May 8) confessed that to have imposed on Germany the entire war cost, estimated at 1,000 billions of francs, not only would have broken Germany economically, but would not have improved the position of France and Belgium.[71] Furthermore, the impression was growing, probably encouraged in French official circles, that France was to be given a position of distinct preference by her allies in the receipt of reparations. The *Liberté* announced, May 5, that the distribution of reparations would be on the basis of a quota fixed in proportion to the damage suffered, and this idea was confirmed by the *Temps* (May 8), in its comment on the Reparations clauses. "Thus France secures recognition in the fullest measure of her right to reparations," concluded that semi-official organ.[72] These questions of priority for France in reparations payments, of a broad interpretation of the "damages" categories, and of continued Allied solidarity were matters for future determination, yet at the time the Conditions of Peace were presented to Germany in early May, even conservative circles were not without genuine hope.

3. THE SAAR BASIN

The problem of the Saar Basin was closely linked to that of Reparations, though it obviously had an important bearing on the whole territorial settlement. Tardieu's statement

that this was the only question "that led to disagreement between the French and American representatives",[73] is an exaggeration, but certainly this was the question which caused
the most acute personal controversy between Wilson and
Clemenceau. In waging its battle for the Saar Basin, the
French delegation was handicapped by the fact that it was
demanding something to which allusion had not been made
in the French diplomatic communications, and which the
resolutions of the French Chambers, on the subject of war
aims, had passed over in silence.[74] A stinging reminder of
this fact was thrown into the French Premier's face by Wilson when, in the heat of the controversy, he lashed out with
the remark that no one had ever heard of the Saar until after
the Armistice.[75]

The question of the Saar developed somewhat more
slowly in the public mind than the other major problems
before the Conference. The major reason apparently was
that it was subordinate, in the minds of most people, to one
or the other of the two more important and more general
problems, Reparations and the Left Bank régime. It was
also related, partly, to the question of Alsace-Lorraine, and,
to that extent, was considered an aspect of "restitutions".
As early as November 14 the *Journal* raised this particular
point, in demanding that Alsace-Lorraine be given back
with its Eighteenth Century limits, including Landau, and
the Saar.

On the whole, very little was said on the subject in the
early days after the Armistice. Even when the German government, on November 23, in connection with the evacuation of left bank territories, protested strongly against "the
attempt to snatch away" the Saar Basin territories, the note
itself was carried by very few papers, and comments on it
were equally scattered. The *Petit Parisien* and *Écho de
Paris* were the only important papers carrying it,[76] and the
only comment from these organs was a brief remark by the
Petit Parisien stating that this was another German
maneuver to obstruct the fulfillment of the Armistice. A

few comments from Radical Socialist organs indicated that already, in those quarters, the idea of taking over the Saar territory was gaining a foothold.[77] The *Œuvre* began at once (Nov. 24) stressing the need for the Basin as a means of restoring French industries. Even when the French colors were returned to Saarbrücken and Saarlouis on November 23, the issue of annexation was not generally raised. Isolated remarks were made about the "sacred places" which were being restored from day to day,[78] and brief notes were carried, such as that Saarlouis, "built by Louis XIV, fortified by Vauban, and the birthplace of Marshal Ney", had been torn away from France by the treaties of 1815.[79] But the press as a whole subordinated the issue to other aspects of the settlement.

Before the question reached the Council of Four, however, public opinion had become pretty clearly defined. In late December the discussion in the Chamber of Deputies bore upon this question, and, though the government did not define its position, the overwhelming desire of the deputies for annexation of the Saar Basin was made clear. Marcel Cachin, speaking for the Socialists, December 27, said that in the Commission on Foreign Affairs, which was representative of all the groups, all except the two Socialist members have favored annexation.[80] Two days later, Franklin-Bouillon, speaking for the Commission on Foreign Affairs, argued that the questions of Alsace-Lorraine and the Saar were one problem. The only difference, he said, was that the Saar had been taken in 1815 rather than 1871. To the lively applause of the Chamber he said: "We are entitled to the same reparation and to the same restitution." If the partition of Poland of 1772 could be wiped out, why not the "spoliation of France of 1815"? [81]

The opinion expressed in the Chamber was in fairly close harmony with that in the press. Under the double head of "restitution" and "reparation", justification was found by the press of the Right, Center, and much of the moderate Left, for annexation of the Basin. The 1814 frontier was

claimed under the title of restitution; and control, in one
form or another, of the remaining third of the Basin was
widely demanded under the title of reparation for the damage done to French mines in the north. All opinions con-
verged, said the *Homme Libre* (March 26), in agreeing that
"the Saar must come back to France, if only to indemnify
her for the destructions in the North". Frequently it was
ignored that the 1814 line included only two thirds of the
Basin, as when the *Phare* of Nantes (Feb. 1) charged that
the Saar had been stolen from France in 1815. "Historical"
and "economic" arguments formed the principal basis of the
case for annexation, as was illustrated by the *Débats'* line
of reasoning (March 6), that, in the first place, the Saar
"was torn from us in 1815". In the second place, "the Basin
ought to be exploited for our benefit by way of material
reparation". Yet the *Temps,* which did not hesitate to pass
beyond the limits of Wilsonian principles when deemed desirable, would have added to these the strict indemnity principle. For having begun the war, and having lost it, Germany should surrender the Saar, "quite apart from considerations of justice or historical right".[82]

Occasional questions were raised in the Center concerning the wisdom of annexing the entire Basin; [83] and in
the moderate Left press occasional warnings were issued to
beware of "annexationist" policies. While the *Œuvre*
(Nov. 24) argued vehemently for annexation without pre-
scribing particular lines, and *Europe Nouvelle* (Feb. 8)
calmly assumed that the "frontier of 1814, including the
Basin of the Saar, and the Circle of Landau", would be
voted unanimously, and without debate, the *Dépêche* of
Toulouse (Feb. 26) and the *Populaire de Nantes* (March
12) felt that though the minerals could be claimed, nevertheless, people could not be claimed like minerals. The
Socialists remained firm on what they considered Wilsonian
principles. The coal of the Saar might properly be taken
under the principle of reparation, but any form of annexation was to be resisted.[84]

The French memorandum on the Saar came before the Council of Four on March 28. Loucheur and Tardieu explained the French thesis. Restitutions and reparations were the basis of the demand for political annexation up to the 1814 frontier; and the claim for full ownership of the mines with a special political régime for the remaining third of the Basin rested on reparations. Historical arguments were marshalled, showing earlier connections of these territories with France. It was urged that a strong middle class and peasant element, in the Saar Basin was still passionately attached to the French tradition. The minimum claims of France, under the principle of restitution, would be the frontier of 1814. Under the title of reparation, however, the cession of the Saar Basin was alleged to be indispensable.[85]

During the presentation of the French case President Wilson "wore a quizzical smile that foreshadowed objections".[86] Lloyd George was at once willing to admit French ownership of the mines with a species of "autonomous organization" for the coal basin, though rejecting all political annexation. Wilson was not willing to grant either ownership of the mines or a special political régime, while naturally opposing all idea of annexation. He would consent, on the 28th, only to allowing France the use of the mines for a given period. There was no comparison, he thought, between the case of Alsace-Lorraine, and that of the 1814 frontier.[87]

The French delegation immediately realized the necessity of abandoning the claim for political annexation, and it decided to concentrate on the principle of ownership of the mines with the establishment of a special political organization of the territory. Their memorandum of March 29 was based on these principles, though the political arrangements seemed to anticipate eventual French sovereignty for at least part of the territory. The question of sovereignty was to be kept in abeyance for the time being, but French nationality could be conferred on individuals, and when the majority of electors in a given district had adopted French nationality, that district might be annexed to France.[88] At the end of fifteen years a plebiscite could be held in those districts which had not already elected for France. President Wilson could scarcely sanction these proposals.

It was during these discussions that the relations between Wilson and Clemenceau reached the breaking point. Clemenceau, losing his patience over Wilson's resistance, charged the President with pro-Germanism, and abruptly left the Council session. Discussing the incident with Dr. Isaiah Bowman the next morning, Wilson said: "I do not know whether I shall see Clemenceau again. I do not know whether he will return to the meeting this afternoon. In fact, I do not know whether the Peace Conference will continue." [89]

Nevertheless, Wilson gradually moved toward the French position. On March 31 he yielded on the point of ownership of the mines by the French, but still refused a special political régime, insisting on guarantees primarily of an economic character that would permit the exploitation of the mines. On April 2 a special committee of three was appointed, including the American expert, Professor Haskins, for the purpose of inquiring into the details of the régime to be applied. On the 5th the committee reported unanimously that "a special administrative and political régime" would be necessary to put into effective operation the proposals which President Wilson had made. Thus Wilson's position was contested by his own expert.[90] On the 8th the President proposed, as an alternative, the setting up of a Commission of Arbitration to settle differences between French and German interests; but Clemenceau insisted that without a special administrative and political régime, insurmountable conflicts would arise.[91] It was not until the 10th that a compromise satisfactory to Wilson and to the French was reached. On the 12th this was finally approved in its details. The President's Commission of Arbitration had become a Commission of Administration. A special régime under the League of Nations was provided for during a period of fifteen years. A Commission of Five, chosen by the League Council, was to have all powers of government. A Customs Union was to be established between the Saar Basin and France. At the end of fifteen years a plebiscite would be held to determine the future status of the territory; and if, at that time, Germany were awarded the sovereignty, she would be required to repurchase the mines from France.

During the period from March 28 to April 12, in which the Four were deliberating on the Saar question, public opinion was in considerable confusion as to the course of events. No communiqués were issued, and semi-official news items were more meager than ever. Most of these were reprinted from the Anglo-American press of Paris, which suffered from somewhat fewer restrictions than the French press. The reports were frequently misleading and confusing. On March 30 the *Daily Mail* (Paris) quoted a Reuter despatch stating that France was claiming the entire Saar Basin; but this was not reproduced in the French press. The next day the *Temps* carried the report that the Four were discussing a political frontier that would include "territories taken away from France"—apparently referring to the 1814 line in the Saar region. The *Chicago Tribune* of April 1 was quoted by the *Temps* as saying that France was still claiming Saar territory which would include over a million Germans. On April 2 the *Matin* and the *Journal*, and various other papers reported that France was assured of the ownership and exploitation of the Saar mines; but that same evening the *Temps* issued the warning that the question of the Saar coal was not settled. The appointment of the committee of three experts was widely noted in the press of the 4th, but no news of its work appeared until the press of the 10th stated that the committee report had been discussed by the Four.

Meantime, on the 8th, the *Temps* carried an item, obviously of semi-official character, and apparently designed to prepare the public for the acceptance of a reduction in the yield of the Saar diplomatic harvest. Purporting to combat the allegations of the German press concerning the claims of France, it said: "We believe that the French government has not put forward any annexationist claim . . . with regard to any territory inhabited by a German population. This remark applies particularly to the regions comprised between the frontiers of 1871 and 1814." It then capped the climax by adding that it made the announcement all the more willingly "since the *Temps* . . . has constantly avoided encouraging any annexationist tendency". Which, of course, was inconsistent with the facts.[92] The *Œuvre* added to the confusion by saying, the next day, that the note in the *Temps* had aroused a "very lively impression in diplomatic circles", and that at the Ministry of Foreign Affairs it was said to have "no official foundation". (This was not proof, however, that the *Temps* had not received official inspiration for its article.) It added, further, that Clemenceau had always insisted that the Saar problem should not receive "a merely artificial solution", that is, one designed to please everybody, but really satisfactory to none.

During these days public attention became concentrated on the Saar question as never before. The delay in reaching a decision aroused bitter comment. "French opinion", said the *Temps* (April 11), was "cognizant of the fact" that this matter interested almost exclusively France. It wanted to know why the debate was dragging out so. "If the French government has, from the beginning, given its claims a form compatible with the general principles of the Allies, how have such persistent objections arisen?" (Whether the French claims were really compatible with the "general principles" of the Allies was highly questionable.)

Pre-existing trends of opinion were crystallized, and demands were made for the frontier of 1814, with the additional right of exploiting the coal in the remainder of the Basin. Most of the Right Wing press continued to demand

the annexation of the whole Basin. An element of surprise
was the strength of the annexationist demand on the Left.
The *Homme Libre* (which, though nominally of the moderate Left, was very close to the government) felt that
"French opinion could not compromise on the question of
. . . the frontiers of 1814";[93] and the *Rappel* (April 1),
also of the moderate Left, boldly demanded the whole of
the Saar Basin. The preponderance of the Radical Socialist
press was frankly annexationist. The *Œuvre* (April 2)
asserted in heavy type: "THE RESTITUTION TO FRANCE OF
THE SAAR BASIN IS, LIKE THAT OF ALSACE-LORRAINE, NOTH-
ING BUT DIS-ANNEXATION", while the *France de Bordeaux*
(April 9) expressed closely similar views, and the *Dépêche*
of Toulouse pursued a rather equivocal policy.[94] The more
advanced liberal organs, the *Progrès* of Lyons (April 4)
and the *Populaire de Nantes* (April 12) agreed that the
coal of the Saar was all that should be demanded; which
was, in effect, the position of the Socialists.[95]

There was increasing evidence, however, of a willingness,
especially in moderate circles, to accept less than annexation. The real desires of the preponderant Center and Right
Wing opinion, as well as of much of the Left, were expressed by the *Petite Gironde* of Bordeaux (April 2) in saying: "The Saar Basin ought to be entirely ours, for reasons
that have been a hundred times given, of which not one has
lost its force." [96] Yet the *Information* (March 31), which
represented strong middle-class elements, said that full per-
mission to exploit the coal mines of the Saar would be satisfactory; and the article cited from the *Temps,* of April 8,
marked a definite reorientation of that journal's policy.
From that time the *Temps* began writing of the "economic
exploitation" of the Saar, whereas, on April 1, it had felicitated the London *Morning Post* for its "clairvoyance" in
supporting France's claim to annexation of the Saar Basin.
Even the *Matin* seemed disposed to accept the mines without full sovereignty if French control were adequately safeguarded so that exploitation could be effective.[97]

The decisions of the Conference on the subject of the

Saar were made public between the 11th and 15th of April,
though the announcements of the details came only through
semi-official sources, as no communiqués were issued. Even
when Clemenceau, on the 13th, met representatives of the
Radical Socialist group, and expressed his satisfaction over
the settlement of this question, he spoke only in general
terms. The first reports of the terms of settlement, widely
circulated on the 11th, were misleading, as they created the
impression that an autonomous state, comparable in status
to Luxemburg, was to be established, over which France
would have administrative control. On the evening of the
14th, however, the *Temps* gave an accurate semi-official
statement of the terms, which was confirmed by the Conditions of Peace handed to Germany on May 7.

The final solution, everywhere viewed as a compromise,
was damned on the extreme Left as the "monstrous" outcome of the union between "French imperialism and Wilsonian principles",[98] and assailed in patriotic circles as
"neither fish, flesh, fowl, nor good red herring".[99] It was
nevertheless acceptable to the great majority as the best
possible compromise. Important organs, previously annexationist, even hailed it as in line with the principles of the
Allies.[100] The very fact that decisions on a highly contested
point had finally been reached was a source of psychological
relief.[101] It was also recognized that, after all, once France's
claims to the Saar coal were granted, the other aspects of
that question dwindled in importance.[102] Typical of the
general tendency to find a new perspective was the *Intransigeant*, which, on April 12, had characterized the Saar settlement as a "hybrid combination". On the 15th it was able
to write in more philosophical vein: " 'sufficient unto the
day is the evil thereof' ", and to align itself with the majority
in accepting the settlement as a whole, in spite of dissatisfaction with the details.

There were even those who hoped that events might ultimately be shaped to the wishes of patriotic Frenchmen. By
the astute direction of policy perhaps the plebiscite fifteen

years later might be turned to good account. It would depend on French officials, and French industrial leaders, it was said, "not to let the others [the Germans] be regretted", and to make France "desired".[103] A policy of "peaceful penetration" was openly advocated by important organs, with a view to achieving that much-to-be-desired result.[104] "Our hope," said the *Journal* (April 14), "must be to give back to France in the future the regions which were French in former times."

During the post-Armistice period the public appetite with regard to both reparations and the Saar had been markedly and abnormally whetted, a condition which, especially in the case of reparations, was the result of a deliberate and persistent campaign of popular excitation in the press, supported by elements in parliament. In both cases those responsible for provoking popular feelings overshot the mark, and they felt constrained to modify their position somewhat when faced with the stark diplomatic realities. In both cases, likewise, but particularly as to reparations, when disappointment loomed in the "Conditions" of May 7, consolation was found largely in hopes for future arrangements which, as it was made to appear, might be shaped favorably to the beliefs and desires entertained by the great majority of Frenchmen.

NOTES

[1] *Humanité*, March 9, 1918.

[2] Tardieu, *The Truth About the Treaty*, p. 285.

[3] Terrail, G. (Mermeix), *Le Combat des Trois* (Paris, 1922), p. 259.

[4] Tardieu, *op. cit.*, p. 288. On November 1 and 2, Clemenceau insisted that the words "reparation for damages" be included in the Armistice terms. Lloyd George, Bonar Law, Sonnino, Hymans and Colonel House objected, chiefly on the ground that such a matter was a condition of peace, rather than of the armistice. On Clemenceau's insistence that the French people "would not understand our failure to allude to this matter", he had his way. After this the Klotz reservation was cleverly inserted, and became the basis of the later French claim that "as regards reparations, they were not bound by the terms of the pre-Armistice agreement. . . ." *House Papers*, vol. iv, pp. 125-126.

[5] Terrail says that with the Klotz formula "anything could be demanded of Germany". *Op. cit.*, p. 259.

[6] It is obvious that only the fourth category came actually within the range of Wilsonian principles. *Matin* on November 30 added a further eight billions, plus, from such items as "requisitions in kind" made by the Germans during the war; damages for thefts, fires, etc., and forced contributions.

[7] November 16.

[8] November 16, 17.

[9] November 15, 29, 30.

[10] December 6.

[11] December 1.

[12] *Annales de la Chambre,* Dec. 27, 1918, p. 3250.

[13] December 1. On December 28, a leader by Gabriel Séailles again specifically accepted the "indemnity" principle, citing with approval the 1,250 billions of Geddes.

[14] *Annales de la Chambre,* December 3, 1918, pp. 2867-2868.

[15] Jean Bon, *ibid.,* p. 2868.

[16] *Ibid.,* December 19, 1918, p. 3093.

[17] *Annales du Sénat* (Paris, 1917-1919), December 17, 1918, pp. 914-915. Thus, incidentally, was launched the demand that the Allies less touched by the war should share in France's financial burdens arising from it.

[18] *Matin,* February 19.

[19] *Matin,* February 28.

[20] *Annales de la Chambre,* March 7, 1919, p. 934.

[21] *Ibid.,* p. 937.

[22] *Ibid.,* p. 937.

[23] "In advance of all possible indemnities which it may please the other belligerent powers to demand, the duty and interest of France is to claim the reparation of her damages. . . ." *Ibid.,* p. 940.

[24] *Annales du Sénat,* December 17, 1918, p. 914.

[25] *Ibid.,* February 14, 1919, pp. 157-158.

[26] See Auriol's speech, *Annales de la Chambre,* March 7, 1919, pp. 937-943. Bouilloux-Lafont, however, may be said to have had this in mind, stating what he characterized as the French thesis as to reparations: it "would consist in exacting from Germany all that she can pay; in giving certain claims priority, and in dividing among the Allies, in annuities, the balance of the unpaid war expenses". *Ibid.,* March 11, 1919, p. 974.

[27] *Ibid.,* p. 944.

[28] *Ibid.,* March 11, 1919, p. 973.

[29] *Ibid.,* pp. 969-972.

[30] *Ibid.,* p. 971. *André Lebey:* "France has a right of priority!" *Frédéric Brunet:* "A privileged claim! (*Trés bien! trés bien!*)"

[31] *Ibid.,* March 7, 1919, p. 942; March 11, pp. 969-972.

[32] Conference in Paris of "The French National Congress" said to represent 10,000,000 Frenchmen, February 27 to March 1. *Petit Journal,* February 28; pamphlet, *Les Conditions de la Paix et le Sentiment National Française.* Paris, 1919. Hoover War Library; *Esprit Public en France,* Bulletin 16, February 23—March 1, 1919.

[33] *Esprit Public en France,* Bulletin 17, March 2-8, 1919.

[34] February 21.

[35] There were a very few exceptions, such as the *Débats*, March 9, and *Libre Parole*, March 5.

[36] *Journal*, March 7; *Intransigeant*, February 22.

[37] *Matin*, February 21; *Liberté*, February 17; *Petite Gironde*, February 26.

[38] *Temps*, February 18. *Temps* also expressed a view widely held in the conservative press that a control comparable to that formerly exercised over Turkey would have to be established over Germany.

[39] February 21.

[40] *House Papers*, vol. iv, p. 272; Baker, *op. cit.*, vol. iii, p. 61.

[41] Klotz, *De la Guerre à la Paix*, pp. 135 et seq.

[42] Baruch, B. M., *The Making of the Reparations and Economic Sections of the Treaty* (London, 1920), p. 21. It is probable, also, that the absolute sum to which France would be entitled would be reduced, since the total sums due all the Allies would have to be scaled down within range of Germany's capacity to pay.

[43] Miller Diary, vol. xix, p. 265.

[44] *Ibid.*, vol. vi, pp. 30-33.

[45] Baruch, *op. cit.*, p. 26.

[46] Miller Diary, vol. vi, pp. 316-317.

[47] Tardieu, *op. cit.*, p. 292.

[48] Baruch, *op. cit.*, p. 29.

[49] Mordacq, General, *Le Ministère Clemenceau, Journal d'un Temoin*, 3 vols. (Paris, 1921-1931), vol. iii, p. 185.

[50] Lamont, T. W., in House, E. M., ed., *What Really Happened at Paris* (New York, 1921), p. 262. How difficult it would have been for agreement to be reached on a given global sum is illustrated by the fact that whereas the Americans placed the maximum bill to be demanded at from twenty to thirty billion dollars, the British put in totals of 120 billions, and the French talked in terms of 200 billions. *House Papers*, vol. iv, p. 343.

[51] Memorandum of Conference, April 2, at French Ministry of Finance. *Reparation Clauses in Treaty of Peace with Germany, Memoranda and Conferences*. Hoover War Library, pp. 35-52.

[52] *Ibid.*, pp. 35-52.

[53] Memorandum of Conference, April 5, at President Wilson's house. *Ibid.*, pp. 69-76. Colonel House remarked that he thought Clemenceau's position "very close to the American proposal", but Davis interjected that it was "a complete departure from the principles upon which we have been working for three months", which was that Germany should pay all she could "for thirty or thirty-five years at the most".

[54] Memorandum of Meeting at Lloyd George's Apartment, April 7. *Ibid.*, pp. 77-88.

[55] Mordacq, *op. cit.*, vol. iii, p. 212.

[56] *Treaty of Peace with Germany*, Articles 231-244, and Annex I.

[57] *Croix*, April 8.

[58] E.g., *Journal, Œuvre, Radical, Petit Marseillais*, April 11.

[59] *Matin*, April 8, 11, 12, 13, 14, 16, 17. On April 6 and 7 it had ex-

pressed a fleeting hope that satisfactory decisions were coming out of the Conference.

[60] April 8.

[61] *Temps*, April 5, 9.

[62] April 16.

[63] April 13, 14, 16, 17.

[64] Bulletin 23, April 13-19, 1919.

[65] *Matin*, April 11.

[66] *Ibid.*, April 12.

[67] *Ibid.*, April 16.

[68] *Annales de la Chambre*, April 18, 1919, p. 1855.

[69] *Annales du Sénat*, April 18, 1919, pp. 740-742.

[70] *Temps*, May 9, 1919.

[71] The Reparations clauses of the Conditions were among those least criticized by the Socialists. A number of the sections were picked out for special analysis and condemnation by *Humanité*, but only brief and passing reference was made to reparations. Cachin (May 10) condemned the principle of "responsibility" imposed on Germany, and the policy of desiring "to make conquered Germany pay the entire cost of the war". He predicted that they would lead "to the worst financial disillusionments".

[72] *Petit Journal* (May 9) said France had "gained the essentials of reparations" which were due her; and the *Débats* (May 9) agreed that France was getting all she could hope to obtain.

[73] Tardieu, *op. cit.*, p. 250.

[84] Terrail (Mermeix), *op. cit.*, p. 200.

[75] *House Papers*, vol. iv, p. 396.

[76] November 24.

[77] The *Pays* commented, November 25, on the "pretensions" of Germany and her desire to keep "our Saar mines".

[78] *Petit Journal*, November 24.

[79] *Matin*, November 26.

[80] *Annales de la Chambre*, December 27, 1918, p. 3250.

[81] *Ibid.*, December 29, 1918, p. 3329. Though the speaker referred specifically to redressing the "spoliation of 1815", which would have brought France to the 1814 frontier, his references to the "Basin of the Saar" as well as the general tone of his speech would seem to indicate a desire to incorporate the entire Basin. Indeed, the third of the Basin not included within the 1814 line contained the richest coal deposits.

[82] January 24.

[83] The *Lyon Républicain* (Feb. 4), for example, thought there might be disadvantages in annexation, unless the populations consented; and the *Opinion* (March 22) would have been satisfied with the cession of the mines.

[84] *Humanité*, January 29, February 19, March 14; *Populaire*, January 30.

[85] "It is not only reparation for the special damage done to French mines. . . . It is the whole problem of Germany's indebtedness to France." Tardieu, *op. cit.*, pp. 251-261.

[86] *Ibid.*, 252.

[87] *Ibid.*, p. 264.

[88] *Ibid.*, p. 268. Annexation could also take place on the request of the district council. The region was to be placed under the protection of the League of Nations, which should grant France a right of military occupation, with a right of veto on the local administration.

[89] Statement by Bowman, quoted in *House Papers*, vol. iv, p. 396.

[90] Tardieu, *op. cit.*, p. 270. In the matter of the Saar, Mr. Wilson was opposed not only by the French, but also by his own experts, and even by Colonel House. The experts were willing to grant not only the political frontier of 1814, but also an extension to include the remainder of the coal basin; and with them the Colonel was inclined to agree. *House Papers*, vol. iv, p. 383. House recorded on April 2 that Wilson sought to induce him to admit that the solution proposed by the American experts was contrary to the Fourteen Points; to which House replied that "there were many who thought otherwise". *Ibid.*, vol. iv, p. 397.

[91] "Every economic measure, however indispensable, taken by the French government, would be indefinitely held up by the German authorities. . . ." Germany would thereby be given a permanent means of obstructing French operation of the mines. Tardieu, *op. cit.*, p. 272.

[92] E.g., *Temps,* January 24, April 1, 1919.

[93] April 1.

[94] It states on April 7 that the Saar Basin ought to come to France as reparation. It had previously expressed satisfaction with the acquisition of the coal.

[85] *Humanité,* April 2.

[96] *Journal,* March 31, characterized as a "bastard régime" the proposal to give France the ownership of the mines, while leaving to Germany political sovereignty.

[97] March 29; April 1.

[98] *Humanité,* April 15. On May 9, *Humanité* characterized these clauses as "the most criminal part of the Treaty, that which conflicts most strongly with justice".

[99] *Œuvre,* May 11, argued that heavy charges would be inflicted on France, and that there would be no appreciable advantage, since the value of the coal extracted would be deducted from the German debt.

[100] E.g., *Petite Gironde,* April 15; *Temps,* May 8.

[101] "Decisions at last!" said the *France de Bordeaux,* April 15, expressing a general sense of relief.

[102] *Paris-Midi,* April 14, warned the Conference not to lose sight of the forest in the midst of the trees.

[103] *Revue des Deux Mondes,* May 15.

[104] E.g., *Journal de Rouen,* April 13, which said that the plebiscite was included only "to flatter Mr. Wilson". *Action Française,* April 14, confessed to the belief that it was unlikely that the plebiscite would go against France.

CHAPTER VII

GUARANTEES

"[What] we are seeking is a peace that we can all unite to guarantee and maintain."
(Woodrow Wilson, Address, February 11, 1918.)

"The problem of the defense of civilization is the problem of the defense of France."
(Senator Henri Michel, in *Petit Provençal,* January 28, 1919.)

"Monroe Doctrine or not, it is on the banks of the Rhine that the fate of all of us will be determined if war should some day break out again."
(*Temps,* April 2, 1919.)

1. THE PROBLEM OF SECURITY

THROUGHOUT the Conference public thought and discussion were constantly coming back to the basic problem of all: that of French security. "Guarantees, Guarantees, Guarantees", was the cry of the Radical Socialist press shortly after the signing of the Armistice.[1] "Guarantees" was the dominant theme of Clemenceau's pronouncement of December 29; and the widespread approval which greeted his speech demonstrated fairly clearly that this was the matter of primary concern to most French people. But what should be the nature of the guarantees, and how were they to be attained? There were two major approaches to the solution of the problem. One was the indirect approach, emphasizing as of first importance the organization of peace and security through such institutions as the League of Nations. This was the method favored especially by Socialist opinion, and also by advanced liberal elements. The other was the direct approach advocated farther to the right. This consisted of a variety of expedients. The disarmament of Germany and the impoverishment of that country under a crushing indemnity, as already indicated, were aspects of this program. Of more permanent importance were: (a) Germany's future political relations with Austria, (b) German unity, (c) the status of Germany's Western frontiers, and (d) the question of actual alliances with France's wartime allies. These will be dealt with in this chapter.

In this connection, the failure of the French program in the League of Nations Commission had important repercussions. If the Bourgeois proposals for armaments control and for an international military organism had been adopted, considerable wind would have been taken out of the sails of nationalistic propaganda in favor of more drastic guarantees of the direct sort, and a more moderate peace settlement would have lain in the logic of events.[2] In fact, the "weakness" of the February draft was, within two weeks after its promulgation, used as a primary argument for pushing ahead the program of French security based on geographic and military guarantees,[3] thus emphasizing the remark of André Tardieu that "To make certain her safety was the first duty of France".[4]

2. THE QUESTION OF AUSTRO-GERMAN UNION

In the memorable debate of December 29, Clemenceau stated that France, after first being assured of strong frontiers and military alliances, would gladly accept other guarantees of a "supplementary" character, one of which, he said, was the League of Nations. Two others which he did not mention, but which were no less a part of French policy, were the prevention of the union of Austria with Germany, and the effective loosening of the bonds of German unity. Both of these took on new importance after the Armistice. In the heyday of the Fourteen Points and other Wilsonian principles preceding the Armistice, nothing had been heard of either subject, whether in the press or in statements of government policy. Had not the principle of "self-determination" been acclaimed by Allied leaders as well as by President Wilson? And could the peacemakers legitimately interpose to nullify the operation of that principle, whether by preventing one political group from joining another, or by forcibly tearing apart others desiring to maintain common political bonds? In the weeks following the Armistice a great deal was heard of both these issues, and with a large section of opinion they took a leading place among the "supplementary guarantees".

The French government's policy on the subject of Austro-German union was disclosed by Foreign Minister Pichon in the debate of December 29. Pichon informed the Chamber that there were means within the government's knowledge, of solving the problem "in such a manner that it will not offer our enemies the compensations and resources which they are pleased to hope for. . . . It will be for the Allies to make dispositions which . . . will remove from it [Germany] the possibility of finding, on the side of the Austrians . . . that which they have lost by reason of our victory. . . . (Applause.)

Pierre Renaudel: But what if the German Austrians proclaim it themselves?

Pichon: Do you not believe that the victory gives us these rights over the vanquished? (Applause. Lively interruptions on the Left.)

Renaudel: Not those rights! (On extreme Left: That is not the Wilsonian doctrine.)" [5]

Though no further elaboration of this point was vouchsafed by the Foreign Minister at that time, the direction of French policy was clear.

Meantime public opinion was in a state of considerable uncertainty and perplexity. From the November Armistice to the February crisis it was generally assumed that Austro-German union was inevitable, and that there was slight hope of preventing it. Such widely divergent organs as the *Victoire* and *Œuvre* agreed that the issue was foreclosed, that Allied intervention to prevent union was out of the question. As early as October 27, the patriotic *Victoire* stated that if the German Austrians decided to attach themselves to Germany, it would be impossible to oppose their decision. "We cannot, after invoking democratic principles all through the war . . . throw them overboard today, because these ideas happen to inconvenience us." The *Œuvre,* a month later (Nov. 21), called attention to the inconvenience of the principle of "self-determination", noting that some "most serious colleagues" would like to introduce into the preface of the Treaty the statement: "All nations have a right to dispose of themselves, except the Germans and the Austrians." During this period, most of the press remained silent on the subject, while a majority of the journals that commented did so in the mood of deploring an inevitable necessity rather than in the hope of preventing its consummation. Important provincial organs as far apart politically as the *Nouvelliste de Lyon,* and the *Dépêche* of Toulouse, abstained from all comment. They merely carried brief news items on the drift of events in Austria, apparently resigned to the inevitable. Others, of practically equal importance, and at the same distance from each other, politically—such as the *Ouest-Éclair* and the *France de Bordeaux*—manifested considerable anxiety.

Apparently no one looked forward to the event with pleasure, and, as the February crisis developed, opposition grew bolder. The position of the Socialists was equivocal. The *Populaire* and *Vérité,* after the Austrian election of February 16, hopefully expressed the view that the Socialist triumph meant that Austria would remain an independent Socialist republic, abstaining from joining Germany.[6] Though *Humanité* on various occasions, stated its desire to respect the principle of self-determination, it frankly admitted that it viewed the union as "dangerous", adding, however, that "if Austria wishes it, there is no means of preventing it".[7] At the other extreme, the *Action Française* thought the problem "the greatest question of the peace". "Germany will soon recover her strength if Austrians are added." The Allies were said to have put into movement forces which they did not understand. "The famous prin-

ciples of the Allies have created things which now alarm
them." "What a splendid formula for a conquered people
is the 'Right of Nations'!" [8] The *Matin*, of the Center, was
equally outspoken (Feb. 16). Permitting Austria to be
added to Germany, it said, amounted to saying "that Germany, in losing 1,800,000 Alsace-Lorrainers, and 3,500,000
Prussian Poles, will recompense herself by the incorporation
of about 9,000,000 German Austrians. And all in the name
of Wilsonian principles!" The Radical Socialist *Petit Provençal* (Feb. 16) disconsolately remarked that while the
League Covenant—"the first act of the Conference"—was
emerging, Germany was about to annex Austria.

On all sides it was anticipated that the Allies would, in
the near future be presented with a *fait accompli,* yet there
developed an increasing unwillingness to accept this result
without an effort either to prevent it or to offset its consequences. Bitter recrimination was directed at Allied policy for permitting things to go as far as they had. "Why
have the victorious Powers allowed things to come to this
pass?" was asked by numerous organs from Right to moderate Left. It was alleged that the Allies could easily have
given a different orientation to events, on the morrow of the
Armistice.[10] "The Allies have been very wrong and weak
in not putting their foot down betimes," said another.[11]
"We should not put up with German-Austria entering the
Empire of the Eberts, or into any other camouflaged democratic edifice, . . ." said the *Ouest-Éclair.* "We should not
put up with it under any circumstances." [12] Even the
Œuvre, which had earlier ridiculed the right of the Allies
to interfere [13] changed its tune with the progress of events.
When on March 4 the Austrian Assembly proclaimed its
desire for union with Germany, that paper frankly stated
that before the consummation of the union "the Entente
must intervene".[14]

Serious efforts were made to discredit the elections. They
were attacked on the ground of fraud.[15] Violent propaganda from Pangerman and Social Democratic sources in

Germany was said to invalidate the election result.[16] Germans resident in Austria were said to have been allowed to vote, "thus vitiating the results of the election".[17] "Pressure", presumably brought by the Berlin government on that of Vienna, was discussed and condemned, and the Entente was called on not to recognize the Austrian Assembly if, on investigation, the reports were corroborated.[18] The *Croix* (Feb. 24) distributed the blame among the women, the Czechs voting in Vienna, the Jews, and the workmen, all of which groups were alleged to have voted Socialist, for questionable and transient reasons. The *Temps* (Feb. 22), which for weeks had been waging a campaign against Austro-German union said: "To recognize its [the Assembly's] right of annexing seven or eight million people to Germany would be to give a reward for fraud and blackmail."

Doubts were raised, even in liberal quarters, as to the genuineness of the Austrian desire for union, and the "necessity for preserving the European equilibrium" was invoked as a means of preventing it. Otherwise, it was suggested, it would be necessary to "go the full length of Mr. Wilson's principles", and, after informing the Austrian people fully of the consequences, proceed to "a widespread and free plebiscite".[19]

Various other proposals were made with a view to solving or to avoiding the difficulty. Some leading organs urged that Austria be set up as a perpetually neutral state, this neutrality being guaranteed by the "present members of the League of Nations".[20] Economic and financial action was urged. Austria should be told that if she allowed herself to be annexed by Germany she "would have a double load of reparations".[21] The theoretical and the practical aspects of the problem might be harmonized. Although in theory France could find no pretext to obstruct this sudden "love marriage", in practice, Austria had incurred obligations toward the various Allies, and for her "complicity in unchaining the war . . . the Allies are entitled to invoke certain sanctions against Austria". This could be done, it was urged, without the "Wilsonian doctrine having suffered even the slightest eclipse".[22]

It was food policy, however which gradually came to be regarded as the most hopeful instrument of control and obstruction. "Do we send food to Austria only that the Germans may have the pleasure of annexing a well-fed country?" it was asked.[23] The use of this instrument of control was widely advocated.[24]

The precise policy of the American delegation on this subject is not clear. However, Pichon, in his interview with the journalists, February 16, threw some light on the diplomatic status of the problem, saying that though the matter had not been formally discussed, the French government had declared itself opposed to the union of Austria with Germany. He then added, significantly: "but it is possible that other Allies have a different opinion".[25] Commenting on this, the *Ouest-Éclair* said that the United States and Great Britain were, presumably, the parties referred to. Colonel House records that on February 23 Clemenceau discussed the problem with him, and insisted that the Austrians would not join the Germans "if they received an intimation from the Allies that they did not wish them to do so".[26] At the discussion in the Supreme Council of March 5, Colonel House was apparently favorable to the use of the revictualling policy to affect Austria's decision. "All reports indicated," he said, "that the sending of food to German Austrians would weigh heavily in the scale" when they "came to decide whether or not they would throw in their lot with Germany".[27] When Pichon gave his next interview to the journalists, March 9, he seemed more optimistic on this question. The union of Germany and Austria, he said, could not take place on the sole desire of Germany and Austria, and it was for the Conference to decide. Furthermore, he added, "it is certain that it will decide contrary to the wish of the Germans".[28] It was in the latter half of April, writes Tardieu, that the French thesis finally triumphed. This, he says, was one of the "essential guarantees, demanded in vain up to that time, by Clemenceau". In Article Eighty of the Treaty Germany "acknowledges" and undertakes to "respect strictly" the independence of Austria.

3. GERMAN UNITY VS. GERMAN DISMEMBERMENT

The post-Armistice opinions and policies with regard to German unity were likewise markedly different from those that had gone before. The Revolution of November 1918, and the elections of January 1919 brought into power a democratic and socialistic régime which, instead of returning to the particularism of pre-Imperial days, threatened to carry much farther the work of national consolidation which Bismarck had begun. Consequently grave fears were aroused that in a subsequent crisis the striking power of the German Reich might be greater and more effective than ever before. Tardieu, in his book on the Peace Conference defends the government, of which he was a member, against the attacks of those who criticized it for failing to secure the dismemberment of Germany. The very ardor of his defense attests to the weight of the criticism against which he was defending his chief and himself. He points out in no uncertain terms that "the disintegration of German unity was never one of the war aims of the Allies. . . . At no time during the war did the Governments, the Parliaments, or even the Press demand the destruction of German unity." [29] Furthermore, he adds, quite correctly, that during the critical days of 1918, "To have announced . . . what has been called the 'vivisection of Germany', would have been a terrible imprudence, would have been playing into the hands of German propaganda." Had not, indeed, Lloyd George, in his January 5, 1918 speech, disavowed the desire to "dismember Germany"? And had not Wilson, in his speech on the Fourteen Points, stated that "We do not pretend to suggest to Germany the alteration or modification of her institutions"? "Nobody," he pointed out, "protested, either in October or on November 11", against the action of the Allies in dealing with the Reich as a unit, rather than with its constituent parts. Nevertheless, Tardieu frankly admits that "France would far rather not have at her very doors, and bound together by a common will and consciousness of unity, a people from which she has so often suffered"; [30] and he explains that the policy of the government actually was to support "autonomous tendencies" whenever they "manifested themselves spontaneously". Naturally, the degree of spontaneity of a given movement would be a matter of interpretation.

As above suggested, not only was the government silent, by necessity, during the pre-Armistice months of 1918, but the press also, for the most part, held aloof from discussing a problem so thorny with diplomatic difficulties.[31] With the coming of the Armistice there soon appeared evidences of a movement aimed at weakening Germany internally, either by the break-up of Prussia, or by the appeal to separatism in other parts of the Reich. The *Temps* and *Action Française* led the way. On the morrow of the German Revolution and before the actual signing of the Armistice, the *Temps* began a campaign that lasted throughout most of the Conference. The Revolution seemed almost to be regretted. Particularistic tendencies could be found, it said, in the old dynastic system, but this would be impossible "under a Germany levelled by the wheel of revolution".[32] In any case, the Revolution was not enough. ". . . the entire system incarnated by the Hohenzollerns" must "crumble to its very foundations." [33] "We talk of German liberty, and we continue to conceive of Germany as a centralized state under Prussia. . . . We must get out of this habit." [34] "The cult of the ideal must not obscure the facts. . . . Germany is not a homogeneous people. . . . Our rôle will consist in seeing to it that . . . the German countries most capable of governing themselves are not absorbed or oppressed by the Prussian State. . . ." [35] And so the campaign continued, becoming stronger in its demand for the use of pressure by the Allies. The Social Democrats were regarded as "More centralizing than the Hohenzollerns", for persisting "in unifying Germany at a time when it is necessary to give autonomy to the different German regions". The Allies were urged to use the food relief program to further separatism.[36] Recurrently throughout January and February it came back to the same theme.[37] Preaching against the danger of letting things drift, and accepting the developments as "inevitable", it urged that "Even though there was only one chance in a hundred thousand of affecting the soul and the structure of Germany, we should have seized this chance".[38]

The *Action Française* was equally persistent and even more emphatic than the *Temps*. The Allies were advised to negotiate peace, not with the central government, but with each of the twenty-six states of Germany.[39] Dismemberment, it insisted, took precedence over reparations.[40] Other powerful organs lent early support to the campaign. The *Croix* (Nov. 13), leading Catholic organ, and *Écho de Paris* (Dec. 2) threw their support to the movement. The *Débats* (Dec. 9) strongly urged the breakup of Prussia, though it did not hope for the general success of separatism. The attitude of the *Œuvre* was interesting. René Pichon said he knew "many publicists—and not the least important—who would not stop at any obstacle" in imposing dismemberment on Germany. He frankly hoped for the success of the separatist movement; but instead of force, he would use more subtle types of pressure: the threat of heavier financial terms, the use of the economic boycott, and prolonged military occupation as reminders that "separatism" was the best policy.[41]

Though there is little doubt that a highly decentralized, if not dismembered, Germany was desired by practically all groups, there arose a baffling dilemma: If the largest possible indemnity were desired, would that not presuppose a strong centralized régime to make payment possible? "If, on the other hand," as it was sometimes put, "we prefer above everything else to assure universal peace, we must reduce

Germany to powerlessness, and to that end there is only one means; it is to divide it, according to the old French tradition." [42] Fear was occasionally expressed lest a disunited Germany would be unable to pay war costs; [43] though the *Débats* insisted that the individual units of Germany, whatever their relations, should be held for their entire responsibilities. [44] The *Action Française*, [45] *Écho de Paris*, [46] *Homme Libre*, [47] *Paris-Midi*, [48] and *Œuvre* [49] frankly recognizing the dilemma, argued that reparations were of secondary importance, and that they should yield to the exigencies of greater security. In general, however, there was a disposition not to face the problem frankly, and it is doubtless true that most Frenchmen would have preferred to enjoy the fruits of both policies. [50]

In spite of hesitations and dilemmas the demand for loosening the bonds between the various units of Germany became more widespread and insistent during the February-April period. Though a number of journals (especially in the provinces) made no comment, there is no reason to suppose that they did not feel the danger so insistently pointed out by leading organs. The growing intensity of feeling is illustrated by the changed tone in the Radical Socialist press. The *Œuvre*, which in the November period, had abjured the use of force, now permitted General Verraux, in repeated articles, to demand the annihilation of Prussia. "Germany in Prussia," he said. "Let there be no more Prussia." [51] The *Dépêche* of Toulouse, which earlier had made no comments, now became insistent. "We have at our gates an enemy which remains, in spite of everything, powerful. . . . Germany will always remain a very disagreeable neighbor." The reduction of her strength was therefore, it thought, "an imperative necessity", and it should take the form of a "territorial splitting up". [52] A number of provincial recruits lent vigorous support to the demand of the *Temps* for the creation of a Rhenish-Westphalian State, with the Rhine as its axis; [53] in fact, the *Phare* of Nantes campaigned for the use of this territory as the neutral center for the League of Nations.[54] Aside from the exceptional case of the *Victoire,* which opposed dismemberment on the ground that it would render Germany incapable of paying reparations, only the Socialist press openly opposed that policy, expressing the fear that Germany might thereby be pushed to despair and anarchy.[55]

It seems clear that the French government was not quite so neutral in its attitude as Tardieu has suggested. On the very day of the Armistice Gabriel Hanotaux, former Minister for Foreign Affairs, handed to General Headquarters, and later to the Foreign Office, a plan for the dismemberment of Germany, which would have cut it up into six or eight states of about ten millions each. The only connection between the states would have been a central Diet, with extremely limited powers, so that the *ensemble* would be in the nature of a loose confederation, patterned on that of 1815.[56] The government did not adopt this extreme policy, but its program of November 1918 did state its interest "in favouring Federalism".[57] Indeed, Colonel House records that Clemenceau would have gone considerably beyond that, for on February 23 the Premier demanded the establishment of a Rhenish Republic, which he would exempt from the payment of any indemnity, and which he would favor in every way so that they would not want to join the German Federation; "and if they have such a desire," it was added, "they will not be permitted to do so".[58]

In the debates of the Council of Foreign Ministers, March 27, on the feeding of Bavaria, this question came to the fore. Pichon urged that Bavaria be supplied with food directly in order "to diminish Prussian influence". Lansing remarked that "the real question was one of policy. Did we want to separate Bavaria from Germany?" Hoover pointed out that contracts had been made with the central German government for the distribution of supplies throughout Germany. The whole German people were thus responsible for payment. A separate arrangement with Bavaria would mean a separate means of payment. There were also diffi-

culties of transportation which he envisaged. Balfour agreed
that Lansing's point was fundamental. Pichon urged the
importance of preventing Bolshevism in Bavaria, and of
encouraging those men there who were favorable to the
Entente; which brought from Lansing the reply that "if our
object was to get rid of Bolshevism, the best way was to
consider the Berlin government, which was certainly not
Bolshevist. He doubted the expediency of interfering with
the internal affairs of any country." [59]

The French design to detach Bavaria by a separate revictualling arrangement was finally dropped when the
Supreme Economic Council, April 25, reported it economically impracticable,[60] but the persistence of the aim to open
the way to dismemberment of Germany was manifested by
their proposal, April 29, that the German plenipotentiaries
be required to have credentials from each of the constituent
States. The basis of the French argument was that, with
the collapse of the Empire, the pre-Empire diplomatic personality of the various component states had revived.
Clemenceau and Cambon recalled that in 1871 Bismarck
had asked for the adhesion of Bavaria, Württemberg and
Baden to the preliminaries of Versailles. To these precedents
Lansing opposed that of Algeciras, in 1906, when France
had not demanded the signature of any single German State,
not even of Bavaria which had retained a certain right of
diplomatic representation. As Mermeix puts it, the French
thesis met "an insurmountable resistance" at the hands of
the "American Allies". Unfortunately for the French design, the various dynasties, which had been the real centers
of particularistic resistance in the States, had been swept
away by the November Revolution, and these States themselves did not demand the special representation which the
French would have forced upon them.[61] Likewise, in the
meetings of the Committee for the Verification of German
Credentials, May 2 and 4, the French insisted on their
thesis, limiting it this time to the special case of Bavaria,
demanding that its special adherence to the Treaty be re-

quired.[62] But the American delegate (Mr. White), supported by the British, was no less unyielding, and the French delegates finally consented to treat with only the central German government. "In spite of the resistance of our [French] plenipotentiaries," says Mermeix, "German unity, so dangerous to the peace of the world, was thus safeguarded by our Allies, especially by the Americans. . . ."[63]

The proceedings of the Supreme Council on this subject were not made public at that time; therefore they were accompanied by no repercussions in the press.[64] But the susceptibilities of public feeling on this subject were strikingly revealed by a final significant episode—the declaration of the so-called "Rhenish Republic".[65] On June 1 proclamations were posted in Aix-la-Chapelle, Mayence, Spire and Wiesbaden proclaiming "an Autonomous Rhenish Republic", basing itself on the German left bank territories, along with a strip on the right bank. Its desire was stated to be to remain within the framework of Germany, but to cut itself off from Prussian militarism. The moment had arrived, it said, to establish a peace of peoples, and the Rhenish peoples, desiring a peace of reconciliation, thought it their highest duty to work for general and permanent pacification. Dr. Dorten, chief delegate of the Committee, sent a note to the Allies stating the desire of the Rhinelanders to separate themselves from "Feudalism and Prussian Militarism", and asking for recognition.[66]

The interpretation of these events by the patriotic press of France was a remarkable illustration of wishful thinking. Almost without hesitation, and without raising questions, the press of Paris and of the provinces (with a few exceptions, mostly on the extreme Left) hailed the appearance of the posters in certain Rhineland areas occupied by Allied troops as though the new republic were already an accomplished fact. From the Center and Right Wing press came a jubilant welcome. The "health of the new German Republic" was drunk with a "glass of Rhine wine".[67]

The "monstrous hiatus" which the Allies had left in the Peace Treaty was thus deemed to be filled.[68] The Rhenish people were thought to "have had enough of Prussian domination".[69] The movement was hailed as a triumph for the "good administration and polite manners of the French".[70] It was saluted as "entirely in harmony with the Wilsonian principles".[71] Even the *Temps* and the *Débats* wrote gravely, and in solemn acceptance of the presumed *fait accompli*. It was the "logical result of 1815", which was a work of violence, said the *Débats* (June 3). "It consists in reestablishing the natural course of history," wrote the *Temps* (June 3). "They invoke the 'rights of peoples'. They bring a guarantee of peace. This right, is it not our principle? This peace, is it not our aim?" The editorial columns of this semi-official organ were even less critical than the reports from its own correspondent in the Rhenish territories. In answering his own question whether the act constituted the establishment of a state, the correspondent wrote: "Does the posting of an anonymous appeal, and its publication by the journals constitute the characteristic elements of such a fact? Time will tell." Yet in a nearby column the *Temps* (June 6) was protesting editorially against the conduct of the German government in taking measures to check the movement. "It could not be admitted," it said, "that the Berlin directors should impose a governor on a people who desire to govern themselves, or should prosecute a man [Dorten] who enjoys the confidence of his fellow-citizens." This judgment was expressed after several days of the Republic, during which the Rhineland, in spite of Allied occupation, had not been swept with enthusiasm for autonomy; after the Pangermanists, on one side, and Socialists and workers, on the other, had taken definite positions against the movement; after the movement seemed clearly to be limited to certain Catholic circles, and to commercial and industrial groups whose interests would benefit by a separation from Prussia, and a rapprochement with France; and also after the Rhenish representatives both at the Constituent Assembly and in the Prussian Landtag had, on June 3, joined in condemning the movement. It was even a day later than this that the *Homme Libre* (June 7), which for several days had somewhat ostentatiously reserved its judgment, abandoned all skepticism, and accepted the separatist movement as *bona fide*, delving into history to prove that the Rhinelanders had always hated the Prussians.

The majority of the Radical Socialist press showed considerable interest and enthusiasm. The *Dépêche* of Toulouse (June 3, 6), saw in it "an event of prime importance for the calm of Europe", and thought it a manifestation of the disintegration, bit by bit, of the German Empire. While the *Petit Provençal* and the *France de Bordeaux* ardently welcomed the new Republic,[72] the *Progrès* of Lyons (June 9) and the *Populaire de Nantes* (June 11) were more careful, avoiding blind acceptance of the genuineness of the movement, though they manifestly desired to be convinced. The *Œuvre* likewise seemed rather cautious though hopeful of developments. Democratic principles, it said (June 2), "which the Allied armies have again carried there", "possess a fortunate power of contagion". *Europe Nouvelle,* a liberal weekly, several days after the appearance of the posters in the Rhineland, felicitated the Rhinelanders without reservation (June 7) on having themselves "shaken off the yoke" of Prussian domination. Only the Socialists manifested complete skepticism. *Humanité* marveled at the gullibility of the press as a whole, and its failure to take account of the previous connections of the Republic's promoters, who, it asserted, were for the most part reactionary clericals strongly annexationist and anti-French during the war. A striking contradiction, it said, was the anti-democratic and anti-Socialist character of the movement.[73] The Republic was proclaimed, it wrote, after a few conversations among persons of the Catholic Center Party, and after councils with the military authorities of the Army of Occupation.[74]

The question of the relation of French officialdom to the movement was a ticklish point. The press of the Center and Right was particularly careful to emphasize the spontaneity of the movement. The very day of the appearance of the news, and before confirmation was possible, the *Écho de Paris* (June 2) began asserting that "France had done nothing to bring about this result". These protests of innocence continued after charges had been made by the German government that the occupying authorities had openly supported the movement, and after documents had been published implicating the General Staff of the 8th French Army.[75] Such charges were indignantly repudiated by the conservative press. Interviews with Dr. Dorten were carried in which he asseverated that the French had nothing to do with the movement.[76] In private conversation well-informed French conservative journalists admitted the complicity of the French officials;[77] yet the *Figaro* solemnly affirmed that "the only French influence has been the French spirit of benignity and moral greatness, her smiling firmness, uprightness and intelligence which has purified the atmosphere and made the people see that something was changed in the world and that there might be something to change in Germany".[78]

On all sides the economic implications and possibilities of the movement were stressed, and it was frankly recognized that economic motives had played a large part in the promotion of the movement. Opinion was divided as to whether the reparations burden of the so-called Republic should be lightened or not.[79] But great hopes were entertained, even in the Radical Socialist press, that the establishment of the Republic would mean definite economic advantages to France.[80] Most of the hopes, however, seemed to be built on the assumption that the degree of autonomy would be greater than was actually anticipated by the promoters of the scheme.

Demands were made in moderate Left circles, as well as farther to the right, that the Allies should not stand idly

by. The occupation by Allied troops of the territories concerned (thus giving free rein to the movement) did not
seem sufficient. That the Allies should at once recognize it,
was the demand of the nationalistic press. "With us, principles and interest converge," said the *Ouest-Éclair*, "in
urging us to recognize the Wiesbaden government." [81] Support of the movement "ought to be the object of all our
efforts and all our propaganda", said the *Figaro* (June 3).
Responsibility for the success of the movement was placed
squarely on the shoulders of Wilson, Clemenceau and
Lloyd George. The Conference was rebuked for ordering
the Armies of Occupation to maintain a position of strict
neutrality in the Rhineland, thus "letting them down after
they had fought five years against Prussian oppression." [82]
The great fault of France and the Conference was said to
be too great apathy and indifference. [83]

The Conference was bound to disappoint the hopes of
those who looked to it for aid in promoting the Rhenish
adventure, for the enterprise had already been badly compromised before its official proclamation. On May 22 President Wilson had received, through General Pershing, a message from General Liggett of the American Army of Occupation to the effect that the French General Mangin had
been endeavoring to promote "the establishment of an
Independent Rhineland Republic". [84] On Wilson's protest
to Clemenceau, the incident was investigated and the French
Premier, having recognized the abuse of authority, wrote
General Mangin that "Such a use of military authority is
absolutely inadmissible", and imposed on him "strict observation [*sic*] of complete neutrality". [85] That Clemenceau
would have been glad to see the establishment of such a
Republic, there is no doubt. The expression of his desire on
this subject to Colonel House in February is conclusive.
But that he was involved in the episode in question is
scarcely credible. In his *Grandeurs et Misères d'une Victoire* the Premier waxes bitter, and adduces evidence to show
that the only way in which the French government was di-

rectly involved was through the person of the French President. It was to Poincaré that General Mangin sent the Dorten telegram announcing the establishment of the Republic, and it was through Poincaré that the official message came to Clemenceau—the Minister of War. The comment of the French President, in sending the message to Clemenceau, was significant. "I suppose," he said, "that General Mangin would not transmit this address to me if the movement were not serious, and if it is serious, I hope that the Allies will not force us to suppress it. Furthermore . . . there would seem to be nothing in it which could shock President Wilson. It would be, in my opinion, very vexatious for us to take sides against these still very timid desires for independence." [86] The fact that the Mangin message did not come through the regular channels—to Clemenceau as Minister of War—but that it came rather to Poincaré, the "discreet but resolute partisan" of the seizure of the Rhineland, would seem to be persuasive evidence that the Premier had abandoned as hopeless that particular approach to the solution of the French security problem.

Events proved that Allied neutrality was not enough; and the hope of giving the *coup de grâce* to German unity gradually slipped away by reason of the inaction of these powers, much to the disgust of patriotic opinion which agreed with the correspondent of the *Journal*, who persisted to the end, saying that if they would only "push a bit the whole question would be solved in a trice", and a "durable peace could thus be hoped for."[87]

4. The Left Bank: The French Program

Whatever the importance of preventing Austro-German union, and of encouraging German dismemberment, it was the location and the organization of Germany's western frontier which inevitably loomed up as fundamental, and ultimately epitomized the problem of guarantees in the minds of most patriotic Frenchmen. As Victor Bérard put it, compromises could be made on the financial clauses, but for the daily welfare of the people, nothing could completely replace "security" on all frontiers.[88]

The policy of the French government on this subject was formulated toward the end of 1916, following the suggestions of Sir Edward Grey in September and November of that year that the Allies should make known to each other their war aims. In a note of January 1917 the Briand government demanded the 1792 frontier for Alsace-Lorraine, plus the Saar Basin; along with the creation of a neutral buffer state on the left bank of the Rhine.[89] Early in 1917 the Comité d'Études, headed by the historian, Ernest Lavisse, and composed mostly of historians and geographers, was established for the purpose of preparing reports on various peace problems. The conclusion presented to the government by this group was that, as regards the political frontier, the minimum claim of France should be the 1814 line, with certain extensions in the Saar to include the coal basin. From the military point of view, however, the only frontier "which assures France a durable peace . . . is the frontier of the Rhine".[90] The military was thus to be separate from the political frontier, and the territory in between the two was to be organized into a special political régime from which German forces would be entirely excluded.[91] The general conclusions of the Comité d'Études were strongly endorsed by Marshal Foch, who carried them somewhat farther and applied them in detail in a series of memoirs and in personal appeals to his government and to the Conference.[92] In his first memoir of November 27, 1918, the Marshal argued that nature had provided that the Rhine should be the natural frontier of western Germany. He proposed, therefore, that all the peoples on the left bank were to be grouped in a single military organization prepared to resist the "German peril". All of the states on the left bank were to follow a common policy "controlled by certain ones among them" (France, England and Belgium being designated). The bridgeheads as well as a neutralized zone on the right bank were to be occupied by

Allied contingents right up to the complete execution by
the enemy of the treaty obligations.[93] In his note of January 10 the Marshal sought to justify his proposals by
giving them a League of Nations dressing. The League
must have time to develop. In the meantime it must be given
"a sufficiently secure basis and an especial strength that
will insure its development". The Entente which was the
"embryo League of Nations" would have to take "emer-
gency precautions" against a Germany which would remain
"dangerous and threatening" for European peace. The
states on the left bank would have to be provided with new
"outlets for their economic activities", and they should be
united "with the other western states in a common customs
régime". "Under the protection of these defensive measures
. . . the League of Nations . . . would be strengthened,"
and it could gradually develop "by the successive adhesion
of other nations".[94]

In his third memoir, of March 31, the Marshal followed
somewhat the same arguments, though he omitted reference
to the common military organization of all the left bank
peoples, as well as to customs union with France.[95] The
theses of the Comité d'Études and of Foch became those
of the French delegation. As Gabriel Terrail puts it, "Clemenceau did not think differently either from the Marshal, or
from Poincaré, or Briand, or Doumergue or any other
Frenchman." [96] The French case, drawn up by Tardieu, and
presented to the Allies February 26, was even more highly
embellished with an adornment of internationalism. The
French proposals, it was insisted, involved "no selfish character". The question involved was "a problem of general
interest", although France was most exposed to the danger.
The last war had made it plain that the safety of western
and overseas democracies required that they should forbid
Germany access to the left bank of the Rhine, should fix
her western frontier at that river, and should occupy the
bridges with Allied forces.

This necessity was all the more urgent in view of the

inadequacy of the guarantees to be anticipated from the limitation of German armaments and from the League of Nations. Germany could not be expected honestly to fulfill its military obligations, as was shown by its "total lack of morality" in placing at its head "such men as Ebert, Scheidemann, Hindenburg", etc. The concerted support from League members, in case of attack, could not be expected to materialize sufficiently rapidly, since the processes leading to such action required decisions by League organs and then by the individual states. This would involve costly delay.

Therefore France must have a physical guarantee. There was *"only one such guarantee,* the guard of the Rhine bridges by an inter-Allied force". France "claimed nothing for herself", she did not want to annex the left bank of the Rhine. Great Britain and the United States claimed that their great fleets were of vital necessity to themselves though they were protected by the seas from a Germany whose fleet had been surrendered. France looked to "an inter-Allied occupation of the Rhine" for the same results that Great Britain and the United States "expected from the maintenance of their naval forces".

Such was the formidable argument of the French case which ran through twenty closely typed pages. This policy has been labeled by Georges Michon, biographer of Clemenceau, as "scarcely disguised annexation", and as "an unprecedented violation of plighted word, since it was not proposed to consult the six million inhabitants who spoke only German".[97] Indeed, Tardieu, in the Chamber of Deputies, later admitted that the French policy "called into question one of the essential principles" accepted as a basis of the peace: the right of self-determination.[98]

5. THE LEFT BANK: DEVELOPMENT OF OPINION

"In all this question of the left bank of the Rhine," says Michon, "the will of the nation was systematically flouted, for the immense majority were not concerned with it at

all." [99]   It could plausibly be argued that the majority of
the population remained relatively unconcerned as to the
precise application of any one of the major principles of
the peace settlement. It is probable that the average "man
in the street" thought very largely in general terms with
regard to Germany, asking only for "security", and "guarantees" without presuming to apply the principles to particular cases. There is good evidence, however, of a widespread feeling that this security was closely linked with
the status of the left bank. This is conclusive if one accepts
as evidence expressions by leaders of organized groups and
by the press, which in the long run tend to dominate national
policy and to sway the relatively inert masses. It is nevertheless true that the policy espoused by the government was
considerably in advance of that demanded by public opinion in the weeks immediately following the Armistice.

Since 1915 a vigorous campaign had been carried on by
nationalistic groups such as the League of Patriots and the
Committee of the Left Bank for annexation, open or disguised, of the left bank. The columns of the *Écho de Paris*
had been freely used by Maurice Barrès to propagate annexationist views.[100] During 1918 preceding the Armistice,
however, the press of the Right remained silent on this
issue, and naturally the pronouncements of the government,
which were scanty at best, did not broach the subject. The
Wilson program, which was perhaps a trifle ambiguous, and
seemed to imply a reservation even as to Alsace-Lorraine,
would obviously have been affronted by annexationist designs. After the Armistice activity revived in certain nationalist circles, though expression of opinion was frequently
so vague that it was difficult to conclude whether open annexation or whether a military frontier or some other special
régime was preferred. Nevertheless, such leading organs
as the *Action Française, Croix, Ouest-Éclair,* as well as the
Libre Parole, Rappel, Éclair de l'Est and *Dépêche* de Lille
seemed clearly favorable to outright annexation in the early
days after the Armistice.[101] A much larger body of opinion

was disposed to favor either a military frontier on the Rhine or a prolonged military occupation; and advocates of one or the other of these policies, which were, indeed, not far removed from each other, came not only from the Right, but largely from the Center, and to a remarkable degree from the Left. During the November-January period such leading organs as the *Temps, Petit Parisien, Petit Journal, Matin, Petit Marseillais, Nouvelliste de Lyon, Figaro, Liberté, Homme Libre* and *Paris-Midi* definitely aligned themselves in favor of a policy either of a military frontier, or of prolonged military occupation, either of which could be characterized, perhaps, as a policy, if not of "disguised annexation", at least as one giving rise to the hope, eventually, of close political ties between that territory and France.[102] The question was generally approached with caution and finesse.

The glories of history, "perhaps too unfamiliar", were appealed to. The French Revolution "had the glory of achieving the work of Richelieu, and of bringing France right up to the borders of the Rhine". Danton had said: " '. . . the limits of the Republic are marked by Nature. We obtain them along the Rhine.' " The Rhinelanders had drunk of the "poisoned cup of Pangermanism", and would have to be disintoxicated. Nevertheless, said the *Petit Journal* (Dec. 2) imprudent "forecasts and predictions" should be guarded against, for at that time there was a question of merely military occupation by Allied forces, and the Peace Conference would fix the ultimate character of the occupation. "But the Past is not dead."

As the Allied soldiers approached the Rhine, memories of the more distant past were stirred. "In a few days," wrote the *Temps* (Nov. 25), "the soldiers of all the Allied nations will mount guard on the banks of the Rhine, which was the natural frontier of Gaul in the times of Cæsar and Vercingetorix." It was a heroic rôle which had been cast for France, and it was at times certainly not without a note of idealism. It was France, said the *Homme Libre* (Jan. 13), who would be in the first line of western democracies to withstand the first shock of Oriental barbarism. She was the "Old Guard" of civilized peoples, and when she claimed guarantees, it would be not merely to protect herself against future aggression. It would also be to safeguard the League of Nations to which she would in future remain loyally attached, as in the past she had been "the rampart of civilization".

The question of the military frontier was persuasively put. A letter from a "high officer" was quoted with approval by the *Temps,* in which he exposed the thesis that the military barrier of the Rhine was necessary, and "in the interest, indeed, of America herself—so that her arrival will not be too late" next time. Though the military frontier would have to be on the Rhine, he argued, the political frontier might be elsewhere. "The author of this letter sees the problem in its reality", was the comment carried in the *Temps.*[103] It was the Foch thesis which had been thus analyzed and approved.

Somewhat similar views were aired in the moderate Left Wing press of the provinces, where it was insisted that the occupation of the left bank should continue at least "till the moment when all the conditions imposed on the defeated enemy" were fulfilled,[104] and where there were hopes that before the expiration of the occupation the Rhenish people would become enamored of "liberty, which they have not previously possessed", with the result that they would want to unite with France.[105]

Thus it appears that during the early days after the Armistice a majority of the most influential journals of Paris and the provinces manifested very definite sympathy for the idea of at least indefinite military control of the Rhineland. In spite of this fact, it seems clear that this did not represent a minimum demand. It was not a *sine qua non,* except with the more nationalistic press of the Right Wing, where the demand for direct annexation found favor. It likewise seems clear that at that time the pro-

gram of the French government was markedly more nationalistic than the demands of its public. This is emphasized by the debates in the Chamber late in December 1918,
in which the demands of the various groups were revealed.
The vital interest of all groups in the Left Bank question
was apparent, and all were united on at least one "minimum demand". This was the program of military neutralization of the left bank. Speaking for the Commission of
Foreign Affairs, which, on this question, was able to register
unanimity, Franklin-Bouillon said: "all that we demand"
is that in future the left bank "shall never serve as a base
for Prussian armies". "Not a German soldier, not a German
military establishment, not a fortress on the left bank of
the Rhine, or within a radius of thirty kilometers on the
right bank." This, he said, was the "minimum" of guarantees which would be acceptable to France and to this
minimum he hoped that other guarantees, such as the
League of Nations, would be added.[106] That even the
Socialists were largely in accord with the proposed régime
was pointed out by Cachin who, on December 27 remarked
in the Chamber, "We agree that on the left bank of the
Rhine all the forts should be razed; that not a single soldier
should be camped there; that it should be a zone entirely
neutralized." [107]

During February and March the demand for a strong
Rhenish frontier became more widespread and more insistent. This was largely due to the fears which had been
aroused with regard to German recovery, and probable
German resistance, and also to the fact that the League
Covenant failed to provide the guarantees unanimously
hoped for in France. Added to this was the fact that the
United States was clearly manifesting a disposition to
weaken the already feeble bonds between League members.
The feeling that the League of Nations was "not enough"
was expressed not only on the Right,[108] and in the Center,[109] but also in the liberal press.[110] Relatively few voices
were raised, however, for outright annexation. The *Action*

Française continued frankly and openly to demand it, lamenting that nowhere was "covetousness" so feeble as in France.[111] But even among staunch republicans the tradition of the French Revolutionary period weighed heavily and inclined them to look with favor on the idea of a return to the "natural frontiers" of the Rhine. "France on the Rhine has, since the National Convention [1795], been the policy of French Revolutionary patriots," wrote Du Mesnil, of the *Rappel* (March 11).

For the most part, the weight of opinion had concentrated upon the military frontier policy, or that of prolonged occupation.[112] This was probably due to the realization of the fact that the government was not, after all, demanding outright annexation. Indeed, the *Débats*, on March 6, severely rebuked "numerous Parisian papers" which had adduced "historical, economic, ethnical, strategical or sentimental" arguments in favor of the Rhine frontier, and had written as though the government were asking for a political frontier on the Rhine. The "essential flaw", said the *Débats*, was that the project did "not enter into the program or the ideas of Clemenceau". All that France wanted, it said, was the occupation of the left bank till Germany had fulfilled the peace terms. But after the occupation the territories were not to be returned to Prussia.

At this time the campaign was led chiefly by the powerful Catholic organ, *Croix*, and by the *Écho de Paris* and *Matin*. The *Croix* seemed to be interested not only in the fact that the Rhine furnished a "strategical frontier", but also in the fact that "The Rhineland was decidedly Catholic"; and the people of that region were, it was argued, hostile to "Lutheran Prussia".[113] Maurice Barrès continued his glorification of the French Rhineland tradition in the *Écho de Paris* (Feb. 9, 28), and he averred that the desire for the Rhine had "taken on new force and inspiration", after the arrival of the French army and the awakening of the French energy "which had accumulated" during France's "apparent sleep". The *Matin's* campaign was frankly for the military

frontier advocated by Foch, as was emphasized by an interview with the Marshal on March 21. "Yes, the Rhine is
our only good line of defense," the Marshal was quoted
as saying. "I do not demand annexation, but if we do not
have this military frontier, we should have fought in
vain." [114]

Not only was this propaganda in favor of a strategic
Rhine frontier supported actively by the other leading
organs of the popular press,[115] but organs of the moderate
Left manifested marked sympathy. "France and Belgium
must have a barrier in the West", in order to "protect themselves against a return of the Boche flood", wrote the
France de Bordeaux (March 24). The hoped-for aid from
a distance would not materialize at once, for there would
be serious delays of procedure. Likewise, *Europe Nouvelle*
(Feb. 8) argued that it was the possession of the Trans-
Rhenan territory which had "facilitated the brigandages of
Germany", and concluded that Germany must be thrown
back beyond the Rhine. Not only that. France would also
demand of the Conference that there should be no obstacle
to "France's legitimate hope that she might exercise in the
Rhenish territory her full intellectual and moral ascend-
ancy", and "the superior attraction" of her genius. The
people should, at the expiration of a given time choose "between the two affinities". "No annexation! No conquest!
No oppression! But a policy which would be tractable,
humane, democratic; characterized by discretion, preparation and transition." This indicates how deeply tinged even
liberal elements were with the belief in the tradition of the
French Rhineland, as well as the superiority of French cul-
ture. Radical Socialist opinion which did not call for a
strategic frontier on the Rhine was insistent on absolute
neutralization, coupled with the hope that an autonomous
Rhineland would be formed.[116]

The Foch program was also supported at this time by
popular demonstrations. Among other manifestations was
that of the "French National Congress", said to represent

one hundred and fifty different associations, and twelve million Frenchmen, and which called itself "The Estates General of France". It held its convention in Paris, February 27 to March 1, and was presided over by M. Bonnet, who was also chairman of the Radical Socialist Federation, and one of the leading spirits of the "Committee of the Left Bank".[117] The resolution of the Congress demanded that there should be "no longer a German soldier on the left bank of the Rhine", which should be "detached politically and economically from Germany". The Rhine should be the frontier of Germany, the bridgeheads should be occupied and France should exercise a protectorate on the Rhine State detached from Berlin. It was the Foch thesis in its purest form.[118] On March 9 Clemenceau was interviewed by a delegation from the "Republicans of the Left", one of the "moderate" groups of the Center of the Chamber of Deputies. Though the press widely reported that they had asked for annexation of the Rhine,[119] Barthou denied that outright annexation had been asked. Presumably a military frontier was satisfactory to them.[120] Only the Socialists vigorously opposed the nationalistic tendencies which became increasingly strong during February and March[121] though an occasional voice was raised in other sections of the press warning against annexation.[122]

6. The Left Bank: Negotiations

During this period the French government was pursuing its Rhenish policy quietly and persistently in informal conversations outside the Council of Ten, and the public knew little, if anything, of what was taking place. The government, apparently, was giving comparatively little direction to the semi-official press as to the line of policy to be followed.

These facts perhaps largely explain why public opinion, in the period preceding the critical days of late March and early April, did not become more excited than it did on this subject of such deep interest to France. It has been said that the Clemenceau government held itself more aloof from the press with regard to the Rhine policy than on any other major subject, and further, that if there was relatively less manifestation of popular interest in the military frontier on the Rhine (than, for example, on Reparations) it was not because the majority of French people were not then favorable to such a policy. "It was rather because official and semi-official circles abstained from arousing popular feeling on such a delicate subject." [123] The preceding weeks of the Conference had been a period of exploration and inquiry, during which policies were gradually crystallizing. It is difficult to say how far Wilson, uninfluenced by British policy, would have gone in yielding to French demands on the Rhine. Tardieu implies that the Americans would have gone farther than the British. At any rate, as early as December he and Clemenceau had presented the French claims to Colonel House, who, says Tardieu, "appreciated their importance".[124] Likewise, Wilson "seemed to acknowledge" the "weight" of the French arguments in his talks with Ambassador Jusserand on the *George Washington* in December 1918; and as late as early March he was reported by his "most intimate collaborators" as not having "any definite objection to them".[125] It is naturally impossible to draw precise conclusions from these statements, but there appears to be no doubt that Colonel House was favorable to the creation of a buffer state on the left bank. The suggestion that there could be a future plebiscite and a decision by the League of Nations silenced any qualms which he might previously have had on this score.[126]

With regard to demilitarization of the left bank, there was never, apparently, any serious question. This principle "seems to have been taken for granted by the representatives of the Principal Powers from an early date in the Preliminary Conference".[127] Whatever Wilson's earlier inclinations were as to other phases of the problem, he was, on his return from the United States (March 14), quick to join forces with Lloyd George to oppose the French theses.

In lieu of the French demands that the German political
frontier be fixed at the Rhine, that the Rhine be occupied
by an inter-Allied force under a League mandate, and that
the left bank territory constitute one or several independent
states, Wilson agreed with Lloyd George (though contrary
to the views of Lansing, White and Bliss of the American
delegation) in offering demilitarization plus an Anglo-American promise to come to France's aid in case of German
aggression.[128] Without denying the great significance of the
Anglo-American offer, Clemenceau would not yield, at least,
on the point of military occupation of the Rhine; and only
very reluctantly did he abandon his demand for an independent state on the left bank.[129] On the 17th the French
government proposed a compromise. It would accept the
proposed alliance plus complete demilitarization of the left
bank and a fifty-kilometer strip east of the Rhine, if, in
addition, the Allies would concede a right of rigorous inspec-
tion of Germany's military status, and also the occupation,
for at least a thirty-year period, of five Rhine bridgeheads.
If, after that period, war should threaten as a result of
German violation of her pledges France should be permitted
to advance her troops to the Rhine.[130]

Between the French and the Anglo-American theses, the
arguments were pursued from March 17 to April 22, when
agreement was finally reached. The issues were tightly
drawn on March 26 and 27 when Lloyd George and Wilson
made their replies in almost identical terms to Clemenceau's
note of the 17th. Demilitarization, plus the proposed Alliance, along with the protection which the League of Nations
would increasingly offer, were considered a sufficient guarantee for France. From that time it was a fight principally
over the question of occupation; and not till the 14th and
15th of April were compromises reached on the fifteen-year
period of occupation, with British and American participation for a brief initial period. It was not till April 29, however, that a provision was added, as a safeguard for France,
providing for a delay in evacuation in case the guarantees

were not deemed to be sufficient at the end of the period of occupation.[131]

7. THE LEFT BANK: PUBLIC ANXIETY

Toward the end of March the Rhineland issues debated in the Council of Four began to define themselves in the press, though a rather imperfect picture continued to be presented until the 16th of April. It was generally accepted at this time (end of March), on the one hand, that the demilitarization of the left bank had been conceded, and, on the other, that the program of annexation had been abandoned. The impression remained that there was a strong probability of establishing a military frontier along the Rhine. The Paris *Daily Mail's* reference, on March 30, to three kinds of frontiers—political, military and economic —with the statement that the military frontier would "almost certainly be the line of the Rhine", was given wide currency, and naturally stimulated hopes for the attainment of this objective. On April 3 the same organ stated that France continued to maintain that the only status which would give it absolute security on the Rhine was "not any form of neutralization [demilitarization] but a neutral state". Nothing was publicly known, at that time, of the proposed alliance, hence the picture created was that of the French delegation struggling for minimum security demands against uncompromising Anglo-American opposition. It is not surprising that the alarm of practically all of the patriotic press became intense. The unanimity with which the leading organs close to the government joined in a concerted demand for stronger guarantees leaves little doubt that they were, at this time, responding to suggestions emanating from official sources. The *France Libre,* of the Socialist press, scarcely exaggerated in saying: "The Paris press . . . which takes its orders [from the Quai d'Orsay] has multiplied its strategic, ethnic, economic and sentimental arguments to justify the annexation of the left bank of the Rhine." [132] As a matter of fact, although these arguments were freely used, the conclusions drawn from them were generally limited to the demand for a military Rhine frontier, along with inter-Allied cooperation in occupation.

All the leading organs of Paris, without exception, as far to the left as the *Œuvre,* vigorously supported the minimum program of a strategic frontier on the Rhine, with an autonomous state (or states), on the left bank. The *Figaro* was perhaps the most persistent and emphatic, beginning on March 30 and keeping up a violent campaign until the middle of April. The arguments of the Tardieu memorandum were repeatedly paraphrased and insisted on. The Rhine was the only possible military frontier. Proposals for limitation of German armaments and for various controls offered only slight promise.[133] It was "nothing less than the very future" of France which was at stake.[134]

The sentiments of other leading organs were practically identical. Either a military frontier, or an autonomous left bank with some sort of control by France, was demanded in all the most influential circles.[135] "The politicians" were advised to yield to the "impartial military experts" in deciding what was indispensable.[136] Wilson was assured that the "most scrupulous" of French republicans believed that in detaching the Rhinelanders from Germany and in creating a neutral state, there would be no serious infringement of their rights, for "there would be no annexation".[137] The *Journal* (April 8) asserted that all other questions paled in importance in comparison with the permanent occupation of the left bank, and even the moderate *Information* (March 30) was equally convinced that the minimum which France could accept was "the occupation of all the bridges over the Rhine and a large strip of territory on the right bank".

That there was official encouragement for the press campaign is scarcely open to question, but it is equally clear that the widespread interest was not merely artificially stimulated. The sympathetic attitude of such moderate Left organs as the *Œuvre,* the *Dépêche* of Toulouse, the *France de Bordeaux,* the *Petit Provençal* and *Europe Nouvelle,* indicate the depth and sincerity of the feeling. The *Dépêche,* for example (April 2), was convinced that the Rhinelanders wanted a neutralized republic under French protection, and it also thought that this solution was compatible with a military frontier on the Rhine. "In the hands of Germany," it said, "the left bank has been an offensive force; in the hands of France it will be a pledge of security." Aside from the Socialist press, only an occasional and relatively less influential voice was raised to condemn or question the Foch Rhine program. "Our reactionaries and chauvinists still persist in their blind designs," wrote *Humanité,* April 2. "They exact as a minimum, permanent military occupation of the left bank of the Rhine. . . ." [138]

But there was not merely the question of occupying the left bank. There was also the question whether France's allies, especially the British and Americans, would assist in maintaining "the Guard on the Rhine". That they should do so was ardently desired by the great majority, for two important reasons. In the first place, it would limit the obligation incumbent upon France, thus releasing much of her man-power. In the second place, it would be the constant, visible and reassuring sign of Allied solidarity. If the occupation were maintained under the ægis of the League of Nations it would be equally, if not more, satisfactory, for it would carry with it the imprimatur of even broader international authority. With the progress of events during the first half of April this aspect of the Rhine problem came increasingly to the fore.

Whatever the military guarantees agreed upon, said the *Temps,* April 2, "The primordial necessity" was that "all of the interested States should cooperate in maintaining them"; that is, France, Belgium, Great Britain and the United States. On April 3 it referred with approval to the recommendation of "the inter-Allied Command" (Marshal Foch) that "military forces occupy the Rhine permanently". The occupation of the Rhine was said to be "a pledge for the common debt of the Allies". "But if the debt is common, why should we be alone in safeguarding the pledge?" "Allied solidarity" and maintenance of their guarantees by means of a "common bond of unity, politically, militarily and economically": these were the indispensable minima, not merely in the view of the *Temps*,[139] but also in that of all other leading organs except those of the Socialist press.[140]

The reports of April 15 and 16 that occupation had been agreed on for a fifteen-year period, but that the Allies would participate only during the first year or two, were received with mixed feelings. The concession of occupation, even for a limited period, was a source of relief, coming as it did, after the stress and strain of the preceding weeks. Nevertheless, the prospect of the withdrawal of British and American forces at an early date left a feeling of grave anxiety as to the future.[141] Not only would France be left facing her historic enemy alone, and bearing the entire burden of the occupation, but the period itself was felt to be too brief.

These feelings were given free rein in the Senate in the debates of April 18 when that body voted unanimously (227 being present) a resolution demanding that the government, in cooperation with the Allies, "secure all of the military guarantees that are indispensable to the security of France and to the liberty of the world".[142] In its original form, as proposed by Senator Paul Doumer (later President of France) and thirty-eight of his colleagues, the resolution demanded the insertion in the Peace Treaty of "the military guarantees recommended by the inter-Allied High Command", that is, by Marshal Foch.[143] On the intervention of the Foreign Minister, however, this reference was stricken out and Senator Doumer accepted the modified form, assuring the Senate and the country that the modified resolution expressed the substance of the original.[144]

When Senator Flaissières, of the Senate Left Wing, sought to amend the resolution by adding words repudiating "energetically every project of territorial annexation, disguised or open", (stating explicitly, also, that Alsace-Lorraine did not come in either category, as it was merely returning to her nationality of 1870), "exclamations" were heard from his colleagues.

Several Senators: This is odious!

Senator Flaissières: I hear from this side of the chamber (the Right) the cry: "This is odious".

Numerous voices: From all sides!

When the Senator explained that he simply wanted to remove from the Germans every pretext for subsequent complaint, disturbances and protests were aroused on "a great number of benches"; and his proposal to amend the resolution by adding the clause renouncing territorial annexation, "disguised or open", received only eight votes out of 226 cast.[145] M. Pichon, Minister of Foreign Affairs, intervened personally against amending the Doumer resolution as it was then phrased, and he assured the Senate that the government was doing its best to obtain the results demanded by the authors of the resolution. These objectives, as expressed by various speakers on that occasion, in speeches which received warm applause throughout the Senate, included, as a minimum, the military barrier of the Rhine for a long period of time—at least until all the obligations of the Treaty were fulfilled.[146] To the applause of his colleagues, Senator Savary, also of the Senate Left Wing, insisted that this guarantee was as important as the restitution of Alsace-Lorraine, for without it Alsace-Lorraine could not be held.

The Doumer resolution was apparently an attempt on the part of its authors to call public attention to the gap between the "Guarantees" program of Marshal Foch, and that which appeared to be prevailing in the diplomatic councils of the Allied leaders, although a semi-official statement denied this to be true. The *Œuvre* (April 19) thought the denial protested too much. It observed that the French military High Command did not think the Treaty was providing sufficient military guarantees, and added somewhat skepti-

cally: "We only hope they are wrong." [147]   The *Temps*
(April 20) interpreted the episode, probably correctly, as an
indication of the "general nervousness" of the public.

8. THE TRIPARTITE ALLIANCE

Meantime, reports were becoming public of the Anglo-
American offer of assistance to France in case of German
aggression, and opinion was gradually being reoriented as
to the left bank régime. It is probable that a few organs
close to the Foreign Office had for some time known of the
discussions between Clemenceau, Lloyd George and Wilson
on this subject. The *Temps*, for example, on April 3, seemed
to be preparing public opinion for future developments by
carefully raising the question whether, before deciding the
Rhine question, the Allies should not be asked to give other
guarantees than occupation. Why could not the governments
of London and Washington promise that "any German aggression against France, against Belgium or against the
region of the Saar, would be considered a declaration of war
against Great Britain and the United States"? [148]   On
April 14 a few organs close to the Foreign Office for the
first time carried the suggestion that there was a probability
of supplementing the Rhine guarantee with something in the
nature of an alliance. In a special box on its front page,
with the heading: "What one must not say", the *Matin*
(April 14) quoted from the *Liberté,* of the previous evening,
the gist of statements reported to have been made by Clemenceau to the Radical Socialist delegation on the 13th.
The whole left bank régime was to be "guaranteed not only
by the League of Nations, but by an interplay of alliances".
The negotiations on the subject were apparently not then
sufficiently advanced to warrant giving them full publicity,
and the publication of the report by a very few papers was
in the nature of an indiscretion. [149]   The project being thus
somewhat in the vague, most leading organs refrained from
assuming that the alliance was a fact, and skeptical commentators refused to count their chickens before they were

hatched. Their editorial remarks continued for a time to reveal their anxieties. An alliance between England, the United States and France was more necessary than ever, said the *Journal* (April 14), as it appeared that the Allies were not to participate in the occupation of the Rhine. "Never did the necessity for serious guarantees seem more imperious." *Écho de Paris,* the same day, suggested that if England and the United States would guarantee the treaty by an "actively defensive alliance" then France could more easily accept a decision by England and the United States not to participate in permanent occupation. The *Temps,* which had preached Allied solidarity almost as insistently as the *Écho de Paris,* demanded, on the 14th, that the treaty text on which the Allies were working should constitute, "first and foremost, a treaty between the victorious powers". The next day it observed that the peace would demand, as imperiously as the war itself, "a close union between the Allies. Let us put in common therefore, as many things as possible." *Paris-Midi* (April 14) reflected moderate opinion in hoping that "the perpetual grouping of the Western Democracies" might transform the "fragility of a material frontier" into the "solidity of a political and moral frontier".

Several days later, the promise of an alliance became more definite, and the semi-official press was able to write more freely and confidently. On the 16th Lloyd George appeared before the House of Commons and spoke reassuringly on this subject. "We have not forgotten that she [France] has a right, not only to be guaranteed against a return of a like attack, but to have the feeling fully that she is guaranteed." These "words of an ally", said the *Temps,* with great satisfaction, meant that Great Britain and the United States were undertaking "to support France in case she should be attacked again by Germany".[150] Leading organs of the Center and Right urged the importance of supplementing the League with the alliance. The *Journal,* which was representative, said, April 19, that "though it goes without saying that the Treaty will be guaranteed by its signatories, in the words of Talleyrand: 'It goes much better if it is said.' " [151]

Comment, at that time, was somewhat reserved. For one reason, the precise form of the Allied undertaking was not known, hence its exact bearing on the Rhine situation could not be appraised. A more important reason was the delicate situation arising out of the question whether Wilson could induce the American Senate to accept the defensive alliance. Traditional American aloofness with regard to commitments in Europe, in addition to Wilson's political weakness arising from Republican control of Congress, could not fail to arouse misgivings. The too frank exposure of these anxieties was frowned upon by the French government,[152] hence the press was cautious. The *Écho de Paris* however (April 19), took account of the difficult political situation, and urged that Wilson and Lloyd George, even though a formal alliance might be difficult, should at least bind themselves, in the spirit of Sir Edward Grey and of the *Entente Cordiale*, and say "We are in honor bound." On April 20 the *Petit Journal*, under a headline announcing: "The Treaty will comprise a defensive alliance between France, England and the United States!" called attention to the difficulties by reproducing a despatch from New York announcing that the Senators opposed to the League were equally opposed to an alliance. The American press, it said, could not believe that there had been talk of a special treaty of guarantee. This delicate aspect of the problem was also carefully raised by the *Temps* (April 21), in insisting that a defensive alliance should be superimposed on the League. "A generation at least" would pass before rival peoples could be induced to take their quarrels before an international organization. The British constitution certainly authorized such an alliance. "Is it the same for the United States?" On the 24th, however, the *Temps* wrote more reassuringly. "The union of the Western Powers has never been closer." In case of new aggression, Germany would find arrayed against her, "the forces of Great Britain and the United States as well as those of France". But the fundamental French thesis should not be forgotten: "The more powerful the guarantees of peace, the smaller will be the probability of having to call upon them."

9. CHANGED PERSPECTIVES

The prospects of a demilitarized Rhineland, occupation for fifteen years, with temporary Allied cooperation, and the tripartite alliance produced a notable change of tone with regard to the left bank program. Though satisfaction was not complete, anxiety was visibly relieved in patriotic circles. The alliance terms were not actually published until July 2, though announcement was made, semi-officially, at the time of handing the peace conditions to the Germans on May 7, that the defensive agreement was definitely agreed upon. Reviewing the situation, the *Temps*, May 8, enumerated the guarantee provisions: (a) Reduction of German forces to 100,000; (b) demilitarization of the left bank and fifty kilometers on the right bank of the Rhine; (c) inter-Allied occupation for fifteen years, with the possibility of retarding the evacuation under certain contingencies; (d) obligation of Germany to submit to investigation by the Council of the League in the enforcement of the military clauses; (e) the Anglo-American alliance—"in virtue of a particular stipulation, which has not figured in the treaty, but to which, without doubt, public allusion will be made". Such, said the *Temps*, were the securities offered to France. "Public opinion will say whether they appear negligible, as certain individuals have pretended." This was a distinctly different tone from that of early April.

Yet a considerable portion of the Right Wing press did not follow the *Temps* in its appraisal. There was a marked feeling that while of course the promised alliance should be accepted with alacrity, it was, nevertheless, an admission that the guarantees were inadequate.[153] One would have "to make the best of a bad bargain," said the *Écho de Paris* (May 8). The *Journal de Rouen* (May 10) referred with approval to a cartoon in the *Rire*, showing a little French soldier keeping watch on the Rhine while, on the other side, an enormous German soldier patrolled back and forth. Two American soldiers, on the point of departure, were saying to the French soldier: "If he jumps on you, telegraph us in America. Then three years later we shall come speeding to your aid as we did last time." The *Journal de Rouen* thought it a sufficiently exact picture of the situation.

Even in the Center and on the Left dissatisfaction was expressed by important organs concerning the inadequacy of the guarantees. France was said to have not much more security than in 1914,[154] and Clemenceau was condoled with for his "despairing efforts" to "bind the obstinacy of the impenitent idealist", President Wilson.[155] Even the *Œuvre* and the *Dépêche* of Toulouse were not pleased, the former (May 11) feeling that the guarantee clauses were not workable, and the latter (May 10) fearing that Germany would do its best to avoid executing the treaty. Germany, it thought, remained "the country of Hegel and Treitschke".

There is no doubt, however, that a fair majority found the guarantee clauses of the treaty tolerably satisfactory, although the Socialist press condemned the arrangements generally as too militaristic.[156] A number of the most important organs which had earlier demanded the strategic frontier on the Rhine now joined with the *Temps* in finding the result either completely satisfactory, or as nearly so as could have been anticipated. This included not only most of those organs which were closest to the government, such as, the *Petit Parisien, Homme Libre, Petit Journal, Figaro,* and *Liberté,* but also some of those which were more independent of the Foreign Office, such as the *Croix, Intransigeant,* and the *Débats*. The *Figaro*, which had led the campaign for the Foch program, said the result represented "the greatest possible approximation" of a really definitive settlement, though it thought that the hope of the future lay in the degree of firmness which France would manifest.[157] This sentiment was echoed, not only in the conservative press, but also in that of the Left. The provisions were acceptable to the *France de Bordeaux,* for example (May 9), on condition that France pursued "a policy of prudence and firmness". The *Petite Gironde,* which had been almost as annexationist in its tendencies as the *Figaro,* proclaimed itself "profoundly satisfied" with the result, and felt that France had found "inestimable securities" in the peace.[158]

That the promised treaty of alliance played an important part in moderating views and in making the final provisions more acceptable, there is no doubt. The *Ouest-Éclair,* previously ultra-nationalistic, felt that the "good news" of the treaty would be "received with profound joy by all friends of peace", and that it would be the "surest of guarantees".[159] The *Petit Journal* (May 8) said it was "hardly necessary to emphasize the capital importance" of that engagement, and the *Petit Provençal* (May 9) said that the best part of the treaty was what it did not contain, namely, the "hope of an alliance beween the United States, England and France."

It could not be said, however, that there were no misgivings with regard to the future of the alliance. The informal nature of that guarantee was distinctly unsatisfactory,[160] and the real value of the proposal was regarded as still to be revealed.[161] That there were "suspicious individuals" was pointed out by the *Figaro* (May 8), which made a subtle appeal to British and American pride, saying that, "if English honor with its imperious exactions, if the American ideal, so magnificently shown in its prodigious efforts, are not a sufficient guarantee, then there is no hope left on earth, no reason for living, no human civilization". The prevailing sentiment of early May was well expressed by the *Paris-Midi* in its conclusion that "If the parliaments ratify the guarantee pact we can affirm that the good germs in the Treaty will develop, and that there will be fruit where blossoms were before."[162]

In the matter of guarantees, as in that of reparations, the contingencies of the future played a dominant rôle. France fell far short of obtaining what was sought by the government and ardently desired by patriotic opinion in the questions of German unity and the régime of the left bank. On the other hand, the prohibition of the union of Austria with Germany was more than had been generally hoped for at the time of the Armistice, while the Anglo-American alliance was, until the critical days of March and April, beyond the wildest dreams of any Frenchmen, official or unofficial. It is significant that those parts of the French program where attainments fell short of hopes, lay primarily in the field of the tangible and substantial, while those as to which the gains (apparent, at least) exceeded expectations were relatively more intangible, more dependent upon the imponderables of international politics, and less subject to direct control by France. Most significant in this latter category was the promise of the alliance which had been accepted in lieu of the most substantial of all the guarantees sought by France, namely, the establishment of a special political régime on the left bank, a régime which, under French control, would have been an important safeguard for an indefinite period. The alliance, it is true, was potentially far more important for the security of France, but its consummation lay in the future and the prospects for its ratification were already clouded with doubt. It is not surprising that informed opinion regarding guarantees was lacking to a degree in genuine enthusiasm and confident hope.

NOTES

[1] *Dépêche of Toulouse,* November 24, 1918.

[2] In the debate in the Supreme Council, February 12, on the renewal of the Armistice, Clemenceau, in opposing the immediate fixing of the final military terms of peace, argued that if the League of Nations "gave guarantees that were expected from it", the military terms would be different from what they would otherwise be. Miller Diary, vol. xiv, p. 334.

[3] See Tardieu's February 25 memorandum on the Left Bank. Tardieu, *op. cit.,* pp. 147 *et seq.*

[4] *Ibid.,* p. 280. "France's security precedes every other consideration," said the *Intransigeant,* March 30, 1919.

[5] *Annales de la Chambre,* December 29, 1918, p. 3334.

[6] February 20, 1919.

[7] February 23.

[8] January 28, 31; February 8.

[9] E.g., *Temps*, February 15; *Croix*, March 7; *Petit Provençal*, February 16; *Figaro, Écho de Paris*, February 17.

[10] *Matin*, February 16.

[11] *Débats*, February 17.

[12] February 19.

[13] November 21, 1918.

[14] March 9.

[15] *France de Bordeaux* charged fraud designed to insure a majority to the Socialists who desired the union. February 22.

[16] *Croix*, February 16; *Figaro*, February 13; *France de Bordeaux*, March 17; *Petit Provençal*, February 17.

[17] *Journal de Rouen*, February 17; *Petite Gironde*, March 1.

[18] *Petit Provençal*, February 17.

[19] *Europe Nouvelle*, March 1, 1919.

[20] *Débats*, February 17; *Temps*, March 7; *Phare*, February 24.

[21] *Temps*, February 22; *Pays*, March 7.

[22] Albin, Pierre, in *Petit Marseillais*, March 8.

[23] *Temps*, March 7; *Liberté* did not approve of worrying about Austrian stomachs unless they belonged to an independent Austria. March 7.

[24] *Croix*, March 7; *Écho de Paris*, February 17; *Journal*, March 6; *France de Bordeaux*, March 30.

[25] *Lyon Républicain*, February 17.

[26] *House Papers*, vol. iv, p. 335.

[27] Miller Diary, vol. xv, p. 152.

[28] *Nouvelliste de Lyon*, March 10.

[29] Tardieu, *op. cit.*, p. 364.

[30] *Ibid.*, p. 375.

[31] May 19; July 2, 1918. Exceptions were *Temps*, May 19, July 2, 1918; *Figaro*, January 6, September 27; October 5, 1918.

[32] November 10.

[33] November 11.

[34] November 17.

[35] November 20.

[36] January 8, 1919.

[37] "It is in the centralization of Germany that the danger lies!" *Temps*, January 16.

[38] February 23. Should not the Allies, it asked, "treat directly with the regional governments of Württemberg, Baden, Hesse, Saxony", etc., and should they not encourage the creation of regional authorities, where they do not exist, even in Prussia itself? February 24, 1919.

[39] November 26, 1918.

[40] December 1.

[41] November 20.

[42] *Cri de Paris*, January 12, 1919. The choice in this case in favor of the latter alternative, seemed pretty clear.

[43] E.g., *Victoire*, March 15.

[44] November 10, 1918; March 10, 1919.

[45] December 1, 1918.

[46] December 2.

[47] January 30, 1919.

[48] February 24.

[49] November 20, 1918.

[50] A great many journals, especially of the provinces, abstained from comment on this particular aspect of the problem, though there was no lack of demands of a general character for adequate security provisions. E.g., *Ouest-Éclair*, November 11, 14, 25, 28, 1918; *Petite Gironde*, December 12; *Figaro*, November 23. Some fear was expressed that the "guarantee" of separatism might tend to weaken other guarantees regarded as more solid and direct. E.g., *Écho de Paris*, February 25, 1919; *Current Summaries*, March 3, 1919.

[51] March 9, 10, 14, 1919.

[52] February 28; March 19.

[53] *Ouest-Éclair*, March 8; *Éclair de l'Est*, April 3; *Temps*, February 25, March 3, 27, 1919.

[54] January 31; March 5.

[55] *Current Summaries*, February 17, 1919.

[56] Hanotaux, G., *Le Traité de Versailles* (Paris, 1919), p. 199.

[57] Baker, *op. cit.*, vol. ii, p. 15.

[58] *House Papers*, vol. iv, p. 334.

[59] Minutes of the Supreme Council, March 27, 1919. Miller Diary, vol. xv, pp. 510 *et seq.*

[60] Baker, *op. cit.*, vol. ii, p. 97.

[61] *Le Combat des Trois*, pp. 162-165.

[62] *Ibid.*, pp. 168 *et seq.*

[63] *Ibid.*, p. 177.

[64] When the Conditions of Peace were handed to Germany, however, there was some protest from conservative organs over the failure of the Allies to deal individually with the various German States. *Action Française*, May 7, 9, 13; and *Temps*, May 9, continued their campaigns. *Avenir* averred that the Allies had "consecrated the unity of Germany", after France had for fifty years opposed it as her greatest peril. May 9, 1919.

[65] Feelings on this subject were also revealed by the negotiations of late March and early April over the security régime for the left bank. This will be discussed in the succeeding sections on the left bank.

[66] *Matin*, June 2, 3, 4.

[67] *Paris-Midi*, June 3.

[68] *Phare* of Nantes, June 4.

[69] *Matin*, June 3.

[70] *Journal*, June 3.

[71] *Liberté*, June 3.

[72] June 3, 6.

[73] June 3, 5.

[74] June 3, 6. *Vérité* also saddled responsibility on the military authorities. June 6.

[75] *Current Summaries*, June 4, 5, 7.

[76] E.g., *Matin*, June 6.

[77] *Current Summaries,* June 9.

[78] June 12. See *Current Summaries,* June 3 to 12.

[79] *Current Summaries,* June 3 to 12.

[80] *Petit Provençal* and *France de Bordeaux,* June 4; *Matin,* June 3; *Écho de Paris,* June 4.

[81] June 3. Also *Action Française,* June 3; *Liberté,* June 5.

[82] *Petit Provençal,* June 8.

[83] *Matin,* June 14; *Journal,* June 11, 15.

[84] Baker, *op. cit.,* vol. ii, p. 87.

[85] *Ibid.,* vol. ii, p. 90.

[86] *Grandeurs et Misères d'une Victoire,* pp. 188-189.

[87] *Journal,* June 8, 9. "France and the Allies are abandoning the young Rhenish Republic," he said, "and the hopes of peace which it bears in its bosom will change into fermentation of war."

[88] Bérard, Victor, *La Paix Française* (Paris, 1919), pp. 179, 289. *Temps,* March 15, said "the entire problem of peace" hung on the military and geographic aspects of the settlement.

[89] Terrail (Mermeix), *op. cit.,* p. 191.

[90] *Travaux du Comité d'Études* (Paris, 1918), vol. i, pp. 319-324. "So long as we allow the enemy the possibility of an assembling place on the left bank of the Rhine, we shall have, from the military point of view, only an artificial frontier, forcing us to maintain a formidable defensive organization."

[91] *Ibid.,* pp. 319-324.

[92] It is well known that the Marshal had the full support of President Poincaré.

[93] Terrail (Mermeix), *op. cit.,* pp. 204 *et seq.*

[94] *Ibid.,* pp. 210 *et seq.*

[95] *Ibid.,* pp. 219 *et seq.*

[96] *Ibid.,* p. 194. Recouly quotes Foch as saying: "The French government at once made my thesis its own." Recouly, Raymond, *Foch, My Conversations with the Marshal* (New York, 1929), p. 191.

[97] Michon, G., *Clemenceau* (Paris, 1931), p. 219.

[98] September 2, 1919. Quoted in Michon, *op. cit.,* p. 219.

[99] *Ibid.,* p. 227.

[100] The Comité du rive gauche was representative of a considerable body of opinion, including among its lists even men of Radical Socialist affiliations, such as Professor A. Aulard; and its official organ was the Radical Socialist paper, *Rappel.*

[101] *Écho de Paris* continued to carry Maurice Barrès' annexationist articles, though Pertinax stressed alliances rather than annexation. *Libre Parole,* a journal of minor importance, conducted an "inquest" among public leaders of the Right Wing, most of whom favored annexation. *Rappel,* organ of the "Committee of the Left Bank," resumed its advocacy of annexation immediately after the Armistice.

[102] It should be recalled that a considerably larger group, including *Œuvre,* was favorable to the idea of an autonomous Rhineland.

[103] December 11. "We cannot disturb the United States and England every fifty years, or less, even though they are now convinced that in

defending us they are defending themselves." That there were doubts as to the realization of these hopes was illustrated by the *Petit Parisien's* comment (December 2): "If it [the Rhine] does not become the political frontier let it at least become—and this is absolutely necessary—a military frontier, and an insurmountable barrier behind which Germany is kept back by strong bonds."

[104] Editorial by General Heymann in *Dépêche* of Toulouse, December 1, 1918.

[105] *Est Républicain,* December 15. *Progrès de la Somme,* December 5. The *Œuvre,* December 9, thought the Rhinelanders would want to "come back" to France. One reason for the demand for crushing indemnities was to permit an indefinite occupation of the Rhine.

[106] *Annales de la Chambre,* December 29, 1918, p. 3329. It is not to be supposed that some of the groups of the Center and Right would not have demanded more than this minimum. But it is notable that this demand was for less than what was finally achieved by the government, the right bank zone being ultimately fixed at fifty rather than thirty kilometers.

[107] *Ibid.,* December 27, 1918, p. 3250.

[108] E.g., *Figaro,* March 10.

[109] *Petit Parisien,* March 4.

[110] E.g., *France de Bordeaux,* March 24.

[111] February 7; March 4; April 2.

[112] This might, in effect, ultimately yield fruits comparable to that of annexation.

[113] March 1. Also March 18, 21.

[114] See *Matin* also, March 4, 29, 31.

[115] *Petit Parisien,* March 4; *Petit Journal,* February 25; *Journal,* March 17; *Intransigeant,* March 4.

[116] *Populaire de Nantes,* March 12; *Dépêche* of Toulouse, March 19.

[117] *Débats,* March 1.

[118] *Journal,* March 1. The representative character of this Congress was doubtless exaggerated, but it is interesting from the point of view of the participation in its councils of leading figures of the moderate Left.

[119] E.g., *Temps,* March 9.

[120] *Esprit Public en France,* Bulletin 18, March 9-15, 1919.

[121] *Populaire,* February 18; *Humanité,* March 10, 14.

[122] The *Lyon Républicain,* for example, of the Center, while remarking that it was "a very popular" view in France that "the political and military frontier of Germany" should be the Rhine, expressed the conviction that the river was not really a frontier. It was an obstacle, it said, but not a frontier. Such a régime could not, it thought, bring security. February 25; March 4.

[123] Statement to author by Saint-Brice, of the *Journal,* August 13, 1931.

[124] Tardieu, *op. cit.,* p. 170.

[125] *Ibid.,* p. 171.

[126] *House Papers,* vol. iv, pp. 334, 383.

[127] Annotations in Miller Diary, vol. xix, p. 56.

[128] Tardieu, *op. cit.,* pp. 175-177. Colonel House was apparently entirely

favorable to the project at first. *House Papers,* vol. iv, p. 394. On March 27, however, his three colleagues, Lansing, White and Bliss, dissented strongly from the idea of the alliance on the ground that it would be "absolutely fatal to the success of the League of Nations". Miller Diary, vol. vii, pp. 258 *et seq.* This seemed to modify the Colonel's views, as he recorded, on that day, his own view that the alliance might be looked upon "as a direct blow at the League of Nations". *House Papers,* vol. iv, p. 394.

[129] The left bank, it was argued, March 17, was "different from the rest of Germany", and was "conscious of its economic independence", though this "economic independence" had been practically admitted to be non-existent in the French note of March 12, which would have required Germany to furnish every year to the left bank state or states sufficient coal for their industries. Tardieu, *op. cit.,* p. 176.

[130] *Ibid.,* p. 181.

[131] *Ibid.,* pp. 206 *et seq.* Article 429 of Treaty with Germany.

[132] April 3. It is not necessary to assume that a concerted campaign was "ordered". Suggestions from Quai d'Orsay and from the press bureau at rue François-Premier would be sufficient.

[133] March 30.

[134] April 1. April 5: fears were expressed that a "crushing disappointment" was in store for France, and that "the indispensable guarantees" were being jeopardized. April 6: The time had come for the Allies to listen to France with regard to the "legitimate demands" which she was making. April 9: "The military frontier of the Rhine is indispensable" to prevent a repetition of the German offensive. April 10: The most important question was "the occupation of the left bank of the Rhine". It was a matter of "life or death". April 11: "The Rhine is the natural and historical division between the two lands. The Rhine is a solid military frontier—the only one. . . ." April 13: Provisions regarding the Saar and reparations would be as "nothing" unless the left bank were occupied.

[135] "To neutralize without occupying . . . is as good as ordering the inhabitants of the moon to respect our civil law," wrote the *Écho de Paris* (April 1). "Neutralization by the setting up of independent states" was the preference of the *Petit Parisien,* April 2, and the *Petit Marseillais,* April 2. "France will not have the Rhine as her political frontier," wrote the *Intransigeant,* April 1, "but she demands that it become a military frontier." Unless the bridgeheads of the Rhine were under international control France could not go to sleep without risking a "cruel awakening".

[136] *Débats,* March 30, thus supported the Foch thesis.

[137] *Victoire,* April 1.

[138] See also *Petit Bleu,* April 9, and *Progrès de la Somme,* April 10; *Esprit Public en France,* Bulletin 22, April 6-12, 1919.

[139] April 9.

[140] E.g., *Écho de Paris,* March 31; *Débats,* March 30; *Œuvre,* April 5. The *Rappel,* organ of the "Committee of the Left Bank", was equally insistent, April 15, that all the weight of the military burden should not fall on France alone.

[141] The *Intransigeant,* April 15, asked whether the United States and England feared that "they might be accused of imperialism if they collabo-

rated with France on the Rhine", and *Œuvre*, April 16, raised the question whether France would "remain alone facing Germany". See *Current Summaries*, April 16.

[142] *Annales du Sénat*, April 18, 1919, pp. 736-738.

[143] *Ibid.*, April 17, p. 706.

[144] *Ibid.*, April 18, p. 736.

[145] *Ibid.*, pp. 736-738.

[146] *Ibid.*, p. 737.

[147] The *Matin*, April 19, used the occasion for another vigorous editorial flourish in favor of a long inter-Allied occupation of the left bank.

[148] *Écho de Paris*, which had, throughout the Conference, led the way in insisting vigorously on an alliance policy, stated on March 29 that the political complement to the left bank régime should be "a military alliance with Belgium, England and the United States" which should "come into play automatically as soon as the adversary makes the slightest move to recover the Rhine line".

[149] The episode illustrates the vagaries of the censorship. The *Matin's* main article in which it apparently attempted to give the same information was heavily censored. *Petit Journal*, however, on the same day, was allowed to carry the item.

[150] April 18.

[151] See also *Current Summaries*, April 19.

[152] Statement to author by M. de Marsillac, of the *Journal*, May 1931.

[153] E.g., *Action Française* and *Écho de Paris*, May 8.

[154] *Journal*, May 10.

[155] *Progrès du Nord*, May 10.

[156] *Humanité* and *Populaire*, May 9.

[157] May 8, 10.

[158] May 9.

[159] May 9.

[160] E.g., *Matin*, May 8.

[161] *Intransigeant*, May 9.

[162] May 8.

CHAPTER VIII

THE ENIGMA OF RUSSIA

"The treatment accorded to Russia by her sister nations in the months to come will be the acid test of their goodwill."
(Woodrow Wilson, in the Fourteen Points.)

1. THE PROBLEM BEFORE THE CONFERENCE

THE problem of Russia dogged the peacemakers from the beginning of the Conference to its close. Even before the Conference opened, leaders of policy and of opinion were convinced that peace with Germany could be organized only in the larger context of a solution of the enigma presented by the new Soviet régime. It has been stated that "Russia played a more vital part at Paris than Prussia".[1] Whatever its relative importance, it is significant that at the first meeting of the Supreme Council the Russian question was up for discussion, and that the first major decision of the Conference, aside from questions of procedure, had to do with this baffling question. "It is impossible to make peace for Europe," said Lloyd George, in the Supreme Council, January 16, "without settling the Russian question." [2]

On all sides, in France, demands were repeatedly made for the formulation of a policy toward Russia. The degree of French public interest in this matter is pretty well illustrated by the fact that, during the December-January period, no fewer than nineteen of the *Temps'* leaders were occupied directly with this subject; and in editorial columns from Right to Left it was a frequently recurring theme. The *Temps* led the way in the demand for the crystallization of a policy. December 6: "Why do we fear Bolshevism in Germany?" "Because we have allowed it to flourish in Rus-

sia." December 7: "The chaos in Berlin would continue"
unless the Allies knew how to reorganize Russia. December
12: If we disinterested ourselves in Russia, the affairs of
Germany would become a "barrel without a bottom". On
the day of President Wilson's landing in France, it pressed
its demand for a "positive policy".[3] On December 26 it
wrote: "If the Allies do not occupy themselves with the
reorganization of Russia . . . Russia will either one day
be reorganized by the Germans, or the Russians will dis-
organize Europe." In February that paper was continuing
the same theme. "Now Germany has been poisoned and
infected by Russia." "Russia's influence is incalculable." [4]
And so it continued throughout the Conference. The Socialist press was equally insistent on the formulation of a policy,
though the policy it desired was radically different from that
advocated by the *Temps*.[5]

As early as July 1918, President Wilson had indicated to
Colonel House his difficulties in framing a Russian policy.
"I have been sweating blood over the question what is right
and feasible to do in Russia," he said. "It goes to pieces
like quicksilver under my touch." [6] On the eve of the Conference it was, apparently, still like quicksilver. American
troops had been sent to Northern Russia and to Eastern
Siberia, although, in July 1918, the Secretary of State, in a
note to the Allied ambassadors, had refused to intervene in
Russia, or to "sanction it [intervention] in principle." [7]
But now hostilities against Germany had ceased, and American troops were still on Russian soil. Did this situation have
any *raison d'être,* in view of principles of "rights of peoples"
and "self-determination"?

The French government had less difficulty in making up
its mind on the Russian problem, for it had fewer "idealogi-
cal" qualms of the sort which troubled the American President. "Rights of peoples" and "self-determination" were
phrases which easily translated themselves into the urgent
need for active interposition to safeguard the "right" of the
"real" Russian people to dispose of themselves. Further-

more, the war was not really over. It was only in a state of suspended animation, and war-time measures must be relentlessly pursued. As Clemenceau later remarked, the Conference period was "only a lull in the storm".[8] For the French government it was not so much a question of knowing "what were good to do", but rather, of getting the necessary support from the Allies and from its own people for doing what was considered desirable. The result was a compromise policy based on what seemed to the government to be attainable.

During the middle period of December it was commonly accepted in the public press that the government favored military intervention in Russia, though the ministry refused to be drawn out on the subject by the Socialists in the debate of December 11. It was apparently waiting for conversations with the Allies before committing itself.[9] This expectation of Allied intervention was heightened by the publication in the *Temps*, December 23, of a Reuter despatch from London which, as the *Petit Journal* said, December 24, gave rise to the presumption of "a decisive intervention" and the organization of "a great expedition to bring the Bolsheviks to reason". Yet two days later the *Temps* regretfully remarked that "The Allies have apparently renounced making any military effort in Russia",[10] and coincidentally Pichon went before the Commission on Foreign Affairs of the Chamber of Deputies and stated that a military expedition to Russia was not envisaged.[11] The assumption was that Great Britain and the United States would not go along with a policy of military intervention.[12] In the Chamber debates, December 27 and 29, French policy was stated somewhat more fully by Pichon, after the government had been attacked from both sides. Commenting on Cachin's statement that apparently "the government was renouncing military intervention in Russia", Pichon stated somewhat ambiguously that he had said nothing of the kind. The press "had misinterpreted" his remarks.[13] Presumably, intervention was not renounced.

It was simply not intended, at that time, to send a further military expedition. Franklin-Bouillon, Radical Socialist, and head of the Commission on Foreign Affairs of the Chamber, also attacked the government policy, but rather on the ground that it was not sufficiently vigorous. "We cannot abstain from intervention in Russia," he insisted. It would need to be military in character and also to involve material and staffs.[14]

Replying to all his assailants, Pichon explained the existing government policy to be that of the *cordon sanitaire*. Clemenceau's instructions of December 13 to French Generals on the Russian front were quoted, indicating that the inter-Allied plan of action was not offensive in character, but that it was designed, rather, "to prevent the Bolsheviks from having access to the Ukraine, the Caucasus, and Eastern Siberia, which are economically necessary for their existence. . . ." It was a question, first of a "defensive front". If an offensive became necessary in order to reduce Bolshevism, it would have to be executed ultimately by Russian forces who would be given material aid by the Allies.[15] Such was the *cordon sanitaire*. It was, in short, the policy of blockade, in the hope of thus starving out Bolshevism.

The French government, in its general desire for a forward policy in Russia, had the warm support of patriotic French opinion, though the Socialist and Labor press repeatedly and vehemently stigmatized the project as "criminal intervention". *Humanité* and *Populaire*, which, before the Armistice, had opposed the interventionist policy, denounced the "Russian War", even more bitterly afterwards. Cachin argued that Pichon's "pretext" for sending soldiers to Russia, namely, the necessity of forming an Eastern front against Germany, had now collapsed. The expedition against Russia was "dangerous, suspect, and destined to raise against us the entire country".[16]

Farther to the right there was general agreement that interposition in some form should take place, but the form which it should assume was the subject of great controversy and the source of grave doubts. A fact which caused much Left Wing opinion to favor some form of intervention was that it could be justified on really idealistic principles. Albert Thomas, of the Socialists, for example, had, since July 1918, been an advocate of intervention for the purpose of acting with the "democratic elements for the salvation of Russia". "No objective of an internal political character" was envisaged.[17] On November 27 he expressed the same views in *Humanité*, though the use of force was apparently disavowed. "By all economic and moral methods, by the methods which President Wilson defined in his Fourteen Points concerning Russia, we have still the right to intervene." Much Left Wing opinion was thus to be found, along with that of the Center and the Right, in the camp of the interventionists, though there was no unanimity as to the method to be adopted. "Intervene?" asked *Dépêche* of Toulouse (Dec. 13). "Yes, but under what form and in what degree?" As to the basic principle, the *Dépêche* was clear. Whatever the form adopted, it said, the common aim and limit of intervention ought to be "to restore to the Russian people the right of self-determination".

The form which interposition should take was equally debated in the conservative and nationalist press. On the extreme Right the *Action Française* vigorously opposed military intervention, proposing the alternative of blockade, thus allowing Russia "to stew in its own juice".[18] The *Victoire, Débats,* and *Écho de Paris* led an active campaign for military intervention. "Who is it among our Chiefs of State that refuses to go to help Russia?" asked the *Victoire*. "Is it you, Mr. Lloyd George? Is it you, M. Clemenceau? Or, could it be you, Mr. Wilson?"[19] The same journal frankly proposed that the "young American army" would be the logical one to use for the purpose, along with some volunteers from other Allied countries.[20] The *Débats* averred that intervention was "dictated by a duty toward humanity",[21] and *Écho de Paris* insisted that only a few men—say, 200,000—would be needed for the task" if it were undertaken at once.[22] The *Temps* hammered on a policy clearly implying military action, without too openly saying so. The *cordon sanitaire* proposal of the French government was vehemently condemned (Dec. 13) as "immoral" and "dangerous". We should not allow a former ally "to stew in its own juice". Furthermore, "To abandon Russia would be . . . to hand it over to German influence", for one could not "erect a water-tight compartment between Russia and the West". The same organ appealed subtly to President Wilson's pride by repeated suggestions that the prestige of the League of Nations (not then organized) was at stake. "A fine beginning for a League of Nations!" [23] In February and March it continued strumming the same chord.[24]

In spite of the vigorous campaign on the Right for military intervention, it was the policy of the *cordon sanitaire* which apparently met with greatest favor, for it seemed to promise the solution of the problem without involving the sending of French troops to Russia. Demands for demobilization were growing, and further sacrifice of French lives was looked upon as highly undesirable. Leading organs of the heavy press pronounced strongly on this. Was France, who had "sacrificed so many of her sons", who had "suffered so many ruins", was she "to shed her blood again?" asked the *Petit Journal,* December 24. Her first need was thought to be "to preserve all that are left of her children in order to realize the victorious peace which she has deserved". The *Matin,* December 25, noted the swing of policy away from military action, and said the Entente governments did not wish to impose a painful expedition on soldiers tired by years of war. Moderate Left Wing organs [25] were happy over the reports of the abandonment of military intervention, and looked with satisfaction on the plans for supplying money and materials for the achievement of economic encirclement.

2. PRINKIPO

The French government, though backed by most of its own public in its Russian policy, encountered serious resistance from British and American sources. The British opposition was first completely revealed by the publication of the famous "Pichon note" in *Humanité*, January 11. Lloyd George, about the first of January, had proposed that the warring elements in Russia be called upon to agree to a truce during the Peace Conference, and to send representatives to Paris. Pichon lost no time in stigmatizing this as a complete abandonment of all that had been held dear in previous Allied policy toward Russia. Recalling the Allied policy of "furnishing . . . all the aid and succor which it is possible to give to the healthy, faithful, honest elements in Russia, in order to help them to escape from the bloody and disorderly tyranny of the Bolsheviks", he solemnly announced: "The French government . . . will not come to terms with crime." No objections were raised to the representation at Paris of the various anti-Bolshevik groups, but the existing Moscow régime would have to be rigorously excluded.[26]

President Wilson had also become an advocate of the idea that the Bolsheviks should be given a hearing, and he threw his powerful support to the proposal of the British Premier. In the first meeting of the Supreme Council, January 12, a clash occurred over the question of the representation of Russian interests at the Conference. Pichon favored calling in various representatives of the old régime, but Lloyd George, supported by Wilson, protested "strongly against the Conference choosing representatives for one hundred million Russians".[27] On January 16 the Supreme Council considered the British proposal to bring to Paris representatives of the "different governments now at war within what used to be the Russian Empire". The Great Powers, after hearing these representatives, "would then try to find a way to bring some order out of chaos". The only alternatives to this policy, said Lloyd George, were military intervention, and the *cordon sanitaire*. As to the first, was there anyone who proposed to put down the Bolshevik movement, even though it was a danger to civilization? As to the *cordon* policy, the members of the Supreme Council could not, "as humane people" envisage it. "It would starve the wrong people—our friends." Wilson agreed with Lloyd George's diagnosis, as well as his proposed remedy. He had no sympathy "for the brutal aspect of Bolshevism", yet there was a growing impatience with the slowness of reform in the political and economic world dominated by "large vested interests". They would be playing against the principle of the free spirit of the world "if they did not give Russia a chance to find herself along the lines of utter freedom".[28] At Pichon's request, the Supreme Council heard Noulens, former French ambassador to Russia. On January 20 he gave his impressions of the Soviet régime—impressions which had already been published in lurid detail (Jan. 12) by the conservative press, apparently as an answer to the publication of the Pichon note. The reign of terror was described: "The fortresses were full of prisoners who were dying of starvation . . . it was a regular thing for the guards to take from ten to twelve of these poor prisoners every day and shoot them so as to make room for more." "Not only men but women had been shot. There had been atrocities, drownings, the cutting off of noses and tongues, mutilations, burials alive . . . rape and pillage everywhere."[29] Scavenius, the Danish minister to Russia, was also heard. Intervention, he thought, should come about quickly. Famine was forcing many to become Bolsheviks.[30] No testimony favorable to the Bolshevik régime was heard.

The bitter opposition from the French was not without effect. Wilson now came forward with a compromise proposal for convening the various representatives at some distant place, perhaps Saloniki, perhaps Lemnos. Even this was strongly objected to by Clemenceau, who regarded the Bolsheviks as "criminals", and who thought the meeting would only "increase their prestige". His preference was, he said, to set up a barrage between himself and the Bolsheviks and let Bolshevism work itself out. Nevertheless, he would yield, especially if Wilson would draw up a "short, clear, substantial paper in which it was stated that it was not the wish of the Allies to interfere in the internal affairs of Russia".[31]

The next day the Supreme Council accepted the amended proposals of President Wilson. Disclaiming any intervention in Russia, and professing friendship for the Russian people, the Conference invited "every organized group" then exercising political authority in Russia (excluding Finland) to send representatives, not to Saloniki or Lemnos, but to Prinkipo (Princes Island) in the Sea of Marmora. Meantime, there would be a military truce, and a free conference would seek to bring about understanding and agreement among the various Russian elements, and to establish "happy cooperative relations . . . between her people and the other peoples of the world". Thus the famous Prinkipo proposal was launched upon the Conference waters.[32]

This decision of the Supreme Council was one of the major sensations of the Peace Conference. It was the occasion of no little surprise, coming, as it did, when conservative opinion was beginning to hope that the testimony of Noulens and Scavenius, whose anti-Bolshevik views were well known, would divert the Conference from the proposals to listen to Bolshevik representatives.[33] The massive headlines of the *Matin*, announcing it as a *coup de théâtre*, suggested the nature of the public reaction.[34] The *Petit Parisien* described the "astonishment" of "an important part of public opinion" as the resolution adopted,[35] and the *Croix* said: "The least that one can say is that we were far from expecting this proposal." [36]

Socialist circles were jubilant,[37] and a few of the more advanced liberal organs seemed pleased.[38] But moderate Left Wing opinion was, for the most part, hesitant and skeptical. "The invitation is vast and vague," ambiguously commented the *Œuvre*, calling attention to the "diplomatic lazaret" to which the delegates had been summoned.[39] The *Petit Provençal* (Jan. 24) and the *France de Bordeaux* (Jan. 25) were cautious and reserved, while the leading

Radical Socialist organ, *Dépêche* of Toulouse (Jan. 26) frankly regretted that the invitation implied an interruption of military operations which, it averred, were at that time unfavorable to the Bolsheviks. Nevertheless, it concluded, "we are at the Conference of Paris prepared by Mr. Wilson in his messages. We have subscribed to the preface; are we free to tear up the book without having turned over its leaves?"

The press of the Center and Right did not conceal its indignation. "A perilous decision", "a disastrous compromise",[40] "a disconcerting solution",[41] "a deplorable act",[42] "A hazardous attempt at reconciliation",[43] a "triumph for Lenin",[44] were typical characterizations. "An impression of stupor" was created by the proposal, said another.[45] The only comfort which the *Temps* (Jan. 24) and *Écho de Paris* (Jan. 23) got out of the affair was that the Bolsheviks had not been invited to Paris. The Bolsheviks, it was alleged, were the only parties who would profit by the affair—an impression which was widely expressed. The heavy press was uncompromisingly against the proposal. Though the *Petit Journal*, organ of Pichon, was somewhat cautious and reserved, the *Petit Parisien, Journal* and *Matin* boldly fought the project. "Were the Allies not already sufficiently documented on Bolshevism?" asked the *Petit Parisien*. As for reconciliation between the opposing factions, that was out of the question. One possible ray of hope remained: perhaps the move was another Wilson "maneuver", which would ultimately make it obvious that direct action was necessary.[46]

The press of the Right was vitriolic. The choice of the meeting place for the Conference was lampooned. It might have occurred to the writer of a farce, averred *Action Française* (Jan. 23). "The fact is," said the *Croix* (Jan. 24), "that we have actually recognized, and almost approved the régime of assassination, pillage and terror which has desolated Russia for a year; we have sacrificed the elements of order to a band of unavowed anarchists." "Idealism, ignorance and politics, these are the evil guests at the Quai d'Orsay," lamented *Écho de Paris* (Jan. 23). "What an image of the League of Nations they are giving us."

Wilson became the subject of bitter comment. "Fears" were confirmed "that certain spirits, full of the best intentions, but filled with ideology, would get the Allies to make dangerous decisions".[47] The *Victoire* (Jan. 23) thought it not necessary to announce that the proposal came from President Wilson, as it bore "the stamp of this good judge of international peace. The sermon which he addresses to the different Russian parties is the same that he addressed with evangelical patience to the belligerents during two years of the great war before deciding to take part in the quarrel." [48] Several papers accused Wilson of introducing mercantilist considerations to strengthen his case. The *Daily Mail,* of Paris, January 24, carried a news item stating that "one of the underlying motives . . . was that of retrieving the enormous sums of money loaned to Russia by the Allies [over thirty-nine billion francs, it said]".[49] Accepting this as authentic, the *Débats,* January 25, delivered a violent attack on the President, expressing surprise that he had not perceived "the moral impossibility of dealing with the Bolsheviks". "When one is striving for the creation of a League of Nations founded on the sacred respect for mutual engagements, can one extend one's hand to brigands, and invite them to a conference? Whatever the material advantages, we must answer: 'No.' We have always appreciated the elevation of spirit of Mr. Wilson, and the nobility of his character. But, we must confess, we should lose a good part of our confidence in his wisdom if we should see him recommend negotiations with the Bolsheviks." [50] The *Phare* of Nantes, under a heading: "THIRTY-NINE BILLIONS IS A FINE LITTLE SUM", stigmatized the Conference for the "flagrant contradiction" between its action and its words, and sarcastically asked whether the *Daily Mail* wasn't wrong, "for had not Wilson said 'The Peace Conference will not be a market-place for bargaining'?" [51]

3. THE FAILURE OF PRINKIPO

The Prinkipo proposal was simpler in conception than in execution. President Wilson and Lloyd George could propose, but they could not dispose in such a matter, where hostile influences were rampant. Had all five of the Great Powers been in agreement as to the desirability of holding the Conference, and had they worked harmoniously for its realization, there seems little doubt that it could have been consummated. Granting acceptance of the project by the Bolsheviks, whom the Entente did not control, acceptance by the other groups, who were largely dependent on the Entente, could have been assured by firmness and a certain amount of pressure. But this solidarity was notoriously lacking, and the French government, which was bitterly opposed to the whole program, occupied the most strategic position for bringing about its defeat.

That it at least connived at the defeat of Prinkipo seems scarcely open to question. As early as January 25 Ambassador Page, in Rome, telegraphed to the American Commission at Paris: "Opinion here, in which I concur, seems to be that Sazonoff is extremely pro-French, and probably working with them in opposition to Prinkipo." [52] W. C. Bullitt, who was closely in touch with House and Lansing at the Peace Conference, stated in his testimony before the Senate Foreign Relations Committee on this subject, that "the French Foreign Office had communicated to the Ukrainian Government and various other anti-Soviet Governments that if they were to refuse the proposal, they [the French] would support them and continue to support them, and not allow the Allies . . . to make peace with the Russian Soviet Government". [53] Both George D. Herron and William Allen White, the American Prinkipo delegates, believed that the anti-Bolshevik opposition to Prinkipo was largely inspired by the French government, and particularly by Pichon, with the knowledge and consent of Clemenceau. [54] Herron wrote that the representatives of each of the anti-Bolshevik factions claimed that French officials "persuaded or commanded them not to go".[55]

The governmental press did its part in bringing about the defeat of Prinkipo. Far from accepting the decision and working for the project's achievement, the most powerful organs close to the Foreign Office used their influence to discredit the scheme and to prevent its consummation. The *Bataille*, Labor organ, called attention, January 26, to the "campaign of the reactionary press" against the Prinkipo proposal, and to its exploitation of "the *'noble candeur'* of the President".[56] The *Petit Parisien, Matin, Journal, Figaro, Écho de Paris* and *Débats*, of the most influential press, studiously and carefully undermined the program; while the *Temps* and *Petit Journal* somewhat more cautiously threw their support in the same direction. The *Victoire*, with whom military intervention against the Bolsheviks was a consuming passion, was convulsed with rage, and repeatedly vented its wrath in long editorials stigmatizing the presumed wickedness of the scheme.[57] All Frenchmen "except the curates and sacristans of the Orthodox Socialist Church", were disconcerted and indignant, it wrote (Jan. 25); but "the noble President Wilson has the excuse of being American, and thus is unable to appreciate European realities".[58]

Various devices were resorted to for the purpose of circumventing the Wilson-Lloyd George scheme. The "lively emotion in Russian circles of Paris" was immediately played up, and "general indignation" was reported to prevail.[59] Statements of Russian "patriotic" groups were prominently carried, indicating their horror and amazement at the proposal. A ringing protest to Clemenceau from the "Council of the National and Democratic Bloc of Russian Political Organizations Abroad", including eight "Patriotic Leagues", was widely carried. Deploring the failure of the resolution to allude to "the terror which reigns everywhere", it said: "We should be men without courage and without honor if we accepted for a single moment a truce such as is proposed to us when everything that is near and dear to us is in danger of death." [60] Publication was given to a "Reform Program" for "democratic Russia", addressed to Pichon by the "Russian Political Conference", representative of various anti-Bolshevik elements in Paris. Equality before the law, solution of the agrarian problem, decentralization, etc., were promised. [61] Interviews with various well-known anti-Bolshevik Russians were prominently carried. The *Matin*, in particular, played these up in order to drive home its message. An interview with Sazonoff, former Czarist Foreign Minister, was headlined: "The murdered ones have only to meet their murderers"; and Sazonoff was quoted as saying his group would never meet the Bolsheviks. [62] Bourtzeff, a Social Revolutionary, was quoted as saying that the Prinkipo proposal was the "heaviest blow the Russian people had received since the beginning of the war". [63] Maklakoff, former Russian ambassador to France, on being interviewed, said he would "not express any opinion on the decision of the Powers". Then he proceeded to note the "profound humiliation experienced" by patriotic Russians, adding further that the truce would not stop the terror, and would benefit only the Bolsheviks. [64] Sazonoff was prominently quoted by most of the conservative press, and various other interviews found their way into the news columns.

News stories of diverse character hostile to the Soviets were given especial attention during this period. Reports were carried of Bolshevik defeats on various fronts. [65] "Increasing aversion to Bolshevism" was said to be developing "among all classes". [66] Revolts in the Bolshevik army were reported from Helsingfors. [67] News coming from Copenhagen told of the delight in Bolshevik circles over the "unhoped-for success" which the invitation seemed to them to represent. [68] A "radio message" from Moscow, giving the Bolshevik program, was given prominence. Excerpts referring to the "merciless combat" against capitalism and aspects of the class struggle were put in italics, with the comment; "when one invites guests, it is well to know whom one is inviting".[69] A wireless from Tchitcherin to Vorovsky, the Bolshevik representative in Stockholm (and identically, to the *Populaire* in Paris) inquiring whether the invitation to Prinkipo was really *bona fide*, was denounced as "an evasive Bolshevik reply",[70] "an insolent refusal",[71] and characterized as manifesting a "tone of audacious cynicism".[72] Unauthenticated stories with gruesome details of the death of the Russian Royal Family were published. The *Petit Parisien*, for example, carried an italicized column with the introductory note: "Here is unpublished information taken from a source which we have every reason to believe to be serious, and which we reproduce exactly, in spite of the horror of some of the details." The details were gruesome enough: "One of the children was cut in half, covered with oil, and burned." [73]

The receipt of Tchitcherin's reply of February 4 was the occasion for another flood of righteous indignation. The Russian note stated that in spite of its "increasingly favorable military situation" the Soviet régime was ready to enter immediately into pourparlers to put an end to hostilities. Furthermore, it indicated its willingness to recognize the financial obligations of the old régime, to grant various mining, lumbering and other concessions, and to enter negotiations on the subject of territorial arrangements. As to propaganda, while it could not "limit the freedom of the revolutionary press", it was willing to agree to a pledge of non-interference in the internal affairs of the Entente Powers.[74] There was no denying that this note constituted an acceptance of the Allied invitation, and such it was generally stated to be. Indeed, this very acceptance was used against them.[75]

Of the journals to the right of the Socialist press, only an occasional voice was raised in favor of taking the reply seriously.[76] All of the leading organs of the Center and Right were solidly against it. It was variously characterized as "astute and insolent"; [77] as "full of ambiguous terms"; [78] and as using "the language of force".[79] "The document is drawn up in a spirit of propaganda, and . . . its author has not missed an opportunity of openly mocking the Allies," said the *Figaro* (Feb. 7). "Its authors are convinced that the offer of the Allies was an avowal of discouragement," wrote the *Temps*.[80] "They still maintain their system of trafficking, bluff and equivocation," said the *Petit Journal*.[81] The wolves had put on sheep's clothing, thought the *Débats*. "They are the accomplices and the collaborators of Germany. . . . Let no one forget that." [82]

A vigorous pronouncement of "The Russian Political Conference" was widely publicized in the press of February 8, protesting against the terms of the Soviet reply, and denying the right of the Bolsheviks to speak in the name of the Russian people. On the same day, leading organs displayed prominently an interview with Tchaikovsky, of the Archangel government, condemning the Bolsheviks in the name of Wilsonian principles. From official circles it was reported, "the Soviet message is not considered a sufficient response".[83] Fortunately, most of the anti-Bolshevik contingents had already refused to go to Prinkipo, and, as the *Matin* said, the French government "believes that the Conference of the Isle of Princes has no point if only the Bolsheviks participate".[84] In fact, two days after the receipt of the Bolshevik acceptance, and the day following the announcement of the names of the American and other delegates to Prinkipo, Pichon, in a press interview, solemnly announced that the conference no longer had any *raison d'être,* since the anti-Bolshevik factions had refused to participate.[85]

The official demise of Prinkipo was never announced by the Supreme Council. The project simply passed gradually and quietly out of the picture. There was, however, some further discussion of it by the Supreme Council. On February 14, Churchill, of the British Ministry, attended the Council and demanded that a policy toward Russia be formulated, suggesting that there was little use in the Prinkipo meeting if only the Bolsheviks attended. He warned also that the military situation was getting worse for the Allied soldiers in Russia, and that the Russian anti-Bolshevik elements were deteriorating.

President Wilson thought the Allied soldiers were doing no good in Russia. "They did not know for whom or for what they were fighting." The existing forces could not stop the Bolsheviks, and "not one of the Allies was prepared to reinforce its troops". "If the Allies were asked what they were supporting in Russia, they would be compelled to reply that they did not know." [86] As to Prinkipo, "he would be quite content that informal American representatives should meet representatives of the Bolsheviks".[87] His conclusion therefore was that the Powers ought to withdraw their troops from all parts of Russian territory. He had explained to the Council how he would act if alone, he said. "He would, however, cast in his lot with the rest." As to the question of arming the anti-Bolshevik forces in Russia in case Prinkipo failed, the President hesitated to express any definite opinion.

The next day, after President Wilson's departure for America, Mr. Churchill urged the preparation of a program of military action against the Soviets, to be called into play in case of their failure, within ten days, to cease hostilities and withdraw their forces on all fronts.[88] Clemenceau (and Sonnino) favored the immediate adoption of the military proposals, explaining that he had been "quite opposed to the whole [Prinkipo] policy, and he now thought the Conference should get out of it as discreetly and simply as possible". He would prefer to send no further messages to the Bolsheviks, for he "was in favor of the policy of encirclement". Furthermore, "French opinion had been unanimously opposed to the Prinkipo policy", and the Allies must now abandon it. Colonel House, in the President's absence, revealed his sympathy for the Clemenceau theses. "He had never been in favor of the Prinkipo proposal", and thought that the question now was "how to finesse the situation against the Bolsheviks".[89] The matter was thereupon adjourned to the 17th, at which time it was again adjourned, apparently, indefinitely.

By common consent the Conference of the Isle of Princes was thus quietly relegated. Foreign Minister Pichon, in his weekly interview of the 16th, had already forecast the fate of the scheme in stating casually that the matter was no longer of interest.[90] Only the Socialists mourned its demise. For them "all the hypocrisy and duplicity of the Allies" were again confirmed.[91] "The governments have not even taken the trouble to give the slightest explanation" of their silence on the project. "It is the worst sort of secret diplomacy." [92] The remainder of the press was apparently glad to "let sleeping dogs lie", and some annoyance was shown over the fact that the Supreme Council discussions of February 14 and 15 had dragged the project from the oblivion into which it had apparently sunk.[93]

4. PRINKIPO REVIVED

The passing of Prinkipo from the stage did not endow the Conference with a Russian policy, though it left the leading members of the Conference with their individual policies, consisting generally, in the maintenance of troops in various quarters of Russia, and in supporting anti-Bolshevik forces. The question remained, said Pichon, in his interview of February 16, of determining a positive policy toward Russia. A step in this direction was taken by Clemenceau in the Supreme Council of February 18, in proposing to bring Tchaikovsky, of the Archangel government, before the Council. Balfour inquired whether it was "part of a systematic plan to get evidence from all parts of Russia"; and Lansing suggested the "danger that only one part of the evidence be heard". The matter was adjourned, and thus the French move in the direction of a reinforced *cordon sanitaire* policy was blocked.[94]

The leading organs of the Center and Right Wing press continued to demand the adoption of a strong forward policy. The *Temps,* which was representative, devoted repeated leaders to the subject. February 17: "Before concluding peace with Germany, it is absolutely necessary to have a clear policy in Russia. . . . The Prinkipo proposal was a failure before it really started." February 20: "Petrograd must be occupied." March 6: "The Russian problem is becoming increasingly grave, and is throwing the German problem out of joint." "To make a durable peace, Russia must be pacified. . . ." March 20: "To draft a treaty for Germany without having a Russian policy would be to throw the fruits of victory into a barrel without a bottom." March 22: "The Allies ought to have one united military front from the Baltic to the Black Sea." And so it continued.

Prinkipo was dead; but its ghost was destined to walk the Conference stage again. About the 26th of March W. C. Bullitt returned from Russia with a set of proposals from Tchitcherin for the reestablishment of relations between the Entente Powers and the Soviets. Bullitt had been sent by the American delegation, in pursuance, doubtless, of the policy suggested by Wilson in the Supreme Council, that "he would be quite content that informal American representatives should meet representatives of the Bolsheviks".[95] His mission was made known only to the British, with whom (at least with Mr. Philip Kerr, Lloyd George's confidential secretary) agreement had been reached as to terms which would be acceptable as a basis for a renewal of relations.[96] The terms agreed to by Tchitcherin were practically identical with those which Bullitt had formulated in agreement with the British.[97]

After conferences with Colonel House, Secretary Lansing, Mr. White and General Bliss, Bullitt found them all apparently desirous of attempting "to bring about peace on this basis".[98] On the morning of the 28th he breakfasted with Lloyd George who also, apparently, found the terms satisfactory. Unhappily, however, Lloyd George had before him a copy of that morning's Paris *Daily Mail* with a flaming

editorial by Wickham Steed on "THE INTRIGUE THAT MAY
BE REVIVED". Referring in bitterest terms to the original
Prinkipo proposal, with its alleged commercialism, Steed
continued: "That intrigue failed. It may be revived. Lenin,
who is a sinister fanatic, would promise any price to secure
the recognition he needs in order that his agents . . . [might]
encompass the ruin of ordered democratic civilisation."
"Bolshevism is a plague that must be fought in the name
of democratic freedom, social justice, economic progress and
political morality." Lloyd George was immobilized. The
political repercussions of a revival of Prinkipo looked too
ominous. " 'As long as the British press is doing this kind
of thing how can you expect me to be sensible about
Russia?' " he asked.[99]

The disclosure of the American and British diplomatic
feelers was a torch thrown into inflammable material. Public opinion was already somewhat panicky over the Russian
problem. Hungary had, only a few days previously, gone
Bolshevik, which naturally accentuated the general fear of
the Soviets' influence. Throughout the press of Paris and the
provinces, even in liberal circles, the demand was made for
a vigorous policy. The *Populaire de Nantes,* for example, of
advanced political views, demanded a "clear Russian policy".
"Either trade with the Bolsheviks or make open war." The
worst of all was "the hypocritical attitude of doing both half-
heartedly".[100] Conservative opinion was naturally more bitter. The debates on Russia in the Chamber, March 25 and
26, further contributed to the general anxiety. The government had been attacked from both sides, and Pichon sought
to defend it. The French policy, he said, was the same then
as in the preceding December when he had presented it
as that of the *cordon sanitaire,*[101] and in this policy France
was united with the Allies. The Russian problem was, above
all, "an inter-Allied problem". France could take no separate action, either "militarily, financially, politically, or
morally". The solution of the problem depended on an
agreement between them. "I can say nothing on this sub-

ject. I don't know what solution will come." [102] But the Russian problem would have to be examined again, by the Conference, "for it is not possible . . . not to settle it if we want to assure peace in the world".

Into the midst of this atmosphere the rumors of a revived Prinkipo came as a severe shock to patriotic circles. [103] The *Écho de Paris* (March 28) fulminated in a highly censored article. "We were talking yesterday of how we might smash the Bolsheviks. Now it appears that the old question, which we believed dead and buried, is again debated. . . . MR. PRESIDENT OF THE COUNCIL THE HOUR HAS COME FOR YOU TO SPEAK TO ENGLAND AND AMERICA!" The *Temps,* congratulated the *Daily Mail* for speaking out, and trained its heaviest batteries on the threatened revival. It would not make "any indiscreet revelation", or indulge in any "personal polemic", but tragic consequences would follow the revival of Prinkipo. The first result would be the consolidation of the Bolshevik régime and the collapse of democracy. Ultimately, those Russians whom Bolshevism could not satisfy would turn to Germany as their only hope. Furthermore, "Lenin would not recognize the debts of the old régime. . . . Would American and English merchants go and enrich themselves in Russia?" "To treat with the Bolsheviks would be an act of fear. And, as an American Statesman has said, 'cowardice cannot assure the peace'." [104] Other organs of the Center and Right were equally bitter, and "complicity, complacency and indulgence" outside of Russia were charged with the responsibility for the continuance of Bolshevism. [105]

The facts lying behind the rumpus were not then known to the public, and the *Journal du Peuple* undertook to make an "indiscreet revelation". "An American Commission" had returned from Moscow and given Wilson "edifying reports on the Russian situation", "Mr. Wilson feels it his duty to treat with the Russian government. . . . Lloyd George, as a good business man, cannot see England left out of such a good business deal." [106]

But the "business deal" did not go through. The hue and cry was so great, and Wilson was so preoccupied with more critical Conference matters that he did not take time to give the matter serious consideration. Bullitt had breakfasted with Lloyd George, but he did not get to see the President who, on one day, "had a headache", and who later said he "had a one-track mind" and that he was so occupied with Germany at the time that he could not think about Russia. Consequently, he left the matter in the hands of Colonel House, who, though he appeared at first to be interested in this scheme, had, in the Supreme Council February 15, admitted his profound suspicion of the original Prinkipo proposal.[107] At any rate, the Colonel soon became more interested in the Hoover-Nansen scheme for feeding Russia. As for Lloyd George, his ardor had been dampened by the editorial outbursts of the English press, and his interest was completely dissipated by protests from members of the British Parliament.[108] Consequently, the question was never placed before the Conference.

It was under the guise of the Hoover-Nansen proposal that, in April, the ghost of Prinkipo once more walked the Conference stage. Under this scheme the Russians were to be supplied with food, "on condition that the Bolsheviks cease their military operations".[109] Even Clemenceau, contrary to the wishes of his own Foreign Office, had been induced to consent to the American proposal that Nansen be charged with the undertaking. But any policy suggesting rapprochement with the Bolsheviks was doomed in advance to a hostile reception from the great majority of the French public. A fortunate stick was at hand with which to beat this particular dog. The whole project, allegedly, was a gigantic scheme of commercialism on the part of the United States, aided and abetted by Great Britain, and (horror of horrors) with the collaboration of German bankers. The leading conservative organs saw the apparition approaching. The *Temps* (April 5) warned of a scheme of American and German bankers for the exploitation of Russia. The *Écho de Paris* (April 9) wrote bitingly of the "offensive with food-stuffs" which the Americans were planning against the Bol-sheviks; and the moderate weekly, *Opinion* (April 12), re-ported dealings of American and German bankers for the exploitation of Russia.[110] The scheme was damned as being, not Nansen's at all, but really of American origin. For weeks, allegedly, American tradesmen had been fighting over the spoils of France's former ally, and had "pocketed concessions in direct negotiations with Lenin".[111] Nor did denials by the American Embassy as to concessions calm the storm. The *Débats* wrote that in spite of these, the names of Russians had only been borrowed, and they were but men of straw. "The supplying of Russia with food is not a humanitarian work. It is exploiting humanitarian sentiments for political ends. . . . The profiteers, who have a guilty conscience, dissimulate and deny." [112] Other lead-ing organs wrote equally bitterly,[113] while even the Socialist press was skeptical over the ingenuousness of the pro-posal [114] and the press of the moderate Left was dubious as to its desirability.[115] Discredited, as it clearly was, by the taint of "commercialism", and opposed by anti-Bolshevik groups, the project died quickly when the Bolshevik reply of May 7, posed the condition, unacceptable to the Entente, that a general conference be called to discuss all political and military problems involved.

5. KOLCHAK

All policies of conciliation having failed of application, or of whole-hearted adoption, it only remained for the Con-ference to give practical recognition to the anti-Bolshevik leader who seemed to offer greatest promise. The fortunes of Admiral Kolchak suddenly loomed up brightly during late April and early May, with the result that by the middle of May a formidable demand among leading Center and Right Wing organs was made that recognition be accorded him.[116] The time had come "to finish with the Bolshevik conflagration", wrote the *Écho de Paris* (May 15), urging that the "Council of Statesmen" then at Paris be recognized as the official representatives of Russia. "Kolchak has proved to be one of the best men to stand up against Bolshevism," wrote the *Temps* (May 17). "His government in Omsk has some stability and is aided by English and Americans." It should be recognized. Other leading organs seemed to think the psychological moment had come. Bolshevism was apparently in retreat, and it remained but to give it the *coup de grâce* by contributing openly to the material and moral forces of its opponents. In a three-column article the *Figaro* (May 16) urged continuing the starvation policy against the Soviets. Kolchak, "who knows Russia best, and whose aim is to resuscitate the real Russia", was begging the Allies to tighten the blockade on the Bolsheviks. Meanwhile the bogey of probable German reorganization of Russia was continually played up.[117]

The trend of events gave rise to the belief that important decisions were in process, and that recognition of Kolchak would soon follow. On May 23 the *Temps* wrote that the recognition of Kolchak was practically decided upon, and added that the interests of all the Allies would suffer if this were not done. While the Socialist press was chagrined and infuriated, denouncing the "stab in the back" apparently to be given the Russian democracy, and charging Wilson with playing the part of Pontius Pilate,[118] the nationalist press assailed the President equally bitterly for appearing to hesitate over the decision, and to ask for guarantees from Kolchak. ". . . in the name of his principles", had not Wilson "always resisted doing anything which might bring the slightest harm to the Bolsheviks"?[119] The proposal to submit Kolchak's opinions to an inquest was looked upon as "dangerous".[120] Furthermore, it was "the Manchester and American idealists" to whose profit it was "that Russia should remain in anarchy".[121] The liberal press, though strongly anti-Bolshevik, was in somewhat of a dilemma when faced with Kolchak. *Bonsoir*, for example, (May 27), envied those who could make a clear choice between Kolchak and Lenin. In its opinion neither one could be recognized. Likewise, *Europe Nouvelle* (May 31) felt that to support Kolchak would mean a definite failure of the "Entente democratic program", and it advocated supporting the liberal anti-Bolshevik elements. The liberal press of the provinces remained practically silent on the subject during this period.

The final note of the Great Powers to Kolchak, June 12, 1919, came at a time when he was in full retreat before the Bolsheviks. Up to about the end of May the *Temps* had consistently reported Kolchak gains over the Bolsheviks, and it was during this period (May 26) that Wilson joined with the Allied leaders in a note to the Admiral offering assistance to him and his associates "with munitions, supplies and food to establish themselves as the government of all Russia, provided they receive from them definite guarantees that their policy has the same object in view as the Allied and Associated Powers".[122] Kolchak replied on June 4, giving assurances concerning the summoning of a constituent assembly. Meantime, it was obvious that the military tide had turned, for even the *Temps'* columns, hostile to the Bolsheviks, were regularly reporting Bolshevik victories over the Admiral's forces. On June 8 a Berlin despatch reported that Kolchak had lost 45,000 men to the Soviet forces. Yet the Allied and Associated leaders saw fit, on June 12, to inform the anti-Bolshevik leader that they were satisfied with his assurances and that they were therefore willing to extend to him and his associates "the support set forth in their original letter".[123]

That the note amounted to practical recognition was the interpretation of practically all of the press, though this was the only point of agreement between radical opinion and that farther to the right. It was now the Socialists' turn to shout "commercialism", to damn the "maneuver" of the Supreme Council as "a policy directed by high finance and bondholders",[124] and to stigmatize the message as "a salutation to Czarism".[125] Liberal opinion, also, while not com-

pletely disillusioned, was inclined to suspicion and skepticism.[126] The note was said to represent a policy of compromise, and *Bonsoir* rather pointedly remarked that the Allies
had picked out the man who was the most regularly
beaten.[127]

But, for the most part, the Allied note was warmly acclaimed by patriotic opinion, which hailed the message as
amounting to actual, if not avowed, recognition.[128] The
Conference was congratulated on having finally come out of
its *laisser-aller* policy with regard to Russia; [129] and the
Temps (June 14) glowed with satisfaction over the leading
rôle which France had played in bringing the affair to a
consummation. But the Entente Powers were warned that
this was only the first step in the policy of action which
patriotic opinion had so long demanded. The Allies had embarked upon a policy which consisted in "reconstituting the
national unity of Russia". It would now be necessary to
show that "Allied aid is not a vain word", and to furnish
"war materials, economic aid and political cooperation".
In this enterprise the United States would be able to contribute powerfully "toward filling up the gaps".

Unfortunately for the advocates of this policy, Admiral
Kolchak and his forces passed off the stage before Allied
aid materialized, and soon thereafter the policies of the
Entente Powers took on a different orientation.[130] Thus the
Russian enigma, which, during the course of the Conference, had recurrently stirred deep currents of popular feelings, and which had constantly baffled the statesmen, was
left as unsettled at the close as at the beginning of negotiations. The Entente leaders ultimately followed the easiest
course, which was the comparatively negative one of passing
the problem on to the foreign offices of the various Powers
to be solved as their respective national interests might
subsequently dictate.

NOTES

[1] Baker, *op. cit.*, vol. ii, p. 64.

[2] Minutes of the Supreme Council, January 16. *Treaty of Peace with Germany*. Hearings before Senate Committee on Foreign Relations, U. S. Senate, 66th Congress, 1st Session, Senate Document, 106, p. 1235.

[3] December 16.

[4] February 24.

[5] "What is the attitude of the Ministry on the Russian Revolution?" asked *Humanité*, November 27, 1918. The *Populaire du Centre* (December 29) said the government refused to avow its policy because "it would be a contradiction to the successive declarations which the ministers have brought to the Tribune during the past four years".

[6] *House Papers*, vol. iii, p. 398.

[7] United States. Department of State. *Papers Relating to the Foreign Relations of the United States*. Supplement, *Russia, 1918* (Washington, 1933), vol. ii, p. 287. The note stated that military action in Russia would be admissible "only to help the Czecho-Slovaks consolidate their forces . . . and to steady any efforts at self-government or self-defense in which the Russians themselves may be willing to accept".

[8] Interview in press of February 10.

[9] *Allied Press*, vol. v, no. 8, January 1; vol. v, no. 9, January 8, 1919.

[10] December 25.

[11] *Temps*, December 26.

[12] *Allied Press*, vol. v, no. 9, January 8, 1919.

[13] *Annales de la Chambre*, December 27, p. 3250.

[14] *Ibid.*, December 29, p. 3330.

[15] A subsequent telegram, December 21, confirming the previous one, stated: "The plan of action of the Allies is to realize simultaneously the economic encirclement of Bolshevism and the organization of order by the Russian elements." *Ibid.*, December 29, p. 3335.

[16] November 16, 1918. "Each week Allied intervention in Russia becomes more scandalous," wrote Longuet, December 17, in *Humanité;* and each succeeding week brought repeated protests from the Socialist press.

[17] *Humanité*, July 8, 1918.

[18] December 12, 17.

[19] December 13.

[20] December 23. The idea of using the American army in Russia was a rather popular one in interventionist quarters. For example, *Paris-Midi* said: "What are we waiting for? The English fleet is intact. It is able to debark in a few days on the quays of Petrograd an American army which, come to Europe to re-establish order, has scarcely got into action." January 10.

[21] December 23.

[22] December 20.

[23] December 27. On December 29: "How can we promise liberty to the peoples so long as we allow Lenin to advance? How can we found a League of Nations when our own League is incapable of acting?"

[24] February 20; March 18. Others also made this same subtle appeal

concerning the League. E.g., *Débats,* December 24: ". . . nothing resembling world peace or a League of Nations can be established while Russia remains in a perpetual state of civil war and anarchy." *Victoire,* January 21, invoking League action in Russia, asked: "What prestige will the League of Nations have if from the beginning it shows itself infirm, deaf, blind and lame?" It is interesting to note that the Radical Socialist *Dépêche* of Toulouse, consistently urged that "The principles of right" ought to compel the League of Nations to "come to the help of this great victim". December 13; January 13, 16.

[25] E.g., *Progrès* of Lyons, January 11, and *Populaire de Nantes,* January 12.

[26] *Humanité,* January 11.

[27] Minutes of the Supreme Council, January 12, 1919. B. C. A-1.

[28] *Ibid.,* January 16, 1919. B. C. 3.

[29] *Ibid.,* January 20, B. C. 5.

[30] *Ibid.,* January 21. B. C. 6.

[31] *Ibid.,* January 21. B. C. 6-A.

[32] *Ibid.,* January 22. B. C. 7-A.

[33] *Current Summaries,* January 22. The communiqué of the 21st said that a decision would be made on the 22nd. In view of the fact that no more witnesses were to be called in addition to Noulens and Scavenius and that no witnesses favorable to the Bolsheviks had been heard, it seemed that the Council was already convinced of the necessity for positive and direct action. See *Croix,* January 23.

[34] January 23.

[35] January 23.

[36] January 24.

[37] *Humanité* hailed the proposal as a recognition of the Russian Revolution, and paid "homage" to "the philosopher" who was deemed to have "come out of his ivory tower". "Again the man *à la noble candeur* comes to point out the way to the world." January 23, 24. *Populaire's* only regrets were that the anti-Bolshevik groups had thus won implied recognition, and that the conference had not been planned for Paris. January 23, 24. The *France Libre,* January 24, said that the proposal had received the approval of all the Socialist press.

[38] The *Populaire de Nantes* (January 25, 26), and the *Progrès* of Lyons (January 26) expressed warm approval, the *Progrès* acclaiming Mr. Wilson as "not only an idealistic University man", but also, as "a clever statesman". *Europe Nouvelle,* January 25, also expressed satisfaction. See *Allied Press,* vol. v, no. 13, February 5.

[39] January 23.

[40] *Gaulois,* January 23.

[41] *Débats,* January 24.

[42] *Nouvelliste de Lyon,* January 25.

[43] *Figaro,* January 23.

[44] *Journal,* January 23.

[45] *Phare,* January 24.

[46] January 24. This idea that perhaps, after all, Wilson was out-flanking the Bolsheviks as he had outmaneuvered the Germans in October,

cropped up in several papers, and softened some of the bitterness. In fact, *Intransigeant*, by way of exception in the conservative press, was frankly favorable to the project on these grounds. January 24. Also *Progrès de la Somme*, January 25.

[47] *Nouvelliste de Lyon*, January 25.

[48] Hopes were expressed "that the generous views of that sublimated Christian, Mr. Wilson", would not "end in a recrudescence of Oriental fanaticism revived from the Middle Ages". *Liberté*, January 23.

[49] Evidence is lacking as to the authoritativeness of the *Daily Mail* report.

[50] He had, of course, already, not only recommended them, but had fought the proposals through to adoption by the Supreme Council.

[51] January 25. See also *Petite Gironde*, January 26. The Conference was bitterly assailed in the Center and Right Wing press for delay, indecision and improvisation. The policy was characterized as one "of least effort". *Petit Marseillais*, January 23. The Conference was accused of having lost days in a maneuver which it thought to be ingenious, but which no one outside could understand. *Journal de Rouen*, January 26.

[52] Miller Diary, vol. iv, p. 178.

[53] Bullitt testimony, *Treaty of Peace with Germany*. Hearings before Committee on Foreign Relations. U. S. Senate, 66th Congress, 1st Session. Document 106, p. 1245.

[54] Briggs, M. P., *George D. Herron and the European Settlement* (Stanford University and London, 1932), p. 145. Mr. White is quoted by Briggs as saying to him, in 1929: "I don't think that Wilson abandoned the project. The French craftily made it impossible."

[55] *Ibid.*, p. 145. "Even two delegates from the Caucasus yesterday told me that the French agents in the East told them to have nothing to do with the Conference."

[56] The *Progrès* of Lyons also called attention to the campaign. "Our great press of information has received the initiative of Mr. Wilson very badly. What inspirations have the papers obeyed? It would be lengthy and vain to seek them, for as in everything human, there are noble reasons and reasons less noble." January 29.

[57] E.g., January 23, 24, 25; February 5, 7.

[58] February 5.

[59] E.g., *Temps*, January 24.

[60] *Matin*, January 25.

[61] *Temps*, January 30.

[62] January 24.

[63] January 25.

[64] January 25.

[65] *Petit Parisien*, January 24, 25, 27.

[66] *Temps*, February 2.

[67] *Temps*, January 4.

[68] *Temps*, January 29.

[69] *Figaro*, January 25.

[70] *Petit Parisien*, January 26.

[71] *Figaro, Journal*, January 26.

[72] *Débats,* January 27.

[73] February 4. *Figaro,* February 1, devoted a leading column and a half to an equally lurid and unauthenticated story. "It is said that they burned the bodies of their victims, and threw the ashes to the wind."

[74] *Temps,* February 8.

[75] The *Débats* expressed the prevailing view in saying that they had "seized with haste the opportunity offered by the Allies for a conversation". February 8. "They threw themselves on the proposal like shipwrecked people on a plank," said the *Victoire,* February 7.

[76] *Homme Libre,* curiously, was one of these, timidly suggesting that perhaps all groups should go to Prinkipo. February 8.

[77] *Gaulois,* February 7.

[78] *Éclair de l'Est,* February 9.

[79] *Temps,* February 7.

[80] February 7.

[81] February 7. "Beware," said the *Petit Parisien* (Feb. 8), warning against illusions. "They hope that between the Prinkipo Conference and the recognition of their régime there is only a shade of difference."

[82] February 8.

[83] *Petit Parisien,* February 7.

[84] February 6.

[85] *Éclair de l'Est,* February 10.

[86] Minutes of Supreme Council, February 14. Miller Diary, vol. xiv, pp. 423 *et seq.* Concerning Churchill's suggestion that "volunteers, technical experts, arms, munitions, tanks, aëroplanes, etc.," be sent to Russia, "the problem was to know what use would be made of the forces and supplies". "In some areas they would certainly be assisting reactionaries."

[87] "The President manifested some annoyance over the references in the Bolshevik reply to such matters as the payment of debts and concessions— matters, which, he said, had not been referred to in the invitation. These references, he said, were "uncalled for" and "insulting". He was apparently piqued by this, owing to press references to American selfish commercial and financial aims. *Ibid.,* vol. xiv, pp. 423 *et seq.*

[88] A species of ultimatum was to be sent to the Bolsheviks, making these demands for cessation of hostilities, etc. If they accepted it, a some- what similar request would be sent to the anti-Bolshevik factions. *Ibid.,* vol. xiv, pp. 445 *et seq.*

[89] The idea of preparing a military program was acceptable to him, so that, "if eventually the Allies were compelled to embark on military oper- ations, they would be in a stronger and better position".

Balfour agreed, urging the desirability of taking steps "to put the Bol- sheviks in the wrong". *Ibid.,* vol. xiv, pp. 445 *et seq.*

[90] *Éclair de l'Est,* February 17.

[91] *Populaire,* February 17.

[92] *Humanité,* February 27.

[93] E.g., *Journal,* February 16.

[94] Minutes of Supreme Council, February 18. Miller Diary, vol. xiv, p. 498.

[95] Minutes of Supreme Council, February 14. *Ibid.*, p. 423.

[96] See Bullitt testimony, *Treaty of Peace with Germany*. Hearings before the Committee on Foreign Relations, U. S. Senate, 66th Congress, 1st Session, Document 106, p. 1247.

[97] Hostilities were to cease on all fronts; *de facto* governments were to remain in control of their respective territories until the peoples concerned should speak; the economic blockade was to be lifted and trade relations re-established; the Soviet government was to have the right to transit on all railways and the use of all ports of the former Russian Empire; nationals of the respective parties were to have free right of access to territories of the other; amnesty was to be given by the Soviets to all political opponents; troops of the Allied and Associated Powers were to be withdrawn; and the financial obligations of the former Russian Empire were to be recognized. *Ibid.*, p. 1248.

[98] *Ibid.*, p. 1260.

[99] *Ibid.*, p. 1260.

[100] March 25.

[101] *Annales de la Chambre*, March 26, 1919, p. 1306.

[102] *Ibid.*, p. 1308.

[103] The Socialists actually dared for a moment to hope for a reconciliation. *Populaire*, March 29.

[104] March 29.

[105] *Débats*, March 29. "The madmen of Russia and the bleary-eyed statesmen of the Conference," said *Victoire*, were preparing a tragic train of events. Wilson and Lloyd George, like Pontius Pilate, had rejected "Russia's appeal" and were washing their hands of the affair. March 29, 31. *Current Summaries*, March 29.

[106] March 29.

[107] Bullitt testimony, *Treaty of Peace with Germany*. Hearings before Committee on Foreign Relations, U. S. Senate, 66th Congress, 1st Session, Document 106, p. 1264. It should be noted that Mr. Wickham Steed, author of the violent article in the Paris *Daily Mail*, was a close personal friend of the Colonel, and indeed acted at times as a sort of go-between for House with the British and French delegations. See Steed, W. C., *Through Thirty Years*, chapter on the Peace Conference.

[108] Fischer, *The Soviets in World Affairs*, vol. i, p. 173.

[109] Hoover had suggested to Wilson that if hostilities could be stopped, there might be some hope of stabilizing the peace temporarily established along the frontiers, and the Russian people might swing back to moderation. *Ibid.*, vol. i, p. 175.

[110] Even the Socialist press made occasional references to the "commercial maneuvers" of the United States. E.g., *Vérité*, April 15.

[111] *Écho de Paris*, April 18.

[112] April 19.

[113] *Current Summaries*, April 18, 19.

[114] *Humanité*, April 19.

[115] The *Dépêche* of Toulouse, for example, carried a message from Stockholm quoting an alleged statement by a member of the Russian Supreme

Economic Council to the effect that "on the insistence of Wilson, pushed by American capitalists who want to get possession of the Russian market, the Allies have decided to lift the blockade on Russia". April 17.

[116] Some journals, while insistent on pursuing an interventionist policy in Russia, were dubious as to the desirability of giving specific recognition to Kolchak before he had made more definitive gains. E.g., *Débats*, May 23; *Journal*, May 25; *Information*, May 22.

[117] E.g., *Action Française*, May 19; *Démocratie Nouvelle*, May 17.

[118] *Humanité*, May 15. On May 21 *Humanité* published a ringing manifesto by Kerensky and his supporters against the proposals to recognize Kolchak. *Populaire*, even more bitter, repeatedly assailed the Entente policy. "In spite of the censor and the systematic campaign of false news, we know that the Entente governments have not abandoned their criminal designs against the Russian Revolution." May 15.

[119] *Gaulois*, May 24.

[120] *Matin*, May 27; June 4.

[121] *Action Française*, May 24.

[122] Cumming, C. K., and Pettit, W. W. (editors), *Russian-American Relations, March, 1917-March, 1920*, Documents and Papers (New York, 1920), pp. 337-339. Quoted from *New York Times*, June 13, 1919.

[123] *Ibid.*, p. 343.

[124] *Humanité*, June 14.

[125] *Populaire*, June 15.

[126] E.g., *Œuvre*, June 13; *Pays*, June 15.

[127] *Bonsoir*, June 14. Not only was the Bolshevik army not a phantom, said the *Europe Nouvelle*, but the entourage of Kolchak was not above suspicion. "Around this man are strange persons . . . whose hearts remain profoundly imperialist." June 14.

[128] *Homme Libre*, June 13; *Écho de Paris*, June 13. The headlines of *Petit Parisien*, *Journal* and *Petit Journal* (June 13), stated somewhat more cautiously: "The Allies promise assistance to Kolchak."

[129] *Figaro*, June 13.

[130] Vernadsky, G., *A History of Russia* (New Haven, 1929), pp. 269-273.

CHAPTER IX

OPEN COVENANTS OPENLY ARRIVED AT

"Open covenants of peace, openly arrived at, after which there shall be no private international understandings of any kind but diplomacy shall proceed always frankly and in the public view."
(Woodrow Wilson, in the Fourteen Points.)

"There are only two ways of dealing with a democratic press. The best way is to tell them everything; that bores them stiff. The second best way is to tell them nothing, which at least provides them with the glory of a 'secrecy' stunt, which provides a highly pleasurable form of news value. The worst method is to tell them half-truths in the form of conciliatory leakages."
(Harold Nicolson, *Peacemaking, 1919*, p. 124.)

1. OPEN DIPLOMACY UNDER FIRE

PRESIDENT WILSON's commitments to open diplomacy and to democratic processes gave rise to the belief "that the Peace Conference would be an open conference";[1] and the influx into Paris of some five hundred foreign journalists emphasized the general conviction that the peace negotiations were to be conducted under closer public scrutiny than that to which any previous diplomatic parley had ever been subjected.[2] It is fairly certain that the President never admitted such broad implications as were commonly drawn from his first point, and Winston Churchill overstates it in saying that if it meant anything "it surely meant a vast world debate upon the war settlement; and that all the 'plain people' in all the lands . . . should consciously and intelligently participate in the grand solution".[3] Nevertheless, it is doubtful whether Wilson was himself perfectly clear as to the precise application of this principle to the processes of the Peace Conference, for his statements on different occasions lend themselves to varying interpretations. In a memorandum for the Senate, June 12, 1918, he explained that he meant "not that there should be no private discussions of delicate matters, but that no secret agreements should be entered into"; [4] and Mr. Baker quotes the President as saying at the beginning of the Conference that while he wanted all the open diplomacy he could get, yet he feared that if "partial results" were announced, or "one decision at a time, it might easily result in bloodshed". [5]

The debates on this subject in the Supreme Council, just preceding the formal opening of the Peace Conference, suggest that Wilson desired to go somewhat farther than above indicated. On January 15 the President proposed that the press representatives be admitted to the "Peace Conferences", in order to avoid the danger of "publicity by leak". He qualified his proposal, however, by pointing out that the Great Powers would determine beforehand what should be brought before these large conferences. [6] The next day he asked for "complete publicity of all that happened", though he later conceded the inadvisability of publicity for the small preliminary conferences. Yet the large conferences would be given an important rôle, for presumably they would have the function of accepting or rejecting the preliminary decisions reached by the Great Powers in small conference. [7] Tardieu is approximately correct in saying that Wilson "had never intended open negotiations, but only open debates upon all decisions arrived at before the latter became final". [8]

Mr. Wilson's proposals were unacceptable to his colleagues in the Supreme Council, who argued that if the proposed publicity were allowed the differences of views among the Great Powers would be unduly stressed in public, and, further, that the debates of the Conference would be intolerably prolonged by reason of the fact that representatives of small and large states alike would feel called upon to make long speeches. So great was the opposition that the President yielded the principle on the first day's debate, remarking that though he had raised the point for discussion, he would not press it. It was agreed, therefore, January 15, that a brief official communiqué would be issued to the press, and that the members of the Supreme Council would enter into a gentleman's agreement not to discuss on the outside anything not contained in that statement.[9]

This important decision was far from acceptable to a great majority of the world's press representatives, and especially to those from the United States. C. T. Thompson, of the Associated Press, characterized it as "a strange reversion to old-time secret diplomacy",[10] and William Allen White says the Americans "realized that if our Government bound itself not to discuss with the press subjects not mentioned in the daily communiqué, the President thereby had lost his chance to appeal to the idealism of humanity as against the organized nationalism of the world in its actual governments. So the American newspaper men blew up".[11] In any event, the American journalists led a revolt, lodged a vigorous protest with President Wilson, and called a conference of all newspaper men.[12] At this conference the American proposals were the most radical, demanding unlimited access to the diplomatic discussions, or, alternatively, representation by a small committee, and circulation of a verbatim report of the proceedings. The British favored a more restrictive principle, being satisfied that Sir George Riddell should sit in as their representative, "withdrawing when matters of necessary secrecy were discussed". He would afterwards meet with the press correspondents and supplement the communiqués.[13] The weight of the French press, doubtless under pressure of the government, was thrown against both the British and American programs, in favor of greater secrecy. Since the French group had no definite program, a committee of three of the more conservative French journalists was appointed to suggest a plan for obtaining "the maximum publicity practicable".[14]

The Supreme Council had, meantime, settled the issue by adopting, on the 17th, the system of "communiqués" as its guiding principle in its relations with the public. This meant that a brief statement of decisions arrived at would be made public, from time to time, though without giving a summary of the discussions, for this might disclose divergencies of opinions. A certain mitigation of this régime was suggested in the statement that representatives of the press would be "admitted to the meetings of the full Conference", though it was provided that, upon "necessary occasions", the deliberations of the full Conference might be held in secret.[15] Mr. Thompson accurately observed that "after all, the Peace Conference is well on the way to the abandonment of the first of the Fourteen Points".[16]

The French public had not been led to anticipate a literal application by the Conference of the principles of "open covenants, openly arrived at". The war-time censorship had accustomed them to restrictions on their access to news. The overwhelming desire of all Frenchmen was for an early peace settlement. A great many were convinced that open discussions, would lead to embarrassing displays of divergent policies, which might enable Germany to drive a wedge between the Allies and thus endanger the peace as well as postpone its advent. This inclined the great majority to accept with comparative complacency a restricted application of the principles of open diplomacy. Only the Socialists demanded a literal application of Wilsonian principles in this particular. In the Chamber, December 27, 1918, Cachin asked the government whether "the deliberations and the conclusions" of the Conference would immediately be made public. The government had adhered to the Fourteen Points. "Was it a mere verbal adherence?"[17] Pichon's reply that the government had "no objection to publicity of agreements",[18] was far from satisfying the Socialist inquiry. Yet most organs of opinion, including those of the moderate Left, agreed on the necessity of limiting publicity. The *Dépêche* of Toulouse, for example, felt (Jan. 1) that there was "great inconvenience in public discussion", and agreed that a middle ground must be found. The *Homme Libre* expressed the prevailing view of conservative and even liberal opinion in saying (Dec. 31, 1918), that though diplomacy ought not to be secret, it could not be exercised on the public square. "Treaties should be published, but they should not be elaborated with doors open."

It is not surprising, therefore, that the French press representatives, for the most part, stood out against the American proposals for full publicity of Conference proceedings. Nor is it to be wondered at that the Supreme Council's decision restricting publicity was received with general satisfaction. Only a few voices were raised in protest, and these came almost exclusively from the ranks of the Socialists and advanced liberals.[19] An important exception to this was the *Débats*, from which (Jan. 18) came a portentous warning. A policy of secrecy would not be workable, said Gauvain, if a government believed it to be "its duty to divulge this or that fact in what it judges to be a superior interest". To guard against hearsay and rumors he urged that the substance of the deliberations should be published as soon as possible, so that opinion might not be led astray. Though virtually without support in the Center and Right Wing press at that time, this point of view was not without honor in the later stages of the Conference.[20]

A certain tone of superiority pervaded the comments of the Center and Right Wing press. The decision was hailed as a triumph of French "good sense".[21] The French press realized, it was said, that such matters could not be treated in public.[22] The discussion of diplomatic matters was "not like discussing the purchase of a cow".[23] The proposals of both the Americans and the British were characterized by the *Écho de Paris* as equally chimerical, and though the final text conformed to "the political wisdom of all times", it regarded the reference to plenary sessions as "rather absurd", and illustrative of the "contradictions into which inevitably those fall who have the pretension of regenerating the political universe".[24] *Action Française* (Jan. 18, 20), in somewhat similar vein, suggested that "in order to satisfy some simpletons the Conference would have to put on some framed-up performances", and prophetically compared the Conference to the fable of Phœbus and the north wind: the harder the winds of publicity blew, the more the Conference would swathe itself in its mantle of secrecy. Emphasis was frequently laid on the importance of preserving the "unity of the diplomatic front" of the Allies;[25] and *Paris-Midi* (Jan. 17) closed the argument by saying that "in order to shut the door to the Boche, one has to shut the door to all the world".

It is highly probable that the complacency on the part of some of the leading journals was due in large measure to their close relations with the government, and to the fact that, whatever the régime of silence imposed, they anticipated being able to keep well informed by reason of their special contacts. Such organs could well reproach their foreign colleagues for being out of touch with realities, and could safely indulge their own sense of moral superiority arising from their presumably more realistic view of the proper relation of the press to the Conference. There is no doubt, furthermore, that much of the press was in complete agreement with the view of the French government, that the realization of French national aims depended not so much upon public discussion as upon shrewd diplomacy. The fact that the government "controls a certain element of the French press by unabashed government subsidy", as pointed out by William Allen White,[26] and as generally admitted by French journalists, is likewise of importance in this connection.

2. The Régime of Communiqués

Until March 24 the Conference, organized in the Council of Ten, carried on under the régime of partial publicity represented by intermittent communiqués. The value of these communiqués as sources of enlightenment on the work of the Conference was not very great. This has already been illustrated in the case of the Commission on the League of Nations.[27] Their usefulness in regard to other matters before the Conference was little, if any, greater. During the last days of January, for example, the problem of mandates was being bitterly fought over in the Supreme Council, and President Wilson was struggling against the annexationist designs of France, Japan and the British Dominions. On the 27th the communiqué relating to this subject ran as follows:

> The meeting of the afternoon followed up the exchanges of views in regard to the former German colonies of the Pacific and the Far East. Representatives of the Dominions and China were heard.[28]

The communiqués of the 28th and 30th were equally barren of significant information,[29] although on these days occurred one of the bitterest clashes between the old imperialism of annexation and the new idea of trusteeship of backward peoples.

During the days immediately preceding Wilson's first departure for the United States on February 14, the communiqués were even less informative. On the 12th of February, for example, the discussion came to a head relating to the renewal of the armistice with Germany. Should it be renewed for another month, and should new and heavier conditions be introduced into it, as urged by Clemenceau? Or should it be renewed for an indefinite period without the addition of new terms, as ardently desired by Wilson? Should final military and naval terms be drawn up immediately and presented to Germany, as urged by Wilson, so that Germany could be disarmed at once and Allied Armies be demobilized? Or should such incentives to Allied demobilization be deferred until Germany had been forced to accept the important territorial and financial terms, as passionately supported by Clemenceau? These issues were bitterly fought out on that day.[30] The official communiqué of that day ran as follows:

> The Supreme War Council met this morning from eleven to one o'clock, and resumed its session this afternoon from three to five-thirty.
> The conditions of the renewal of the armistice were drawn up.[31]

These communiqués, however, did not represent the sole source of news concerning Conference activities, and in this situation lay one of the chief disturbing elements in the Conference's relations with the public. It was inconceivable that the pious wish of January 15 should be carried out, and that the members of the Supreme Council, and their attachés, should permit no additional word of their doings to escape to the outside and anxious world.

In fact, "publicity by leak", the danger to which Wilson, as well as some French commentators, had called attention, became a recurring source of embarrassment. As early as January 15 Lloyd George complained that statements made by him in the privacy of the Supreme Council had been misquoted in the French press, much to his embarrassment and annoyance;[32] and on January 17 President Wilson cited the fact that a private conversation concerning the Adriatic question, in the intimacy of his own house, had been reported with much accuracy in the *Daily Mail*.[33]

On January 30 both Wilson and Lloyd George came to the Supreme Council with serious grievances. Wilson stated that each morning in the English press of Paris there appeared a great deal more information regarding the meetings than was given in the official communiqué. He referred especially to comments concerning his own "idealistic views". He said that if these articles continued to appear, he would find himself compelled to publish his own views. So far, he had spoken only to people in that room and to the members of the American delegation. He and his colleagues had been extremely scrupulous that nothing should come from them implying that there were divergencies of view; yet the press had, that morning, disclosed that there was, apparently, a Dominion point of view, and that the United States of America was in some way or other standing out against that view. (All of which was true.) "If these articles continue to appear," he added, "a public discussion would become inevitable, and such a public discussion would be fatal" at that time.[34]

Interestingly enough, on the same day, Lloyd George also complained against the English press of Paris. The *Daily Mail*, he said, had published a "very monstrous report, which represented the whole of the delegates as being at loggerheads. . . . The article in question gave the impression of a royal row between America, Japan, Great Britain and her Dominions, France and everybody else." Correct quotations were given from some of the speeches. Though the account was "grossly inaccurate", yet it was "accurate enough to have been supplied by somebody who either directly or indirectly had inside knowledge". He did not see "how the Conference was to be conducted at all if such statements were allowed to continue".[35]

In spite of all warnings and elaborate arrangements to maintain secrecy in the small meetings, there was, as pointed out by Mr. Baker, continued leakage.[36] During the second week of February the exasperation of President Wilson was such as to cause him to threaten to move the Conference away from Paris;[37] and it was the dramatic clash of March 21 over the leak of Lloyd George's remarks on the Polish terms that brought the whole problem to a head and contributed to a change of procedure.[38] Balfour at that time made the point that leakage was also taking place in the commissions and committees as well as in the Supreme Council, with the result that the members who expressed an opinion on any subject were later lectured by outside parties. This view was emphatically confirmed by Wilson, who said that with regard to a certain decision about to be reached by a commission, he had learned of it from outside parties against whom the decision was going to be given.[39]

On the whole, the view was fully confirmed that the methods of the Council of Ten were no guarantee against embarrassing leaks when it was felt by a given national group that the interests of its particular country might be served thereby.

The system of haphazard "leaks" was but an aspect of a somewhat better organized system of "drippings" from the

Conference board. The American, British and French delegations maintained, for a time at least, a limited contact
with their respective press representatives by means of
conferences between journalists and certain members of
the delegations. The comparative reticence of the delegates
on such occasions reduced the value of these conferences
very markedly. Even these conferences were further restricted in the later stages of the Conference, and Tardieu
records that in March the Supreme Council requested that
they be abandoned.[40]

Other less official contacts were nevertheless maintained
between the delegations and the newspaper men. The
French system was divided into two branches. The "Service
de la Presse" maintained one branch at the Quai d'Orsay,
the seat of the Foreign Office, under the direction of Charles
Corbin. The other was at rue François-Premier, where
Sabatier d'Espéyran was in charge. The Quai d'Orsay
branch was reserved for those few who enjoyed the special
favor of the Foreign Office. Practically every evening at six
a chosen few—Pertinax (André Géraud), of the *Écho de
Paris,* Herbette of the *Temps,* Sauerwein of the *Matin,* and
Bassée of the Havas news agency—forgathered with Foreign Office officials, and sometimes with Pichon himself.
There they were given an intimate review of the details of
the work of the Conference. They were also advised what
things it would be desirable to emphasize, and what things
it would be well to omit. At rue François-Premier the majority of the French journalists gathered around Sabatier
d'Espéyran, who performed a function somewhat similar to
that of Foreign Office officials. All of these officials "interpreted" the news of the day from the point of view of the
Foreign Office, which throughout the Conference, was
strongly anti-Wilsonian in its policies.

It was at such conferences as these that *"directives",* or
suggestions, were passed out to certain organs as to the line
of editorial policy to be followed. It was here, likewise,
where the work of the censor was supplemented, and the

journalists were requested not to comment on particularly embarrassing episodes of the Conference, as, for example, Wilson's threat, in early February, to move the Conference from Paris, or his summons of the *George Washington* in April.[41]

The régime of communiqués, with the supplementary procedures, official and unofficial, for maintaining an imperfect contact between the public and the Conference, became increasingly less satisfactory to French opinion. One major reason for this was the fact that restrictions imposed by the French government on the sources of information and freedom of expression of the French public were far more drastic than those existing in Allied countries, especially Great Britain and the United States. Whereas, in Allied countries these restrictions had been largely removed with the coming of the Armistice, in France they continued even after the Peace Conference. The right of the Chamber of Deputies to interpellate the government on its foreign policy during the Conference was restricted,[42] whereas the British Parliament and the American Congress could debate freely.

The censorship of the press, which not merely restricted access to news, but also limited the newspapers' right of discussing freely what they knew, or thought they knew, became peculiarly irksome when the Allied press was under no such handicap. In the January debates in the Supreme Council concerning the publicity régime to be adopted, Pichon argued that the censorship should extend equally to the British and American press. But his efforts were unavailing,[43] and when the Conference decided on relative secrecy, the only serious criticism levied against it by the Right and Center press of France was the disadvantageous position of the French as compared with the British and American news organs.[44]

The effect of this situation on the French press was strikingly signalized by the *Daily Mail* of Paris (Jan. 17), in saying: "Yesterday's French newspapers published practically nothing concerning the Conference except the official bulletin. Indeed, a stranger arriving from a far country, who did not know hostilities had ceased, would have had some difficulty in realizing, from a perusal of yesterday's Paris journals, that the most portentous Congress the world has seen had commenced its sittings."

The Conference was not many weeks old before its procedures were pretty largely discredited. Perhaps the major reason for this was the growing conviction that the Conference was conspicuously ignoring its major task, and that the vital interests of France were being sacrificed on the altar of Wilsonian ideology and Anglo-American commercialism.[45] Patriotic opinion was convinced that the early emphasis on the League of Nations amounted to putting the cart before the horse, and this was thought to result in the subordination of the immediate material interests and security of France. Long-term planning, as typified by the League, should, it was argued, be postponed until after the solution of the problem of Germany. Already, at the beginning of February, it was noticed by the British General Staff press service that there was "a certain undercurrent of feeling perceptible that France is in too weak a position at the Conference; that her interests risk being neglected or placed in the background".[46]

On all sides the Conference methods were scored, and alarm spread throughout patriotic opinion. The communiqués were likened to those given out during the war: "The peace communiqués give us daily, along with the names of the ten sitting members, excellent time-tables: the hour of opening and closing, and sometimes, also, the date of the next sitting, all written with the elegant discretion so pleasing to diplomats who are conscious of the gravity of words." [47] "Indiscretions flourish," said the *Figaro* (Feb. 10), pointing to articles appearing in the *Daily Mail*, but indiscretions for which it felicitated the *Daily Mail*, while deploring the limitations on French journals. "Among all the peoples of the Alliance," said the *Temps* (March 31), "only the French have not received information as to the claims which its government has brought forward."

These feelings found clamorous expression in the debates on the credits in the Chamber of Deputies. Speaking with the unanimous mandate of the Commission on Foreign Affairs, Franklin-Bouillon, a fiery leader of the Radical Socialists, scathingly denounced the methods of the Conference and of the government. For three months, he said, the Chamber of Deputies and the country had been kept in absolute ignorance regarding French foreign policy and the negotiations of the Conference. The policy of silence on the part of the Conference and the government had produced a wave of uneasiness throughout the country, where a general feeling prevailed that French interests were being jeopardized. The Conference had neglected its main task, and, instead of beginning at the beginning with the territorial and financial aspects of the peace, it had begun at the end with the League of Nations, and had simultaneously taken up "all the problems of the world", without arriving at solutions of any of them. Two days previously he had spoken to the Premier concerning the weakness of the French strategic position, and had, though without avail, expressed "the unanimous wish of Parliament to bring to the government a new force which would enable him [Clemenceau] to negotiate usefully" with the Allies.[48] The policy of secrecy and silence could perhaps be justified, he thought, if it had met with striking success, but in this respect it was a conspicuous failure, so far as French interests were concerned.

Patriotic opinion had now become convinced, in other words, that the régime of communiqués and practical secrecy, combined with the restrictions on the French press, operated very seriously to prejudice France's case at the Conference. Franklin-Bouillon accurately reflected the prevalent feeling that if more information were available, and if greater freedom were allowed, public opinion would then be able more effectively to press French claims upon the Allies.[49]

It is highly probable that wider publicity of the Conference proceedings would have had a doubly beneficial effect upon the negotiations as a whole. First, it would doubtless have improved the methods of the Supreme Council by imposing more effective controls on the discussions, thus making agreement somewhat easier. Second, it would have given the public more confidence in its work by revealing the inherent difficulties of the problems with which it was coping, and would thereby have brought understanding and sympathy to its task. Quite probably, also, it might have dictated greater moderation in the demands actually insisted upon by certain Allied governments.

The effect of the procedures adopted was actually to produce a poorer opinion of the Conference and its work than was really deserved. A great deal of important work during the early weeks of the parley (some of it preliminary in character, though necessary), passed almost unnoticed, and entirely unappreciated by the public. Early in February, for example, when the Conference had practically settled the Mandates question, had appointed a great many commissions and committees for special investigation and report, and was forging ahead with the League of Nations, while struggling with the problem of renewing the German Armistice and with problems of social unrest in various parts of Europe, it was said already to be stagnating. The peacemakers were charged with adopting only "wait and see" policies, after studying "numerous questions: Russia, Poland, the Banat of Temesvar, the German colonies, Turkey in Asia, without counting questions of a general order, such as the League of Nations and International Labor Legislation".[50] Such a judgment was clearly premature, and rather unfair, yet it is understandable in view of the methods of procedure adopted by the negotiators.

As the weeks dragged along these feelings inevitably became more pronounced, and perhaps they had more justification. In early March the system of "letting everybody stew in his own juice" was thought to be getting the upper hand, and the Conference was regarded as "dancing on a volcano".[51] Critical week succeeded critical week, each offering a ray of hope at the beginning, but each, in turn, closing with the hope extinguished. Toward the end of March the *Esprit Public en France,* a careful review of the drift of French opinion, noted that the public uneasiness, which had been increasing for some weeks, was becoming alarmingly grave.[52] A divorce between public opinion and the Conference was appropriately signalized by the *Petit Provençal* (March 23), a moderate Left organ. "People no longer believe in it. More than that, people are beginning to think it is leading us to catastrophe."

The prevailing pessimism and anxiety over the methods of the Conference did not, however, bring about a demand from the malcontents of the patriotic press for the application of the Wilsonian principles of "open covenants openly arrived at". On the contrary, while omitting to clarify their own ideas as to the precise régime desired, they turned upon the President, holding him primarily responsible for the alleged delays, shortcomings and tergiversations of the Conference. Only the Socialists supported Wilson at this time, and exempted him from all responsibility for the slow progress of events.[53] "Ideology" and "demagogic diplomacy" were assailed even in the moderate Left press.[54] Wilson's influence in the Conference was deplored as being out of all proportion to the sacrifices of the United States. Satire strode prominently through the columns of leading organs. Wilson was mocked openly as a fake healer. The legendary "Marius", of Southern France, called upon the President, seeking to turn his attention to curing the ills of the weather, which, thought Marius, were not less curable than the other ills of the world which Wilson had essayed to remedy. The President felt honored, and confided in this mythological visitor: "my policy in regard to this will be exactly the same as in other great world questions: wait and see. Just fancy,

I have discovered that Spring always follows Winter. That is the secret of my policy. I can also tell you another of my profound views, namely, that the weather will improve more quickly than will Europe. But this is a diplomatic confidence. Don't repeat it." [55] "It is not fitting," wrote another leading provincial organ, "that the man who does not pay the bill should order the dinner." [56]

3. The Régime of Official Silence

On March 24 appeared the last communiqué of the Council of Ten. It stated that the Supreme Council had met from four to six P.M., and had discussed the question of German submarine cables, adding that the future régime of the cables had been agreed upon. Brief reference was also made to the work of the Commission on Teschen. Immediately following this communiqué the *Temps*, on the afternoon of the 25th, carried a brief note to the effect that information from English and American newspapers (of Paris) indicated that the meetings of the Council of Ten would be supplanted by conferences between the four heads of delegations. Unofficial items were quoted from the Paris *Daily Mail* and *New York Herald*, stating that the decision was made with a view to expediting the work of the Conference and completing the peace conditions in the near future.

Thus, quietly and unostentatiously, the Council of Ten was dethroned, and the Council of Four assumed supreme command.

The change was not quite so abrupt as it seemed. Indeed, the transition had been practically achieved before the public became aware of it. For some days the new institution had been developing out of informal meetings between the four leading heads of delegations. The need for a change of method had become increasingly apparent to all, though perhaps Wilson was not so convinced of its urgency as were some of the others. As early as March 7, during the President's absence, Colonel House began having meetings with Clemenceau and Lloyd George, and on the 10th his diary records that he would urge Wilson to continue the private conferences on his return.[57] Apparently the President was convinced, for private conferences began, at first with Clemenceau and Lloyd George, on March 14, the very day of his return from the United States, and gradually became a regular procedure.

The statesmen had taken a heroic step. The rising tumult of discontent on all sides, and the onslaught of violent criticism of its methods drove the Conference to drastic action.[58] It decided, therefore, in the words of Saint-Brice, of the *Journal* (March 25), "to drape its wounded dignity in absolute mystery", hoping that out of the intimate discussions among the four heads of governments, satisfactory solutions would quickly come. It was "the last stage in the abandonment of the Fourteen Points", said C. T. Thompson.[59]

The next three weeks, which marked the most critical period of the Conference, were indeed weeks of comparative silence and mystery. With two exceptions, the official communiqué ceased to shed its tiny flicker of light on the doings of the Conference. On April 2 a brief official note stated that General Smuts had been sent to Hungary to inquire into certain problems raised by the Armistice. The nature of the problems was not suggested.[60] On April 3 a somewhat more significant item indicated that the Yugoslav delegates had been heard by Messrs. Wilson, Clemenceau and Lloyd George. Orlando (unwilling to attend because of Italy's conflicting claims) "had amicably explained to his colleagues the reasons why he could not take part in it".[61] Thus casually was a fleeting ray of official light thrown on the bitter controversy between Italy and Yugoslavia.

Not only was the stream of official information dried up, but the unofficial news was much further restricted, especially so far as the French were concerned, though not so drastically as regards the Anglo-American press. On the afternoon of March 27, for example, the *Temps* news column on the Conference said, "the French press continues to be deprived of all information; we reproduce those items published by our American and British colleagues, who are not submitted to the same treatment." Again on the 28th the *Temps'* news items noted that "the Council of Four continues to publish no information concerning the subjects of its meetings"; and on several subsequent days similar notes were printed. On April 1 it recorded that, "The English language newspapers appearing at Paris continue to be favored with certain confidences."

Gleanings of a semi-official and semi-indiscreet character which the Anglo-American press of Paris had been able to gather from the entourage of the Conference were therefore carried daily in the news columns of the *Temps* as well as in those of other French papers, though the reports were much less ample than formerly, and also less reliable.[62] After the first few days of the new régime the French journals close to the Foreign Office apparently repaired their lines of communication to a certain extent, so that they too were able to carry brief items concerning the work of the Conference, which, though provokingly meagre, became, toward the middle of April, fairly good guides to the main lines of the work of the Conference. The Council of Four, however, remained throughout this period officially ensconced within its "ivory tower" in unbroken silence, although Lloyd George gave an optimistic interview to the *Matin* on April 6, stating generally that all was well. On the 13th Clemenceau likewise sounded a reassuring note to a delegation of Radical Socialists; and Wilson, on the 14th, spoke hopefully of an early "definitive solution".

The first reaction of French opinion to the reduction of the Ten to the Four, was, for the most part, amazement and indignation, bordering on stupefaction. The Conference was already viewed universally as out of touch with public opinion, hence the drawing of this additional veil of secrecy served at first only to increase the general fears with regard to its capacity to deal responsibly with its problems. Attacks equally bitter came from the Right and from the Left. The most bitter opponents of "open covenants openly arrived at" found the decision intolerable. The *Écho de Paris* (March 25) caustically remarked that since they had not been able to stand the light of day "the plenipotentiaries were deciding to burrow down". The diplomats, meeting in private from place to place, were likened to Abdul Hamid, who changed his abode every night in order to avoid assassination. The *Figaro* vented its wrath in violent tirades on the 25th and 26th, expressing the prevalent view of conservative circles, that when the governments needed more than ever to be supported by public opinion, "they raise a veritable Chinese wall between the public and themselves". Likewise the *Journal* (March 25), while avowedly in favor of "diplomatic secrecy", argued that where it was a case of taking decisions "imposed by publicly known events", one could not think of "shutting one's self up in a cellar without provoking interpretations infinitely more dangerous than any revelation".

One of the principal reasons for special indignation and, indeed, chagrin throughout most of the French press, was the manner in which the new régime was given publicity, and the inferior position, relatively to the Anglo-American press, from which the French press suffered. In a scathing article on the evening of the 25th, the *Temps* denounced the whole procedure. "That which happened this morning is scandalous," it said. "A capital decision is taken. It is concealed from French readers, but it is given to British and American readers, and doubtless to Italian." The following day it vigorously supported the Chamber of Deputies in its apparently unanimous desire to know more of the Conference, and to pass judgment on what was happening. The initiative of the *Temps* was warmly seconded by a wide circle of papers of varying opinions. The *Intransigeant* (April 4) struck a common note in remarking on the sadness of being reduced to seeking in the foreign press arguments in favor of the French cause. "We are forced to it," it concluded, "since all information is refused us here, and comment is impossible on news of which we are ignorant."

Sometimes even items quoted from the Anglo-American press were whitened by the censor.[63]

"Triple-plated secrecy," denounced so bitterly by the *Populaire* (March 27), of the extreme Left, was distasteful to all, and the *Intransigeant,* of the Center, remarked on the 27th, that "the great anger provoked by the Four in their decision on secrecy had not died down". It was with no little satisfaction that *Humanité* (March 26) took note of the complaints of its journalistic colleagues, who, earlier in the Conference, had accepted "the most odious infringements on the freedom of the press".

In spite of the distastefulness of the new secrecy procedure to practically all of the press, much of the bitterness was allayed by semi-official assurances from Conference circles that the new technique was designed to hasten the advent of peace. Moderate and conservative circles were ready to accept almost any régime that offered fair promise of eliminating delay, which had come to be regarded the greatest enemy of all. The *Information* (March 27) in fat headlines, expressed this point of view in demanding "RESULTS", whether the Council consisted of One, or Four, or Ten. It added, however, that surely the Council could not seriously mean not to publish any official communiqué, for the total absence of news would risk leading public opinion astray, and would thus defeat its own purpose.

Official influences were plainly brought to bear to calm feelings and to raise hopes for better results in the near future. The *Petit Parisien,* for example, on the 26th, under a headline: "To FINISH QUICKLY", said the idea was that the Four would quickly complete a set of preliminaries. On the 28th, its headline said: "PATIENCE, THE FOUR ARE WORKING", and on the 30th it continued its mollifying course with a reassuring note under the headline: "THE FOUR ARE GETTING RESULTS". The *Petit Journal, Homme Libre,* and *Liberté* pursued somewhat similar courses. Thus, for a few days there was almost a rebirth of hope and a restoration of public confidence in the work of the Conference. Some important conservative organs, which had at first been bitterly critical of the Four, were a few days later expressing satisfaction with the apparent progress being made.[64] Leading organs of the moderate Left, however, were far from convinced of the validity of the new régime. The *Petit Provençal*, for example, demanded the end of "the politics of mystery", and remained unconvinced by the soothing words of semi-official statements.[65] Likewise, the *France de Bordeaux* denounced the "curtain of steel" which the Conference had drawn between itself and the public, and protested against being punished like school children. But it spoke for a wide constituency in saying that it could pardon the Conference for even that if, within four or five days, it could produce a finished treaty.[66]

The Conference had, in effect, been given a few days of grace after the French public recovered from the first shock of the "curtain of steel" drawn between it and the Four. When these days expired, the secrecy régime was unmitigated, and the conviction grew that the results predicted were far from being achieved. The depth of the general discontent with the methods of the Four can be gauged by the violence of the *Temps* (April 5) which, in spite of its close relations to the government, could not refrain from pointing out the deceptions from which the public was suffering. Each day, it said, the "public was terrified" by the contradictions between the news announced and the anticipations of the preceding evening. France had a right to know not only what sort of peace was being prepared, but also how its interests were being safeguarded while the peace was being made. "Is it not true that a whole crowd of equivocations and obstacles would vanish with the first ray of light?" Thus the "openly arrived at" clause in the first of the Fourteen Points was taking on added meaning.

The results of bolting and barring the doors of the Council of Four proved satisfactory to no one. Least of all to Wilson, who was reported to be finding it a "sort of Frankenstein" turned to the accomplishment of ends contrary to the purposes espoused by him.[67] Furthermore, the personal relations of the members were greatly embittered, and soon reached such a point that Wilson remarked to certain of his experts that he did not know whether he would see Clemenceau again, and he did not know whether the Peace Conference would continue.[68] About the same time Clemenceau exploded to Wickham Steed, saying that Wilson was intractable, believing that he was the first man who, for two thousand years, had known anything about peace on earth. "I have done everything to gratify him. I receive him at the foot of the staircase as though he were the King of England; still he is not satisfied." The Premier added that he was on the point of throwing up his hands and quitting.[69] To another friend Clemenceau remarked: "I am disgusted. . . . Wilson acts like a cook who keeps her trunk ready in the hallway. Every day he threatens to leave." [70]

4. EPISODE OF THE "GEORGE WASHINGTON"

The idea of breaking with the Allied leaders and returning permanently to the United States had doubtless occurred to President Wilson during the earlier days of the Conference. His February threat to have the Conference moved from Paris was an indication of his feelings at that time, and [71] William Allen White records that there were days in February when Wilson was tempted to tell the Allied heads that since they had no intention of keeping the contract with Germany, he was going to wash his hands of the matter and return to Washington.[72] On March 28 he considered the possibility of a break but remarked to Mr. Baker that it could not be risked at that time.[73] On the 30th Henry White, of the American delegation, urged the President to make the American position clear to the French, and to give them to understand "that if an agreement be impossible" the only course for the American delegation would be "to retire from the Conference".[74] On April 5 Mr. Tumulty cabled the President from Washington urging that something be done to clear up the situation.[75] The occasion, he thought, called for "audacity" and a "bold stroke". The President's feelings must have been aggravated, and his decision hastened by the continued deadlock in the Council of Four, and by a recurrent outburst of violent criticism from the Center and Right Wing press. The press campaign was open and obvious enough. Nevertheless, the *Petit Journal* (April 6) significantly remarked that if the press and the people did not complain more openly about the delays at the Peace Conference, it was "from political considerations *vis-à-vis* its great neighbor".[76]

On the morning of April 7 Admiral Grayson informed the Press Bureau, thus publicly telling the world, that the President's ship, the *George Washington,* had been ordered to sail at once for Brest. Though there has been some difference of opinion as to the precise significance attached to this act by the President, the evidence seems to be fairly conclusive that it was done with forethought and deliberation, and was planned as a dramatic gesture to indicate to the world in general, and the French government, and perhaps the French public, in particular, that the American President had reached the limit of his patience, and that if satisfactory concessions were not soon made he would feel compelled to take the drastic step of withdrawing with the American delegation from the Conference. "It was Wilson's ultimatum," says Baker, and was "thoroughly meant".[77] Henry White agreed with this interpretation, saying that the President summoned the ship in order to be prepared for any eventuality.[78]

The precise effects of this gesture on the course of events are somewhat difficult to appraise. Mr. White thought it filled the French with consternation, though Lincoln Steffens thought they regarded it as a bluff.[79] Professor Seymour, discounting its importance, says it had no effective results on the negotiations. It is true that Wilson apparently went farther to meet the French views in the next few days than did Clemenceau to meet those of Wilson, but it would be an

overstatement to suggest that Clemenceau made no concessions.[80] It is quite probable that in addition to the concessions obtained from Clemenceau during the ensuing days,
another factor tending to give pause to the President was
advice against precipitate action coming from the United
States. On April 9, for example, Tumulty cabled the President suggesting that the gesture looked like an act of impatience, and counselling that withdrawal at that time would
be "an act of desertion".[81]

That the French authorities were at once clear as to the
implications of the gesture, was evident from the sarcastic
comment of the representative of the Foreign Office, the
evening of April 7, in saying to the journalists that he had
heard rumors that some delegations were "going home to
mother".[82] That these authorities also saw immediately the
importance of minimizing France's annexationist aims, is
well illustrated by a significant item appearing in the
Dernières Nouvelles (latest news) section of the *Temps,*
the afternoon of April 7, the very day on which the news
broke concerning the *George Washington.* The leading item
in this section was a semi-official statement to the effect that
France had "no annexationist pretensions" concerning any
territory "inhabited by any German population", referring
particularly, it added, "to the regions comprised between the
frontier of 1871 and the frontier of 1814", by which, reference was obviously made to the Saar, the problem then causing the most acute difficulty for the Council of Four.

That official French circles recognized the explosive possibilities of the situation is revealed by the manner in which
it was handled in the French press. By all the canons of
journalism the episode constituted a major sensation, certainly one of the two or three greatest sensations of the Conference. Its full significance was at once recognized by the
American press. The *New York Times,* for example, on
April 7, carried on its front page the following six-column
headline: WILSON SUMMONS HIS SHIP, THE "GEORGE WASH-
INGTON," and it was said to mean that Wilson was "prepar-

ing for possible unpleasant eventualities, but with the hope that they will not occur". On the following day the *Times* carried the following two-line streamer across the entire front page: PEACE CONFERENCE AT CRISIS, EARLY RESULTS EXPECTED: WILSON'S PLANS FOR RETURN INTERPRETED AS WARNING, and an Associated Press dispatch from Paris said Wilson's act was construed "as preliminary to a determined move to force an agreement at any early date. . . ." On the 9th a *Times'* article announced prominently that the President's order had created "a sensation in all quarters", and stated, furthermore, and contrary to the reports of "certain persons", that the President was not bluffing. On the 10th the *Times'* columns asserted that the tension had been relaxed in the Council of Four and that the President's order had "cleared the atmosphere".

The New York *World* gave equal prominence to this startling news. In banner streamers across its front page, on April 8, it blazoned forth: "WILSON WARNS HE WILL MAKE NO MORE CONCESSIONS. AMERICANS INTIMATE THEY MAY QUIT CONFERENCE." Likewise the New York *Tribune* (April 8, 9, 10) gave sensational publicity to the news, though somewhat less than that of the *Times* and the *World*. On the 9th Frank Simonds reported from Paris that the final crisis had been precipitated and on the 10th the *Tribune* said that though the compromises then in prospect could not with certainty be attributed to the President's order, it was "at least a coincidence that the main difficulties began to dissolve from the time that his decision became known".

How did the French press handle this episode? The contrast reveals not only the anxieties harbored in official French circles, but also the stringency of the French control of their press, whether through the censorship or through friendly official guidance. On the afternoon of April 7 (dated April 8) the *Temps* carried inconspicuously the following tiny item: "President Wilson has telegraphed for the *George Washington,* now in the United States, to leave for Brest." Seventeen words. No comment. The following day its news columns carried brief excerpts from the Paris *Daily Mail* and *New York Herald,* the first suggesting that the President anticipated a rapid conclusion of the peace, and that from the *Herald* indicating that Wilson might leave for the United States in fifteen days, even though the peace were not completed. The latter also stated, rather innocuously, that while the Four were agreed in principle, there were some differences of application.[83] On the afternoon of the 9th a brief item in the *Temps* cryptically noted that a telegram from New York announced that the sailing date of the *George Washington* had been advanced from the 14th to the 11th, and added an ambiguous note to the effect that the reason for the change of date was that Admiral Benson had cabled "asking when the ship would be ready to leave". Two days later the *Temps* announced briefly that the *George Washington* had sailed, and quoted the Paris *New York Herald* as saying that some stir had been caused by the departure on it of an eminent surgeon, Chalmers da Costa.

Such was the treatment of the episode by the leading organ of the French press. That of the other journals of the heavy press was equally significant. The *Petit Parisien,* on the 8th, under the heading "The Intentions of President Wilson" noted very briefly that the President had telegraphed for the *George Washington;* and on the 9th printed a brief statement quoting Tumulty and Franklin Roosevelt as denying the receipt of an order for the departure of the ship. *Écho de Paris* (April 8) and the *Petit Journal* (April 9) each carried one inconspicuous item on the subject, that of the *Écho de Paris* saying that the rumor that the President intended to go away as soon as possible was without foundation. The columns of the *Journal* carried no reference whatever to the episode. All of these papers yielded gracefully to the directions of the Foreign Office in minimizing the significance of this sensational episode. The *Matin,* however, went somewhat further than the others in minimizing the incident. While carrying three brief news items (April 8, 9, 10) it also took editorial notice of the incident (April 9), bitterly condemning those—"perhaps of the Hearst press"—who had circulated the "ridiculous rumors" suggesting that possibly the President would not ratify the French demands.[84]

As far as the public at large was concerned, its information was restricted to the brief quotations from the Anglo-American press of Paris which, at most, presented two alternative interpretations of the incident, one favorable and the other unfavorable. For the most part, the patriotic press was content, outwardly at least, to accept the favorable interpretation, and to follow the lead of the semi-official press. A few organs, however, were less inclined to "discretion", and, for one reason or another, were permitted a limited freedom in the expression of their views. The *Information,* for example, in an article (April 9) partly whitened by the censor, was allowed to comment satirically on Wilson's insistence on his Fourteen Points, and to remark that, "In any case the arrival of the *George Washington* will be an event for the Peace Conference." [85] The *Liberté* also, very friendly with the Foreign Office, and very nationalistic, was permitted (April 9) to write even more frankly than its more influential colleagues. France, it affirmed, could make no concessions. "The coming of the *George Washington* will not be able to influence her. Would that it might bring with it the ideas which would animate George Washington himself if he were on board the ship which bears his name!" The press of the extreme Left surmised that where there was so much smoke there must be some fire; and the *Vérité* (April 11) carried an interview with a "well-informed American" who categorically affirmed that the call for the ship was due to the fact that Wilson had been unable to "recall the Allies to a truer point of view". Hopes were expressed by this press that Wilson would not leave, for however bad the peace was apparently going to be, it would doubtless be much worse if his influence were taken away.[86]

5. THE "CLOSED DOOR" RÉGIME DISCREDITED

The real meaning of the call for the *George Washington* was obvious enough to journalistic circles, though the gesture was doubtless suspected of containing a certain amount of bluff. Such was the weight of official influence, however, in limiting news and in guiding editorial comment, that the public at large remained almost unaware of the significance of the events, as was appropriately pointed out by Marcel Sembat who wrote that there was no real current of opinion, "nor, indeed, any opinion at all, since the peoples are ignorant of everything that is going on".[87] If Wilson had hoped to reach the ear of the French public in order to gain its support against the policies of Clemenceau, which, from the President's point of view, were deadlocking the Conference, he sadly failed to do so. Secret diplomacy, combined with rigid control of the press in France, had shackled the President, and stricken from his hands his most useful weapons. News of the *George Washington* episode was so limited, and comment on it in all the influential press was so controlled that the French people got no picture of an exasperated American President struggling as sincerely and vigorously as anyone against the delays of the Conference in the name of moderation and justice. The French public, except on the extreme Left, remained convinced that within the Council of Four Clemenceau was heroically defending the unquestioned rights of France, and that President Wilson was ruthlessly obstructing in the name of a visionary ideology.

This picture was sedulously painted by the patriotic press during the trying days of April, although, in order to prevent a complete collapse of public confidence, occasional injections of optimism with assurances of progress, were carefully administered. It is not surprising, therefore, that during this period, and with undoubted official encouragement, a violent campaign, chiefly against Wilson, swept most of the influential organs of the Center and Right Wing press.[88] Veiled satire and innuendo often gave place to open outbursts against the President. His "ideology" was assailed. The fight within the Council was said to have been actually one between "reality and illusion".[89] His illness was imputed to his futile efforts "to adapt his dreams to reality".[90] The delays in the Conference were said to be due to "a *trop candide* (too simple) idealistic conception".[91] His return to the Council, April 8, after his illness was said to have had a bad effect on the Council's labors, by re-introducing indecision, and calling into question decisions already made.[92] "A certain statesman" was assailed as attempting to play the moderating rôle of a Lord Castlereagh.[93] Veiled attacks were made on his good faith, and he was accused of having failed to adhere to his own principles.[94] His theoretical discussions were said to have served the cause of Bolshevism.[95] The "noble President of the Great American Republic" was "too preoccupied in making a peace of justice", to appreciate the "realism" of Clemenceau; and Wilson's ignorance of Europe and its affairs was the "greatest obstacle" to the peace.[96] The President had begun as "the Apostle of Peace" but was, presumably, ending by "discontenting everybody".[97]

The constitutional position of the President in the United States was pointed to as a source of serious embarrassment to the Allies. On the one hand, he was irremovable until 1921, whereas his colleagues at the Conference could be removed at any time by their parliaments. This fact, supposedly, gave the President an unfair advantage over the others by destroying the equality of status and giving him a rôle of supreme arbiter.[98] On the other hand, the President had lost control of his Congress, and to a very considerable extent was politically discredited at home. Even the semi-official and cautious *Temps* (April 12) raised this embarrassing point, reminding the President that in the new government he was in a minority. The *Démocratie Nouvelle* insisted repeatedly during this period that Wilson was politically discredited and, further, that opinion in the United States hostile to him had not been allowed to reach France.[99]

The Council of Four itself, with its atmosphere of secrecy and mystery, completely lost public favor. It was characterized variously as an "Ivory Tower", a "Tower of Babel", a "Council of Olympians", "a fight of niggers in the dark".[100] The liberal *Œuvre* (April 8) likened it to Leon, the philosopher, whose lands were ravaged by the enemy while he was writing a book on tactics to do away with war. The press of the extreme Left had, of course, from the beginning, denounced secrecy and all its works. The remainder of the press now became equally convinced of the bankruptcy of the Four's methods. In large type the *Information* (April 14) arguing, as always, for "reasonable publicity", shouted that the underlying error was an error of method, and that the resulting evils were THE CONSEQUENCES OF SECRET DELIBERATIONS.[101] If the general anguish was increasing from day to day, said the *Matin* (April 10), it was "because of the mystery with which the Four" surrounded themselves. The *Petite Gironde* (April 13) cited with approval opinions from various papers showing the extreme discontent with the Four's secret procedures. Even the most nationalistic pens could now invoke "popular mandates", "open diplomacy", and "the rights of peoples".[102] The *Temps* (April 12) expressed the universal disillusionment in saying that the policy of the closed door stood condemned. If at the beginning of the Conference, in January, Wilson and open diplomacy were under suspicion in moderate and conservative circles, in April, when the Four were struggling in an apparently hopeless deadlock, Wilson and the diplomacy of the "Closed Door" were totally discredited.[103]

The activities of the chambers and of the commissions of parliament reflected these same feelings. Following a telegram from four hundred members of the British House of Commons to Lloyd George demanding a parliamentary discussion of British peace policy (to which Lloyd George acceded), commissions of the French Senate and Chamber made similar demands upon Clemenceau and Pichon. A resolution from the Senate Budget Commission, and one from the Commission on Foreign Affairs of the Chamber of Deputies, demanded a strong peace, and demanded further that Clemenceau and Pichon discuss, before competent parliamentary commissions, the proposed terms of peace before submitting them to Germany. These resolutions of the parliamentary commissions received the heartiest endorsement of the press, which, with one voice agreed that the peace terms ought to be discussed fully with the representatives of parliament.[104] But the Premier took refuge in a constitutional technicality, which he stretched somewhat, and refused the request, saying he would submit the treaty to the entire parliament, which could approve or reject it as a whole.[105]

Down to the middle of April the wave of pessimism and the campaign of disparagement continued unabated. On the 15th, however, Colonel House went to Clemenceau with assurances that the fifteen-year occupation of the left bank of the Rhine would be acceptable to Wilson. This difficulty had remained as the chief obstacle to an agreement between Wilson and Clemenceau. The Colonel, at the same Conference, complained of the press campaign that had been carried on against the President. The Premier, gratified by the President's concession, and feeling somewhat more generously inclined, intervened at once. Calling his secretary, and speaking in French, he told him with much emphasis, says House, "that all attacks of every description on President Wilson and the United States must cease; that our relations were of the very best and that there was no disagreement between our two countries on the questions before the Peace Conference". The *Écho de Paris, Petit Journal, Petit Parisien, Figaro, Temps* and *Liberté,* along with certain others whose names were not recalled, were to be given special directions along this line.[106]

The effect was instantaneous. The following day the President had a "good press". At any rate, most of the leading organs amenable to official influences (and that included the large majority of the important papers) became suddenly very friendly, and even grateful to the President for his contributions to the peace. The *Petit Parisien,* for example, fairly reeked with the odor of official inspiration. It was time, it said, to destroy the legend which represented Wilson as working against the interests of France! Indeed, "Champion of right, Mr. Wilson has desired that our rights should suffer no wrong. . . . The man who threw his country into the war *for France,* has been during these latter days, and remains, the real friend of France." The *Journal* (April 16) praised the President as a man of great initiative. No one had shown "greater will than he to found the peace on right". Even those organs which had shown unusual hostility to the President breathed appreciation. The *Figaro* and *Gaulois* recognized that Wilson was desirous of showing his sympathy for France, and the *Écho de Paris* (April 16) carried the inspired quotation from "a well-informed person" to the effect that never had the understanding between the United States and France been closer. This was said to be due to "the spirit of equity and high loyalty of the President of the United States". The *Liberté* (April 16), quoting "a high authority" to the effect that Wilson's assurances regarding guarantees were fully satisfactory, continued somewhat unctuously, saying that the longer it took the President to reach a decision, the firmer was his attitude once he had reached it.

That these encomiums were forced and artificial, evincing no serious change of opinion in Center and Right Wing circles, was demonstrated by later events of the Conference. That the distrust of the Council's methods, furthermore, was not eradicated, is also clear, for shortly thereafter, lamentations were again heard that France was the only victim of the mystery enveloping the deliberations of the Conference.[107]

6. Over the Heads of Governments: The Italian Episode

The régime of communiqués and, much more so, that of complete secrecy, had been condemned by patriotic Frenchmen because French interests seemed to be endangered. Mr. Wilson also found the diplomacy of the "closed door" increasingly an obstacle to the achievement of his program.[108] His gesture in summoning the *George Washington* was in the nature of a break toward the open to escape from the intolerable restraints imposed by the "Ivory Tower" of the Four; and it was probably of some value in its results on the Conference. For reasons convincing to himself, the President did not carry through the threat implied in the call for his ship, but chose rather to meet Clemenceau more than half-way in a policy of compromise.

When the Adriatic question came to a head in the latter half of April, the Italian delegates found Wilson in a much less compromising mood. The readjustment of the frontiers of Italy "along clearly recognizable lines of nationality" was stipulated in the ninth of the Fourteen Points; and the granting to Serbia of "free and secure access to the sea" was provided for in the eleventh. True, the Italian representatives, in the November 1918 pre-Armistice discussions, had objected to Point Nine, proposing to modify it in such a way as to bring in "national, geographic, strategic and historic factors" as a basis for the rectification of frontiers,[109] and thus rendering it quite vague and meaningless. Nevertheless, after repeated failures to change it, they let it pass as it stood.[110]

President Wilson had, as a matter of fact, made a significant and perhaps disastrous compromise on the Italian frontier question, before the development of the April crisis. Probably as early as January he had agreed to the cession to Italy of the Brenner Pass, and with it some 240,000 German Austrians, which was a serious infraction of his "nationality" principle.[111] It has been said that "If Wilson could swallow the Brenner, he could swallow anything".[112] Nevertheless, when the questions of Fiume, in the northeast Adriatic, and the Dalmatian strip along the eastern shore of the Adriatic, became acute, the President chose to stand by his principles.

Unfortunately, the situation had been complicated by a division of opinion within the ranks of the American delegation, which led Orlando and Sonnino to believe that eventually they could win both the Dalmatian strip which the Treaty of London did give, and Fiume, which it did not give. "The Italian delegates were undoubtedly encouraged by some Americans to believe," wrote Mr. Lansing, that the President would ultimately yield on this point as he had in the case of the Tyrol.[113] On one side were Colonel House and Dr. Mezes, who advocated a compromise which would give Fiume to Italy as a free port and would apply Italian strategic theses to the eastern shore of the Adriatic.[114] On the other side were ranged Lansing, White and Bliss, along with the six American experts most directly concerned with the territorial and economic problems involved in those regions.[115] The experts proposed the so-called "American line", giving Fiume and the Dalmatian strip to Yugoslavia, and urged the President to stand firmly on it.[116] "Never," they wrote, "did the President have such an opportunity to strike such a death-blow to the discredited methods of the old diplomacy." [117]

In the midst of these divided counsels the Italian delegation devoted itself to arousing an uncompromising spirit at home, in support of Italian demands, and to pursuing Fabian tactics with Wilson, relying on their ultimate ability to force his hand. Some concessions, in addition to the Brenner Pass compromise, the President was disposed to make. On April 14 he told Orlando he would consent to making Fiume an international port, with a large degree of autonomy, and on April 19 he offered to place Fiume and Northern Dalmatia under a régime of the League of Nations somewhat comparable to that of the Saar.[118] Farther than this he would not go; but neither proposal was acceptable to Orlando.[119]

Meanwhile, Clemenceau and Lloyd George were standing by, bound by their obligations under the Pact of London to yield Dalmatia to Italy. This pact Wilson refused to recognize, on the grounds of its inconsistency with the Fourteen Points.[120] As to Fiume, Lloyd George and Clemenceau were in general agreement with Wilson, though, as Baker appropriately remarks, not for Wilson's reasons, but rather "for traditional interests based on the concepts of the Old Order".[121]

Despairing of reaching a satisfactory compromise within the Council of Four, Wilson decided to cut through "the endless tangle of controversy by a bold appeal to the people of the world".[122] On April 23, when Orlando threatened that if he did not obtain satisfaction by the following day, he would return to Rome, Wilson made public his dramatic message to the Italian people, calling upon them to bear in mind "the new order" which Italy had played "so honorable a part in establishing", and begging them not to ask for anything which could not be made "unmistakably consistent" with the principles which, on America's initiative, had become the basis of the peace.[123]

Wilson's eloquent appeal to the Italian people over the heads of their government at once became the sensation of the Conference, and for nearly a week all other issues took second place. With a magistral gesture the veil of secrecy had been temporarily drawn back from the Council of Four, revealing the degree to which it was dominated by the Old Order of imperialism rather than by the New Order of which President Wilson had become the prophet.

There were a number of factors which determined the reaction of French public opinion to the merits of the Italian case. Most of these can be summed up under the heads of political expediency, sentiment of Latin solidarity (which, perhaps, was largely a creation of the moment), and money. The first and the last were by far the most important. Italy had come into the Allied fold on considerations of expediency,[124] and it was felt that if she were to be kept there, it would be on the same basis. "Principles" should therefore not be allowed to weigh too heavily. Italy's claims were probably exaggerated. Some nationalistic French organs openly admitted that they were. But even so, Italian good will was regarded as too precious a prize for France to risk losing it "by gambling on the question of Fiume".[125] The question of expediency weighed heavily even with the liberal *Dépêche* of Toulouse, which (May 4) warned of the danger that Italy might turn pro-German if she did not obtain what she wanted, and concluded that France should support the Italian claim to Fiume.

Closely connected with expediency was the sentiment of solidarity of the Latin peoples which was fostered during this period. This cropped out in most of those organs favorable to the Italian case, and on April 24 five deputies laid before the Chamber of Deputies a resolution addressing to the Italian nation France's assurance of her friendship for her Latin sister, and her unalterable fidelity to her engagements. The resolution was reported, doubtless with some exaggeration, to have been greeted with unanimous applause.[126]

A very liberal use of money by Italian authorities with responsible organs of the French press was also, without doubt, an important factor in the direction of opinion in France at the time of the crisis. The statement of a high official, early in 1919, that "unfortunately our press accepts money", is a conviction that is widely held by those in a position to know, though, naturally, few care to be quoted in public. General Mordacq, secretary to Clemenceau, frankly says that Orlando forgot nothing to make the claims of his country triumph, and, most of all, did not forget the French press which, he says, received "ample rewards" for supporting the Italian case.[127] Another high official stated confidentially at that time that the Italians had spent 8,000,000 francs on the French press; and a responsible

journalist said that when a member of the Italian delegation reproached Clemenceau for being personally less friendly
than the French press to the Italian cause, Clemenceau
turned to him and threatened to go before the Chamber and
tell at the tribune how much it cost Italy to gain the back-
ing of the French press. "I have the list in my pocket!"
Clemenceau is quoted as saying.[128]

Another closely related aspect of this picture was the
flood of Italian propaganda largely to the exclusion of that
of the Yugoslavs during this period. The *Débats,* on
March 9, in a censored article, said there was at that time
"a debauch of [Italian] propaganda which recalls the worst
days of Crispi". On April 23 the *Politique,* also cut by the
censor, referred to imperialistic Italian propaganda and affirmed that "a few months ago this country was perfectly
indifferent to Fiume". And the *Correspondant,* a conservative and friendly weekly, remarked (May 10) that "to gain
Fiume, Italy has flooded the foreign press with suggestive
information". The columns of the *Temps* illustrate this very
well. Between April 16 and 24, for example, they carried
sixty-four column inches of material, of various sorts, favorable to the Italian case (including one editorial advocating
the granting of Fiume to Italy) while nothing whatever was
carried favorable to that of the Yugoslavs.

Taking these various factors into account—expediency,
sentiment, and pecuniary considerations—it is not surprising that when the crisis broke in late April, French opinion
seemed to be staunchly in support of the Italian claims. It
had already been observed, on April 16, by the press review
of the British General Staff that "a slow modification of the
French view of the rights of the Yugoslav State is apparent
in the press, and signs of a growing rapprochement with Italy
become ever more noticeable".[129] The *Esprit Public en
France* remarked at the time of the crisis that "the greater
part of opinion appears to support the Italian claims", though
it added that the Socialists and the liberals supported President Wilson.[130] This appraisal seems to accord with the

facts. When Wilson's pronunciamento broke the silence of the Four and precipitated the public clash, all of the heavy press was to be found in the Italian camp—the *Matin, Journal* and *Écho de Paris* very clamorously so, and the *Temps, Petit Parisien* and *Petit Journal* with somewhat more caution and restraint. France could not admit, said the *Matin* (April 24), "that the only other great Power called upon to mount guard on the frontier of liberty, should be separated from her by misunderstanding"; and the *Écho de Paris*, which had always insisted on the primary importance of the Italian alliance, averred (April 24) that if upholding the Treaty of London brought about "a revision of certain foolish stipulations, which ideology and commercialism have imposed on us, our Italian friends will not be the only ones to profit by the affair".

Practically all the other influential organs of the Center and Right joined forces with the heavy press, with varying degrees of vehemence. *Action Française, Figaro, Gaulois* and *Liberté* played leading rôles, and Gustave Hervé, the stormy petrel of nationalism, conducted an unrelenting pro-Italian campaign in the *Victoire*. On six of the seven days of that week his trenchant editorials alternately pleaded the Italian cause and heaped sarcasm upon the President. "The noble thought and evangelical spirit of the document" were said to be "worthy of the previous pastoral manifestoes to humanity, of which he has constituted himself the good shepherd".[131] Hostile reactions in Italy to Wilson's pronouncement were given special emphasis by this press, and counter-demonstrations in Yugoslavia were almost totally ignored. The *Temps* of April 25, for example, carried forty-eight inches of pro-Italian news, including a statement by Orlando, but carried nothing giving the Yugoslav point of view.

In spite of this redoubtable array of support for the Italian cause, it cannot be said that the pro-Italian sentiment was overwhelming. The Left Wing press, despite all considerations of expediency, sentiment, etc., was about as solidly for the Wilsonian position as the Center and Right press was against it. "We love our Italian allies," said the *Œuvre* (April 24), "but not more than justice"; and the liberal review, *Europe Nouvelle* (April 26), said that the ideas of Wilson represented the true desires of the people of Europe. Socialist and labor opinion was solidly Wilsonian. On April 26 the Administrative Commission of the General Confederation of Labor unanimously agreed, not only to appeal to Italian labor in the name of the rights of peoples, but also to send an open letter to Wilson assuring him that his protest against the Italian pretensions had met with unreserved approbation "in the conscience of French working classes".[132]

Even among conservative organs, there were notable defections from the Italian cause. Chief of these was the *Débats,* which, guided by the able journalist, Gauvain, throughout the months leading up to the crisis, had watched with grave concern the growing appetite of Italy and the spreading propaganda. On April 25 it counseled its colleagues that they were talking too much of the danger of setting Italy against France and too little of the danger of setting the United States against France.[133] Furthermore, several moderately influential organs of the Center press, such as *Paris-Midi, Information* and the *Intransigeant* assumed distinctly neutral rôles in the controversy.

By and large, in spite of the strong pro-Italian press campaign led by the most influential papers, it seems reasonable to conclude that there is much truth in the opinion expressed at that time by Albert Thomas, that "at bottom, all of France thinks as Gauvain [of the *Débats*] does". On this question, perhaps, more than any other at the Conference, there was a divorce between the patriotic press as a whole and public opinion.[134]

7. REFLECTIONS ON THE NEW DIPLOMACY

So much for the merits of the Italian case, for which no satisfactory solution was found. What shall we say of the unprecedented diplomatic methods resorted to by the President for the solution of the crisis? There was, not unnaturally, a strong tendency for those who agreed with the President's general objective, to sanction the means resorted to for its attainment, and, conversely, a natural inclination on the part of those who disapproved of his ends, to denounce the means by which he sought to gain them. Even the nationalistic *Démocratie Nouvelle,* which in this particular case sympathized with Wilson's territorial objectives, rejoiced (April 25) that an end had been put to "the intolerable secrecy and hidden maneuvers of the Conference". Socialists, joined by some advanced liberals, breathed a welcome to the "fresh air" which had finally arrived.[135] The General Confederation of Labor in an open letter to the President fervently applauded his gesture in "calling to the peoples themselves by a discussion in full daylight, in order to permit them to formulate their judgment".[136] But there was a note of sadness among the Socialists. "Ah, Mr. Wilson, why have you waited so long?" plaintively queried *Humanité* and *Populaire* (April 25). In all justice, it was felt, his new methods should not be limited to this one episode, but should be extended to problems of imperialism closer home.

As above suggested, those who disapproved of Wilson's aims in this particular matter, were inclined to find the method dangerous, if not sinister. Nor was this disapproval altered by the fact that they had unanimously objected to the Stygian proceedings of the Council of Four. The anathemas which they had heaped upon The Four were no prophecy that the rough and ready "shirt sleeves" diplomacy of the best American tradition would be viewed with anything other than alarm. The fact is that the President's methods, in this affair, were more severely and more generally criticized than his proposed solutions, for, though important groups in the Center and Right were at bottom lukewarm if not hostile to the Italian case, they were much less neutral concerning the unprecedented diplomatic technique.[137] Their remarks in condemnation of the President's unwonted diplomatic methods can therefore be taken much more nearly at their face value than can corresponding comments in favor of the Italian case.

Throughout most of this press the new technique of the President was viewed with great alarm. He was accused of having substituted himself for the Conference in this case.[138] He was charged with attempting to arouse one government against another within the Council, and, by his public messages outside the Council, with endeavoring to "stir up the peoples against their governments".[139] According to others, he was attempting to dictate to Europe and the world.[140] His manifesto was said to be the result of studied lack of realism; [141] and he was charged with issuing it when conciliation was about to be reached.[142] *Paris-Midi* expressed a widely felt sense of alarm (April 25) that such an appeal should have been launched on the eve of the arrival of the Germans; and the *Revue Politique et Parlementaire* also reflected much moderate and conservative opinion in saying that though there was some merit in Wilson's case, that did not justify his act of "breaking the windows" with such "truly American brusqueness and lack of ceremony".[143]

The possible dangers involved in an appeal to the popular masses over the heads of their governments was a matter of serious concern. It was urged that an appeal to popular passions, contrary to all the diplomatic traditions, would envenom the conflict rather than calm it.[144] Saint-Brice, of the *Journal*, argued (April 25) the matter plausibly and somewhat at length. Assemblies were more sensitive to passion than to reason, he said. That was the great danger of debate on the public square as instituted by President Wilson. Did the President believe it would be easier to impose a compromise on the popular masses than on experienced statesmen? The whole American maneuver was founded on the idea that, in the presence of a conflict, the Italian people would abandon their government. No more serious psychological error could be committed, he thought. Instead of forcing the government to yield, the populace would form a solid block of national resistance. The force of Saint-Brice's words was soon fully realized in the developments in Italy. Viewing this as the first act of the "new diplomacy" even the *Dépêche* of Toulouse (April 26) felt that the world would deplore that it "was not a happier one".[145]

In promulgating his Italian note President Wilson had only sought to break a deadlock, and not to establish a new procedure for the Conference. It was not a deliberate harking back to the "open covenants openly arrived at" of early Peace Conference days. No suggestion was made of a general change in Conference methods. The secret councils of the Four or the Three continued as before the pronunciamento, and public opinion was no more enlightened than formerly as to its doings. Hence, while dividing into definite majority and minority blocs on the subject of Wilson's Italian gesture, the public remained fairly united in its disparagement of the Conference procedure as a whole. The "wind of folly" still blew over Paris, in the words of the *Petite Gironde* (April 28) and from day to day the Conference of the world's "élite" was said to continue its "inexplicable groping and tergiversations".

Auguste Gauvain, of the *Débats,* was one of the few commentators to present a thoughtful analysis of the problem; and his views are worthy of note as they are representative of those held in moderate circles. The problem brought to a climax in the Italian affair was, he believed,[146] due to an original and fundamental defect of procedure: the failure at the beginning of the negotiations to take positions frankly and publicly. Clarification of positions was postponed, and discussion of principles was delayed in the hope that at the last moment miraculous bargains could be struck. The Conference had "neither programs nor principles. There were not even any résumés of its proceedings. There was fear of registering the substance of the discussions of the Ten, the Five, the Four, and the Three. In meetings on which the attention of the entire world was fixed, no delegate made declarations which left any public traces. Everything took place in darkness." The fatal disaster was therefore, inevitable.

Some months later,[147] re-appraising the procedures of the Conference, he criticized those who laid the blame for the defects of the treaty on the new diplomacy, and who mourned the neglect of the old methods. This tendency, he averred, was ridiculous, for never had there been more maneuvering in darkness and secrecy than in 1919, and never had a few men so completely imposed their omnipotence. The only innovation was that those who made the treaty were politicians rather than diplomats. "If the treaty of June 28," he said, "contains so many regrettable compromises, it is because its authors, instead of discussing their problems as responsible men, have comported themselves as did Metternich or Napoleon III. And yet, we do wrong to Metternich —the Congress of Vienna was less secret than that of Paris."

Mr. Wilson's procedure in dealing with the Italian crisis may have been necessary and salutary. It was so regarded by practically all of Left Wing opinion, and by important moderate elements farther to the right. It was certainly an act of unprecedented diplomatic brusqueness. It was, doubtless, a natural outcome of the unwise organization and procedure of the Conference which gradually pushed the public farther and farther away from its counsels. These methods became increasingly unsatisfactory to all parties concerned. Therefore the President's isolated and irregular venture into the domain of public diplomacy may be regarded not merely as a tragic reflection, but also as a solemn condemnation, of the preceding failure of the Conference to work out a reasonable application of the principle embodied in the first of the Fourteen Points.

Yet it must not be assumed that any method of procedure could have saved the Peace Conference and made it worthy of the idealism in the name of which the war was ostensibly fought. Gauvain was correct in saying that the defects of the treaty should not be blamed on the "new diplomacy". He scarcely exaggerated in suggesting that the new diplomacy became a tawdry phrase rather than an effective reality. But he erred in assuming that any technique, whatsoever, could have rescued the Versailles settlement from failure and ultimate collapse. The disease of European and world politics was too persistent and deep-rooted to be exorcised by any diplomatic legerdemain, and a radical attempt to apply the "new diplomacy" might have precipitated further international disorder even among the erstwhile Allies themselves. Perhaps the most significant commentary suggested by an examination of the proceedings of the Paris Conference is the testimony which it offers as to the incompatibility of a democratic diplomacy with the demands of undemocratic national policies.

NOTES

[1] White, W. A., *Woodrow Wilson, the Man, His Times, and His Task* (New York, 1924), p. 394.

[2] Nicolson, Harold, *Peacemaking, 1919* (London, 1933), p. 123.

[3] Churchill, *The World Crisis, The Aftermath*, p. 136.

[4] Baker, *op. cit.*, vol. i, p. 137.

[5] *Ibid.*, p. 138.

[6] Minutes of Supreme Council, in Hoover War Library, B. C. 2, January 15, 1919.

[7] "It was hardly conceivable," he said, "that the big conferences would be obliged to accept the decisions of those present if the principle of: 'one nation, one vote' were adopted." To which Mr. Balfour made the pointed rejoinder that "surely the President did not propose to permit the Great Powers to be outvoted by the small Powers". *Ibid.*, B. C. 3, January 16, 1919.

[8] Tardieu, *op. cit.*, p. 108.

[9] Minutes of Supreme Council, in Hoover War Library, B. C. 2 and 2-A, January 15, 1919.

[10] Thompson, *op. cit.*, p. 102.

[11] White, *op. cit.*, p. 397.

[12] The President was told that a limitation of information to "things accomplished" would deny to the public the right of following through the development of issues, and of being informed of the position assumed by the various elements within the conference; "and public opinion will thus have no chance to function in the way that you have always advocated, and that you define in the Fourteen Points. We stand where you stand," they urged: "Open Covenants of peace openly arrived at." *Daily Mail*, Paris ed., January 17, 1919.

[13] *Ibid.*, January 17, 1919.

[14] Statement of Saint-Brice, one of the French Committee, in the *Journal*, January 19. Other members were, Marcellin, of the *Liberté*, and Bassée, of the *Agence Havas*.

[15] Minutes of Supreme Council, in Hoover War Library, B. C. 4-A, January 17, 1919. This reservation of the right even of the full Conference to exclude the press indicated a lingering fear on the part of the Supreme Council that the plenary sessions might conceivably assume some of the supervisory and deliberative functions which Mr. Wilson had previously envisaged for them. All such misgivings were soon put to rest as the comparative barrenness and formality of the plenary sessions revealed themselves.

[16] Thompson, *op. cit.*, p. 113.

[17] *Annales de la Chambre*, December 27, 1918, p. 3247.

[18] *Ibid.*, December 29, 1918, p. 3332.

[19] *Humanité*, January 18; *Vérité*, January 19. The *Œuvre*, the *Progrès* of Lyons, and the *Populaire de Nantes* also were skeptical.

[20] The *Intransigeant*, January 17, also had some fears over the nondescript régime of secrecy, on the ground that the governments might be compromised by what the papers might erroneously write.

[21] *Éclair de l'Est*, January 26.

[22] *Journal*, January 18.

[23] *Temps*, January 17.

[24] January 16, 18.

[25] E.g., *Liberté*, January 17.

[26] White, *op. cit.*, p. 398.

[27] *Supra*, p. 117.

[28] *Débats*, January 29.

[29] The communiqué of the 28th:

> The exchanges of views related to the German colonies of the Far East, of the Pacific, and of Africa.
>
> The representatives of the Dominions were present at the two sittings.

.   .   .   .   .   .

> In the morning the delegates of Australia, of New Zealand, of Japan and of China were heard.
>
> In the evening, M. Henry Simon, French minister for colonies, expressed the views of his department on the colonial questions.
>
> In addition, the principles of the League of Nations, and the application of these principles were considered.
>
> *Débats*, January 30.

The communiqué of the 30th:

> The exchange of views continued on the question of the German colonies in the Pacific and in Africa, in the presence of the representatives of the Dominions, of M. Henry Simon, French minister for colonies, and M. Salvago Raggi.
>
> A provisional and satisfactory arrangement has been reached with regard to the régime to be applied to the German colonies. . . .
>
> *Débats*, February 1.

[30] Minutes of Supreme Council, Miller Diary, vol. xiv, pp. 374 *et seq.*

346 POLICIES AND OPINIONS AT PARIS, 1919

[31] *Débats,* February 14.

[32] Minutes of Supreme Council, Hoover War Library, B. C. 2, January 15, 1919.

[33] *Ibid.,* B. C. 4, January 17, 1919.

[34] Minutes of Supreme Council, Miller Diary, vol. xiv, p. 73.

[35] *Ibid.,* p. 126.

[36] Baker, *op. cit.,* vol. i, p. 152.

[37] *Ibid.,* p. 153.

[38] Lloyd George had objected, on March 19, to the support of the Polish Commission, arguing heatedly that it proposed to turn over too many Germans to Poland. The communiqué of the 19th stated simply that the Council "discussed the western frontiers of Poland, and listened to the report of the Commission on Polish affairs". *Débats,* March 21. A number of French newspapers, and particularly the *Temps, Journal* and *Écho de Paris,* gave much fuller accounts of the proceedings, combining these with rather bitter comment, directed, this time, chiefly at Lloyd George.

At the session of March 21 Lloyd George's wrath exploded because of the "garbled account" of his statements, for which he held French sources responsible. Furthermore, he said, disclosures were daily occurring which were causing the greatest harm in Germany and stiffening her resistance to the Treaty. If similar disclosures were to be repeated, he would much prefer not to take any further part in the discussions. The influence of the local press on the proceedings of the Conference were such, he suggested, as to raise the question whether the Conference should be continued at Paris. As was well known, the *Temps* was supposed to be in such close touch with the government that the article in question would be doubly mischievous, and it ought to be possible to prevent responsible officials from giving away such information, especially when it was deliberately altered in order to make it the ground for a violent attack on one of the Allied countries.

Clemenceau somewhat contritely admitted the justice of the criticisms of Lloyd George, and promised to make a vigorous protest to the directors of the *Temps.* He said that though there was a press censorship in France, the government did not dare enforce it too rigorously. Minutes of Supreme Council, March 21, 1919. Miller Diary, vol. xv, pp. 464 *et seq.*

[39] *Ibid.,* p. 467.

[40] Tardieu, *op. cit.,* p. 110. M. Pichon's fatal interview of March 16, in which, contrary to the statement of President Wilson the preceding day, he denied that the League of Nations would go into the peace preliminaries, was apparently his last appearance in a press conference.

[41] Again, when the proposed Treaty of Guarantee was announced, the press was requested not to comment on Wilson's constitutionally weak position in the United States. Statement based on confidential conversations with responsible journalists and officials, May to September, 1931.

[42] M. Clemenceau informed the members of that body, January 16, 1919, that though he did not "suspend" the right of interpellation, he would expect them to use it "with moderation". *Annales de la Chambre,* January 16, 1919, p. 8.

[43] Baker, *op. cit.,* vol. i, p. 143.

[44] The prevailing feeling on this matter was well expressed by the

Figaro, January 16, in saying that the régime of communiqués could not be criticized if it were maintained toward everybody equally, in France as well as abroad. "While the censor rules in Paris," wrote the *Intransigeant*, January 18, "one reads in the *Daily Mail* information that was censored in the *Intransigeant* on the 16th."

[45] See e.g., *Allied Press*, vol. v, no. 14, February 12, 1919; and *Esprit Public en France*, Bulletin 21, March 30-April 5, 1919.

[46] *Allied Press*, vol. v, no. 13, February 5, 1919. This feeling was well reflected in the *Petit Provençal*, February 25, in saying that "for the first time the Conference is taking up something that directly concerns France".

[47] *Figaro*, February 10.

[48] *Annales de la Chambre*, March 25, 1919, pp. 1280-1281.

[49] *Matin*, March 28, noted with regret that public opinion had been prevented from pressing the claims of France; and the *Intransigeant*, March 29, feared that France was now the victim, rather than the leader of the discussions.

[50] *Petit Provençal*, February 8.

[51] *Débats*, March 9.

[52] Bulletin 20, March 22-29, 1919.

[53] The Socialist view was, rather, that Mr. Wilson was resisting unjustifiable demands of the Allies. *Humanité*, April 3, e.g.

[54] E.g., *Petit Provençal*, February 4; March 23. "There are times when goodness [of Mr. Wilson's variety] is a crime," said the *Progrès du Nord*, February 5.

[55] *Petit Marseillais*, February 9.

[56] *Phare* of Nantes, February 26. An episode of March 15 illustrates how inadequate publicity led to misunderstanding of essential facts, and reacted against Wilson. On his return from America the President asked for time to peruse the military terms drawn up during his absence. An ill-tempered outburst from various organs was directed chiefly against Mr. Wilson, as well as against the Conference methods. *Figaro*, March 16. *Matin*, March 16, caustically remarked that "out of deference to the President of the United States, the Council decided to adjourn the deliberations". Even *Œuvre* (March 16) was sarcastic, and the Paris *Daily Mail* (March 17) remarked on the "misinformed and, in some cases, malevolent, comment".

[57] *House Papers*, vol. iv, p. 357. A memorandum in the Miller Diary, vol. vi, p. 316, notes that at House's suggestion it was agreed between Clemenceau, Lloyd George and the Colonel that on the President's return, the three Prime Ministers and the President would meet regularly in private. Mordacq says that on the 9th or 10th of March Clemenceau had said the Council of Ten system would have to be changed. *Le Ministère Clemenceau*, p. 164. Allan Nevins ascribes the change in procedure to Lloyd George. *Henry White: Thirty Years of American Diplomacy* (New York, 1930), p. 417. House later recorded, on the 17th, that the President was not so clearly impressed with the importance of speed on the German treaty, feeling that peace should be made simultaneously with the other defeated powers. *House Papers*, vol. iv, p. 385.

[58] Colonel House, on March 22, wrote in his diary: "From the look

of things the crisis will soon be here. Rumblings of discontent every day. The people want peace. Bolshevism is gaining ground everywhere."

Again on the 24th: "I saw the President for nearly an hour at his residence, and pointed out the necessity of forcing the Conference out of the rut into which it has fallen." *Ibid.*, p. 389.

[59] Thompson, *op. cit.*, p. 266.

[60] *Temps*, April 4.

[61] *Ibid.*, April 5.

[62] E.g., the *Daily Mail's* statements concerning the "military, territorial and economic frontiers" of the Saar, in *Temps*, March 31, and the *Chicago Tribune's* item concerning reparations, in the *Temps*, April 2.

[63] See e.g., *Progrès de la Somme*, March 27.

[64] "The general impression is that all goes well," said *Ouest-Éclair*, on the 28th, after having previously criticized it harshly. The *Nouvelliste de Lyon*, March 28, likewise reversed itself. After referring to a semi-official communiqué stating that peace with Germany would soon be ready, it optimistically announced that the decision of the Four to deliberate in secrecy was right. The new system was working better than the old. See also the *Petite Gironde*, and *Petit Marseillais*, March 25-30.

[65] March 25, 26, 27, 29.

[66] March 29. See also the *Œuvre* for same period.

[67] Thompson, *op. cit.*, p. 286.

[68] Statement by Isaiah Bowman, in House, E. M., *What Really Happened at Paris*, p. 464.

[69] Steed, *op. cit.*, vol. ii, p. 310.

[70] Confidential correspondence in Hoover War Library.

[71] Baker, *op. cit.*, vol. i, p. 152.

[72] White, *op. cit.*, p. 430.

[73] Baker, *op. cit.*, vol. ii, p. 40.

[74] Nevins, *op. cit.*, p. 436.

[75] Baker, *op. cit.*, vol. ii, p. 57.

[76] See also *Current Summaries*, April 4-7. It is notable that all parties agreed that there had been unnecessary delays in the Conference, though views differed as to responsibility.

[77] Baker, *op. cit.*, vol. ii, p. 59.

[78] Nevins, *op. cit.*, p. 438. Even Professor Seymour, who says that Mr. Wilson "evidently regarded the cable as an incident of small importance" —because, says Seymour, House says nothing about it in his diary— nevertheless says that the cable was probably sent after a meeting of the President with the Commissioners in which it was decided "that if nothing happened within the next few days Wilson would tell the Prime Ministers that he would have to go home or have the conferences in the open". *House Papers*, vol. iv, p. 404. Lincoln Steffens, however, tells of discussing the matter with House who inquired, in behalf of the President, what would be the political effects of such an act on the various governments. Steffens says the President thought he was calling at last to the peoples of Europe. Steffens, Lincoln, *Autobiography* (New York, 1931), p. 786.

[79] Nevins, *op. cit.*, p. 438; Steffens, *op. cit.*, p. 786.

[80] Seymour says: ". . . it was Mr. Wilson and not the French or British

who made concessions during the following four days." *House Papers,* vol. iv, p. 404. See discussions, *supra,* p. 210, e.g., concerning the Saar.

[81] Baker, *op. cit.,* vol. ii, p. 62. Steffens also says that the British brought strong pressure to bear on Wilson. Steffens, *op. cit.,* p. 786.

[82] Thompson, *op. cit.,* p. 291.

[83] It is evident that the French censor exercised a restraining influence even on the Anglo-American press of Paris, though this was never so drastic as on the French press. Frederick Moore reported in the *New York Tribune* of April 10 that the censor had interposed on this occasion.

[84] These "American propagandists", said the *Matin,* had seen "in this *natural* order" (of the President's) an opportunity for blackmail, and had devoted themselves, "with the disapprobation of all the American friends of France, to an audacious maneuver of intimidation". April 9.

[85] On the following day it was permitted to suggest that the episode really was meant as "a discreet warning".

[86] *Humanité,* April 9; *Populaire,* April 10; *Bataille,* April 10.

[87] *Heure,* April 10.

[88] It is of course true that many of the papers needed no suggestion or encouragement from official sources for a campaign against Wilson.

[89] *Figaro,* April 14.

[90] *Croix,* April 7.

[91] *Gaulois,* April 11.

[92] *Journal,* and *Liberté,* April 10.

[93] *Écho de Paris,* April 8.

[94] *Homme Libre,* April 13; *Liberté,* April 10.

[95] *Liberté,* April 10; *Victoire,* April 9.

[96] *Victoire,* April 9, 11, 13.

[97] *Croix,* April 7.

[98] *Action Française,* April 11.

[99] There is some truth in the latter statement, as the French government maintained a censorship which restricted the news coming from the United States. André Géraud (Pertinax), of the *Écho de Paris,* says there were two Americans in charge of the censorship of news coming from the United States. Interview, September 3, 1931.

[100] *Current Summaries,* April 14; also, *Allied Press,* vol. v, no. 24, April 30.

[101] The *Débats* (April 10, 12) continued, as from the beginning, to deplore the Conference methods, and hoped that responsibility for the errors would not be imputed to the democratic régime, which, it argued, was "innocent of the faults of the autocrats who, for three weeks, have sat on Sinai".

[102] *Démocratie Nouvelle,* April 16.

[103] The primary reason for the increasing anxiety was the feeling already noted, that French interests were being compromised by the secrecy régime. Clemenceau would be much stronger, it was claimed, if he were surrounded and supported by the majority of French public opinion. *Intransigeant,* April 14. It was especially feared that France, while denied adequate territorial and financial guarantees, would be left as the "sole sentinel of the Western powers" on the Rhine. *Gaulois,* April 9. The heavy press expressed

the prevailing belief that the work of the Four was not providing for France reparations and guarantees in proportion to her needs. *Esprit Public en France,* Bulletin 22, April 6-12. The refusal by Wilson to accept the Bourgeois amendments when the revision of the League Covenant was resumed, and, in addition, the apparent deadlock at that time in the Four gave special point to these misgivings.

[104] The *Bataille* pointedly reminded the Premier that the uneasiness came not merely from the opponents of the government, but that all parties were alike "irritated by the governmental silence". April 13.

[105] The *Temps* (April 12) accurately interpreted public sentiment in the caustic remark that the constitution had certainly not intended to put the representatives of the nation in such a vexatious dilemma. *Esprit Public en France,* Bulletin 22, April 6-12.

[106] *House Papers,* vol. iv, p. 407; Mordacq, *op. cit.,* vol. iii, p. 233.

[107] E.g., *Temps,* April 19.

[108] Secretary Lansing stated that in spite of Mr. Wilson's commitments to open diplomacy, he was strongly inclined, in fact, to secret methods. Against this the Secretary warned him as early as January. Lansing, *op. cit.,* pp. 213 *et seq.* Mr. Henry White was especially fearful of the methods of The Four, and warned the President, accordingly. Nevins, *op. cit.,* p. 419.

[109] *House Papers,* vol. iv, p. 172.

[110] Harold Nicolson says Orlando did not really accept Point Nine; that he merely ceased to protest when it was suggested that this point did not bear upon the Armistice with Germany. Nicolson, *op. cit.,* p. 163.

[111] Mr. White thought this seriously weakened the President's position, and believed that House's influence was determining in the decision. Nevins, *op. cit.,* p. 427. Nicolson says "the consequences were disastrous", for the President had yielded his principle of nationality to the principle of strategic necessity. It also was thought to imply approval of the Treaty of London, of 1915. *Op. cit.,* p. 170.

[112] Nicolson, *op. cit.,* p. 170.

[113] Lansing, *op. cit.,* pp. 222, 228. He says there would have been no "Fiume Affair" if there had been no secret interviews at which false hopes were stirred.

[114] Nevins, *op. cit.,* p. 426; Miller Diary, vol. vi, pp. 451-453. White regarded the Mezes report of March 16 as containing "unjustifiable concessions to Italy upon Fiume and Dalmatia".

[115] Isaiah Bowman, Allyn A. Young, W. E. Lunt, Charles Seymour, Clive Day and Douglas Johnson.

[116] See reports of January 21, and April 17. Miller Diary, vol. iv, pp. 239-242; Nevins, *op. cit.,* pp. 425-427.

[117] Nicolson, *op. cit.,* p. 181.

[118] *House Papers,* vol. iv, p. 445.

[119] Perhaps "the painful concessions" which the President had made to France "in order to keep the Allies together", was another factor (in addition to the appeal of the experts) in inclining him to intransigence. Baker, *op. cit.,* vol. ii, p. 159.

[120] Miller Diary, vol. xix, p. 533.

[121] Baker, *op. cit.,* vol. ii, p. 162.

[122] For several days Wilson had contemplated this act, but was restrained by Lloyd George and Clemenceau in the hope of a final compromise. Baker, *op. cit.*, vol. iii, pp. 287 *et seq.*

[123] *Ibid.*, pp. 287 *et seq.*

[124] Harold Nicolson says that Sir Edward Grey was so disconcerted by Italy's demands leading up to her entrance into the war that "he retired to the country on a plea of illness", leaving the negotiations in the hands of the Permanent Under-Secretary. This official, in his discussions with the Italian Ambassador, used an expression of "contemptuous realism" which caused the Ambassador to remark: "You speak as if you were purchasing our support." "Well," said the Under-Secretary, "and so we are." Nicolson, *op. cit.*, p. 160.

[125] *Correspondant*, May 10, 1919, p. 571.

[126] *Journal*, April 25.

[127] *Le Ministère Clemenceau*, vol. iii, p. 232.

[128] Statements based on confidential documents in Hoover War Library, and on personal interviews. A leading publicist quoted a remark of an Italian made one day when a major semi-official organ printed an article that was not entirely satisfactory: "Four hundred thousand for forty-eight lines! That is a bit dear!" A leading semi-official organ is quoted as having sent a representative to Trumbitch of the Yugoslav delegation, asking why he didn't publish anything in that organ. Trumbitch is said to have replied: "You know very well you don't publish anything we send you without submitting it to the Italians"; whereupon the journalist representative replied, "The right of replying would only cost you 150,000 fr." See also Raffolovitch, A., *L'Abominable Vénalité de la Presse* (Paris, 1931), *passim.*

[129] Papers which formerly had nothing but friendly references to the Yugoslav nation, it said, "now concur in Signor Orlando's labelling of it as 'a people which fought against Italy up to the last moment'." *Allied Press*, vol. v, no. 23, April 16.

[130] Bulletin 24, pp. 20-26, April 1919.

[131] April 24. Two days later it remarked that if it weren't for the respect which the press entertained for Mr. Wilson's person there would be a "regular howl" over his action.

[132] *Humanité*, April 27.

[133] It ought to be noted that most of the leading organs sought to placate the American point of view, and appealed to the spirit of conciliation. The *Démocratie Nouvelle,* under the influence of André Chéradame, maintained a consistently pro-Yugoslav position, so much so that M. Chéradame was much surprised to find himself practically in agreement, for the one and only time, with President Wilson.

[134] Thomas said there was a divorce between the press and public opinion on this question. Another high French official expressed the same idea in saying that "As to Italy, the papers do not represent opinion, which is very hostile to Italy." Confidential papers in the Hoover War Library.

[135] *Vérité*, April 24; *Œuvre*, April 24; *Heure*, April 25.

[136] *Humanité*, April 27.

[137] The *Petit Parisien* and *Petit Journal,* for example, though sympathetic to the Italians, for reasons of expediency or otherwise, had ex-

pressed relatively mild and conciliatory views as to the merits of Italy's case. Yet as to Wilson's technique they both deeply deplored (April 24) that it had been such as to expose the conflicting views of the Italians and Yugoslavs.

[138] *Matin,* April 24.

[139] *Écho de Paris,* April 25; *Correspondant,* May 10.

[140] *Liberté,* and *Victoire,* April 25; *Action Française,* April 26.

[141] *Action Française,* April 25.

[142] *Gaulois,* April 25.

[143] May 1919, pp. 202 *et seq.*

[144] *Avenir,* April 24.

[145] The *Correspondant,* May 10, said that if the President had wished to prove "that diplomacy should be conducted within a well-closed room [and such was that journal's conviction] and not in the forum open to all the winds of passion, he would not have acted otherwise than by this striking act".

[146] *Débats,* April 24, 25, 27.

[147] *Ibid.,* October 9.

CHAPTER X

PEACE CONDITIONS AND THE TREATY

"I do not know whether war is an interlude in peace, or whether peace is an interlude in war."

(Clemenceau, Senate debates, October 11, 1919.)

1. CONDITIONS OF PEACE

ON May 7 the Conditions of Peace were handed to the German delegation in a plenary session at Versailles.[1] The time was not deemed to have arrived however, for diplomacy to "proceed always frankly and in the public view". The Big Four were not prepared to reveal the complete document to their own peoples. Only a brief summary of its terms was given out, and the press of the 8th stated, semi-officially, that the complete text would be published only when it had obtained the German signature.[2]

That the failure of the Four to make public the complete text did not immediately cause a great outcry in France was due partly to the fact that the summary given to the press did provide a fairly good outline of the peace settlement, and thus provided the public with food for thought for at least a few days. Another probable reason was suggested by the *Dépêche* of Toulouse, in saying (May 21) that the public was becoming somewhat accustomed to such acts of "stupidity" on the part of the administration.

The anomalous situation soon became extremely vexatious. No sooner had the Treaty reached German hands than it was translated and distributed to the members of the German National Assembly at Weimar; after which it was published in the German press. Apparently the Germans felt that full publicity of its terms would not hurt their cause. Having been published in Germany it was only another step for the Treaty terms to recross the frontier into France and other Allied countries. Yet the press of France was sternly forbidden to reprint even translations of the details of the Treaty from the German papers.[3] *Bonsoir,* a radical journal, was repeatedly seized during the middle of May for attempting to violate this edict.[4]

Parliamentary circles soon became exasperated. On May 16 Marcel Sembat, supported by some 150 colleagues of the Left, introduced a resolution pointing to the fact that whereas the French deputies had seen only the summary given to the press, in Germany the complete Treaty had for some time been in the hands of the members of the National Assembly. The resolution called upon the government to supply the members of Parliament with complete texts of the Treaty.[5] The attitude of the Radical Socialist Party was defined in a statement to the effect that it was "scandalous to see the German press in possession of documents refused even to the French Parliament".[6] The Commissions of the Chamber on the Budget, on Military Affairs and on Foreign Affairs sought to obtain texts of the Treaty for special examination.[7] All these efforts were unavailing. Clemenceau, in reply to the Commissions, pretended that he was prevented by constitutional provisions from complying with their requests, inasmuch as the Treaty had not been accepted by the Germans nor passed upon by the French President.[8] The fact that the Treaty was soon broadcast, not only in enemy countries, but also among neutral and even Allied peoples was a source of increased vexation in France, and a stimulus to parliamentary oratory.[9] To heighten the comedy of the situation, *Bonsoir* imported a large number of copies of the Treaty, which had been translated into French, and distributed them to members of the Chamber of Deputies, explaining that they could be bought on the streets of Berlin for a few sous.[10] The eventual publication of the full Treaty text, on June 20, before it had even been signed, revealed the hollowness of Clemenceau's earlier objections to giving it to the parliamentary commissions.

The summary of the peace terms of May 7 was sufficiently definitive to indicate clearly the major lines of the proposed settlement, and sufficiently reassuring to allay many fears which had agitated patriotic circles during the greater part of April. Although the nationalists on the Right found the peace proposals too weak, and the Socialists labeled the terms imperialistic, for the great majority in between these extremes, the terms were as satisfactory as one could have hoped for, though there were few, if any, who would not have improved it in one direction or another. By and large, those organs subject to the inspiration of official circles contrived to give the Conditions of Peace a good press, regardless of what they may have previously claimed as indispensable for French national interests. The semi-official *Temps* set the tone of press comment.[11] "France is entitled to restitutions, to reparations and to guarantees," it pontificated. "She finds them in the treaty which was communicated today to the German plenipotentiaries." The following afternoon, again speaking apparently with the voice of the government, it breathed assurances that the Conditions consecrated the principles for which France had fought. The Treaty conformed not only to the war aims of France, but also to the Fourteen Points of Wilson.

For the most part, opinion of the Center and moderate Left and Right, reflected these views. As the *Esprit Public en France* put it, "the most general expression is that of contentment".[12] The "peace proposed to the Germans" was hailed as "a French peace".[13] The "atmosphere of contentment and satisfaction" in the corridors of the Chamber of Deputies was commented upon, with the assurance that the guarantees were sufficient to remove all fear of a rebirth of German hegemony.[14] Gauvain, of the *Débats* (May 9), wrote almost rapturously, saying that the proposed terms were "glorious and comforting", and that they gave France all she had a right to hope for. Even the *Figaro, Gaulois* and *Victoire*, farther to the right, glowed with satisfaction. "No Frenchman can read the Treaty without a feeling of just pride," wrote the *Figaro* (May 8); and Hervé chanted in the *Victoire* (May 8) that the peace was the sort of which he had dreamed, and shouted a hosannah to Wilson as well as to the Tiger, Foch and the poilus.

Moderate, and, especially, liberal organs, made a special effort to demonstrate that the terms were in conformity with democratic principles. Professor Aulard, writing in the *Pays* (May 9), affirmed that this would be the first great treaty in the history of the world which breathed the spirit of justice and liberty; and the *Dépêche* of Toulouse (May 10) averred that the terms were entirely free of traces of imperialism.

The nationalists, led by the *Action Française* and *Écho de Paris,* found the terms too much of a Wilsonian compromise, and far too weak in guarantees, whether against future aggression, or for securing the enforcement of the financial clauses of the treaty; and a few important organs of the Center were inclined to share the nationalist views on this score.[15] The proposed tripartite alliance offered by England and the United States, while it was viewed with much hope, was deemed to be proof of a gap in the treaty in the matter of security.[16] Pertinax, of the *Écho de Paris* (May 8), voiced nationalist sentiment in saying that France would simply have to trust to the Providence "which exists for shortsighted politicians", and be ready to take advantage of all future occasions to remedy the weaknesses of the Treaty.

The Socialists likewise damned the Conditions as a compromise—"a bastard compromise between Wilsonian idealism and imperialism". At a party demonstration on May 11 a resolution was adopted asserting that principles of justice had been violated "in nearly every sentence" of the terms.[17] The Socialist press proclaimed that the Conditions were imposing a peace of "oppression and injustice", of the same vintage as that of Brest-Litovsk;[18] and *Humanité* (May 9) at once affirmed that no Socialist deputy would be able "without total abdication", to ratify such a diplomatic instrument which history would certainly regard as a breach of sworn faith, and an assault on morality and justice. The principal objections coming from Socalist quarters related to the League of Nations, the reduction of German armaments, Polish frontiers, the Saar, Reparations, and the German colonies. The League was said to be a "league of governments, rather than a society of free peoples". The reduction of German armaments, however desirable in itself, should, it was argued, be only an aspect of immediate general reduction of armaments. The Polish frontier arrangements violated the rights of peoples, and were a dangerous source of future difficulties. The Saar provisions savored of "annexation and capitalistic exploitation", and were called the "most criminal part of the Treaty". The disposal of the German colonies could be regarded only as an "imperialistic division of the spoils". The Reparations total should have been fixed at a precise figure, and within the capacity of Germany to pay. "Assuming that Germany is responsible for the war," wrote Cachin in *Humanité* (May 10), and that she therefore ought to pay all its costs, "answer this: if she were a thousand times more culpable (and we do not pretend in any way to minimize her fault) could she then pay 500 billions?" [19]

With regard to the financial aspects of the Treaty, the Socialists agreed with opinion farther to the right that the terms were hopelessly inadequate; and this impression was all the more marked because of the distressing necessity faced by parliament of raising huge new credits by loans or taxation. The chairmen of the budget commission of the Chamber and Senate were pulling long faces over the prospects,[20] and even the Socialists were glad to consider any plan which would guarantee France against any possible default by Germany, and which would lighten the crushing burden of debt which was darkening the horizon. The French demand for some form of inter-Allied solidarity had had the united support of all groups, and the apparent failure to realize it brought a chorus of disappointment from the extreme Left as well as from liberal, conservative and reactionary groups. Socialist spokesmen joined with others in urging that the Allies could have relieved the grave situation by means of an international financial consortium, and that the League of Nations lacked reality without carrying with it "financial consequences".[21] The very basis of inter-Allied negotiations, wrote the liberal *Europe Nouvelle* (May 10), should have been a financial settlement of the war, based upon "the division of war costs in proportion to efforts expended, to human capital sacrificed and to the effective productive capacity of the contracting parties on November 11, 1918, the date of the Armistice".[22] Farther to the right, *Opinion,* ordinarily moderate in tone, was openly belligerent. "If France is allowed to encounter financial disaster," it threatened (May 17), "she will go into bankruptcy. So be it. She will not be alone."

2. ACCEPTANCE OR REJECTION

The French public had but little time in which to speculate abstractly upon the merits or defects of the peace terms, for very shortly the question whether Germany would accept them changed the entire perspective of events. This problem was posed as soon as news of the reception of the Peace Conditions floated back across the Rhine, and for many days it remained the all-absorbing topic in the news and editorial columns of the French press. A campaign of resistance to the terms was soon detected by French commentators.[23] German political leaders and the press were apparently united in unmeasured denunciation of the proposed terms. Fehrenbach, president of the German National Assembly, Chancellor Scheidemann, President Ebert, Hermann Mueller, Majority Socialist chief, and other prominent leaders contended that the terms condemned Germans to slavery, and predicted a war of revenge. The moderate Erzberger undoubtedly expressed overwhelming national feeling in saying that "The Treaty of Versailles is the work of the devil", and that radical modifications would be necessary before any government could sign it.[24] Only the Independents seemed to feel that it would be better to sign, regardless of the terms. Haase argued that though the terms were unbearable and incapable of execution, yet it was necessary to sign in order to live.

French commentators, except on the extreme Left, pretended not to take the German protests seriously. The German demonstrations were but a "maneuver" aimed to intimidate and weaken the Allies. Indeed, the public was led by the patriotic press to believe that the scene in Germany was unrolling precisely as was to be expected. As the *Petit Journal* (May 10) put it, "No one in France will take seriously the cries of our enemies, nor their attempts at bluff, blackmail and bargaining. They will cry out . . . and they will sign." Perhaps the Scheidemann government might resign, but the Independents would come in and Germany would sign.[25]

Of course there would be protests and, if the Allies permitted, there would be interminable discussions.[26] Unflinching Allied solidarity would overcome this difficulty, and only when Germany realized that this was a fact, would she yield.[27] In this connection there was some anxiety concerning Wilson's attitude, for a careful German propaganda campaign was thought to be trying to estrange the President from France.[28] Large sums were presumably being spent by Germany in the United States on anti-French propaganda.[29] Germany was said to be bringing her batteries to bear on Wilson, and was counting on the support of high American commercial and financial circles which were anxious that Germany should be able to buy American merchandise.[30] Fears were expressed that Wilson's profound respect for German scientific achievements would incline him toward a softening of the peace terms,[31] and attention was called by the press of May 24 to appeals from Berlin to the American people against the "economic destruction, moral degradation and political dishonor" which the peace terms would allegedly bring upon Germany.

In order to counteract German maneuvers and silence

Socialist criticisms, particular stress began to be laid (even in quarters which had received the Conditions with a sigh of relief) on the inadequacies of the terms, which, as they were, merely secured the bare "right of existence", as the organ of the Ligue Civique put it.[32] In the more nationalistic circles a clamor was raised in favor of making the terms more rigorous.[33] The Chamber of Commerce of Rennes expressed disillusionment over the failure to satisfy France's territorial claims, as formulated "almost unanimously by French Chambers of Commerce".[34] The Committee of the Left Bank, protesting against the failure to gain the frontier of 1814, against the weakness of the League of Nations, and the inadequacy of the reparations, called on the government to secure a revision in conformity with "the interests and sacred rights of France".[35] The Right group of the Senate and two Right groups of the Chamber expressed great dissatisfaction that the Treaty had been "denuded" of guarantees, and asked for improvements.[36] The Federation of National Leagues for the Defense of the Rights and Interests of France, claiming to represent ten million Frenchmen, wrote to the members of Parliament urging the non-ratification of the Treaty unless it were altered to provide for the permanent occupation of the left bank, as well as the occupation and exploitation of the Ruhr until all reparations were paid.[37] The University Union placarded the billboards of Paris, June 2, in protest against "the Catastrophe", as it stigmatized the Peace Conditions, condemning particularly the military frontier and reparations clauses.[38]

Toward the 20th of May the probability of a German refusal to sign appeared to be stronger.[39] Solemn warnings were therefore issued to Germany by the patriotic press suggesting the serious consequences which she might anticipate from such a refusal. The inconveniences for Germany would be enormous. The Allies would be bound by no engagements, and would have the right to impose far more stringent terms. "As to the Saar and the left bank, we would demand much more radical solutions." [40] The *Temps* (May 20) and *Information* (May 22) joined with more nationalistic organs such as the *Gaulois* and *Action Française* in threatening to negotiate with the individual German states, and thus to break up the Reich. Further military occupation and tightening of the blockade were also envisaged as appropriate and effective weapons for the purpose of forcing the German hand. [41]

The general drift of opinion during these first few weeks revealed clearly that what was wanted above all else by the overwhelming majority of Frenchmen was the German signature to the Treaty as it stood. Its terms were unsatisfactory enough in certain respects, but if the German protests and manifestations prevailed, the treaty would risk being emasculated. Hence liberals, conservatives and even nationalists joined in common defense of the document, demanding that it be accepted by Germany in its May 7 form. Even the Socialists advised the Germans to sign, hoping for later revision. [42]

3. COUNTER-PROPOSALS

Anxieties as to the nature and extent of Germany's revisionist demands were brought to a head May 29 when the full text of her counter-proposals was received by the Allies, and made public in summary. [43] A lengthy introduction argued the fundamental inconsistency of the proposed terms with the Fourteen Points and the "solemn promises" of Allied statesmen. The various terms were then attacked in detail and counter-proposals were made.

Immediate entrance into the League of Nations "as a power with equal privileges" was demanded by Germany. The military, naval and air clauses would be accepted, on condition that this was "the beginning of a general reduction of armaments", and on condition of German entrance into the League on a basis of equality. Instead of the proposed Saar régime, Germany would guarantee to deliver to France sufficient coal to compensate her for the destroyed coal mines in the North of France. French ownership of the mines and the plebiscite at the end of fifteen years were bitterly opposed. A "free plebiscite" was asked for in Alsace-Lorraine, Germany admitting that she had erred in not consulting the people in 1871. The fifteen-year occupation of the left bank would "destroy the unity of the German people for years to come", and was unacceptable. The occupied territory should be evacuated within six months after the signing of the Treaty. The reparations categories were said to be too broad, and Germany would accept responsibility only for damage caused to civilians in occupied portions of France and Belgium. Furthermore, she would undertake to pay a sum not to exceed 100 billions of marks, without interest, of which twenty billions could be paid before May 1, 1926.

Strenuous objections were made to the Polish frontier proposals. Upper Silesia could not be ceded, nor could she consent that East Prussia should be cut off from the rest of Germany. Facilities could be granted to Poland through German territory in such a way as to assure her free access to the sea. The loss of her colonies, the surrender of her merchant marine, and the demand for the surrender of the former Emperor for "criminal prosecution" were the subjects of vigorous protest and counter-proposals; and other less important provisions of the Conditions were also attacked.[44] The above comments and proposals were accompanied by an urgent request for oral discussions on the various points at issue between Germany and the Allied and Associated Powers.

As was to be expected, the German counter-proposals encountered a storm of disapproval and righteous indignation everywhere in France, except on the extreme Left, where radical revision of the Treaty was demanded.[45] Throughout the patriotic press Germany was said to be attempting to escape, morally and materially from the consequences of the war brought on by her.[46] "Arrogance", "German defiance", "Monument of impudence", "odious piece of buffoonery",

"height of audacity and insolence", were typical characterizations of the German conduct in various quarters.[47] Germany was not only questioning fundamentals of the Treaty,
but was also attempting to divide the Allies and to dictate
terms of peace to the conquerors.[48] She was alleged to be
trying to disengage herself immediately from the position of
international inferiority which constituted the "characteristic trait of the project of the Allies".[49] Count Brockdorff
was charged with acting as though "the peace of 1919 were
a peace of reconciliation", whereas, in fact, "it is a peace
of reparation".[50]

The liberal press was, apparently, equally appalled by the
"cynicism" of the German tactics.[51] Professor Aulard, writing in the *Pays* (May 30), said that though he was not
given to insulting the vanquished, nevertheless, the only
words which he could find for Brockdorff's note were
"indecency and lack of conscience".

The charge by Germany that there were serious discrepancies between the proposed terms and the Fourteen Points
prompted leading organs to flatter and cajole President
Wilson, in order to induce him to stand firm. Was Wilson
not "one of the principal authors of the Treaty"? it was
asked. Count Brockdorff would surely find some difficulty
in convincing him that he did not understand himself.[52]
What was "the use of the Germans' arguing about the Fourteen Points"? Mr. Wilson, having helped to draw up the
Treaty, and having approved and signed it, would naturally
be "the man best qualified to interpret the meaning of his
Fourteen Points".[53] The "arrogance of the Germans" in
assuming to interpret to Wilson his own ideas was held up
to ridicule;[54] and the German response was held to be "a
veritable insult to the President of the United States". "We
do not think," said the *Matin* (May 31), "that Mr. Wilson
will remain silent before such a caricature of his most generous thoughts."

Non-Socialist groups were therefore, for the most part,
insistent that a peremptory "No" must be the Allied reply

to the German proposals. Neither oral discussion, nor any important changes of the text could be tolerated.[55] "To allow Germany to discuss our principles is both a moral and a material impossibility," wrote the *Homme Libre* (May 31). "It is time to finish this comedy and deal severely." The *Débats* (May 31, June 2) expressed the prevalent view that the Treaty could be re-examined by the Allies only to clear up incoherencies in the drafting or to adjust matters of detail. As to concessions, Germany was reminded again that the terms were "already inadequate". France, in a spirit of conciliation, had agreed to compromises. In return, said the *Débats,* "We shall demand of our allies that they remain faithful to that which has been agreed to in common accord, and reject *en bloc* the German counter-proposals." With this view liberal opinion was in entire harmony. Agreeing that discussion was out of place, and that the Treaty provisions were already dangerously weak, the *Dépêche* of Toulouse (May 29, June 2) suggested that Brockdorff-Rantzau was only feigning intransigence in the hope of capitalizing the "idealism of Mr. Wilson" and the "mildness of Lloyd George".

The *Temps* (May 30, June 5) spoke for a wide constituency in warning the Four "to make no mistake": public opinion expected "firm language". The only possible excuse for altering the Treaty, it said, would be in case a clause violated one of the Fourteen Points. But "If there had been any violation of the Fourteen Points, Mr. Wilson would have been the first to draw attention to it." In a long and scarifying outburst, the *Temps* (May 31) gave eloquent expression to the moral indignation of all patriotic opinion in a scathing indictment of the whole German case. "Germany, scarcely camouflaged in democracy, and still represented at Versailles by a minister of William II, was pretending to teach a lesson to the nations which have rescued the liberties of the world from her, and to instruct these nations as to the means of 'establishing a durable peace'." Germany was seeking to use, in her own behalf "the prin-

ciples which the Allies have been compelled to defend against
her. . . ." "The problem which is posed for the chiefs of the
Allied and Associated Governments," said the *Temps*, "is
neither a territorial, nor a financial nor a political problem. . . ." "It is the honor and dignity of the Allied and
Associated Peoples" which is at stake.

There appeared to be real "danger" that the Allies might
make important concessions. Rumors of modifications to be
made in the Treaty were floating in from various quarters.
On May 30 several papers cited despatches from Washington indicating that notable changes were to be made. Special reference was made to reparations, Upper Silesia, the
Saar, and German entrance into the League of Nations.[56]
The following day various papers commented on the dangerous trends. The Four were sorrowfully reported as apparently once more "on the way to making concessions"; [57]
and, although vague denials were made, these were regarded
as quite insufficient. "These intrigues must be cut short,"
said the *Journal* (May 31).[58]

The tension everywhere increased. As noted by General
Mordacq, great nervousness prevailed in public opinion, as
well as in military and political circles.[59] The source of this
anxiety was the danger, first, that Germany might not sign
the terms as they were, and second, that France's allies
might actually force through serious concessions to Germany. The possibilities of military coercion of Germany had
long been envisaged. As early as April 8 the Four had put
this question to their military and naval advisers, and from
time to time the matter was discussed by the Four, as well
as in conferences with Marshal Foch.[60] Another matter
which agitated the Council of Four during this period was
the question whether the fifteen-year period of occupation
of the Rhineland should be reduced, as was repeatedly,
though unsuccessfully, urged by Lloyd George, with the
support of at least some of the American experts.[61] This important controversy, however, was kept entirely out of the
press.

The censor was never more active than at this time. Every day his interdictions whitened portions of news and editorial columns. The situation was well illustrated by a cartoon in the *Matin* (June 7) showing the censor mercilessly slashing the press. "It is prohibited to publish what Marshal Foch says," commented the *Matin*. "It is prohibited to publish what Lloyd George thinks. It is prohibited to publish the Treaty of Peace with Germany. It is prohibited to publish what is going on at. . . . And in order to be very certain that nothing will be published, the censor holds up all the despatches." Under the title "WHITE EVERYWHERE", the *Temps* (June 10) voiced the general uneasiness over the short-sighted régime of the censorship, which wrongly "imagined that it was serving the national interests of France". Even "an unjust criticism", it argued, "could contribute to the solution of a problem", by putting people on guard, and encouraging the quest for remedies. But, as it was, facts, presumably concealed, were spreading "in uncontrollable rumors, with the result that they are deformed and made more irritating". The motivation behind this and similar criticisms was the fear that Clemenceau might be forced into a policy of compromise.

Interestingly enough, Wilson was not, at that time, the chief source of uneasiness. The line-up in the Council of Four had changed perceptibly, for the pressure in favor of yielding to the German demands came almost exclusively from Lloyd George. General Mordacq records that on the evening of May 30, after the Council meeting, Clemenceau's exasperation with Lloyd George flamed out. "The task," said Clemenceau, "is becoming veritably impossible. For weeks and weeks I had to fight Wilson and his famous principles. Finally, with much patience, and also with much diplomacy, I came off triumphant, and in that matter Lloyd George aided me powerfully. Now it is England which is obstructing the way and changing her mind as to everything that has been decided." [62]

President Wilson's attitude toward the German counter-proposals was expressed in a meeting with the other American delegates and the experts, June 3. The American experts apparently favored making the Reparations figures definite, also reducing the period of occupation of the left bank, and modifying the Upper Silesia terms. While not unqualifiedly opposed to any change, the President said he would not be frightened into concessions by the German threat of a refusal to sign the Treaty. "The time to consider all these questions," he thought, "was when we were writing the Treaty, and it makes me a little tired for people to come and say now that they are afraid the Germans won't sign." [63]

For the first time since the opening of the Conference the President had a predominantly "good press" in conservative circles, as the information seeped out that he was, for the most part, supporting Clemenceau against Lloyd George. He was said by the *Matin* (June 4) to be manifesting "the most remarkable lucidity" in the important debates; and it was "affirmed" that the President was no less intransigent than Clemenceau himself. [64]

The fate of Upper Silesia and the question whether Germany should be promised admission to the League of Nations absorbed most of the public's attention at this time, and the debate on the question whether the reparations total should be definitely fixed was given relatively less notice, though condemnation was visited upon the Socialist group of the Chamber for proposing to fix a precise sum. The current argument against the Socialist view, as well as against the German counter-proposals, was that an immediate appraisal of the total was impossible. [65]

A strong Poland was regarded, by non-Socialist opinion, as second only in importance to a strong France. It was natural, therefore, that Lloyd George's proposal to alter the Upper Silesia Polish frontiers in Germany's favor should meet with resolute opposition. Powerful arguments were adduced. The danger of weakening "the barrier to Germany's access to the East" was stressed. [66] "The setting up of a strong Poland economically independent" was a "vital question", as it constituted an integral part of the guarantees

demanded by France.[67] "Only the counter-balance of a
strong Poland" permitted France "to give up the military
frontier of the Rhine". Germany was accused of concen-
trating her chief efforts on the revision of these frontiers
because she realized that a strong Poland would be the
greatest obstacle to her recovery.[68] "As long as Russia remains foundered in its ruins," said the *Écho de Paris*
(June 6), "it will be for Poland to hold back Germanism
on the Eastern part of our continent. . . ." Even a plebiscite
was generally unwelcome in non-Socialist circles. "Plebiscites are, in general, dangerous things," wrote the *Écho de
Paris* (June 7). "If the precedent were started it might endanger most of the existing states. Suppose one were held
in Ireland, for example, or India, or Egypt!" [69]

The suggestion that Germany be promised admission to
the League of Nations likewise raised a storm in moderate
and nationalist circles. The German counter-proposals had
asked that Germany be admitted to the League "as a power
with equal privileges" as soon as the Peace Treaty was
signed.[70] It was shocking to patriotic French opinion that
Germany should thus boldly demand a status of equality
with the Allies before she had given proof of moral regeneration. As the *Homme Libre* put it (May 31), Germany
was like a desperate criminal, who, having robbed and murdered his victims, was now demanding a place among his
judges. Before promises could be made, a necessary period
of regeneration was imperative.[71] Not only was Germany
far from "aspiring to justice", wrote the *Temps* (June 12),
but she actually delighted in her "iniquity". Yet she "dared
to ask for admission into the League of Nations". The idea
that allied nations should be called upon to associate in
the League with Germany was most distasteful. "The immense majority of Frenchmen" were unwilling, said the
Débats (June 11), "to submit to the repugnant contact"
with Germany. "Does one think it possible," solemnly asked
the *Gaulois* (June 12), "to make cannibals and civilized
people live together under one roof?"

It was not merely a moral problem. There were perhaps even more important material considerations. If Germany were admitted into the League on a footing of equality, she would, it was believed, succeed in evading her various obligations to the victors.[72] The *Matin,* for example, in a highly censored article (June 9), said that the Treaty, which was already a great disappointment for France, would mean her ruin if Germany were allowed in the League; and the *Journal* (June 8) argued that such admission would mean "the suppression of the régime of legalized suspicion on which the whole Treaty is based". It might also result in Germany's claiming "the same guarantees as to her ethnic minorities separated from their homeland" (in Alsace-Lorraine, for example) as other countries might claim. Furthermore, it would reestablish the economic régime on a basis of reciprocity. Indeed, "the principle of equality would not stop even before a general limitation of armaments and the abolition of conscription".[73] Even the moderate Left press found it "repugnant to the honor of the French Republic to admit Germany immediately".[74] Anglo-Saxon "merchants and financiers" again appeared as the evil geniuses of the peace. In behalf of these " 'philanthropists' " it was presumably deemed necessary to deal gently with Germany—"to receive her into the bosom of the League of Nations".[75] German membership in the League [76] would give her a footing of equality with all, "with the exception . . . of America and England, to whom the domination of the sea, and economic power assure special protection. . . ." The suggestion that Germany might, in the near future, attain a position of equality with France could make little appeal to most Frenchmen, for the idea of inequality, moral and material, lay at the very basis of the Treaty.[77]

4. THE TREATY SIGNED

The Allied reply of June 16 (given to the press in full), revealed that the Four had not yielded much ground in the face of German demands. Certain ameliorations were introduced into the reparations clauses without altering the basic principles: Germany was granted the right, through a commission of her own, to present relevant data to the Reparation Commission, and the Entente Powers promised not to withhold the "commercial facilities" essential to a "resumption of German industry".[78] Germany was assured of membership in the League after proof was given of her willingness to observe her "international obligations".[79] A plebiscite was granted for Upper Silesia in place of outright annexation of that territory to Poland; [80] and the Schleswig plebiscite zones were slightly modified in Germany's favor.[81] An extension of time was conceded for the reduction of Germany's military establishment, and the arms limitation clauses were reassuringly stated to be "the first steps towards" general reduction and limitation of armaments.[82] A modification of the Saar régime had already (May 24) granted to Germany the right, at the end of the fifteen-year period, and under certain conditions, of buying back the coal mines without paying necessarily in gold; [83] and now a joint declaration of Wilson, Lloyd George and Clemenceau (not given to the press) expressed a willingness to consider shortening the Rhineland occupation when Germany had given proof of her good faith.[84] A few other less important modifications completed the list.

These concessions, though important, were by no means a "surrender" to German demands. They were not sufficiently serious either to disturb patriotic opinion very greatly, or to satisfy Socialist demands. Though the nationalists damned them as "disastrous" and the Socialists acclaimed them as "fortunate",[85] the governmental press as a whole was disposed to regard the peace terms as remaining substantially intact.[86] This attitude of complacency toward the concessions was encouraged by a scarifying covering letter to the German delegation which characterized the conduct of Germany as almost "without example in the story of humanity", and in which the Allies scathingly denounced the entire German case.[87] "Never had the responsibilities of

Germany been more strikingly exposed," wrote the *Temps* (June 18) with great satisfaction. Nevertheless, the wisdom of the Allied compromises would depend on whether or not they were determined that Germany should sign the Treaty, and keep her engagements.[88]

The Allies were determined that Germany should sign the Treaty as it stood, with the modifications agreed to. The documents of June 16 were to be the "last word". There would be no more parleying. On the expiration of a fixed term—five days, later extended to seven—the Allies would pass from words to acts. Marshal Foch was instructed by the Council of Four to be ready for action on the evening of the 23rd, and considerable publicity was given in the press concerning Allied preparations for military action.

The fact that the Germans capitulated before the expiration of the ultimatum, and, five days later, affixed their signatures to the final Treaty in the ceremonies of the Hall of Mirrors, did not markedly alter the currents of French opinion with regard either to the Treaty itself or to the German conduct. Events of the days leading up to the final ceremonies only deepened the prevailing French distrust of German promises.[89]

The resignation of the Scheidemann cabinet, June 20, owing to its hostility to the peace terms, introduced a week of uncertainty as to whether a responsible German delegation could be found to affix its signature to the Treaty. The attempt of the Bauer ministry to delegate the task to a subordinate official, von Haniel, rather than to responsible ministers was frustrated by the Allies; but it served only to increase French suspicion that this was another maneuver.[90] The Scapa Flow episode, of the 21st, was another case in point. Though the British were blamed for not having guards on board to prevent the scuttling of the seventy-three German ships about to be handed over, the German act was listed by the "patriotic" press as "another act of bad faith", and "a new act of war".[91] The following day witnessed a "New Infamy"[92]—the flag-burning incident in Berlin.

Under the Treaty terms the French flags captured by the Germans in 1870 and in 1914 were to be returned to France. The Berlin Arsenal, which harbored some of these, was invaded by German soldiers, who took them and burned them before the monument of Frederick the Great,—all of which was peculiarly humiliating to French national pride, and was the basis of further demands for the application of pains and penalties to Germany.

The Germans even sought to resume discussions with the Allies over the peace terms. On the 22nd, the day before the expiration of the ultimatum, the German delegation presented another note full of protests, demands and reservations with regard to the Treaty. A fervent appeal was made to the conscience of mankind. The conditions imposed by the Treaty were said to be beyond Germany's capacity to fulfill; and Germany would have to decline all responsibility for the consequences. The demand was made that, in two years, the Treaty should be submitted to the Council of the League for reconsideration and revision. Finally, it was stated that Germany was "ready to sign the Treaty of Peace" but "without thereby recognizing that the German people were the authors of the war", and without undertaking to surrender German nationals accused of having broken International Law. In a brief and peremptory reply the Allies reminded the German delegation that there remained only twenty-four hours in which to accept or reject the Conditions of Peace. The time for discussion had passed.[93]

During this same week preceding the final ceremonies, . German activities in territories assigned to Poland became increasingly a matter of grave concern. Resistance was apparently being offered to the transfer of some of these territories from German to Polish rule. The Council of Four viewed the situation with such alarm that it was spurred to written protest. Germany would be held responsible, it was said, for the withdrawal of her troops from, and the cessation of local agitations in the territories assigned to Poland. Furthermore, the Scapa Flow and the flag-burning incidents would be investigated, and "necessary reparation" would be demanded.[94]

The charge in the Allied note of June 25 that the German conduct savored of "notorious bad faith" was but a reflection of the feeling prevalent throughout moderate and conservative quarters. "Bad faith! Bad faith!" was the leitmotif of the comments coming from all non-Socialist circles, and the promise of German submission, late on the 23rd, did little to allay this feeling. The gratification experienced over the assurance of the German signature was materially reduced by skepticism concerning German performances. Germany was said to be attempting "to avoid her obligations, if not, indeed, to abrogate them", even before the peace was signed.[95] The character of the German delegation sent to sign the Treaty was assailed. "Do you think the Treaty, signed by Müller and Bell, obligates Germany very seriously?" asked *Matin*.[96] Feelings of almost equal intensity came from conservative and liberal quarters. Gauvain of the *Débats*, ordinarily a moderate commentator, wrote (June 24): "The [German] beast can no longer bite, but it snarls, and on its shattered tusks it curls its chops dripping with the blood of all civilized peoples. . . . The beast is waiting only for its wounds to heal in order to escape from the cage and spring at the throat of its vanquisher." Farther to the left the Radical Socialist *Dépêche* of Toulouse (June 26, 27) joined with other patriotic journals in insisting that the Allies had not been sufficiently hard on Germany for her "breaches of faith" as to the ships, the flags and Poland. Germany was "without human sensibilities in victory", and "without grandeur in defeat". It was not wise to count on her promises, for she would "continue to be the great menace to peace unless she renounces once and for all the abominable gods which she has so long and so piously served". Thus, even before the historic ceremonies at Versailles, attention was being concentrated on the enigma of the future, and this tended to color thoughts and appraisals of the final settlement.

Yet for a brief day, the pageantry of Versailles and the glamour of the final ceremonies cast their spell, and absorbed public interest. The tension had been considerably relieved late on June 23, when the Germans submitted to Allied terms and agreed to sign. The dramatic aspects of the final scenes on the 28th, especially the carefully planned setting, and the studied simplicity of the closing act at Versailles, could not fail to stir deep patriotic emotions and to evoke a wave of national pride.[97] As appropriately remarked by the *Esprit Public en France*,[98] in spite of mental reservations, "for the most part, a feeling of solemn and profound joy prevails, caused by the contrast between the ceremony of June 28 and that of January 18, 1871, which, in the same Hall of Mirrors, consecrated the mutilation of France and the birth of German hegemony". Many of the papers made this obvious comparison, and some pointed with pride back to the Treaty of Versailles of 1783, which "freed the young American Republic".[99] There were other causes for national gratification. "The war was won in France under the command of a Frenchman," wrote the *Temps* (June 29). "The peace is being signed in France, under the presidency of a Frenchman. . . . We may well be proud of our country."

5. WHAT OF THE UNITED STATES?

Yet there were "mental reservations", and anxieties concerning the uncertainties of the future. One of these related to the United States. What part would it play in assuring the fulfillment of the obligations imposed on Germany? Doubts were increasing as to the fate of the Treaty, the League and the Alliance in the United States. The June debates in the American Senate were far from reassuring. The Knox proposal to separate the Treaty from the Covenant, with a view to accepting the former and rejecting the latter, the Fall move to declare a separate peace with Germany, and various other anti-Treaty or anti-League developments, chiefly in Republican ranks, had attracted serious atten-

tion. To be sure, the news on this subject was not drama-
tized in French papers, except in the most nationalistic
press. Indeed, there was a disposition, apparently encouraged officially, to minimize its significance. At that stage of
the peace negotiations the only wise course was to give the
American Senate the benefit of the doubt, and to hope for
favorable action.

Fairly regularly, however, brief items bearing upon
American developments appeared in the columns of the leading journals, and commentators of the nationalistic press
warned of the growing danger which, they said, was being
wilfully ignored by the government and by most other
organs of opinion. The Knox resolution to separate the
Treaty from the Covenant was "an official warning to the
Paris Conference", said the *Action Française* (June 13),
"that the Senate will reject the Treaty in its present form".
The following day it wrote: "They may hide away in obscure corners of our papers the fact that the American
Senate is hostile to the Treaty. It is none the less true that
the motion of Mr. Knox was approved, ten to seven, by
the Committee on Foreign Relations. . . . A miracle will
now be needed if the peace is to be ratified at Washington.
It is amazing that people do not take more heed of this
situation." The *Écho de Paris* (June 15) also warned the
country of the danger involved in failing to take account of
the consequences of American withdrawal from Europe; and
the *Matin* (June 17) asked, rather bitterly, what the Treaty
would be worth when the American Senate had "separated
the League of Nations from it".

By the 20th of June there was a growing conviction that
the Republican Party was determined to separate the League
Covenant from the rest of the Treaty, and news reports
were carried quoting "several senators" as saying that the
Senate had "no other alternative than a separate peace".[100]
A week later, however, the tone of the news columns had
perceptibly changed, as reports indicated that the danger
from the Fall and Knox resolutions had receded somewhat.

A *Temps* (June 26) news despatch from Washington affirmed that the attitude of newspapers as well as of Senators indicated that "the chances for the acceptance of the Treaty and of the League project" were increasing rather than diminishing. In the *Débats* (June 27), Lechartier wrote at some length arguing that the Lodge and Knox opposition had largely broken down, and that even the attack on the League seemed to have run its course. He thought that the opposition would be weaker still after Wilson's trip through the West. Despatches on the 29th stated that friction within the Republican ranks had raised the Democrats' hopes; and Senator Hitchcock was quoted as predicting the ratification of the Treaty by a vote of eighty to sixteen.[101] Even the *Action Française* (June 28) seemed more inclined to accept the probability (though not the certainty) of ratification. Indeed, for the great majority of Frenchmen, the idea that the Treaty, embodying the League Covenant, could be rejected by the American Senate was so repellent as to be unthinkable. As *Europe Nouvelle* put it, it was "improbable" that the Republican Party would persist in its opposition to the Covenant. "World opinion," it said, "American opinion itself, will not admit that the interests of peace and the needs of humanity can be sacrificed to considerations of party politics." [102]

If it was unthinkable that America could reject the Peace Treaty, embodying the League of Nations, could the same be said regarding the proposed alliance? Large headlines, on the 29th, announced that the Franco-Anglo-American pact had been signed,[103] and an official communiqué stated that Wilson and Lloyd George had, the previous morning, signed undertakings to come to the assistance of France in case of unprovoked attack.[104]

That such an alliance would have been a more violent break with the tradition against "entangling alliances" than joining a mutual League for the preservation of peace, there was little question. It was conceded, furthermore, that the guarantee proposed by the alliance was in the nature of a revolution in American foreign policy. "We must not lose sight of the fact," said the *Journal* (July 3), "that this renunciation of the dogma of insularity constitutes a veritable revolution."

There is no question that the alliance was generally regarded as a precious supplement to the Treaty with its allegedly inadequate guarantees. The Socialists, to be sure, waxed cynical, accusing Wilson of abandoning his own principles,[105] but they subsequently refused to vote against ratification of the pact. The average Frenchman, however, felt that "the full value of the Treaty could be realized only in the alliance",[106] for hopes of stronger guarantees had failed of realization.

It is significant, in this connection, that Clemenceau had some embarrassing moments in inducing his own official entourage to accept this alliance proposal in lieu of a military frontier of the Rhine,[107] and there is little doubt that nationalist opinion, generally, would have preferred the more tangible and immediate military and territorial guarantees to that offered by the alliance. The reasons are fairly obvious. In the first place, the pact lacked the elements of firmness, permanence and immediate effectiveness deemed essential by patriotic opinion. Its duration was linked with the development of the League guarantees, and it could be annulled by a majority vote of the Council. Was this an adequate safeguard for France? Furthermore, its application was limited to "an unprovoked attack" on France by Germany. But suppose Germany should attack Poland or Czechoslovakia, and France went to their aid? Would this be deemed an act of provocation which would bring America and Britain to France's aid? Obviously these were difficult matters of interpretation, which might in the future cause serious embarrassment.[108] There was also the problem that America and Britain were democratic countries, and delay would be involved before the question of "unprovoked attack" could be decided. Meantime, France might be laid waste. More immediate than any of these aspects of the case was the question whether the United States would ratify the pact.

The gnawing doubt on the subject of ratification was concealed by most leading organs. The *Intransigeant* was one of the few which blurted out its misgivings; [109] but for the most part, responsible organs of opinion preferred not to raise any presumptions by expressing doubts. This was clearly the policy of prudence. Even the *Action Française* (June 30), while regretting the narrow limitations of the alliance, professed "not to doubt the good faith of England or the United States". Likewise the *Écho de Paris* (July 3), while pointing regretfully to the "positive guarantees" which had been abandoned for the pact, and deploring its limitations (*e.g.*, its temporary character), nevertheless felt "certain" that in England and America opinion would "interpret the Treaty as a true compact of alliance".

Other leading organs of the non-Socialist press preferred to voice no doubts as to the pact's ratification or of its efficacy. The *Dépêche* of Toulouse (June 30) felt confident that it would be ratified by all parties. By virtue of that instrument, it said, France would escape her greatest danger —that of facing Germany alone. In the words of the *Débats* (July 4) the aims of the alliance were, first, to provide a guarantee for France, and second, to give a warning to Germany. Warm thanks were tendered the British and American statesmen for having given "a fresh proof of their friendship". The *Temps* (July 4) affected to believe that the pact meant the establishment of solidarity among the three great Western powers. "Not only is Alsace-Lorraine given back to us, but, in addition, the alliance of the Atlantic watches over the Rhine." No misgivings were expressed, though the cautious reminder was added, as a footnote, that the *raison d'être* of the pact was the fact that the League of Nations alone did not provide sufficient protection for France.

6. AND OF PRESIDENT WILSON?

Almost before the tumult and the shouting had died
away, following the ceremonies at Versailles, President Wilson departed for the United States. No such multitudes
swarmed around him on his departure as had greeted him
on his arrival. A comparable spectacle was naturally not
to be expected. Nevertheless, the contrast was striking.
General Mordacq, writing of the scene, says that when Mr.
and Mrs. Wilson arrived at the station, a few cries of *"Vive
Wilson"* went up from the spectators, but so scattered were
they that he (Mordacq) and his entourage were struck by
the contrast between the spirit of that occasion and the
exuberance and almost delirious enthusiasm of the people
on the day of the President's arrival. "The popularity of
Mr. Wilson had, indeed, veritably sunk to such a point that
the good people of France had just about forgotten that,
without him, the American legions would probably never
have debarked on our shores." [110]

The picture was much the same in the press, where likewise, accounts could not have been expected to rival those
of his arrival. Even so, the contrast was rather striking.
Instead of pages and columns of news and comments, inches,
or perhaps only a few lines, were spared for the event. Organs of the heavy press gave, on the average, about eight or
ten inches of news space, and these were concerned mainly
with the official ceremonies incidental to the departure. The
Intransigeant (June 30) gave only two inches altogether to
the departures from Paris and from Brest. *Humanité*
(June 29), which on his arrival had dedicated an entire special number to the President, recorded his departure in four
and a half lines. Judging from the news accounts in the
heavy press, the cries of *"Vive Clemenceau"* and the *"Vive
Poincaré"*, were certainly as numerous as those of *"Vive
Wilson"*.

Shortly before his departure, President Wilson again ex-
changed toasts with President Poincaré, on the occasion of

a farewell dinner tendered the American President by the President of France. Warm salutations were extended by the French President to the American soldiers for their valorous service. On this occasion, however, as on that of the preceding December 14, the keynote of Poincaré's toast was "Allied solidarity". The Treaty was about to be signed "in the château where the German Empire, at its birth, hurled defiance in the face of justice". Germany was now to be faced with her responsibilities. Close solidarity of the Allies must be maintained. "It was the clear consciousness of the community of our interests which made victory possible; and if we lose this essential idea we should most fatally lose the very fruits of victory." Lifting his glass, therefore, to the American President and to Mrs. Wilson, Poincaré drank to "the indestructible union of all the Allied and Associated Nations".

President Wilson, in reply, first paid his respects, with becoming grace and modesty. During his stay in France, he said, he had received instruction, both for his heart and his mind. He had seen the sufferings and the sacrifices endured by the French people. He had had personal contacts with the leaders of the French people, and he understood better than previously "the motives, the ambitions and the principles which are the springs of action of this great nation". Coming to his main theme, he added: "We have finished making the peace, but we have only commenced the plan of collaboration which, I believe, will be enlarged and consolidated in the years to come. . . . We shall continue to be comrades, and we shall continue to be collaborators in a task which, common to all of us, will evoke . . . a common conception of the rights of man for all races and for all countries." Lifting his glass, in turn, he drank to the welfare of France, "the closer communion of free peoples, and to the consolidation of all those influences which uplift the spirit and the aims of mankind".[111]

Neither the toasts at the Élysées Palace, nor the departure of President Wilson aroused the commentators to enthusiastic ovations. The editorial columns exhibited somewhat the same contrasts as did the news columns and the meager crowd at the railway station. Comment was surprisingly limited. There were few editorial cries of *"Vive Wilson"*. Some of the leading organs preferred to pass over the events in silence. Other organs, close to the government, felt bound to observe the amenities, and to pay their respects in proper diplomatic language. The *Petit Parisien* (June 28), for example, rendered "Homage to President Wilson" in an article, rather defensive in tone, which seemed to take for granted the existence of a strong undercurrent of feeling not any too friendly to the President.[112] The *Temps* (June 28), with its customary finesse, rang the changes of idealism and realism, in bidding a semi-official adieu. Wilson was complimented on agreeing with the French President that the task of establishing the peace "was not finished". Yet the Wilsonian system of cooperation rested entirely on Article 10 of the Covenant, which was "bitterly criticized in the United States" as well as in Europe. "These objections have their importance, and perhaps their merit." Nevertheless, "to recriminate against the past, and continually to call into question that which has been decided, is certain to lead to more serious disappointments than the risks from which escape is being sought". With these reservations duly recorded, the *Temps* then called upon the nations to repudiate "sterile pessimism", and to press forward "with confidence in the way which President Wilson" had pointed out.

In more nationalistic circles the chief source of gratification seemed to be that Wilson had confessed to having gained a better understanding of France and her problems. The experience of the preceding seven months was said to have been "good for at least something".[113] "According to what he himself admits," wrote the *Figaro* (June 28), "he has learned to understand Europe and France better during the course of his long labors," and it added, rather hopefully, that America would "never again shut herself up in any form of splendid isolation". Even the *Débats* (June 28) pointed out that Wilson had apparently learned the difficulty of changing the "German soul", and the *Matin* (June 30) rejoiced that the President had seen for himself that Germany thought only of fighting and that, "far from renouncing revenge", she was "actually preparing for it".

On the extreme Left disillusionment of the deepest hue prevailed. The nationalists on the Right had been suspicious of the President from the beginning, and had probably obtained from the settlement as much as they could have anticipated. The Socialists, however, had seen in Wilson the prophet of a new order, and had dared to hope that he could and would see his program through. Now their hopes lay crushed and all was pessimism and disillusionment. It is true that a few of the Right Wing Socialists, such as Albert Thomas, and those who in 1918 established the *France Libre,* were able to find traces of Wilson's ideals in the Treaty, but the great majority of that party felt that Wilsonism had been sunk without trace.

Yet there was more of sorrow than of anger in the feelings of Socialists toward Wilson personally. He had tried. Not persistently enough, perhaps, but in any case the forces were too strong for him. "The curtain falls," wrote the *Journal du Peuple* (June 28). "The farce is played out. . . . The man of *'noble candeur'* returns, stripped of his illusions, bent under the weight of an immense deception. . . . Meanwhile, capitalism triumphs under the most selfish and uncompromising form." "The disillusionment is complete," said *Humanité* (June 28). "After some weeks of efforts . . . President Wilson let imperialism pass and have its way. Of the noble program proposed by him to the world, nothing has been realized." Yet, after all, Wilson had served the cause of Socialism. "Some have doubted his good faith," it said. "We do not think this a just accusation. . . . His defeat, which is that of all bourgeois idealism, sometimes sincere, but always impotent, shows all peoples that Socialism alone can institute order and fraternity among men."

NOTES

[1] It was a very painful ceremony. Clemenceau, in behalf of the Allied and Associated Powers, told the German delegates that the time had come for a settlement of accounts, and that precautions were being taken that "this second peace of Versailles" should be "a lasting one". There were to be no oral discussions. Any observations which the Germans might desire to make would have to be put in writing. Brockdorff-Rantzau, of the German delegation, replying without rising from his seat, and with unconcealed bitterness, referred to the "spirit of hatred" encountered, and to the terms which, he said, violated pledges given. *Temps,* May 9. Brockdorff's demeanor produced a very painful impression in Conference circles. Clemenceau later confessed to a strong desire to administer a vigorous kick to him, and remarked that Wilson commented several times on the "absolute stupidity" of the Germans. Clemenceau thought the maladroitness of Brockdorff would react well for France in subsequent negotiations. Mordacq, *op. cit.,* vol. iii, p. 263. Colonel House says that if he had been in Brockdorff's place he would have said: " 'Mr. President, and gentlemen of the Congress: War is a great gamble; we have lost and are willing to submit to any reasonable terms.' " *House Papers,* vol. iii, p. 457.

[2] *Dépêche* of Toulouse, May 8. The precise responsibility for the decision not to publish the full treaty text is somewhat in dispute. There seems little doubt, however, that Clemenceau was in favor of publication, and that Lloyd George was strongly opposed, while President Wilson was evidently inclined to the Lloyd George point of view. Mordacq says Clemenceau thought it inadmissible that the Allied peoples should learn the treaty terms through German papers; but that he yielded to the insistence of his colleagues. While Clemenceau was a partisan of secrecy during the preparation of treaties, he was in favor of making them public once they were drawn up. *Op. cit.,* vol. iii, p. 250. Baker says Lloyd George opposed publication on the ground that this would make changes more difficult, while Clemenceau favored it for the same reason. *Op. cit.,* vol. ii, p. 498. Colonel House states positively that Wilson was "not in favor of any publication", though this was contrary to the Colonel's own view. *Op. cit.,* vol. iv, p. 467. Nevins, however, reports that it was Henry White's view that Wilson favored publication, and that Clemenceau as well as Lloyd George opposed it, "fearing a storm of criticism at home". *Op. cit.,* p. 452. This does not seem convincing, as would seem to be borne out by Wilson's telegram to Hitchcock, June 10, protesting against the publication of the Treaty in the United States. "I have considered that it was of the greatest importance not to publish the text of a document which is still the object of negotiations, and which is susceptible of modifications," he said. *Dépêche* of Toulouse, June 11.

[3] *Matin,* May 18.

[4] *Current Summaries,* May 17.

[5] *Annales de la Chambre, Documents Parlementaire,* May 16, 1919, no. 6144.

[6] *Temps,* May 20.

[7] *Ibid.,* May 18.

[8] *Matin,* May 24, 1919. That Clemenceau was not so limited is clear. Article 8 of the Constitutional Law of July 16, 1875, provides that "The President . . . shall negotiate and ratify treaties", and adds that "He shall give information regarding them to the houses as soon as the interests and safety of the state permit". Furthermore, it stipulates specifically that "Treaties of peace . . . shall be ratified only after having been voted by the two houses".

[9] *Annales de la Chambre,* May 27, 1919, pp. 2155 *et seq.; Dépêche* of Toulouse, May 21, June 12; *Matin,* June 10.

[10] *Temps,* June 2.

[11] On the very afternoon of the presentation ceremonies the *Temps* was allowed to outline the main features of the peace terms, ahead of the other evening papers. *Bonsoir,* for example, which sought to print an almost identical review, was prohibited by the censor from doing so. *Humanité,* May 10.

[12] Bulletin 26, May 4-11, 1919.

[13] *Petit Journal,* May 9.

[14] *Petit Parisien,* May 9.

[15] E.g., *Journal* and *Matin.* The *Journal* stated (May 10) that from the point of view of military security, France was scarcely any better off than in 1914.

[16] *Action Française,* May 8.

[17] *Humanité,* May 12.

[18] *Populaire,* May 9.

[19] See *Humanité,* May 12, 13, 20, 30.

[20] *Matin,* May 9, 11.

[21] *Humanité,* and *Bataille,* May 15. The Socialist leader Renaudel, in a speech at Montluçon, called for "an international financial organization" which would divide the war costs of the various nations on a proportional basis. *Temps,* May 13. The *Écho de Paris* (May 17) and other organs of the Center and Right boldly demanded that Great Britain and the United States accept German bonds in immediate payment of France's debt to those countries; and also that France be allowed to issue notes based on what was due to her from Germany. The *Temps,* realizing the practical impossibility of complete inter-Allied solidarity as to debts, expressed the hope (May 10) that a "vast inter-Allied credit operation" might be called into play for the benefit of France.

[22] *Europe Nouvelle* lamented that French negotiators had not been able to resist the "agents of Wall Street and the City". As a result, Frenchmen were faced, it said, with the necessity of sacrificing half their possessions on the altar of their country. See also *Current Summaries,* May 17.

[23] *Petit Parisien,* May 9.

[24] *Current Summaries,* May 10-15. Even former Ambassador Lichnowski, who had denounced Germany's ineptitude in getting into the war, said Germany could not sign without dreaming of a war of revenge.

[25] Even the Socialists, though strongly favorable to ameliorating the terms of May 7, seemed to agree that ultimately the German signature

would be forthcoming. Indeed, *Humanité*, May 24, advised Germany to sign the terms, promising that the Socialists would revise them later.

[26] *Europe Nouvelle*, May 17.

[27] *Figaro*, May 13.

[28] President Ebert was reported by the press of May 15 as making special overtures to American sentiment in appealing for a peace of justice and reconciliation, and in expressing a hope that Germany might still discover that she was not deceived in accepting the Wilsonian program.

[29] *Liberté*, May 15.

[30] *Gaulois*, May 16. This was part of a persistent campaign that was carried on during this period against Anglo-Saxon commercial and financial maneuvers.

[31] *Opinion*, May 17.

[32] *Informateur Civique*, May 15.

[33] *Action Française*, May 9, 28, insisted that there was still time to strengthen the territorial guarantees by taking possession of the left bank and breaking up Germany.

[34] *Ibid.*, May 10.

[35] *Ibid.*, May 17.

[36] *Ibid.*, May 22.

[37] *Matin*, May 25.

[38] *Action Française*, June 3.

[39] The *Matin* correspondent reported, May 20, that the National Assembly had decided not to sign unless decided revisions were made; and the *Journal* correspondent telegraphed, May 23, that the German Council of Ministers had decided to reject the terms if the Allies refused to negotiate.

[40] *Figaro*, May 20.

[41] *Current Summaries*, May 26. Even the moderate *Dépêche* of Toulouse thought that an extension of military occupation against an unregenerate Germany would be justifiable; and it appealed to the "iron will" of the Allies to be firm. May 12, 24.

[42] *Humanité*, May 24.

[43] There had been an intermittent interchange of notes between the German delegation and the Allied and Associated Powers since May 9.

[44] *The German Counter-Proposals to the Draft of the Versailles Peace Treaty* (Berlin, 1919), *passim*. Hereafter cited as *German Counter-Proposals*.

[45] The only surprise in the reception accorded the German response was a change of front on the part of the emotionally unstable Hervé, of the *Victoire*. Having argued, May 30, that the counter-proposals were precisely what was to be expected, and that the Allies should reject them out of hand, the next day he boldly proposed important concessions as to the Saar régime, and the left bank occupation period, and even advised the admission of Germany to the League of Nations. This was a pure aberration, so far as the patriotic press was concerned.

[46] *Matin*, May 30.

[47] *Allied Press*, vol. vi, no. 6, June 11, 1919.

[48] *Petit Journal*, May 30.

[49] *Journal*, May 30.

[50] *Débats*, June 2.

[51] The *Esprit Public en France*, Bulletin 29, May 25-31, 1919.

[52] *Petit Journal*, May 30.

[53] *Débats*, May 30.

[54] *Écho de Paris*, May 31.

[55] The Socialists, while feeling that the German proposals showed some of the "same pettiness of spirit and lack of comprehension" as that of the Allied terms, and while not accepting the entire German case, nevertheless urged a conciliatory policy. *Vérité*, May 30. "It would be pure folly not to discuss the terms with Germany," wrote *Humanité*, May 30. "Let us but confront the text of the Fourteen Points with the text of the Peace Preliminaries. There are contradictions which are striking." The Socialist group of the Chamber issued a statement insisting that important ameliorations of the Treaty terms would have to be made before the peace could become definitive. *Temps*, June 7.

[56] *Journal*, May 30; *Current Summaries*, May 30.

[57] *Action Française*, May 31.

[58] The *Débats* (June 1) noted sarcastically that "strange tendencies" were appearing "in certain quarters not noted for their political constancy".

[59] Mordacq, *op. cit.*, vol. iii, p. 309.

[60] Baker, *op. cit.*, vol. ii, pp. 496, 517; Mordacq, *op. cit.*, vol. iii, p. 311. The anxieties expressed in the press concerned chiefly the questions of Upper Silesia, Reparations, and the German entry into the League of Nations.

[61] *House Papers*, vol. iv, p. 475; Mordacq, *op. cit.*, vol. iii, pp. 315-317.

[62] Mordacq, *op. cit.*, vol. iii, p. 292.

[63] *House Papers*, vol. iv, p. 475.

[64] *Gaulois*, June 4, *Liberté*, June 5, congratulated the President on the firm attitude he had taken.

[65] *Temps*, June 9. The possibility and desirability of fixing a maximum sum, as demanded by the Germans, was totally ignored.

[66] *Petit Journal*, June 5.

[67] *Matin*, June 5.

[68] *Débats*, June 7. *Action Française*, June 6, said that any weakening of the Eastern frontier would only encourage Germany to attack Poland.

[69] The *Temps* repeatedly warned against any concessions in this or any other particular. If a plebiscite were allowed in Upper Silesia, it argued (June 7), the Prussian magnates, who controlled the economic and social life of the country "would use all their influence to induce the popular masses to vote docilely in favor of Germany". "The weakening of Poland . . . would be a danger for the peace of the world. Importunate and indefatigable, the voice of France repeats to the Four: 'Do not yield in the East.' "

[70] *German Counter-Proposals*, p. 28.

[71] In order for Germany to be declared worthy of entrance into the League, said the *Débats*, June 11, "she must have deported herself honestly for a certain length of time".

[72] *Current Summaries*, June 9.

[73] Permitting Germany to enter the League would, in effect, amount to "cancelling the victory", said the *Liberté* (June 10), and if Germany came in, then "France should walk out".

[74] *Dépêche* of Toulouse, June 21; *Œuvre,* June 10.

[75] *Débats,* June 10.

[76] *Écho de Paris,* June 10.

[77] On the extreme Left, opinion was generally favorable to immediate German admission, though there was an inclination to take into account sentimental arguments against it. *Humanité,* June 11; *Bataille,* June 11; *Vérité,* June 12.

[78] *Reply of the Allied and Associated Powers to the Observations of the German Delegation on the Conditions of Peace.* Hoover War Library, pp. 32-36. See also *La Documentation Internationale: La Paix de Versailles,* vol. xii, "Notes Échangées entre la Conférence de la Paix et la Délégation Allemande" (Paris, 1930).

[79] *Reply of the Allied and Associated Powers to the Observations of the German Delegation on the Conditions of Peace.* Hoover War Library, p. 6.

[80] *Ibid.,* p. 14.

[81] *Ibid.,* p. 17.

[82] *Ibid.,* pp. 22-23.

[83] Baker, *op. cit.,* vol. ii, p. 509. This left the substance of French rights practically unimpaired.

[84] Decision of June 16. Miller Diary, vol. xix, p. 489.

[85] *Allied Press,* vol. vi, no. 8, June 25, 1919; *Humanité,* June 18.

[86] Occasional questions were raised, even on the moderate Left, as, e.g., *Dépêche* of Toulouse, June 19; *Europe Nouvelle,* June 21, and *Œuvre,* June 17.

[87] *Débats,* June 18.

[88] *Temps,* June 18; *Revue des Deux Mondes,* July 1.

[89] An unfortunate episode, indicating the feeling of the French masses, occurred the evening of June 16, when the German delegation was departing from Versailles, after the receipt of Allied memoranda. Large crowds gathered along the streets and roadsides, and abused the passengers in the twenty-two automobiles transporting the members of the delegation to the station. Bricks and paving stones were thrown by the crowds, and serious injury was done to a number of the passengers. It was a painful incident, the publication of which was forbidden by the censor until the second day after the episode. *Débats,* June 19.

[90] *Current Summaries,* June 23-27.

[91] *Ibid.,* June 23.

[92] *Journal,* June 25.

[93] *Débats,* June 24.

[94] *Ibid.,* June 27.

[95] *Ibid.,* June 27.

[96] June 27. The *Journal,* June 27, saw "no guarantee of uprightness" in the delegation's composition.

[97] Colonel House remarked on the ceremony at Versailles saying it "was not unlike what was done in olden times when the conqueror dragged the conquered at his chariot wheels". He thought it out of keeping with "the new era" and totally lacking in the "element of chivalry". *House Papers,* vol. iv, p. 487.

[98] Bulletin 33, June 22-28, 1919.

[99] *Matin,* June 29. "This contrast alone," said the *Figaro,* June 29, "would suffice for our national pride."

[100] E.g., *Journal* and *Action Française,* June 20; *Débats,* June 21. Even Lechartier, former American correspondent of the *Débats,* wrote in that paper, June 21, that there seemed to be no longer any doubt that the Republican Party was determined to separate the Covenant from the remainder of the Treaty.

[101] *Matin,* June 29; *Journal,* June 30.

[102] July 19, 1919, p. 1359.

[103] E.g., *Journal,* June 29.

[104] The existence of the promise of assistance had unofficially been a matter of public knowledge since the presentation of the Conditions of Peace, May 7. The document was signed by Wilson the morning of June 28, and laid before the Chamber of Deputies by Clemenceau, June 30.

[105] *Humanité,* July 4. "If the peace of the Four had been what the President solemnly promised the peoples," said *Humanité,* "there would have been no need for these supplementary guarantees."

[106] *Revue Politique et Parlementaire,* July 1919, p. 97.

[107] Mordacq, *op. cit.,* vol. iii, p. 244.

[108] *Action Française,* June 30; *Correspondant,* July 10, p. 184.

[109] Characterizing it as a "very great event" on June 30, it expressed its conviction that there would be "a battle in the Senate in Washington. On this battle," it said, "depends, in great measure, the security of the world of tomorrow." Four days later its headlines boldly asserted: "It Assures Us Security in the Future: All Depends on the Ratification by the American Senate."

[110] Mordacq, *op. cit.,* vol. iii, p. 357.

[111] *Temps,* June 28, 1919.

[112] Mr. Wilson had always pursued a conciliatory policy, it averred. He had been misunderstood. The League of Nations was already a going concern. During the May and June period, when the Treaty was endangered, Mr. Wilson stood firmly by the side of France. Therefore, "it does not seem that the prestige of the President of the United States suffers any diminution".

[113] *Action Française,* June 28. "This phrase pleases us," it said.

CHAPTER XI

AFTERMATH

"Alas, my dear Tardieu, the only certain miracles are those which we ourselves perform."

"An old saying alleges that one is never so vanquished nor so victorious as one seems."

"The future will decide. The mastery resides with him who wills most strongly and most enduringly."

(Clemenceau, in Tardieu, *The Truth About the Treaty,* Introduction.)

"C'est une paix de vigilance. Mais c'est la paix."

(Ajam, in *Dépêche* of Toulouse, August 16, 1919.)

1. REORIENTATION OF PERSPECTIVES

IN spite of deep misgivings in all quarters concerning the wisdom of the peace terms, the presumption and the hope prevailed practically everywhere that the Treaty would be approved by the French Parliament. Though the Socialists at once repudiated the settlement, they congratulated the Germans on having accepted it [1] and assured them that ameliorations would later be made in its terms, "in a spirit of international solidarity".[2] But the Treaty could not, "under any pretext, receive a Socialist vote" of ratification, according to the decision (1,420 to 54) of the National Council of the Socialist Party.[3]

In other circles, where the "Bolshevizing tactics" of the Socialists were condemned,[4] the ratification of the Treaty was looked forward to much more anxiously. Acceptance of the peace terms with all their imperfections was regarded as indispensable. Otherwise, the advantages and opportunities which the Treaty offered might be lost.[5] The prevailing view of patriotic Frenchmen was well expressed by the *Journal* (June 24) in saying: "The past is abolished. We have all we can expect for the present. The weak point is

389

the future." Germany would have to be shown "by acts" that the Allies were "not disposed to permit it to treat the Treaty of Versailles as one more scrap of paper".[6] "Alliances, Alliances, solidly maintained and bound together would be necessary to impose on recalcitrant Germany the strict execution of the clauses against which she is today protesting." [7]

Political and economic considerations of an internal character also weighed heavily in fostering the desire in moderate and conservative, as well as in Socialist circles, for a rapid consummation of the peace. The solution of France's financial problem, the restoration of the devastated regions and the return to normal economic activity were felt to be dependent upon it. Action by Parliament on the Treaty was deemed necessary before the budget for the last quarter of the year could be voted.[8] Protracted debate, furthermore, was regarded as unnecessary because of the fact that the Treaty had to be accepted or rejected as a whole. The time for changes in the Treaty had passed, and Parliament's duty was therefore to ratify quickly, after observing the necessary formalities of examining the document. "Ratification constitutes a duty of conscience," solemnly wrote the *Temps* (July 17), in spite of the fact that the Treaty did not "give all that one had a right to expect from the peace".[9]

2. The Treaty before Parliament

Parliament was in no mood to be hurried in the matter of ratification. For months its wrath had been accumulating because of the failure of the government to take the Chamber and Senate into its confidence. Repeatedly those bodies had protested during the course of the Conference, asking for more light, and urging that France's case with the Allies would be strengthened if the senators and deputies were better informed and thus enabled more intelligently to guide public opinion in support of national interests. The time had now come, they felt, not only to re-state their grievances, but to expose the dangers which, presumably, could have been at least partly avoided if the support of Parliament had been solicited by the government during the negotiations. Before the debates began there was apparently no question as to the ultimate ratification of the Treaty. "In the environs of the Palais-Bourbon," wrote the *Matin* (Aug. 26), "there is no doubt that ratification will be the final outcome; but it is necessary to delay the final vote until a certain number of reservations have been expressed. . . ." It was an excellent opportunity, in other words, not only to air grievances, but also to explain France's case to the world, and to lay bare the weaknesses of the Treaty—weaknesses which might become fatal unless the erstwhile Allies maintained, in the ensuing peace as in the preceding war, a close solidarity that would guarantee the security and stability of France amid the perplexities of an uncertain future. Thus it happened that, after the storm which swept journalistic circles during the peace negotiations had died down, the Chamber of Deputies and the Senate reverberated for weeks with oratorical assaults on the peace settlement.

To all appearances, the prevalent feeling in Parliament was even more bitter than that which had been manifested in the press. In one sense the vehemence of Parliament may be regarded as the final expression of those feelings and desires which, during the preceding months, the press had certainly helped to whip up. It was undoubtedly partly due to the greater freedom of expression which existed in the chambers as compared with the press, where the government, through the censorship or by special favors, could, to a degree, limit or control the free flow of opinion. A growing sense of the precariousness of France's position, and its dependence, as it was felt, on the contingencies of inter-Allied solidarity, was a powerful stimulus to jeremiads upon the future. Furthermore, the certainty that ultimately the Treaty, almost of necessity, would be approved by Parliament, was an added encouragement to unrestrained expression of opinion. It is not surprising, therefore, that, in spite of the general desire for a rapid consummation of the peace, the examination and discussion of the terms in Parliament were long drawn out, so that almost three and a half months elapsed after the signing of the Treaty before final approval was voted by the two houses; and throughout this period there were very few, except those on the government benches, to voice approval of its terms.

The debates in the Chamber did not begin until August 26, although the Treaty had been formally laid before it by Clemenceau on June 30.[10] Before discussion was undertaken the document was subjected to critical scrutiny by a commission of sixty deputies, of which Barthou was *rapporteur*, and on which all groups of the Chamber, except the Socialists, were represented.[11] The report of the commission was made public August 6,[12] but discussion was delayed some three weeks longer, because of the exigencies of domestic politics.[13] During the six weeks of debate in the Chamber representatives from every important group presented their views as to the merits and defects of the proposed terms, and members of the government, in turn, defended the document as best they could.[14]

In spite of the predominantly critical tone of the Chamber toward the peace terms as a whole, there were a few provisions of the settlement which were viewed with general satisfaction, and which, accordingly, consumed relatively little of the time devoted to the discussion of the Treaty. Outstanding among these were the clauses relating to Alsace-Lorraine, the return of which to France was the most universally satisfactory feature of the settlement. Even the Socialists agreed with the majority on this, and refused to support the German thesis of a "free plebiscite", believing, as they did, that the sentiments of the Alsace-Lorrainers were already sufficiently clearly defined.

The reestablishment of an independent Poland was another source of general satisfaction. Socialists joined with Center and Right Wing orators in acclaiming the event. As to important details, however, there were divergencies of view.

The Chamber and Senate commissions appointed to study these matters, and which represented the predominant view of those bodies, expressed unqualified approval. The Allies were said to have been very moderate and to have given Poland only those territories indisputably Polish. The plebiscites provided for in Upper Silesia and elsewhere were noted as an evidence of Allied scrupulousness, though they were neither praised nor condemned. The setting up of Danzig as a free city was also viewed with approval, in spite of the admitted fact that the population was overwhelmingly German.[15] Condemnation of the Corridor and of the Danzig settlement came only from the Socialists. Marcel Sembat thought these "the most serious of the germs of war" contained in the Treaty,[16] and Longuet, while acclaiming the re-birth of Poland, criticized the failure to apply plebiscites more widely.[17]

The Treaty provisions relating to German war guilt and to the personal responsibility of the Kaiser and his military leaders were likewise overwhelmingly satisfactory to both houses. The report of the Chamber commission, prepared by Barthou, devoted its first fifty-two pages to the justification of this section. The war-guilt clause (Article 231) it said, gave the strongest moral and juridical basis to the peace conditions; and although it applied directly only to reparations, it nevertheless "provided the general principle" on which all of the Treaty provisions rested. Likewise Articles 227 to 230, relating to the personal guilt of the former Kaiser and certain military leaders, were emphatically approved, and their "integral application" was demanded.[18] The verdict of the Commission of Sixty was strongly endorsed by the Bourgeois commission of the Senate, which observed that since the essential object of the Treaty was the establishment of justice, it was necessary to give a "striking proof of this to the world, in pronouncing . . . the solemn condemnation which their [the Kaiser's, etc.] crimes merited".[19]

Not even the Socialists came to the defense of the Kaiser,

though many of them doubtless questioned the wisdom of putting him on trial personally. Albert Thomas, for example, said that inasmuch as war had now been labeled a crime, he would not protest against the trial of William II, although he thought the trial of the former Kaiser was not without danger, for, if it were "poorly conducted it might be the occasion for chauvinistic demonstrations, and bursts of *amour propre* from Germany".[20] Several Socialist speakers (Thomas, Renaudel, Sembat) made special mention of Germany's responsibility for commencing the war, and the entire Socialist group admitted the validity of Article 231 as the basis of the reparations clauses.

Other minor territorial adjustments in Germany's frontiers effected by the Treaty were defended by the commissions, and approved by the great majority of both houses. The colonial settlement, which turned the German colonies over to the Allies as mandates under the supervision of the League was likewise defended by the Barthou report and accepted by Parliament as a whole, although the Socialists denounced the mandates scheme as hypocritical and imperialistic.[21]

Throughout the weeks of debate the interest of all parliamentary groups was concentrated primarily on the reparations, financial and guarantees aspects of the peace settlement, and these it was which were universally regarded as the most unsatisfactory. In this respect the senators and deputies were but reflecting, in somewhat heightened colors, the prevailing feeling of the country, which was well described by Barthou in a leading article in the *Matin* (Aug. 9). "Above all", he said, "there are two questions which disturb public opinion: that of the occupation of the left bank of the Rhine, and that of reparations."

3. REPARATIONS AND FINANCIAL PROBLEMS BEFORE PARLIAMENT

It was appallingly evident to senators and deputies that the expectations of the preceding December in the matter

of reparations payments and financial adjustments had not
been realized. Contrary to Klotz's vague promise in the
Chamber debates of December 3, and to the fervent desire
of the great majority of Parliament, Germany was not being
made to pay the cost of the war. Nor indeed, was Germany
being made "to pay first" in the sense that France was to be
substantially relieved of heavy burdens of taxation. Neither
was there at that time any definite evidence of inter-Allied
solidarity in the matter of financial burdens. The question
of reparations remained "the open wound of the Peace
Treaty", as Barthou wrote in the *Matin*, August 9.

Though all parliamentary groups were equally dissatis-
fied with the Treaty provisions relating to these subjects,
there were some cleavages of opinion (primarily between the
Socialists and groups farther to the right) with regard to
particular problems. The principle of German responsibility
for reparations was unanimously acceptable to all groups
from extreme Left to extreme Right. Socialists, however,
would have limited the liability to damages directly caused
in the occupied areas.[22] Even to include such items as pensions and separation allowances, Mistral argued, raised the
bill to outlandish proportions, and, furthermore, decreased
France's percentage of the total, as well as the actual amount
which she would ultimately receive.[23] Other parliamentary
groups overwhelmingly favored the inclusion of war costs
as well as pensions and separation allowances.

The Socialists also argued that the total sum to be demanded of Germany should have been fixed in the Treaty,
and that it should not exceed Germany's capacity to pay.
Furthermore, they urged that care should be taken not to
weaken German credit or morale, in order not to endanger
the fulfillment of obligations.[24] Elsewhere there was still a
tendency to appraise German capacity in astronomical proportions, and other groups were satisfied that the problem
had been left to the Reparation Commission.[25] The failure
to realize inter-Allied solidarity with regard to debts was
also universally regretted. Even the Socialists agreed that

there could be "no League of Nations without financial provisions".[26]

The Barthou report, which represented the preponderant
view of Parliament, emphasized three main points in its ar-
raignment of the reparations settlement: (a) France was
entitled to recover from Germany the entire cost of the war
in all its phases; (b) France should be granted priority in
the receipt of reparations for the devastated regions, and
(c) France's financial obligations should be underwritten
by the Allies, and her liabilities should be shared. The sum
of 350 billions of francs (approximately 70 billion dollars),
it said, would not be an excessive estimate of what the war
had cost France, and her allies would have "to take account
of the exceptional situation, and divide the reparations so
as to assure her the rank to which she is entitled".[27]

In behalf of the government, Finance Minister Klotz on
September 5 sought to reassure the critics of the reparations
clauses. The question of priority was not closed, he said.
All such suggestions could be presented to the Reparation
Commission. Emerging from a complicated set of calculations, he optimistically asserted that if the Treaty were duly
executed, France could hope to receive from Germany, during the succeeding thirty-six years, "the sum of 463 billions
[francs], not counting the restitutions which will have to
be made." Waxing even more hopeful, he estimated the
annual payments from Germany, "after the first few years,"
at "approximately twenty billions of gold marks" (about
$5,000,000,000)! So far as enforcement of the terms was
concerned (which had been a major point of criticism) the
Finance Minister confidently asserted that economic and
military measures could be taken by the Allies to provide
adequately for this. Successful enforcement was merely a
matter of vigilance. Likewise, Allied financial solidarity and
a Financial League of Nations were rosy prospects, according to the interpretation of Klotz. There simply had not
been time, he alleged, to work out plans for a common sharing of the debts. Furthermore, the League was to form a

financial section, and France was already taking steps to arrange for dividing the expenses of the war. When pressed by the Socialists to give evidence of definite achievement along this line, he confessed that there had not, up to that time, been "enough useful discussions" on the subject. The solution of this, like that of all other reparations problems, lay "in the future"; and one was entitled "to hope". On the matter of war costs Klotz manifested one of the few touches of realism displayed by him during the discussion— realism which he had not previously displayed even on this subject. If war costs had been assessed against Germany, he said, "the figure would have been entirely out of reason", and unpayable by Germany; to which the Socialists replied that it was he who had earlier announced that Germany would pay everything.[28]

The explanations of Klotz failed to reassure parliamentary opinion.[29] The report of the Senate commission, which followed after the Finance Minister's explanations, was even more bitter than that of the Chamber, and the debates in the Senate rang with denunciations of the existing clauses, and with injunctions to the government to secure more favorable arrangements from the Allies.[30] Clemenceau's only rejoinder, in his October 11 defense of the peace before the Senate, was to say: "while I recognize that the reparation of France is entirely insufficient, we have been careful to arrange that the negotiations which have been begun shall be continued. That is all I can claim."[31]

4. PROBLEMS OF GUARANTEES BEFORE PARLIAMENT

"The primary question which has haunted the thoughts of all the speakers which have succeeded each other at this tribune, is the question of the security of the country, of its protection against a new invasion." Thus Albert Thomas, moderate Socialist leader, appropriately signalized the grave anxiety felt practically everywhere over the problem of guarantees.[32] There were various types of guarantees. There were moral guarantees and there were those of a material character. There were guarantees for the immediate future, and those for the more distant future. Had the Treaty drawn upon all of these and struck a happy balance between them? None of the senators or deputies, apparently, believed that it had. None of them expressed genuine satisfaction with the régime established. As Charles Benoist, a deputy of the Right, and *rapporteur* for these clauses of the Treaty, was able to say, "the guarantees which we desired we did not get",[33] so Albert Thomas, of the Socialists, commenting upon this remark, was able to reply: "We are in agreement in thinking that the provisions for security are inadequate." [34] The Socialists, for the most part, stressed the inadequacy of the moral guarantees, though recognizing also important material implications of the problems. Non-Socialist groups discounted the moral aspect of the case, and stressed the shortcomings of the material guarantees.

In this connection the problems which engaged the major share of attention during the ratification debates were: German unity; Germany's military establishment; the status of the Rhineland territory; the Anglo-American alliances, and the bearing of the League of Nations on future Franco-German relations.

a. German Unity

The Treaty failed to break up the unity of the German Reich in spite of the widespread yearning for the achievement of that objective. Tardieu, in defending the Treaty on this score, said the government had refused to break up Germany for two reasons: "conscience and prudence". Not only was the war fought for the liberation of peoples, but German disunity would have had to be bought dearly from the individual states, thereby diminishing the military and financial guarantees of the peace. Furthermore, he said, France was bound by the fact that she had not mentioned this as one of her war aims, and that there was not a suggestion of this in the bases of peace accepted by the Allies.[35] But the Chamber and Senate commissions did not mince words in deploring the Treaty terms. Assuming that German unity was but a flimsy structure, and that it could easily have been broken down, the Barthou report argued that dismemberment would have been the most effective means of destroying militarism, as it would have isolated Prussia and put an end to its hegemony over the Reich. Yet the Allies, in negotiating with the Empire as a unit, had given "the military constitution of Germany an official consecration of which the Iron Chancellor would not have dared to dream".[36]

Denunciation was bitter and widespread in both houses of Parliament. This "gap" was stigmatized as the "greatest defect" of the Treaty by Cornudet, of the Democratic Republican Entente,[37] and it was almost universally listed among the most objectionable features of the peace. Only the Socialists were partisans of the existing terms, this being one of the few aspects of the settlement which they wholeheartedly accepted. Not only did they consider that German unity was necessary and desirable in order to enable Germany to pay her reparations obligations, but they also thought the peace had clearly demonstrated that the union of the German states was anything but flimsy, and that to break it up would have created inevitable trouble for the future.[38]

b. The Military Provisions

The military terms of the Treaty were equally, if not more unsatisfactory to Parliament, as was to be expected in view of the enthusiastic support given the Raynaud proposal in March to reduce Germany's military establishment to the status of a mere police force (*supra,* p. 181). In this particular the Barthou report of the Chamber was scarcely representative of the real sentiment of the great majority of deputies and senators, for it expressed general approval of the relevant clauses, though with reservations as to some practical aspects of their application. In fact, the commission practically accepted the point of view adopted by the gov-

ernment on this important section of the Treaty.[39] The
Senate commission was far more skeptical, expressing grave
doubts as to the effectiveness of the measures for limiting
the personnel and material, and concerning the control
features.[40]

The preponderant sentiment of the Chamber, and the
Senate, was clearly with André Lefèvre, a deputy of the
Left Center, who, since January, had fought for complete
disarmament of Germany, and who, in the debates of September 11 and 12, passionately exposed the alleged inadequacies of the military provisions of the Treaty. The thesis
tenaciously held by him was that Germany could have been
disarmed, that she was not, and that there was still time to
achieve this objective.[41] The 100,000 men left to Germany
by the Treaty would provide Germany with an excellent
corps of platoon leaders; and these, along with the members of the police force, who would contribute non-commissioned officers, would constitute the basis of a formidable
military organization. The limitation on material was also
deemed inadequate. Merely to limit the number of cannons
was futile. The only effective method was to forbid the
manufacture of any cannons at all, for it would be quite
impossible to verify and control the number turned out.[42]
The control provisions actually set up were bad, for the commissions provided were only temporary.[43] "When one sees
a nation like Germany," said Lefèvre, "with its personal
and military qualities, manifesting such a spirit, even before
the Treaty is in effect, and not even trying to conceal its
unwillingness to carry out the Treaty provisions . . . I ask
you whether one has not the right to take precautions." [44]

Lefèvre's speech was received with enthusiastic applause,
and his views with regard to more drastic limitation of personnel and material were undoubtedly approved by the
overwhelming majority of the deputies.[45] His proposals for
more permanent and drastic controls were also widely approved,[46] though the Socialists, while accepting the general
idea of supervision, emphasized the inadequacy of any sys-

tem of purely military controls. Moral guarantees, they claimed, would have to be added to material ones.[47] Article 213, it was thought, could function only if there were built up a strong and solid League of Nations.

c. The Left Bank, the Alliances and the League

The Barthou report to the Chamber signalized the general interest in the Rhineland problem by remarking concerning it: "There is no question which has held the attention of your commission more closely. There is none which has more profoundly stirred its feelings, and whose solution engages its responsibility more gravely." If the commission had not been faced with the alternatives of ratification or rejection of the Treaty, said Barthou, and had been able to state its views freely, "by a great majority it would have favored the establishment of Germany's western frontier at the Rhine, and the occupation of the bridgeheads by inter-Allied troops". The overwhelming majority of the commission, in other words, were frankly partisans of the policy for which Marshal Foch had fought so vigorously in the Conference.[48]

The French government had originally adopted the Foch point of view. Why had it renounced it? In answering this question the commission recognized that the French government could not face the problem alone, and that the Allies had consistently refused to yield to French demands, offering, as an alternative, to come to France's aid in case of unprovoked attack from Germany. In addition, demilitarization of the Rhineland was conceded, as was also inter-Allied occupation of the Rhine bridges for fifteen years, with the possibility of prolonging the occupation under certain circumstances. The German military establishment had been greatly reduced, and the League of Nations, by a majority vote of the Council, was given the right to make investigations. Under the circumstances, could France hesitate? In the opinion of the commission, any other government would have had to act substantially as that of Clemenceau had acted.[49] On two points relating to the Alliance pacts serious questions were raised. First, what was the meaning of "immediately" in the promise of intervention? That is, what was the promise of "immediate assistance" worth? Second, how would the agreements be implemented? Should they not be completed by military conventions stipulating precisely the manner in which they would come into operation? The good faith of the promissors was not openly questioned, but the "straightforward generosity" of the American and British peoples was invoked as a guarantee that they would not nullify the effectiveness of the Alliances by refusing to make precise arrangements for carrying them into effect.[50]

The Senate commission reporting on the Treaty likewise felt compelled to yield to the exigencies of the occasion, though it expressed even greater anxiety over the "dangerous weaknesses" which persisted in the terms. Though the guarantees were considerable, their weaknesses could not be denied. The withdrawal of the American and British forces from the Rhine would soon leave France bearing the burden of occupation alone. The League of Nations had only "made war more difficult", and the alliances themselves gave rise to grave uncertainties. A literal interpretation would apply them only to German violations of the demilitarized Rhineland zone, whereas, it was thought, the danger from Germany might arise elsewhere—in Poland, for example. "In a word", concluded the Bourgeois report, "much is provided for, but nothing is yet consummated." [51]

The case for the government was forcefully presented to the Chamber by Tardieu, who explained why it had been impossible to maintain the Foch program in its integrity. Not only was it, in fact, "obviously inconsistent" with one of the accepted bases of the peace (the "right of self-determination"), but the Allies had manifested marked repugnance to the separation of the left bank from Germany, and also against the prolonged occupation of that territory. In place of the French program, the British and American

Allies had made their offer of immediate assistance in case
of unprovoked German attack. This, however, was not accepted by the French government as sufficient in itself.
Other guarantees were demanded, and eventually were added
to that of the alliances: reduction of the German military
establishment; right of supervision on a majority vote of
the League Council; demilitarization of the Rhineland to a
distance of fifty kilometers east of the Rhine; provision that
any violation of this territory would be regarded as an act
of hostility against the signatories of the Treaty, and occupation of the left bank for fifteen years, with the right of reoccupation in case Germany failed to keep her engagements.
"This solution," said Tardieu, "is not what we proposed in
February. Neither is it what our Allies and Associates offered
us on March 14." However, the total result assured to
France "all of the essential guarantees which our first proposal embodied", along with "the inestimable advantage . . .
of the treaties of immediate assistance with Great Britain
and the United States". As far as detailed military agreements for implementing the pacts were concerned, these
would follow naturally after ratification of the treaties had
taken place; but in any case military conventions of the old
sort "made little difference", since, under modern conditions, "to give force to our agreements, only two conditions
are necessary—the word of the governments, and the adherence of the peoples." [52]

The preferences of the Barthou and Bourgeois reports for
the Rhine military frontier were also those of the patriotic
groups of Parliament, which regarded the alternative provisions for security as entirely inadequate.

Louis Marin, of the nationalistic Democratic Republican
Entente, in a two-day speech, elaborated views which were
echoed in Radical Socialist ranks on the Left, and, to a slight
extent, even among Socialists, though few of those who
agreed with him were willing to follow his example in refusing to ratify the Treaty. Neutralization of the Rhineland
would be "a magnificent guarantee" for a people "who know

how to respect their signature. . . . But how can we forget
that we are dealing with Germany, which only yesterday
violated the neutrality of Luxemburg and Belgium . . .?" [53]
The Rhineland occupation would be too brief,[54] and the alliances suffered from three great defects. First, they came
into play "only in case of unprovoked aggression", whereas,
he said, wars in Europe were caused by "indirect attacks".
Second, the meaning of the word "immediately" was vague
and indefinite. Finally, there was "the grave fact that the
League of Nations, by a mere majority vote", could put an
end to the pacts.[55] As for the League of Nations, it would
not be able to prevent a sudden attack, . . . and the guarantees offered by it were unequal to the security offered by
"the occupation of the left bank and the control of the
bridgeheads".[56]

The Radical Socialists, to whose group in the Senate Clemenceau himself belonged, largely shared these sentiments.
The more nationalistic wing of that party, led by Franklin-
Bouillon in the Chamber, accepted the Foch program and
followed the arguments of Marin.[57] The more moderate
wing, however, could not be said to have inclined toward
softness to Germany. Its views were ably presented by René
Renoult in the Chamber and by Debierre and Flaissières in
the Senate. Military aspects of security were not ignored,
but moral guarantees were recognized as important. Renoult
was partial to strong frontiers, and thought the boundary
based on the 1815 line rather than that of 1814, was deplorably weak.[58] The guarantees, in their ensemble, had
brought "real security" to France, but one would have to
recognize that, after all, the quest for absolute security was
doomed to failure, and France should not delude herself as
to Germany's future policy or intentions. "Vigilant and
justly defiant", she "would need to watch Germany".[59]

On the extreme Left of the Chamber "moral" guarantees
tended to take precedence over those of a strictly material
character. Material guarantees were not deemed irrelevant.
In fact, the complete disarmament of Germany, demilitari-

zation of the Rhineland, universal control of armaments and an international force were regarded as most important. But they should be set in a matrix of a general international system, from which they would derive their moral validity.[60]

The Socialists were not unanimous, it is true, in applying the general principles to which they all professed allegiance. Slightly more than a third of the party members in the Chamber were inclined to postpone, for a time, the application to Germany of the strict principles of internationalism, and were disposed to clothe the "moral" guarantees in unmistakably material form, in order to insure Germany's performance of her obligations, and to await her "change of heart". Renaudel, for example, stressed the importance of "immediate guarantees" and "remote guarantees"; and, while he wanted the League to include all peoples, each nation admitted would have to give proof of its "willingness to abide by its engagements"; which would seem to exclude Germany until it could demonstrate its good faith.[61]

Albert Thomas, also of the moderate Socialists, attacked the Treaty provisions relating to security, saying that he found them "frequently insufficient", "frequently precarious", and that he wondered how the government had been able to think "that the sum total of the insufficiencies was able to constitute a solid security for the country".[62] Admiration was expressed by him for the "strong classic lines" of the government program of February 25, which embodied the essence of the Foch plan. Indeed, he inclined strongly toward such a solution of the security problem, including a program of military neutralization of the left bank, leaving it under the occupation of international forces controlled by the League of Nations.[63] Thus the mantle of internationalism, proposed as a cover for the Rhineland régime, had cast its spell, and Thomas responded, with an idealist's enthusiasm, to the solution which would have been international in appearance, and would have offered material safeguards to France.

But the majority of the Socialists had no regrets over the

failure of the Foch program. They did not share Thomas'
faith that the pale cast of internationalism would have made
it any less an imperialistic venture, full of danger for the
future. Mistral argued that even the temporary occupation
of the left bank by Allied forces—"granting that it is necessary"—constituted a source of possible incidents and of friction likely to lead to serious consequences,[64] while Sembat
rebuked the government for having to be called back by the
Allies to fundamental principles.[65]

Neither did the Socialist majority fully share Thomas'
faith in the League. "League of Nations?" "Certainly,"
said Sembat, "but not the caricature which has been presented. 'Embryo' they say? Oh! if it were an embryo, I
should applaud with both hands; but I am afraid it is not
that." To regard it as a "panacea for all wars" was fantas-
tic; and before it could put an end to the sad results of the
pre-war anarchy it would have to embrace all peoples, particularly Germany, and would have to rest upon the good
will of the working masses of the world.[66] Nevertheless, the
League, in spite of its imperfections, was an important beginning, for after all, said Brunet, it was the first "serious
obstacle" which up to that time had been erected against
war.[67]

As for the Anglo-American alliances, these were ignored
entirely by Socialist orators, although the Socialist press had
condemned the principle on which the pacts were based. The
final vote on ratification, however, indicated that these pacts
were less repugnant in practice than in theory, for only one
Socialist vote was recorded in opposition to them.[68]

5. ANXIETIES CONCERNING AMERICAN ATTITUDE

The course of events in the United States, marked by the
consolidation and apparent growth of opposition to the
League and to the special guarantee pact, became increasingly disturbing. Attention was drawn, in the press and in
Parliament, to the grave possibility that these engagements
would fail of ratification in the American Senate. On July 19

the *Temps* appealed to the American people, "for their honor, for the good of humanity", not to "turn back" on the obligations of the Treaty and the Alliance. On August 25, the day before the parliamentary debates on the Treaty began, the *Temps* observed that a majority of the American Senate would probably refuse to ratify the Treaty in its existing form, and noted, further, that "essential provisions" of the League Covenant (particularly Article 10) would be altered. On September 26 its anxiety was still growing. Failure of the United States to ratify the Covenant of the League would endanger the ratification of the Treaty itself, and also of the special treaties of alliance. In fact, so serious did the situation appear that the *Temps* urged the Allies to come together and strengthen the guarantees, in order to avoid the "risk of weakening public confidence".

Other leading organs commented from time to time on the American scene, and, while keenly aware of the danger, were reluctant to believe that the American Senate would actually reject so momentous a peace settlement. Such action would be unprecedented. Even the skeptical *Journal* (July 29) doubted that the Senate would go so far as to reject the Treaty, and the *Débats* reported on August 25 that the pro-ratificationists apparently had the necessary two-thirds, though by a very slender margin. From that time the prospects tended to grow dimmer,[69] and French commentators found themselves in an increasingly embarrassing situation, conscious of the danger of appearing to bring undue pressure on the American Senate. In its appeal for American ratification, the *Temps* (July 19) carefully disclaimed any intention of intervening in the "domestic controversies" of the United States, and other papers followed its example even more cautiously, many of them preferring a policy of comparative silence. The *Débats* (Sept. 26) called special attention to the delicacy of the situation, observing that the attitude of the French press might be of determining importance in the ultimate decision of the United States. **Furthermore, the French Parliament was**

solemnly warned (Sept. 27) that further delay in ratification by France would only encourage the opposition in the
United States.

The deputies and senators were likewise cautious in their
references to the course of American ratification policy.
Though the weaknesses of the alliances, as well as of the
League and other Treaty provisions were relentlessly exposed, and though anxiety was clearly evident over American developments, the orators were generally careful in commenting on ratification prospects in the United States. The
ultra-nationalist, Marin, for example, dissected and denounced the guarantee clauses at great length (Sept. 19 and
23), but carefully abstained from expressing doubts as to
the action of the American Senate. Some speakers warmly
expressed their belief in affirmative American action, thereby
appealing subtly for favorable action, and implicitly admitting their anxieties. But with the progress of the debates
uneasiness was increasingly apparent. Barthou, who on
September 2nd had warmly expressed his confidence in the
alliances, and his "reliance on the loyalty" of the United
States and Great Britain,[70] on September 24th gravely expressed his concern over the future of guarantees and the
prospect of American ratification.[71]

Replying to their critics, September 24 and 25, Tardieu
and Clemenceau felt that optimism was the best policy with
regard to this question. "Every confidence" in ratification
by the United States was expressed by Tardieu. He was
certain that "the immense majority of opinion" in that
"great democracy" which had "done so much to adapt itself
to new conditions" for which its past had not prepared it,
was anxious to affirm its "solidarity with Europe".[72] Clemenceau, in his turn, combined a touch of realism with an
affectation of optimism. It would be "a singular irony of
fate", he confessed, if the United States failed to ratify the
Treaty; but he said that by virtue of certain provisions of
the Treaty [73] France would be able to make new arrangements concerning the Rhine. Furthermore, he thought the

League would be able to carry on even without the United States.[74] The following day (Sept. 25) he was all optimism. The Treaty of Alliance was sure to be ratified at Washington. "The Americans have come. They will not retire. . . . I do not know how they will vote at Washington, but I know they will ratify it, because it is impressed on the hearts of . . . these Americans who have brought us their generous support."[75] In spite of increasing fears of unfavorable American action,[76] the Premier's studied optimism was maintained in his final defense of the Treaty before the Senate, on October 11. He even confessed to a change of heart with regard to the League. Formerly he had "entertained doubts about it". But progress made institutions necessary, and the French people must now apply these institutions in all their rigor, and find men "capable of making them live".[77]

6. THE FINAL VOTES IN THE CHAMBER AND SENATE

When the deputies and senators were faced with the necessity of passing from words to acts, and of accepting or rejecting the peace terms, the overwhelming majority found it impossible to express their dissatisfaction in a negative vote on the Treaty. To do this would have been hazardous, as it might have plunged the country once more into black uncertainty. France, of all the Allies, had most at stake, and could least afford to dally in the no-man's land between peace and war. If the Treaty failed of ratification it would involve great delay in the peace, and a repetition of the agony of peace negotiations. A separate peace with Germany without the Allies was unthinkable. Negotiating another treaty along with the Allies would mean facing the same resistances and the same antagonistic policies as before, so that a better compromise could scarcely be anticipated than the one already achieved. "Imperfections" and "weaknesses" in the Treaty? Undoubtedly. Nevertheless, opinion throughout patriotic circles was in overwhelming agreement with the view expressed by the *Intransigeant*

(Oct. 3) that, "No statesman having the responsibility of the government could undertake to reopen discussions with Germany in such a troubled period. . . ."[78] To reject the Treaty would have been "to open up an abyss", solemnly affirmed the *Temps*.[79]

It is not surprising, therefore, that even such a nationalistic patriot as Maurice Barrès, with all his disappointments, could decide to vote for the Treaty. "How could one do otherwise?" he asked. "The situation is so involved that we are already in a state of peace, and the country, which is aware of the imperfections of this diplomatic instrument, would not follow us if, in rejecting peace, we threw France back into a state of war."[80]

The final vote in the Chamber—372 for ratification, 53 against, with 72 abstentions—disclosed that, with negligible exceptions, the opposition consisted primarily of Socialists, forty-nine of whom cast their votes in the negative. Individual irreconcilable nationalists, Marin, of the Right, and Franklin-Bouillon, of the Radical Socialists, cast negative votes for reasons opposite to those of the Socialists, while two other negative votes were unexplained. Of the seventy-two abstentionists, thirty-three were of the more conservative wing of the Socialists. Eighteen others were Radical Socialists who sympathized with the nationalist views of Franklin-Bouillon but would not go all the way with him into opposition. Most of the other abstainers were among the more nationalistic groups of the Center and Right.[81]

The discussions of October 1 and 2, preceding the final vote, were occupied chiefly with explanations of personal and group votes. The Socialist case against the Treaty was clearly summarized by Ernest Lafont[82] who represented not only the forty-nine who voted against the Treaty, but apparently, also, most of the thirty-three who merely abstained. The unsatisfactory peace settlement was the "inevitable result" of months of ultra-secret discussions. It was but fragmentary. Russia had been left out, and one could not think seriously of reestablishing equilibrium without Russia. The League of Nations had brought "the most cruel disillusionments", for with the exclusion of the enemy belligerents of yesterday, it was "a league built on the principle of the balance of power". General disarmament had been discarded, and France, "crushed with debts, and drained of its best blood", was in danger of being overwhelmed by ruinous military charges. Maritime imperialism had triumphed over the principle of the freedom of the seas. National egoisms had been stronger than the desire of peoples to live in peace. The "right of self-determination" had been trampled, and the Basin of the Saar had been "politically enslaved". German Austria had also "been deprived of the right of self-determination". "The division of the German colonies, under the cover of mandates," had "deprived Germany of precious outlets, and of sources of indispensable activity at the very moment when the financial hopes of the Treaty rest on the development of its material prosperity." Territorial clauses had been "deliberately given first place, at the expense of financial reparations and economic guarantees". "The financial League of Nations on which France had the right to count, after so many sacrifices", was not even shadowed forth. Neither had the economic relations between peoples been any better organized. "On the contrary, tomorrow, as yesterday, tariff barriers will separate peoples, and, in the markets of the world the old competition will revive", and the historic cycle will recommence: "commercial rivalry, diplomatic tension, outbreak of war". The Socialists were excluded from the commission on the Treaty. They now say to the parliamentary majority: "You have wanted the exclusive glory of this Treaty. We leave you also the responsibility for it." [83]

To the right of the Socialists a large majority of every group voted for the Treaty. But each did so with excuses and explanations. Jean Bon significantly remarked a few minutes before the final vote: "There is no one who has dared to say that he was voting for the Treaty with enthusiasm." [84] For them all it was, in varying degrees, a "peace of vigilance".

Of the 156 Radical Socialists, one (Franklin-Bouillon) voted against, and eighteen abstained. The Treaty, as a whole, was more nearly satisfactory to the great majority of this group than to any other. René Renoult, representing this section of the Chamber, explained that, in spite of the defects in the Treaty—primarily involving German disarmament, financial arrangements, Saar frontiers, weakness of the League of Nations, etc.—they would vote for ratification, because the peace terms had really modified "from top to bottom the peril of war which Germany had formerly represented". France, he thought, could greet such a peace with a "large degree of confidence". But at the same time "it was necessary to be watchful" for years to come. [85]

Of the 149 members of the Center, one voted against, and ten members abstained, while, of the ninety-three deputies on the Right, two cast negative ballots and eight abstained. There was practical unanimity of opinion in these sections of the Chamber as to the primary defects of the peace settlement: Failure to destroy German unity; inadequate disarmament of Germany; failure to obtain the Foch Rhineland program; uncertainty as to the reparations settlement, and especially the "unequal position" of France in relation to the Anglo-Saxon allies in the matter of reparations; the "impotence" of the League of Nations, and the absence of a financial League guaranteeing inter-Allied financial solidarity, and, finally, the uncertainties of the Anglo-American alliances. But in spite of these profound objections, the considerations of expediency which had prevailed with Barrès, were also determinative with practically all members of the Center and Right. "We shall ratify it, faced with the unknown mass of dangers which its rejection would create," said the Count de Gouyon, voicing the sentiments of patriotic groups. [86] Consolation and hope were also found in Clemenceau's assurance that the Treaty was "a group of opportunities" which could be improved. [87]

Ratification of the Treaty by the Senate followed on October 11, after three days of debate. Approval was unanimously voted, with only four abstentions.[88] Only two voices in that body were raised in behalf of a spirit of moderation toward Germany; and even they—those of Debierre and Flaissières, on the extreme Left—agreed that Germany was still a danger, and that vigilance would be essential.[89]

The state of feeling in the upper chamber can well be gauged by the speech of Maurice Sarraut, who spoke for the Radical Socialists, and who therefore expressed the dominant view of the Left Wing of the Senate. The decisive factor in their vote for the Treaty was, he said, Alsace-Lorraine, the return of which had freed his generation from "the nightmare which had lasted for half a century". But there were grave dangers lurking in the peace settlement. France, whose mission would be to "mount guard for civilization on the left bank of the Rhine", would be left face to face with a united Germany, "maintained, if not reinforced, by Prussian hegemony. . . ." Events had shown that a "new era" had not been born in Germany. "We are obliged to note, without amazement, but with sorrow, that German militarism is not broken, and that proof is still lacking of a decisive change of her atttitude." Firmness would have to be demanded of future governments, so that none of the clauses of the Treaty signed by Germany should be evaded. Germany was able to pay, and she would have to pay "in its entirety the insufficient obligation" which had been recognized by her. As demanded "unanimously by the Chamber", the disarmament of Germany should be "not merely theoretical". It would have to be "vigilantly controlled". Likewise, the financial gaps of the Treaty should be "repaired by an appropriate policy of agreement with the Allies". The task of the Allies was only half finished. France, impoverished and bled white, was entitled to "that effective solidarity" so "indispensable to her in the economic and financial domain".[90]

Such were the views of the most moderate group of the

Senate. Opinions farther to the right differed from these only in their greater vehemence and bitterness. Admiral de la Jaille, just preceding the final vote, appealed for divine assistance. Amendment of the Treaty had been impossible. France would therefore have to bring to the task of enforcing its terms all her will and resources, with the firm hope that God would do the rest.[91]

In the Senate, as in the Chamber, the decisive factors were, the return of Alsace-Lorraine, the hope of bettering France's future position by means of agreements with the Allies, and by rigorous enforcement of the peace terms, and most important, the absence of any practical alternative. "The brutal fact is," said Bourgeois, "that it is eleven months since the Armistice was signed, and the victory acclaimed. It is necessary that the normal ways of life be resumed in this country. . . ."[92] The force of this argument was irresistible. The Senate, in its unanimous vote of approval, doubtless also shared the philosophy embodied in Clemenceau's final defense of that document: "It is said . . . that this Treaty reduces us to vigilance." "Yes, but life itself condemns us to vigilance!"[93]

7. "Arguments Give Way to Facts"

The ratification debates, though somewhat prolonged, had served a useful purpose. French public opinion, through them, had become more fully enlightened as to the "weaknesses" of the Treaty, and more completely infused with the attitude of "vigilance" which was the leitmotif of the closing exhortations in the Chamber and Senate.[94] Furthermore, they had clarified and emphasized certain aspects of the settlement in such a way that France would presumably be better able to take advantage of her opportunities in the trying ordeal of putting the Treaty into operation.[95] In particular, it was hoped that the debates would assist the "President of the Council in making the French point of view prevail with the Allies".[96]

Even before ratification was finally voted, public interest

was absorbed in the problem of filling the "gaps" and strengthening the terms of the peace.[97] When the Chamber had acted on October 2nd the time for recrimination was deemed to be past. There must be "No more sterile regrets".[98] France had arrived "at the threshold of a new era", and she should enter it "with a new spirit". The Treaty would now have to be applied, and it would be "necessary to make the most of the advantages" which the peace offered.[99]

Unfortunately for France, the application and improvement of the Treaty terms did not lie exclusively, or even predominantly, in her own hands. As had been pointed out in the parliamentary debates and in the press, the most important "ameliorations" of the peace were those for which France would have to turn to "the Allied and Associated Powers".[100] There remained, even after the ratification of the Treaty, the bitter necessity of pursuing further inter-Allied negotiations if France were to hope to gain the military security and financial stability toward which all her policies were directed. Immediately, therefore, after the ratification of the Treaty by the Chamber, that body sought to precipitate matters and to spur the government on to action.

The ratification debates had emphasized the "gap" in the reparations account, and the necessity of a supplementary inter-Allied agreement if that gap were to be filled. Whether Germany would be made to pay, and whether the Allies would come to France's financial assistance were burning questions also in the press,[101] and these were only aggravated by the fact that the franc was falling on the international exchanges. The government having apparently got nowhere in its negotiations with the Allies on this matter, the Chamber, on October 3, unanimously (488 to 0) demanded: (a) priority for France in reparation payments until the damages in the invaded regions were repaired, (b) continued inter-Allied solidarity with a view to assuring the execution by Germany of her obligations, and (c) an inter-Allied agreement for "an equitable settlement of the costs of the war".[102] The fact, not only that this was voted unanimously, but also that it was sponsored by the Socialist, Auriol, indicates how strongly the deputies felt. Yet feelings and desires, however justifiable, had gradually to yield to implacable facts, however bitter, and the *Matin* itself, which had earlier done so much to foster false hopes as to reparations, now frankly pointed out that to expect the United States to assume a share of France's war costs was grossly to delude one's self.[103] Other disillusionments in this and other fields were destined to follow.

Equally contingent upon Allied cooperation was France's military security; and equally vexatious uncertainties were arising on this horizon. German military activities in the Baltic States, so serious in character as to give rise, late in September, to Allied threats of a renewal of the blockade, gave point to a growing conviction that Germany was unwilling to reduce her military establishment according to treaty schedule. The striking analysis of the problem by André Lefèvre during the ratification debates seemed to be justified by the trend of events in Germany. Alarm became widespread, and vigorous support was given Lefèvre's argument that Germany should have been forbidden the manufacture of any cannons whatsoever.[104] Perhaps it was not too late to do something about it. Even the *Temps* (Sept. 26, 27) proposed that the Allies come together hastily before ratification and set up additional security arrangements of a temporary character. Lefèvre, with much support in the Chamber, sought to attach a rider to the Treaty, aimed at dealing with this problem, but Clemenceau, posing the question of confidence, had refused to permit any modification of the Treaty.[105] As soon as the Chamber had acted on the Treaty, however, this matter was again brought before it, and a resolution was unanimously passed (486 to 0) calling upon the signatories of the Treaty to make German disarmament more effective by the absolute prohibition "of certain manufactures", and by other "necessary measures".[106]

A cruel irony seemed to patriotic Frenchmen to be shaping the course of events. "Why is it thus?" asked the *Temps* (Oct. 5). "Why was the Chamber . . . eleven months after the victory, reduced to discussing for an entire session, the disarmament of the German Reich?" Even the *Dépêche* of Toulouse (Oct. 5) cynically picturing England "safe on her rocky barrier", and America, "sheltered by the ocean", remarked that "if the fine promises of yesterday were other than mere effusions of courtesy", the other powers would lend their support to the Lefèvre motion, so that it would not have to be added to the many other "fine phrases which today are without significance".[107]

Here too, desires ran counter to the imponderables of Allied policy, and the French government was apparently aware of the futility of hoping for further improvement of the provisions of the Treaty by inter-Allied action. As a matter of fact, the very basis of solidarity or cooperation in any form between the Allied and Associated Powers appeared to be threatened, as the opposition to the Treaty in the United States gained momentum. It was scarcely credible that the Treaty as a whole would be rejected by the American Senate; yet, by early October, responsible leaders of opinion in France were prepared to believe that ratification would be accompanied by drastic reservations affecting the League of Nations. This eventually, however deplorable, would, nevertheless, have been acceptable to patriotic opinion if the Alliance were duly sanctioned, for this pact, along with the identical arrangement with Great Britain, was regarded not only as a striking symbol of inter-Allied solidarity, but also as a formidable guarantee of France's security. Indeed, the *Temps* solemnly proclaimed that the treaties of guarantee were "inseparable from the Treaty" itself,[108] and other leading organs affirmed that the more drastic the American reservations were, the more France would be compelled to resort to security measures on her own account.[109]

The ratifications of France, Italy and Great Britain, in addition to that of Germany, had made certain the legal validity and effectiveness of the Treaty. This was a source of satisfaction. Yet without the sanction of the United States, "terrible gaps and unbelievable complications" would remain.[110] President Wilson's illness and the doings of the American Senate were followed in France with absorbing interest, and with prolonged hope for favorable action on the Treaty. This hope had been carefully fostered in early October by press reports of interviews with influential Americans, and by encouraging editorial comments; [111] but as the days passed into weeks, and the pageant of Senatorial reservations and amendments to the Treaty lengthened, the favorable prospects grew dimmer, and signs of impatience recurred.[112]

Faltering hope for favorable Senatorial action struggled desperately against rising fears of the uncertainties looming up in case the United States should finally reject the Treaty and refuse to take responsibility for helping to maintain the peace which American leadership had done so much to bring about. Patriotic Frenchmen, including some Socialists, had originally desired a stronger peace settlement. A compromise had been accepted and moral guarantees had been substituted for material safeguards, largely because of the promise that America would not retire once more to political aloofness and irresponsibility. When the inevitable French ratification of the Treaty was finally registered in October 1919, it was no longer expected that the United States would cooperate fully, and up to the limit of the terms of the Versailles system. The question was, rather, whether American cooperation could be anticipated on any terms. That the United States Senate would completely repudiate Wilson and his peacemaking seemed scarcely credible, but it was clear that American domestic politics had largely dissipated the sense of solidarity which had previously bound that country to its erstwhile Allies.

8. RETROSPECT

"Idealism has conquered; but materialism is not yet dead," wrote the *Dépêche* of Toulouse (Oct. 13), suggesting the prevailing bewilderment and disillusionment. It was expressive also, of the abortive results of an unhappy union between the old and the new ideologies. "Open Diplomacy" could be but "sand in the eyes and dust in the bearings" of a diplomatic system geared to the purposes of inflamed nationalism and unregenerate imperialism. Nor could the application of democratic principles be other than farcical among peoples who for years had been held aloof from the facts essential to the formation of an intelligent opinion, and who had been assiduously nourished on a blinding and blighting propaganda.

A realistic appraisal of the factors involved in the peacemaking could scarcely have justified the hopes of the young idealists of the Nicolson [113] and Bullitt schools, however greatly it is to their credit that they sought to convert the promise of a decent peace into a reality. The confusion of purposes and conflict of policies were too great. The lack of clarity as to real war aims was too obvious. As the war proceeded it became increasingly evident that the war aims of the belligerents would not bear frank statement in simple definitive terms, and the fact that this was true of both the Central Powers and the Allies only added to the confusion, for it deprived either party of a well-defined point of departure. Germany had accepted the Wilson program, at first merely as a "basis of discussion", and ultimately only after military collapse. The resistance of the Allies to the Wilson theses in the negotiations preceding the Armistice demonstrated their unwillingness to be bound by definite commitments; and their eventual acceptance of the Presidential pronouncements (with two qualifications), under the pressure of a practical ultimatum, did not alter their determination to pursue individual nationalistic policies, even though this meant distorting or disavowing accepted principles.

But granting the best of intentions on the part of Allied leaders, the task of applying the principles of the new ideology would have been sufficiently baffling, for who could propose an objectively just solution for any of the major issues raised by the war? President Wilson must have sensed this difficulty, not merely when it came to applying his Fourteen Points, but even in the process of framing them, as was evidenced by his repeated efforts to draft a satisfactory proposal for the solution of the problem of Alsace-Lorraine.[114] How, for example, could the principle of self-determination be applied with objective justice throughout the mélange of nationality groupings in Europe? And how could it be made to harmonize with the existing economic realities?

A *bona fide* application of Wilsonism, furthermore, would have required the rapid and almost miraculous birth of good will between peoples who had only tentatively laid aside hostilities. It would have required, incidentally, a much greater degree of harmony and collaboration between the Allies themselves than actually existed. The circumstances of the war had contributed, in an unprecedented fashion, to arousing in the French people the deepest antagonism toward Germany and the German people. The universal involvement of the masses in the business and the risks of war, the colossal losses in killed and wounded, the rigid censorship and the ruthless propaganda had all tended to deprive the peoples of the incentive as well as the means for rational thinking. The German Revolution of November 1918, brought about, in large measure, by pressure from President Wilson, could not have been expected quickly to remove ingrained distrust and hostility. Nor were events in Germany after the Armistice calculated to achieve this objective. How well these suspicions were justified can only be conjectured, but they can easily be understood; and they undoubtedly constituted a serious obstacle to the application of democratic principles of settlement.

The ambiguousness of "open covenants, openly arrived at" was itself a source of confusion and difficulty. Precisely what did this and the accompanying phraseology mean? President Wilson himself did not appear to be clear as to its meaning in relation to the actual processes of the Peace Conference, though he apparently would not have accepted the more radical implications ascribed to it by the Socialist press of France and by the majority of the American correspondents who had flocked to France for the journalistic fiesta.

It is another question whether "open covenants, openly arrived at", literally applied, would have been feasible and wise at the time of the Conference. However much one would like to hope, one cannot suppress misgivings as to the success of an adventure in complete open diplomacy. It is significant that the demand from patriotic French quarters in March and April for more publicity and less censorship was based on the claim that French public opinion would thereby be able to bring more vigorous support to French claims. A more democratic procedure and a more democratic press assuredly would not have meant that the powerful and dominating patriotic organs would have been less inclined to whip up popular feelings. Greater frankness was certainly possible and desirable on the part of the Conference. This, along with more efficient methods, would have helped to maintain public confidence and also to temper national policies. But the clash of policies was at times too fundamental for the negotiations to be exposed at every stage to public scrutiny without risks which no responsible party was willing to take. The new diplomacy could function successfully only in an atmosphere of new conditions and new policies. It could not, of itself, create those new conditions.

Not least important, in its bearing on the prospects of a

Wilsonian peace settlement, were the imponderables of American politics. That Wilson should be heading the American delegation seemed doubly anomalous to the Allied publics. Not only was he a head of State who, as such, would normally negotiate only through diplomatic agents; but his party had recently been defeated at the polls, which, in a responsible parliamentary system (as in England or France), would have shorn him of power in foreign as well as domestic politics. The drift of American policy back to isolation was unmistakable, as was recognized by Wilson himself in his insistence, after his return from the United States in March, on weakening what was already regarded by French opinion as a dangerously weak League. The Wilsonian ideology suffered a double defeat. While antagonistic Allied policies thwarted its complete realization in the treaty with Germany, partisan politics at home, and a hostile tradition of aloofness, combined to prevent that degree of international co-operation by the United States which would have tended to mitigate some of the worst features of the peace settlement.

NOTES

[1] Socialists feared that if the Germans refused to sign it would mean "the postponement of demobilization, the reinforcement of the state of siege and of the censorship, a fresh disturbance of our economic life and the explosion of a new nationalist fury. . . ." *Humanité,* June 24.

[2] Sembat, in *Heure,* June 24.

[3] *Humanité,* July 16; *Allied Press,* vol. vi, no. 12, July 23, 1919. The Treaty was "born . . . in the most scandalous abuse of secret diplomacy", it violated the "rights of self-determination of peoples", and "reduced entire nations to slavery", said the resolution. There were 154 abstentions.

[4] *Esprit Public en France,* Bulletin 33, June 22-28, 1919.

[5] "We are going to put our signature beside that of this pirate," it was said, "because it is necessary to finish the negotiations." *Intransigeant,* June 24, 25.

[6] *Homme Libre,* June 27.

[7] *Petit Parisien,* June 25. Furthermore, said the *Temps,* June 29, a "moral revolution" in Germany was necessary, and for that time was necessary.

[8] *Temps,* July 2, 17; August 29; *Débats,* August 2, September 29; *Matin,* August 26; *Intransigeant,* August 15, 27.

[9] *Débats* insisted repeatedly on rapid ratification. August 2, September 4, 25, 29; *Revue des Deux Mondes,* September 15, 1919, pp. 469-480. The feeling expressed by the *Intransigeant* (Aug. 15, 27) that there was "nothing to do but ratify the Treaty", represented the overwhelming view of the patriotic press, though Maurras, in the *Action Française* (Sept. 27, 28) chirped a rather unconvincing opposition.

[10] In a brief and eloquent address, which was duly placarded throughout France, the Premier invoked the spirits of the departed, and called upon his countrymen "to remain worthy of the great dead" who had sought "to perpetuate France in her noble historic virtues". *Annales de la Chambre,* June 30, 1919, p. 2726.

[11] The Socialists should normally have been represented also, but the eleven representatives of that group resigned as a body because two of their number—Longuet and Mayéras—were rejected from the commission (although they had been nominated by the Socialists themselves) by a special vote of the Chamber. The allegations against them were that they were "pro-German". *Journal,* June 27, 28, July 1, 2, 3.

[12] *Annales de la Chambre,* August 6, 1919, p. 3509.

[13] A factor of primary importance was the meetings of the departmental councils which intervened at this time. In the Senate the Commission on Foreign Affairs, with Bourgeois as *rapporteur,* was assigned the task of studying and reporting on the Treaty. The report of this Commission was made October 3, and debate was undertaken in the Senate October 9.

[14] Only the five members of the Democratic Left failed to be represented in the debates.

[15] Barthou, L., *Le Traité de Paix* (Paris, 1919), pp. 89-93.

[16] *Annales de la Chambre,* September 4, 1919, p. 3730.

[17] *Ibid.,* September 18, 1919, p. 3981.

[18] Barthou, *op. cit.,* pp. 9-52.

[19] Bourgeois, Léon, *Le Traité de Paix de Versailles* (Paris, 1919), pp. 11-16.

[20] *Annales de la Chambre,* August 29, 1919, p. 3665.

[21] E.g., Renaudel, *Annales de la Chambre,* September 26, 1919, pp. 4164 *et seq.* Barthou, *op. cit.,* pp. 72-74, 97.

[22] Speaking for the Socialist group, Bedouce reminded the "German people" of the "wrong . . . done in their name", and told them frankly that it was "for them to repair that wrong". *Annales de la Chambre,* September 5, 1919, p. 3758.

[23] *Ibid.,* September 4, 1919, p. 3735.

[24] Bedouce, in Chamber, *ibid.,* September 5, 1919, p. 3735.

[25] E.g.. speech by Ossola, of the Radical Left, *ibid.,* September 17, 1919, p. 3958.

[26] *Ibid.,* September 9, 1919, p. 3795.

[27] Barthou, *op. cit.,* pp. 112-114. Louis Dubois, *rapporteur* for the reparations and financial sections, demanded, more specifically, that the Allies "either endorse the bonds, the recognition of indebtedness which Germany will have emitted or subscribed", or that they "guarantee jointly the payment of the debt, undertaking that if Germany does not pay it,

they will either pay it themselves, or that all nations shall pay it in a determined ratio". *Annales de la Chambre,* September 19, 1919, p. 3795.

[28] *Annales de la Chambre,* September 5, 1919, pp. 3764 *et seq.*

[29] Longuet expressed the sentiment of the Chamber Socialists (as well as that of patriotic groups) in charging the government with spending too little time on the attempt "to induce England and America to assume part of the expenses of the victory from which they had benefited so greatly". *Ibid.,* September 18, 1919, p. 3982.

[30] Bourgeois, *op. cit.,* pp. 80-102.

[31] *Annales du Sénat,* October 11, 1919, p. 1847. In this connection it ought to be noted that the question of the Saar, in the ratification debates, was of interest primarily as a security problem, since, from the reparations point of view, the régime established was deemed to be satisfactory. It was otherwise as regards the security problem. Except for the Socialists, the Chamber and Senate were practically unanimous in regretting that at least the 1814 frontier had not been gained. See speech of René Renoult, *Annales de la Chambre,* September 30, 1919, p. 4203.

[32] *Annales de la Chambre,* August 29, 1919, p. 3662.

[33] Quoted by Albert Thomas, *ibid.,* August 29, 1919, p. 3663.

[34] *Ibid.,* p. 3663.

[35] *Ibid.,* September 2, 1919, p. 3685. "We considered that German unity was a fact, laboriously prepared from 1804 to 1871, which, in 1919, had had a half century of existence, and that to try to break this up would have paved the way for the most certain German revenge against France."

[36] Barthou, *op. cit.,* pp. 55-61. See also Bourgeois, *op. cit.,* p. 178.

[37] *Annales de la Chambre,* August 28, 1919, p. 3650.

[38] Speech by Thomas in Chamber, *ibid.,* August 29, 1919, p. 3665.

[39] Barthou, *op. cit.,* pp. 123-133.

[40] Bourgeois, *op. cit.,* p. 76.

[41] *Annales de la Chambre,* September 12, 1919, p. 3876.

[42] *Ibid.,* September 12, 1919, p. 3678.

[43] "You have no permanent control, and there is no guarantee that when the commissions are gone Germany will not revert to a different military status." *Ibid.,* p. 3678. Control through the Council of the League, as provided by Article 213, was not taken seriously.

[44] *Ibid.,* September 12, 1919, p. 3881.

[45] *Ibid.,* September 25, 1919, p. 4138; October 2, 1919, p. 4272; September 19, 1919, p. 4016.

[46] René Viviani, of the Socialist Republicans, who naturally desired more drastic limitation of personnel and material, felt that the "fundamental vice" of the Treaty was its failure to provide for permanent supervision (*Ibid.,* September 16, 1919, p. 3924); and René Renoult, of the Radical Socialists, thought that the best hope of safety for France lay in the development of a permanent control over German military activities. *Ibid.,* September 30, 1919, p. 4201.

[47] "In order that war shall die," said Albert Thomas, "in order that a just and durable peace may be brought about . . . it is necessary that the

military clauses be supplemented by other and vaster guarantees." *Ibid.*, August 29, 1919, p. 3663. See resolution of October 3, *ibid.*, p. 4306.

[48] Barthou, *op. cit.*, p. 151. Of course it was added that "No one had demanded the annexation of the Rhenish provinces, in favor of which strong historic reasons might have been invoked. . . . There were other ways of prohibiting military access to the Rhine, and of organizing on the left bank a national régime . . . which would have assured, in accordance with their wishes, the independence of the peoples." *Ibid.*, p. 152.

[49] "Can one deny the imposing force which they [the guarantees] represent?" The Allies (Great Britain and the United States) had "recognized" that France's security was "the condition of the peace of the world", and that the threat from Germany was not merely a danger to France, but was "a common risk which weighed upon them [the Allies], upon Europe, and upon the world". Barthou, *op. cit.*, pp. 156-167.

[50] *Ibid.*, pp. 156-167.

[51] Bourgeois, *op. cit.*, p. 173.

[52] *Annales de la Chambre*, September 2, 1919, pp. 3678 *et seq.*

[53] *Ibid.*, September 19, 1919, pp. 4020 *et seq.*

[54] *Ibid.*, pp. 4020 *et seq.*

[55] *Ibid.*, pp. 4024.

[56] *Ibid.*, p. 4024.

[57] The Left Bank should have been internationalized and erected into an autonomous state, said Franklin-Bouillon. At least the bridgeheads should have been held by the Allies until France had been completely paid by Germany. *Ibid.*, September 3, 1919, pp. 3708 *et seq.;* October 1, 1919, pp. 4230 *et seq.* "The League of Nations, such as it is, is deplorably weak," and, should the United States not come in, it would be "non-existent". As to the Alliance, "Would the United States ratify it?" Even though the United States did ratify it, would that instrument be effective in case Germany attacked Poland, and France went to the latter's assistance? *Ibid.*, October 1, 1919, pp. 4232-4236.

[58] *Ibid.*, September 30, 1919, pp. 4201 *et seq.* Opposed to annexation of the left bank, Renoult apparently endorsed the Foch program as proposed in the memorandum of February 25, believing that it would not have led to outright annexation. Nevertheless, he and the more advanced wing of the Radical Socialists, differed from the almost unanimous view farther to the right in finding considerable satisfaction in the alternative guarantees offered to France by her allies. The Alliance pacts were regarded as of decisive importance, and the League was of immense value in spite of its weaknesses, as to which all Frenchmen agreed.

[59] *Ibid.*, pp. 4206-4207. This "liberal" point of view was ably presented in the Senate by Debierre and Flaissières, who represented the more advanced Radical Socialists of that body. Thus it was the most "radical" view entertained by any members of the Senate. Accepting the material guarantees for what they might be worth, these senators urged the importance, also, of moral guarantees, and recognized the ultimate futility of the occupation of the bridgeheads unless "the spirit of imperialism and the spirit of revenge, which still rule Germany", underwent a change. *Annales*

due Sénat, October 10, 1919, pp. 1819 *et seq.* If Germany should undergo a change of heart, for which they dared to hope (in the midst of disparagements from all sides of the Senate), then France might relax the rigor of her vigil, and the League of Nations might play an increasingly important rôle. Less hope was placed in the alliances than was expressed by Renoult in the Chamber, for alliances, said Debierre, depended on "the changing policies of the powers concerned". *Ibid.,* pp. 1822-1823.

[60] "All the military guarantees which you can accumulate," said Marcel Sembat, "cannot dispense with moral guarantees, which alone can give Europe the hope of finally enjoying peace." *Annales de la Chambre,* September 3, 1919, p. 3730. See also Mistral speech, September 4, p. 3735.

[61] *Ibid.,* September 24, 1919, pp. 4134 *et seq.*

[62] *Ibid.,* August 29, 1919, pp. 3662 *et seq.*

[63] *Ibid.,* p. 3663.

[64] *Ibid.,* September 4, 1919, p. 3736.

[65] *Ibid.,* p. 3731.

[66] *Ibid.,* p. 3734.

[67] *Ibid.,* August 28, 1919, p. 3648.

[68] This was the only vote cast in opposition. 493 were cast for the Alliances.

[69] See *Débats,* September 2, 26; *Dépêche* of Toulouse, September 26; *Revue des Deux Mondes,* October 1.

[70] *Annales de la Chambre,* September 2, 1919, p. 3692.

[71] *Ibid.,* September 24, 1919, p. 4104.

[72] *Ibid.,* September 24, 1919, p. 4093. Tardieu insisted, however, that even though the United States did not ratify the Treaty, the League would go into effect, and supervision would be established over German armaments; though he admitted that the League would "lose some of its significance" if the United States did not enter.

[73] E.g., Article 429, concerning the possible prolongation of the occupation, or the reoccupation of the left bank.

[74] *Annales de la Chambre,* September 24, 1919, p. 4105. This idea that the League could organize without the United States was shocking to Barthou, who characterized the result as a "sort of parody of guarantees".

[75] *Ibid.,* September 25, 1919, p. 4133.

[76] Franklin-Bouillon in Chamber, October 1. *Ibid.,* October 1, 1919, pp. 4232-4236; Debierre in Senate, October 10, *Annales du Sénat,* October 10, 1919, pp. 1822-1823.

[77] *Annales du Sénat,* October 11, 1919, p. 1849.

[78] "Would our Allies have come to Paris for a second deliberation?" asked the *Dépêche* of Toulouse (Oct. 3). "Granted that they would; would they have brought different points of view from those which they caused to prevail, even, at times, at the expense of the vital interests of the nation on which the war weighed most heavily? . . . One can hope. But to believe is a different matter."

[79] September 18. See *Revue des Deux Mondes,* October 15, p. 958.

[80] *Annales de la Chambre,* August 29, 1919, p. 3659.

[81] The remaining twenty-one were as follows: four Socialist Republicans,

one of the Radical and Socialist Republican Union, four of the Radical Left, five of the Republican Left, two of the Democratic Republican Entente, two of the Independent group, three of the Right group. Some twenty other members were absent on leave. *Ibid.*, October 2, 1919, p. 4279.

[82] Four of this group voted for the Treaty, not because they found it satisfactory, but because, as Jobert said, they were in the presence of an "unalterable and definitive document", and because the "single word 'peace' ", contained in the Treaty, was "so precious" that they could not refuse their adherence. *Ibid.*, October 1, 1919, p. 4237.

[83] *Ibid.*, pp. 4275-4276.

[84] *Ibid.*, October 2, 1919, p. 4276.

[85] *Ibid.*, September 30, 1919, pp. 4201-4205.

[86] *Ibid.*, October 1, 1919, p. 4237.

[87] *Ibid.*, September 25, 1919, p. 4132. Ferdinand Bourgère, of the Right, said: "I shall vote for it because it consecrates the end of hostilities, and because, according to the declarations of the government, this Treaty is only a basis for future conventions by which France will obtain fully that which is due her, and which has not yet been recognized as her right." *Ibid.*, October 2, 1919, p. 4274.

[88] *Annales du Sénat,* October 11, 1919, p. 1856.

[89] *Ibid.*, pp. 1819 *et seq.;* pp. 1835 *et seq.*

[90] *Ibid.*, pp. 1851-1852.

[91] *Ibid.*, p. 1853. Jenouvrier also appealed for divine help, expressing the conviction that if other means failed, the "Lord would render certain the execution of the Treaty". *Ibid.*, October 10, 1919, p. 1830.

[92] *Ibid.*, October 9, 1919, p. 1799.

[93] *Ibid.*, October 11, 1919, p. 1841.

[94] *Dépêche* of Toulouse, October 3.

[95] *Revue des Deux Mondes,* October 1; *Temps,* September 5.

[96] *Intransigeant,* October 3. ". . . it is in the best interest of the country," wrote the *Temps,* October 11, "to insist once more on the insufficiency of our guarantees. . . . This is necessary in order to stimulate national energies. It is necessary in order to give to the French government, faced with the task of strengthening the peace, the vigorous support of public sentiment."

[97] The last formalities in the Chamber did not arouse enthusiasm. The *Temps* had warned the Chamber (Sept. 5) that the final vote on the Treaty should not appear to be merely the "tired gesture of an assembly which had yielded to a *fait accompli*". Yet, in the event, it was little else. The contrast with the Armistice period, and with the signing of the Treaty, June 28, was too obvious for comment. The *Matin* (Oct. 3) frankly said the Chamber had, of necessity, bowed before "a *fait accompli*"; and the *Action Française* (Oct. 3) cynically remarked on the "sense of death" which pervaded the ceremonies.

[98] *Intransigeant,* October 4.

[99] *Temps,* October 3. "[France's] forty million children must now work, heart and soul, to win the peace as they won the war," said *Matin,* October 3.

[100] *Temps,* September 5.

[101] E.g., *Temps,* September 7, 11; *Matin,* October 3, 10, 14; *Dépêche* of Toulouse, October 15.

[102] *Annales de la Chamber,* October 3, 1919, p. 4321.

[103] October 3.

[104] *Intransigeant,* September 14, October 2; *Temps,* September 27.

[105] *Annales de la Chambre,* September 30, 1919, p. 4198. The government was, almost necessarily, upheld, but only by a vote of 262 to 188.

[106] *Ibid.,* October 3, 1919, p. 4306 *et seq.*

[107] "Prussian militarism is not dead," said the *Dépêche* of Toulouse, October 9. "Germany does not want to disarm," wrote the *Matin,* October 9. She is "the same as in 1914".

[108] October 4. It also pointed to the fact, that it had been ratified with practical unanimity in the Chamber, 493 votes being cast for it, whereas the Treaty of Peace with Germany had received only 372. This was proof, it added, that it had the unreserved approbation of France.

[109] *Journal,* October 3; *Revue des Deux Mondes,* October 1, p. 712.

[110] *Matin,* October 3.

[111] E.g., *Matin,* October 2; *Intransigeant,* October 2, 5; *Journal,* October 4.

[112] Sometimes a note of resignation was also apparent. E.g., *Intransigeant,* October 26, referring to the proposed reservation concerning "questions affecting national honor and vital interests", said, "Thus if some 'Lusitania' gets torpedoed it will be for the United States to decide whether that constitutes an outrage. . . . Fortunately, we are not dependent [for the legal validity of the Treaty] on the ratification of the United States."

[113] "In the main tenets of his [Wilson's] political philosophy I believed with fervent credulity," wrote Nicolson. *Op. cit.,* p. 36.

[114] Seymour, Charles, *American Diplomacy During the World War* (Baltimore, 1934), p. 286.

BIBLIOGRAPHY

1. OFFICIAL PUBLICATIONS

Allied and Associated Powers, *Reply of the Allied and Associated Powers to the Observations of the German Delegation on the Conditions of Peace*, Paris, 1919. Hoover War Library.

Comité d'Études, *Travaux du Comité d'Études*, 2 vols., Paris, Imprimerie Nationale, 1918.

France. Assemblée Nationale.

Chambre des Députés, *Annales de la Chambre, Session Ordinaire de 1919. Débats Parlementaires; Documents Parlementaires*, Paris, Imprimerie des Journaux Officiels, 1920.

Sénat, Annales du Sénat, Session Ordinaire de 1919. Débats Parlementaires; Documents Parlementaires, Paris, Imprimerie des Journaux Officiels, 1920.

Great Britain. General Staff. *Allied Press Supplement to the Review of the Foreign Press*, issued by the General Staff, War Office, vols. 4-6, June 5, 1918 to July 30, 1919.

Paris Peace Conference.

Minutes of the Supreme Council, BC. A1-BC. 62, January 12 to June 17, 1919. FM. 1-29, March 27 to July 2, 1919. Hoover War Library.

Record of Informal and Confidential Memoranda and Conferences Dealing with Reparations Clauses of Conditions of Peace with Germany. Hoover War Library.

United States Congress. Senate. *Treaty of Peace with Germany.* Hearings before the Committee on Foreign Relations, United States Senate, 66th Congress, 1st session. Senate Document no. 106. Washington, Government Printing Office, 1919.

United States Department of State. *Papers relating to the foreign relations of the United States.* Supplements. *The World War: 1917, 1918. Russia, 1918.* Washington, Government Printing Office, 1928-1933. 2 vols.

2. OTHER DOCUMENTARY MATERIALS

Barthou, L., *Le Traité de Paix,* Paris, Bibliothèque Charpentier, 1919. Report made in name of commission chosen by Chamber of Deputies to examine the Treaty with Germany.

Bourgeois, Léon, *Le Traité de Paix de Versailles,* Paris, Librairie Félix Alcan, 1919. Report made in name of Senate Commission on Foreign Affairs on Treaty with Germany.

Calmette, Germain, *Recueil de Documents sur l'histoire de la question des réparations (1919-5 mai 1921),* Paris, A. Costes, 1924.

Cumming, C. K., and Pettit, W. W. (editors), *Russian-American Relations 1917-1920; Documents and Papers.* New York, Harcourt, Brace and Howe, 1920.

Current Intelligence Summaries, Daily Reports on the French Press, prepared by G. Bernard Noble for the American Commission to Negotiate Peace, during the Paris Peace Conference, 1919. Copy in Hoover War Library.

Dickinson, G. L., ed., *Documents and Statements Relating to Peace Proposals and War Aims, December 1916-November, 1918,* New York. Macmillan, 1919.

La Documentation Internationale: La Paix de Versailles.

Vol. i. *Les Conditions de l'Entente. La Composition et le Fonctionment de la Conférence des Préliminaries de Paix.* Paris, Les Éditions Internationales, 1930.

Vol. ii. *La Conférence de la Paix et la Société des Nations.* Paris, Les Éditions Internationales, 1929.

Vol. iv. Parts 1, 2. *La Commission de Réparations des Dommages.* Paris, Les Éditions Internationales, 1932.

Vol. xii. *Notes échangées entre la Conférence de la Paix et la Délégation Allemande.* Paris, Les Éditions Internationales, 1930.

Germany, Peace Conference Delegations, 1919. *The German Counter-Proposals to the Draft of the Versailles Peace-Treaty.* Berlin, Carl Heymanns Verlag, 1919.

Lutz, Ralph H., ed., *Fall of the German Empire, 1914-1918,* vol. ii, Stanford University Press, Stanford University, California, 1932. Translations by David G. Rempel and Gertrude Renktorff.

Marburg, Theodore, *Development of the League of Nations Idea,*

2 vols., Documents and correspondence, edited by J. H. Latané, New York, Macmillan, 1932.

Miller, D. H., *My Diary at the Conference of Paris*, 20 vols., Appeal Printing Co. (Privately printed.) Hoover War Library.

Official Statements of War Aims and Peace Proposals. Dec. 1916 to Nov. 1918. Prepared under supervision of James Brown Scott. Washington, D. C., Carnegie Endowment for International Peace, 1921.

Shaw, A., ed., *Messages and Papers of Woodrow Wilson*, New York, Review of Reviews Corp., 1924.

The Treaties of Peace, 1919-1923, vol. i., New York, Carnegie Endowment for International Peace, 1924.

3. SOCIETY PUBLICATIONS

Alliance Française, *Bulletin*, January-July, 1919.

Alliance Universitaire Française, *Bulletin Mensuel*, July, 1918-January, 1920.

Association française pour la Société des Nations, Paris.

Tract no. 2, *La Paix Organisée*, undated.

Bulletins nos. 1 and 2, January, February-March, 1919.

Gouttenoire de Toury, Fernand, *Pour la Société des Nations, La Voix des Morts*, Paris, 1918.

Mater, André, *La Société des Nations*, Paris, Henri Didier, 1918.

Association de la Paix par le Droit, *La Paix par le Droit* (monthly magazine).

Alliance Universitaire, 3 posters, 1918.

Comité Catholique de Propagande française à l'étranger.

Bulletin de propagande française, November 1918 to August 1919.

Julien Mgr., *La Société des Nations, une Théorie Catholique*, Paris, Bloud et Gay, 1919.

Emonet, B., *Nos Buts de Paix*, Paris, Bloud et Gay, 1919.

Comité National d'Action pour la Réparation intégrale des dommages causés par la Guerre.

Delombre, Paul, *Les Dommages de Guerre devant le Parlement*, Publication A. a., Paris, undated.

Francq, Léon, *Le paiement et le remploi pour la meilleure reprise de la vie économique*, Paris, April, 1919.

Comité Michelet.
> Driault, Edouard, *La Victoire, Ses Leçons et Ses Promesses,* Versailles, 1919. In Hoover War Library.

Comité National d'Études sociales et politiques.
> *L'Esprit Public en France* (Guy Grand, rapporteur).
> Various bulletins, January 12 to July 12, 1919.

Comité Protestant Français, *Bulletin Protestant Français,* Paris, 1916-1920 (incomplete).

Confédération Générale du Travail.
> *La Voix du Peuple,* Monthly Bulletin, 1918-1919.
> Jouhaux, Léon, *Les Travailleurs devant la Paix,* Paris, undated, November 1918 peace program.

La Conférence au Village, Bulletins, nos. 1, 3, 5, 8, 9. October 1918 to July 1919.

État-Pax, *Rapports Politique, Juridique, Militaire et Financier sur le project État-Pax,* Organisme International permanent et indépendent des Nations pour l'exécution du Traité de Paix et la liquidation des charges de guerre. (Mimeographed.) 1919. In Hoover War Library.

Groupement intersyndicale pour l'Étude des conditions de la Paix, 5 leaflets.

Ligue Civique.
> Bulletins, nos. 1-14, 1918-1919.
> Delobel, G., *Le President Wilson et les Alliés,* Paris, Imprimerie Typographique, 1918.
> Correspondence periodique adressée par la Ligue Civique aux journaux des departements. (1 page.) Undated.

La Ligue des Droits de l'Homme et du Citoyen.
> *Bulletin Officiel,* January-June 15, 1919.
> Buisson, F., *La Constitution Immédiate de la Société des Nations,* Paris, undated.
> Buisson, F., *La Paix Wilson,* Paris, 1918. Pamphlet.
> Guernet, H., *La Guerre et la Paix,* Paris, undated.
> Constant, Estournelles de, *Ce qui peut valoir le pacte de la Société des Nations,* 19th year, no. 10, Paris. May 15, 1919.
> *Bulletin des Droits de l'Homme,* Paris, 1918 and 1919.

La Ligue Nationale Anti-Austro-Allemande.
> *Bulletin,* 4th year, no. 25, April-May, 1919.
> *Congrès National Français: Les Conditions de la Paix et le Sentiment National Français,* Paris, 1919.

Ligue pour une Société des Nations, basée sur une Constitution Internationale.

La Société des Nations, Paris, 1919, nos. 19-21.

Pamphlet no. 6, Paris, 1917.

Ligue Souvenez-Vous.

Carré, Commandant Henri, La Haine Nécessaire, Paris, 1919.

Notre Voix, 1919. Weekly organ of Left Wing Pacifists. In Hoover War Library.

Parti Républicain Radical et Radical-Socialiste, Bulletin, Année 14-15. February 1918 to January 1920.

Union Française: Association Nationale pour l'Expansion morale et matérielle de la France.

Demidousli, P., Quelques Remarques sur la Révolution Russe et le Péril Allemande, Paris, Imprimerie Chaix, 1919.

Union des intérêts économiques.

Scheikevitch, A., L'intérêt allemand et le parti socialiste unifié, Paris, Édition du Reveil économique, 1919.

Union des Grandes Associations françaises contre la propagande ennemie.

Blondel, G., Pour une paix durable, Paris, undated.

Driault, E., La Victoire, ses leçons et ses promesses, Paris, undated.

Feuilles d'Information, nos. 7-21, February-September 1919, Paris.

Bulletin (Comtes-Rendus des Séances), January 7, 1919 to August 5, 1919.

Union Mutuelle Centrale des Victimes des Dommages causés par la Guerre. Revue des Dommages de Guerre, April-August 1919.

Union Nationale Républicain, Brochure, La lumière se fait, Paris, undated.

4. PRESS AND PERIODICALS

Paris daily (French) press. See list, supra, Chapter I, pp. 9-11.

Provincial daily French press. See list, supra, Chapter I, pp. 14-15.

L'Avenir, nos. 35, 37, 38, 39, March-July 1919.

Binkley, R. C., "New Light on the Paris Peace Conference," Political Science Quarterly, vol. xlvi, September 1931.

Le Correspondant, 1918 and 1919.

Le Cri de Paris, 1918 and 1919.

Daily Mail (Paris edition), 1919.

L'Europe Nouvelle, 1918 and 1919.

Price, J. M., "The Influence of Paris on the Comity of Nations," *Fortnightly Review,* Vol. 117, 1922, pp. 977-985.

Literary Digest, "Making War on our Chief Peacemaker," December 14, 1918, pp. 9-12.

New Republic, Editorial Note, November 23, 1918, p. 82. (No title, subject: Wilson's decision to go to Paris for the Peace Conference.)

New York Herald (Paris edition), 1918 and 1919.

New York Times, April 7, 8, 9, 10, 1919.

New York Tribune, April 8, 9, 1919.

L'Opinion, 1918 and 1919.

Revue des Deux Mondes, 1918 and 1919.

Revue Politique et Parlementaire, 1918 and 1919.

Le Rire, 1918 and 1919.

The World, New York, April 8, 1919.

5. BOOKS, ETC.

Adam, G. J., *The Tiger, Georges Clemenceau, 1841-1929,* London, J. Cape, 1930.

Angell, Norman, *The Public Mind, Its Disorders, Its Exploitation,* London, N. Douglas, 1926.

Annuaire de la presse française et étrangère et du Monde Politique, 1919, Paris, Corbeil, Imprimerie Crète, 1919.

Aston, Major-General Sir George, *The Biography of the Late Marshal Foch,* New York, Macmillan, 1929.

Aulard, A.. *Histoire Politique de la Grande Guerre,* Paris, A. Quillet, 1924.

Baker, R. S., *Woodrow Wilson and World Settlement,* 3 vols., New York, Doubleday, Page, 1922.

Baruch, B. M., *The Making of the Reparation and Economic Sections of the Treaty,* London, Harper Bros., 1920.

Beales, A. C. F., *The History of Peace,* G. Bell and Sons, Ltd., London, 1931.

Benoist, Charles, *Les Nouvelles Frontières d'Allemagne, et la Nouvelle Carte d'Europe,* Paris, Plon-Nourrit, 1919.

Bérard, Victor, *La Paix Française,* Paris, A. Colin, 1919.

Bernays, Edward L., *Crystallizing Public Opinion,* New York, Boni and Liveright, 1927.

Binkley, R. C., *Reactions of European Public Opinion to Woodrow Wilson's Statesmanship from the Armistice to the Peace of Versailles*, Stanford University, 1927 (Ph. D. Thesis), Typewritten Manuscript in Hoover War Library.

Bloch, Camille, *Repertoire Methodique de la Presse Quotidienne Française*, Collection Henri Blanc: La Grande Guerre, vol. 6, Paris, Émile-Paul, 1919.

Briggs, Mitchell Pirie, *George D. Herron and the European Settlement*, Stanford University Press, Stanford University, California, 1932.

Buell, R. L., *Contemporary French Politics*, New York, Appleton, 1920.

Bullitt, William C., *The Bullitt Mission to Russia*, Testimony before the Committee on Foreign Relations, United States Senate, New York, B. W. Huebsch, 1920.

Carroll, Eber Malcolm, *French Public Opinion and Foreign Affairs*, New York, London, The Century Co., 1931.

Chambure, A. de, *Quelques guides de l'opinion en France pendant la guerre*, Paris, Colin, Mary, Elen et cie., 1918.

Chassériaud, R., *La Formation de l'opinion publique*, Paris, M. Rivière, 1914.

Churchill, W., *The World Crisis: The Aftermath*, New York, Scribner's, 1929.

Clemenceau, Georges, *Grandeur and Misery of Victory*, New York, Harcourt, Brace, 1930.

Clemenceau, Georges, *In the Evening of My Thought*, 2 vols., translated by C. M. Thompson and John Heard, Jr., Boston and New York, Houghton, Mifflin & Co., 1929.

Creel, George, *The War, the World and Wilson*, New York, Harper Bros., 1920.

Czernin, Count Ottokar, *In the World War*, New York, Harper Bros., 1920.

Dahlin, Ebba, *French and German Public Opinion on Declared War Aims, 1914-1918*, Stanford University, California, Stanford University Press, 1933.

Deherme, Georges, *Les forces à regler, le nombre et l'opinion publique*, Paris, B. Grasset, 1919.

Demartial, G., *La Mobilisation des Consciences: La Guerre de 1914*, 2nd edition, Paris, Les Éditions Rieder, 1927.

Dennis, A. L. P., *The Foreign Policies of Soviet Russia*, New York, Dutton, 1924.

Dillon, Dr. E. J., *The Inside Story of the Peace Conference*, New York and London, Harper Bros., 1920.

Ebray, Alcide, *A Frenchman Looks at the Peace*, translated by E. W. Dickes, New York, Alfred A. Knopf, 1927.

Fabre-Luce, Alfred, *The Limitations of Victory*, translated by Constance Vesey, London, Allen and Unwin, 1926.

Fischer, L., *The Soviets in World Affairs*, New York, J. Cape and H. Smith, 1930.

Fleming, D. F., *The United States and the League of Nations, 1918-1920*, New York and London, G. P. Putnam's Sons, 1932.

Gauvain, A., "La Conférence de la Paix", *Revue de Paris*, vol. 26, pp. 869-894, April 15, 1919.

Graves, Wm. Brooke, ed., *Readings in Public Opinion, Its Formation and Control*, New York, London, Appleton, 1928.

Handbuch der Auslandpresse 1918, Berlin, E. S. Mittler und Sohn, 1918.

Hayes, C. J. H., *France, A Nation of Patriots*, New York, Columbia University Press, 1930.

Herron, G. D., *The Defeat in the Victory*, London, C. Palmer, 1921.

House, E. M., Seymour, Chas., and others, *What Really Happened at Paris*, New York, C. Scribner's Sons, 1921.

Houston, D. F., *Eight Years with Wilson's Cabinet, 1913-1920*, New York, Doubleday, Page, 1926.

Huddleston, Sisley, *France*, New York, C. Scribner's Sons, 1927.

Jouhaux, Léon, *Les Travailleurs devant la paix*, Paris, Édition de la Bataille, undated.

Jouvenel, Robert de, *Le Journalisme en Vingt Leçons*, Paris, Payot et cie., 1920.

Klotz, L., *De la Guerre à la Paix*, Paris, Payot et cie., 1924.

Knight, L. L., *Woodrow Wilson, The Dreamer and the Dream*, Atlanta, Georgia, Johnson-Dallis Co., 1924.

Lachapelle, Georges, *Élections législatives des 26 avril et 10 mai, 1914*, Paris, Georges Roustan, 1914.

Lachapelle, Georges, *Élections législatives du 16 novembre, 1919*, Paris, Georges Roustan, 1920.

Lansing, Robert, *The Big Four and Others of the Peace Conference*, Boston and New York, Houghton, Mifflin, 1921.

Lansing, Robert, *The Peace Negotiations, A Personal Narrative*, Boston, Houghton, Mifflin, 1921.

Lasswell, Harold D., *Propaganda Technique in the World War,* London: Kegan Paul, Trench, Trubner and Co., Ltd., 1927; New York: Alfred A. Knopf, 1927.

Levy, Raphäel-Georges, *La Juste Paix,* Paris, Plon-Nourrit, 1920.

Lippmann, Walter, *Public Opinion,* New York, Macmillan, 1927.

Lippmann, Walter, *The Phantom Public,* New York, Harcourt. Brace and Co., 1925.

Lowell, A. L., *Public Opinion in War and Peace,* Cambridge, Harvard University Press, 1923.

Lugan, A., *Les Problemes internationaux et le Congrès de la Paix,* Paris, Éditions Brossard, 1919.

Martet, Jean, *Georges Clemenceau,* translated by Milton Waldman, London and New York, Longmans-Green, 1930.

Martet, Jean, *Le Tigre,* Paris, Albin Michel, 1930.

Martet, Jean, *Le Silence de M. Clemenceau,* Paris, Albin Michel, 1929.

The Memoirs of Marshal Foch, translated by Colonel T. Bentley Mott, Garden City, N. Y., Doubleday, Doran, 1931.

Michon, G., *Clemenceau,* Paris, Rivière, 1931.

Miller, D. H., *The Drafting of the Covenant,* 2 vols., New York, Putnam, 1928.

Mordacq, General, *Le Ministère Clemenceau, Journal d'un Témoin,* vol. iii, Paris, Librairie Plon, 1931.

Nevins, Allan, *Henry White: Thirty Years of American Diplomacy,* New York, Harper Bros., 1930.

Newton, Lord, *Lord Lansdowne, A Biography,* London, Macmillan, 1929.

Nicolson, Harold, *Peacemaking, 1919,* London, Constable and Co., Ltd., 1933.

Nowak, Karl Friedrich, *Versailles,* translated by Norman Thomas and E. W. Dickes. London, Victor Gollancz, Ltd., 1928.

Poincaré, Raymond, *Au Service de la France.* Vol. ix, *L'Année Troublée, 1917;* vol. x, *Victoire et Armistice,* Paris, Librairie Plon, 1932-1933.

Raffolovitch, A., *L'Abominable Vénalité de la Presse,* Paris, Librairie du Travail, 1931.

Rask-Ørstedfonden, *Les Origines et l'Œuvre de la Société des Nations* (Sous la direction de P. Munch), Copenhague, Gyldensdalske Boghandel—Nordisk Forlag, Christiania, Londres, Berlin, 1923.

Recouly, Raymond, *Foch, My Conversations with the Marshal,* translated by Joyce Davis, New York, Appleton, 1929. (Translation of *Le Memorial de Foch*.)

Renouvin, Pierre, *Les Formes du Gouvernement de Guerre,* Paris, Presses Universitaires de France, 1925.

Riddell, Lord, *War Diary,* London, Nicolson and Watson, 1933.

Scelle, G., *Le Pacte des Nations,* Paris, L. Tenin, 1919.

Schiff, Victor, *The Germans at Versailles, 1919,* with contributions by Otto Landsberg, Hermann Müller, and Friedrich Stampfer, tranlated by Geoffrey Dunlop, London, Williams and Norgate, Ltd., 1930.

Schuman, F. L., *American Policy towards Russia since 1917,* New York, International Publishers, 1928.

Schuman, F. L., *War and Diplomacy in the French Republic,* New York, McGraw-Hill, 1931.

Sembat, Marcel, *Defeated Victory,* translated by Flory Henri Turot, London, Labour Publishing Co., 1925.

Seymour, Charles, *American Diplomacy during the World War,* Baltimore, Johns Hopkins Press, 1934.

Seymour, Charles, *Intimate Papers of Colonel House,* 4 vols., Boston, Houghton, Mifflin, 1928.

Seymour, Charles, *Woodrow Wilson and the World War,* New Haven, Yale University Press, 1921.

Siegfried, André, *Tableau des Partis Politiques en France,* Paris, B. Grasset, 1930.

Steed, W., *Through Thirty Years,* 2 vols., Garden City, N. Y., Doubleday, Page, 1924.

Steffens, Lincoln, *Autobiography,* New York, Harcourt, Brace, 1931.

Tardieu, André, *The Truth about the Treaty,* Indianapolis, Bobbs-Merrill, 1921.

Temperley, H. W. V., ed., *A History of the Peace Conference,* 6 vols., London, Henry Frowde, Hodder and Stoughton, 1920.

Terrail, Gabriel (Mermeix), *Le Combat des Trois,* Paris, Librairie Ollendorff, 1922.

Thompson, C. T., *The Peace Conference Day by Day,* New York, Brentano's, 1920.

Tumulty, Joseph P., *Woodrow Wilson as I Know Him,* New York, Doubleday, Page, 1921.

Vernadsky, G., *A History of Russia,* New Haven, Yale University Press, 1929.

White, W. A., *Woodrow Wilson, the Man, His Times and His Task,* New York, Houghton, Mifflin, 1924.

Wright, Quincy, *Public Opinion and World Politics,* Chicago, University of Chicago Press, 1933.

Yves-Guyot, *Les Garanties de la Paix,* Paris, Alcan, 1918.

INDEX

See Bibliography for authors and titles of books, documents, pamphlets, etc., referred to text.

441

Law, Bonar, 215n.
League for the Rights of Man and the Citizen, 23, 56, 100, 107, 115.
League of Nations, 37, 44, 46, 60, 82, 87, 90, 91, 97n., 99-152, 153, 157, 159, 161, 185n., 211, 219n., 220, 221, 225, 231, 240, 241, 245, 249, 250, 253, 256, 262n., 267n., 274, 279, 295n., 296n., 313, 314, 334, 345n., 346n., 357, 358, 360, 365, 370, 374, 376, 377, 378, 388n., 398, 405, 408, 411, 412, 417, 422, 425n., 426n.
accepted as part of peace settlement, 104.
Aulard on Peace Conference and, 110.
Bourgeois on, 142.
Bourgeois commission on, 101.
British government and, 106.
capital of, 133f., 151n.
Clemenceau on, 37, 88f., 103, 107, 409.
Doumergue on, 142.
Draft Covenant of February 14, 110-121, 133; French criticisms on, 120; French press and public opinion on, 118-121.
establishment threatened, 128.
financial section, 143, 193, 195, 203.
France and, 96, 97n. See also French press; French public opinion; and France: Chamber, government, parliament, Radical Socialists, Socialists.
French interpretations of, 47.
French plan for, 115, 221.
and Germany, 105, 114, 147n., 361, 385n., 386n. See also Germany.
Colonel House on separation of, from Treaty, 149n.
international army, 115ff.
and Preliminaries, 128f., 130ff.
Renaudel on, 145n.
Ribot on, 36.
Smuts on, 108.
union of, with Treaty of Peace, 128-133.
United States and, 124ff., 131f., 149n., 245, 258, 406f., 426n.

League of Nations: Wilson on, 42, 105, 108.
Wilson plan adopted, 108.
See also Covenant.
League of Nations Commission, 113, 118, 133, 134, 135, 136, 138, 141.
Bourgeois on French position in, 147n.
divergent views on, 111.
Franco-American conflicts, 114ff.
and Wilson, 108, 111, 117, 139f.
League of Nations Council, 211, 259, 372, 401, 403, 424n.
League to Enforce Peace, 100f.
Lebey, A., 216n.
Lechartier, Georges, 376, 388n.
Lecomte, G., 22.
Lefèvre, A., 194, 195, 400, 416.
Left Bank, 186, 201, 206, 238-256, 259, 262, 262n., 264n., 265n., 267n., 268n., 360, 362, 385n., 394, 413, 425n.
Barthou report on, 401-403.
Clemenceau on, 249f.
Comité d'Études on, 239.
commission of French Senate on, 402.
compromise on, 250f.
Foch on, 239f., 247.
and France. See French press; French public opinion; and France: Chamber, government, Parliament, Radical Socialists.
French demand for neutralization of, 245.
Colonel House on, 249.
Lloyd George on, 249f.
negotiations on, 248-251.
Tardieu on, 402f.
United States policy on, 250.
and Wilson, 249f., 331.
See also Rhine.
Lemnos, 276, 277.
Lenin, N., 278, 288, 289, 291, 293, 295n.
Lewis, Senator J. H., 97n.
Liberté, La, 9, 64n., 65n., 96n., 108, 118, 131, 146n., 149n., 150n., 152n., 183n., 189, 190, 205, 217n., 243, 256, 260, 263n., 264n., 265n., 297n., 320, 327, 331, 332, 338, 345n., 349n., 352n., 385n., 386n.
Libre Parole, La, 9, 47, 65n., 67, 129, 217n., 242, 265n.